Powers of Freedom

Reframing Political Thought

Nikolas Rose

CAMBRIDGE
UNIVERSITY PRESS

PUBLISHED BY THE PRESS SYNDICATE OF THE UNIVERSITY OF CAMBRIDGE
The Pitt Building, Trumpington Street, Cambridge, United Kingdom

CAMBRIDGE UNIVERSITY PRESS
The Edinburgh Building, Cambridge, CB2 2RU, United Kingdom
  http://www.cup.cam.ac.uk
40 West 20th Street, New York, NY 10011–4211, USA   http://www.cup.org
10 Stamford Road, Oakleigh, Melbourne 3166, Australia

First published 1999

Printed in the United Kingdom at the University Press, Cambridge

Typeset in Monotype Plantin 10/12 pt [wv]

A catalogue record for this book is available from the British Library

Library of Congress cataloguing in publication data

Rose, Nikolas S.
    Powers of Freedom: reframing political thought / Nikolas Rose.
        p.   cm
    'Portions of this book draw on published and unpublished papers' –
Acknowledgements.
    Includes bibliographical references.
    ISBN 0 521 65075 5 (hb)   ISBN 0 521 65905 1
        1. Political sociology.   2. Liberty.   3. Community.   4. Foucault.
Michel – Contributions in political science.   I. Title.
JA76.R645   1999
320'.01'1 – dc21   98–40306 CIP

ISBN 0 521 65075 5 hardback
ISBN 0 521 65905 1 paperback

For Diana

Contents

Acknowledgements

Portions of this book draw on published and unpublished papers.

I have developed arguments first presented in a number of articles co-written with Peter Miller, in particular N. Rose and P. Miller (1992), 'Political power beyond the state: problematics of government', *British Journal of Sociology* 43, 2: 172–205; P. Miller and N. Rose (1995a), 'Political thought and the limits of orthodoxy: a response to Curtis', *British Journal of Sociology* 46, 4: 590–7.

Chapter 1 incorporates arguments from 'Governing liberty, governing modern societies', Green College, University of British Columbia, September 1997.

Chapter 2 is a revised version of 'Towards a critical sociology of freedom', my inaugural lecture for the Chair of Sociology at Goldsmiths College, University of London, which was given in May 1992 (Rose 1992b): thanks in particular to Graham Burchell, Thomas Osborne and Peter Miller for discussion of the issues I raise here and to the participants at the Symposium in Ethics and the History of the Human Sciences, Groningen, November 1996, where this paper was discussed.

Chapter 3 develops arguments first presented in Rose (1996b), 'The death of the social?: re-figuring the territory of government', *Economy and Society* 25, 3: 327–56, and in papers delivered at a Symposium on the Displacement of Social Policies, in Jyväskylä, Finland, January 1997, and workshops on governmentality at the Stockholm Institute of Education, Stockholm, September 1996, and the University of Salzburg, December 1996.

Some of the material incorporated in chapter 4 was first presented in my George Lurcey Lecture and a related seminar at Amherst College in March 1993. Thanks to all who participated for stimulating criticism which was helped me clarify my arguments and to anonymous reviewers of the version published as Rose (1994a), 'Expertise and the government of conduct', *Studies in Law, Politics and Society* 14: 459–67.

Chapter 5 is based upon a keynote address (1997a) entitled 'Between authority and liberty: civil society, communitarianism, third sector', to the Annual Conference of the Finnish Social Policy Association in Helsinki in November 1997, and published in Finnish as 'Vallan ja vapauden välissä: hyveen hallinta vapaasa yhteiskunassa', *Janus* (Journal of the Finnish Society for Social Policy) 1998, 6, 1: 1–33. Thanks in particular to Barbara Cruikshank and Michael Shapiro for advice.

Chapter 6 is an extended version of Rose (1991), 'Governing by numbers: figuring out democracy', published in *Accounting, Organizations and Society* 16, 7: 673–92.

Chapter 7 draws on aspects of a number of the papers cited above, including the papers given at the University of Turku, the University of Stockholm, the University of Salzburg and the University of Jyväskylä in 1996 and 1997. It also incorporates arguments made in a paper delivered to The Future of Forensic Psychiatry, 23rd Cropwood Round Table Conference, University of Cambridge Institute of Criminology, March 1997 and an invited keynote address to Sainsbury Centre for Mental Health Summer School, Oxford University, July 1997. I developed some of these ideas further in a paper on law and control given to the research Institute for Humanities and Social Sciences at the University of Sydney in April 1998, and in discussions with Stuart Scheingold and Jonathon Simon, and the other participants in a workshop on legal pluralism at the Henry M. Jackson School of International Studies at the University of Washington in May 1998.

In my conclusion, I develop some thoughts from a symposium on new forms of governance, held at the University of Toronto in October 1996, and a seminar of the *History of the Present* Research Network, held in London in February 1997.

Thanks to the following for inviting me to give the presentations on which the book is based and for discussions and hospitality: Ruth Benschop, Trudy Dehue, Risto Eräsaari, Richard Ericson, Herbert Gottweiss, Sakari Hänninen, Kenneth Hultqvist, Patrick Joyce, Osmo Kivinnen, Paul Patton, Risto Rinne, Austin Sarat, Stuart Scheingold, Susan Silbey, Russell Smandych, Mariana Valverde and Robert van Krieken.

Thanks to Catherine Max, my original editor at Cambridge, for encouraging me to write this book, to Elizabeth Howard for seeing it through production and to Karen Anderson Howes for meticulous attention to the text which greatly improved the final product.

The ideas I present in this book have been worked out in collaboration with many others. My original work on 'governmentality' was undertaken in close collaboration with Peter Miller, and my ways of thinking about these issues are the outcome of that collective endeavour.

Over the years I have discussed these ideas with many members of the *History of the Present* Research Network, in our seminars in London and meetings elsewhere since 1989. I am truly grateful to my co-workers for this rare extended experience of supportive, critical and committed intellectual work on our present. However, I must stress that, whilst many of my ideas come out of this collective work, this book is in no sense a statement of a collective position. I am glad to say that, whilst there is a kind of thought community mobilized by shared dissatis-factions, and curiosities, there is no governmentality 'school'.

Special thanks to Andrew Barry, Vikki Bell, Graham Burchell, Bar-bara Cruikshank, Mitchell Dean, Barry Hindess, David Owen, Jonathon Simon, Kevin Stenson, Grahame Thompson and William Walters for sharing thoughts and papers with me. Thanks also to all my past and present graduate students for continually forcing me to think, in particu-lar to Lisa Blackman and Martha Michaelidou for making me more aware of the role of popular discourses in governing – an issue I have touched on too rarely in what follows; to Karen Baistow for illuminating the role of behavioural techniques and problems of empowerment; and to Nick Thoburn for helping me understand something of the work of Gilles Deleuze.

In particular, I would like to express my appreciation for the friend-ship and critical support that I have enjoyed from Barry Hindess, Thomas Osborne, Pat O'Malley, Peter Miller and Mariana Valverde over may years, and especially to Tom and Mariana for their generous and insightful comments on the first draft of this book: this work would have been lonelier and poorer without their comradeship.

Introduction: reframing political thought

As we enter the twenty-first century, many of the conventional ways of analysing politics and power seem obsolescent. They were forged in the period when the boundaries of the nation state seemed to set the natural frame for political systems, and when geo-politics seemed inevitably to be conducted in terms of alliances and conflicts amongst national states. They took their model of political power from an idea of the state formed in nineteenth-century philosophical and constitutional discourse. This imagined a centralized body within any nation, a collective actor with a monopoly of the legitimate use of force in a demarcated territory. This apparent monopoly of force was presumed to underpin the unique capacity of the state to make general and binding laws and rules across its territory. It also seemed to imply that all other legitimate authority was implicitly or explicitly authorized by the power of the state. Such styles of thinking about political power also embodied particular ideas about the human beings who were the subjects of power. These were structured by the image of the individualized, autonomous and self-possessed political subject of right, will and agency. Political conceptions of human collectivities also tended to see them as singularities with identities which provided the basis for political interests and political actions: classes, races, orders, interest groups. Within such styles of thought, freedom was defined in essentially negative terms. Freedom was imagined as the absence of coercion or domination; it was a condition in which the essential subjective will of an individual, a group or a people could express itself and was not silenced, subordinated or enslaved by an alien power. The central problems of such analyses were: 'Who holds power? In whose interests do they wield it? How is it legitimated? Who does it represent? To what extent does it hold sway across its territory and its population? How can it be secured or contested, or overthrown?' State/civil society; public/private; legal/ illegal; market/family; domination/emancipation; coercion/freedom: the horizons of political thought were established by this philosophical and sociological language.

These images and vocabularies of politics and power have been fundamentally challenged by contemporary politics itself. Some had predicted that, following the collapse of state socialism, free-market liberal democratic individualism would shape our political future. But, to the contrary, we are seeing the proliferation of forms of politics and of types of contestation which cannot be calibrated in terms of the dichotomies of traditional political thought. The challenges posed to the idea of the nation state by the themes of globalization and localization are too familiar to require much elaboration: the globalization of flows of money, communications, products, persons, ideas and cultures, and the localization of local economic regions, world cities, regional identities, lifestyle sectors and so forth. These challenges disrupt the images of spatialization and communication that underpinned conventional notions of nation states, their territorial unity and governability: the mechanical image of the steam engine or the internal combustion engine, with their associated roads and railways; the semiotic image of a national language and a national currency, the electrical image of the telegraph with its fixed lines relaying signals between fixed points through a single protocol; the organic image of a single national economy, a system of relations amongst discrete economic actors; the sovereignty image of a single source of law, right and authority in a given domain.

As these images of the nation state fragment, in the face of strange new couplings, flows and alliances that spatialize power along very different dimensions, and that establish connections and relations through very different lines of communication, a range of other challenges to orthodox politics are on the rise. New feminisms are articulating, in different ways, the insight of the women's movements of the 1960s, which disrupted the conventional divisions between the political and the personal and between the public and the private. The politics of recognition – of national, cultural, ethnic, religious, linguistic identity – whether in its Western forms of multi-culturalism or its non-Western forms of fundamentalism, disputes conventional notions of the relations of state and citizen, and the sources of political legitimacy and citizenship. A new ethical politics has taken shape – of the environment, of animal rights, of reproduction, of health, of everyday life itself – which refuses the idea that politics is a matter of state, parliament, election and party programme. Anti-political themes are on the rise in right-wing, left-wing and 'no-wing' varieties, stressing the inefficacy, the limits, the inevitable failings of state provision of welfare, crime control, education and much more, and demanding that individuals, families, communities, employers take back to themselves the powers and responsibilities that, since the nineteenth century, have been acquired by states, politicians and legislators. In the face of such events, conventional ways of thinking about the contemporary organization of powers in our societies, and their histories, seem troubled and uncertain. In this context, it is relevant to consider the extent to which these images ever adequately captured the strategies, tactics and techniques through which individuals and populations have been governed in 'the West' since the late eighteenth century.

The aim of this book is to suggest some alternative ways of thinking about our contemporary regimes of government and their histories. In doing so, I hope to introduce some new options into our current political imagination, to amplify the possibilities that are open to us in our present. Of course, in our millenarian moment, many novel theories of culture, power and ethics are being proposed. I do not intend to review or evaluate these. I take my starting point from one particular style of analysis. This has grown out of Michel Foucault's brief writings and lectures on governmentality.[1] In these pieces on governmentality, Foucault sketched some pathways for analysing power that were not transfixed by the image of the state or the constitutive oppositions of conventional political philosophy and political sociology. They defined their problem space in terms of government, understood, in the words of Foucault's much-cited maxim, as 'the conduct of conduct'. Government, here, refers to all endeavours to shape, guide, direct the conduct of others, whether these be the crew of a ship, the members of a household, the employees of a boss, the children of a family or the inhabitants of a territory. And it also embraces the ways in which one might be urged and educated to bridle one's own passions, to control one's own instincts, to govern oneself. Foucault thus implied that, rather than framing investigations in terms of state or politics, it might be more productive to investigate the formation and transformation of theories, proposals, strategies and technologies for 'the conduct of conduct'. Such studies of government would address that dimension of our history composed by the invention, contestation, operationalization and transformation of more or less rationalized schemes, programmes, techniques and devices which seek to shape conduct so as to achieve certain ends.[2]

[1] The best introduction to Foucault's own argument is his essay on governmentality, which is the text of a lecture given at the Collège de France in 1978 (Foucault 1979b, now republished as Foucault 1991).

[2] I am drawing directly here upon Miller and Rose 1995b. For further useful introductions, see Peter Miller's account in his analysis of Foucault's conception of power (Miller 1987); Colin Gordon's introduction to *The Foucault*

Such rationalized practices should be distinguished from the controls on conduct that have, no doubt, existed in all human collectivities at all times and places. This distinction hangs on the elements of thought, intention and calculation. Practices of government are deliberate attempts to shape conduct in certain ways in relation to certain objectives. Attempts at governing may be formally rationalized in programmatic statements, policy documents, pamphlets and speeches – for example, Keynesian economic management, Beveridge's strategies of social insurance, the new forms of risk management coming to shape the provision of mental health services across the English-speaking world in the late 1990s, the programmes of scientific pedagogy developed since the nineteenth century or the multitude of interventions on the family and child rearing. But others are less formally articulated, and exist in the form of a variety of practical rationalities within particular types of practice – for example, much social work or police work is of this type. Governing is a genuinely heterogeneous dimension of thought and action – something captured to some extent in the multitude of words available to describe and enact it: education, control, influence, regulation, administration, management, therapy, reformation, guidance. Nevertheless, it is possible to differentiate the exercise of power in the form of government from simple domination.[3] To dominate is to ignore or to attempt to crush the capacity for action of the dominated. But to govern is to recognize that capacity for action and to adjust oneself to it. To govern is to act upon action. This entails trying to understand what mobilizes the domains or entities to be governed: to govern one must act upon these forces, instrumentalize them in order to shape actions, processes and outcomes in desired directions. Hence, when it comes to governing human beings, to govern is to presuppose the freedom of the governed. To govern humans is not to crush their capacity to act, but to acknowledge it and to utilize it for one's own objectives.

I think it is useful to take Foucault's ideas about government as a starting point for these investigations. But I do not think that there is some general theory or history of government, politics or power latent in Foucault's writings, which should be extracted and then applied to other issues. There are those who seek to be Foucault scholars. That is their privilege. I advocate a relation to his work that is looser, more

Effect (C. Gordon 1991); Graham Burchell's essay in *Foucault and Political Reason* (G. Burchell 1996); and the introduction by Mitchell Dean and Barry Hindess to *Governing Australia* (Dean and Hindess 1998).

[3] Peter Miller's book, already cited, provides an excellent analysis of this (Miller 1987).

inventive and more empirical. It is less concerned with being faithful to
a source of authority than with working within a certain ethos of
enquiry, with fabricating some conceptual tools that can be set to work
in relation to the particular questions that trouble contemporary thought
and politics.

The investigations of government that interest me here are those
which try to gain a purchase on the forces that traverse the multitudes
of encounters where conduct is subject to government: prisons, clinics,
schoolrooms and bedrooms, factories and offices, airports and military
organizations, the marketplace and shopping mall, sexual relations and
much more. They try to track force relations at the molecular level, as
they flow through a multitude of human technologies, in all the practices, arenas and spaces where programmes for the administration of
others intersect with techniques for the administration of ourselves.
They focus upon the various incarnations of what one might term 'the
will to govern', as it is enacted in a multitude of programmes, strategies,
tactics, devices, calculations, negotiations, intrigues, persuasions and
seductions aimed at the conduct of the conduct of individuals, groups,
populations – and indeed oneself. From this perspective, the question
of the state that was so central to earlier investigations of political power
is relocated. The state now appears simply as one element – whose functionality is historically specific and contextually variable – in multiple
circuits of power, connecting a diversity of authorities and forces, within
a whole variety of complex assemblages.

To begin an investigation of power relations at this molecular level,
however, is not to counterpose the micro to the macro. This binary
opposition seems natural and obvious. But it should be treated with
some suspicion. If there are differences between the government of large
spaces and processes and the government of small spaces and processes,
these are not ontological but technological. As Bruno Latour has often
pointed out, the 'macro-actor' is not different in kind from the 'micro-
actor', but is merely one who has a longer and more reliable 'chain of
command' – that is to say, assembled into longer and more dispersed
networks of persons, things and techniques. Indeed, in the analytics of
government, we need to pay particular attention to the ways in which,
in practice, distinctions and associations are established between practices and apparatuses deemed political and aimed at the management
of large-scale characteristics of territories or populations, and micro-
technologies for the management of human conduct in specific individuals in particular locales and practices. For example, the social
insurance regimes for managing insecurity set in place in most Western
nations in the first half of the twentieth century sought simultaneously

to act on the security of the population as a whole, and on the conduct and circumstances of the individual household and its members. The tactics of economic regulation that took shape over the same period sought explicitly to link national prosperity with the self-advancement of individual enterprises and citizens, through tax regimes, accounting practices and the implantation and modulation of particular calculative attitudes in economic actors. The family mechanism has, for at least two centuries, been made up and shaped by legal regulation, moral exhortation, fiscal manipulation and expert intervention in the name of both public good and private well-being. And the regulation of the health of the population, since the middle of the nineteenth century, has established a whole array of linkages between practices aimed at securing the strength and vitality of the nation and its 'manpower', and practices aimed at the maximization of individual and familial health and hygiene. These links between the molar and the molecular have taken a variety of forms, not merely or principally paternalistic attempts at the micro-management of conduct, but more complex and subtle procedures for establishing a delicate and complex web of affiliations between the thousands of habits of which human beings are composed – movements, gestures, combinations, associations, passions, satisfactions, exhaustions, aspirations, contemplations – and the wealth, tranquillity, efficiency, economy, glory of the collective body.

It was these political arts of combination that Michel Foucault tried to capture in his notion of governmentality. 'Governmentality', as the term was used by Foucault, suggested that, from at least the eighteenth century, rulers, statesmen and politicians came to see their tasks *in terms of* government.[4] This 'modern' conception of rule as government differed from earlier forms, such as those exercised by a prince over his territory, a feudal lord over his domain or an emperor over his empire. This is because, drawing on ways of governing conduct that had already been deployed by others, in particular the churches of early modern Europe, authorities came to understand the task of ruling politically as requiring them to act upon the details of the conduct of the individuals and populations who were their subjects, individually and collectively, in order to increase their good order, their security, their tranquillity, their prosperity, health and happiness.[5]

[4] Foucault 1991.

[5] Foucault and his colleagues often suggested that the earliest articulations of this corruption of rule as government were in 'the science of police' and related secular practices of social discipline that took shape in the early modern period (e.g. Pasquino 1991). Ian Hunter has argued that this suggestion seriously underestimates the key role of confessional churches in the

Once political power takes as its object the conduct of its subjects in relation to particular moral or secular standards, and takes the well-being of those subjects as its guiding principle, it is required to rational-ize itself in particular ways. To rule properly, it is necessary to rule in a light of a knowledge of the particular and specific characteristics that are taken to be immanent to that over which rule is to be exercised: the characteristics of a land with its peculiar geography, fertility, climate; of a population with its rates of birth, illness, death; of a society with its classes, interests, conflicts; of an economy with its laws of circulation, of supply and demand; of individuals with their passions, interests and propensities to good and evil. In the same process, ruling becomes a 'reflexive' activity: those who would rule must ask themselves who should govern, what is the justification for government, what or who should be governed and how. Hence 'modern' governmental rationalit-ies, modern ways of exercising rule, inescapably entail a certain invest-ment of thought, however attenuated, and a certain form of reason, however much it may be obscured.

A certain kind of reason, then, makes possible both the exercise of government and its critique. Working along these lines, a multitude of rigorous and innovative studies of specific strategies, techniques and practices for the conduct of conduct have been generated.[6] Thus, rigor-ous empirical studies have been undertaken of emergence of social insurance; education; accounting; the enterprise, economic citizenship and new managerial technologies; crime control; the regulation of unemployment; poverty and insecurity; strategies of development; medicine, psychiatry and the regulation of health; child abuse and sexual offences; and new social strategies of empowerment.[7]

delineation of populations under particular regimes of religious and moral government (Hunter 1998). I return to this issue briefly in chapter 1.

[6] Useful collections of papers introducing these ideas are G. Burchell, Gordon and Miller 1991; Barry, Osborne and Rose 1996; and Dean and Hindess 1988. Barry Hindess has subjected Foucault's arguments to rigorous scrutiny in *Discourses of Power: From Hobbes to Foucault* (Hindess 1996a). See also the work of Mitchell Dean: Dean 1991, 1994, 1999.

[7] See the following: social insurance: Defert 1991, Donzelot 1991, Ewald 1986; education: Hunter 1988, 1994; accounting: Miller 1990, Hopwood and Miller 1994, Power 1993, 1994a, 1994b, 1997; the enterprise, economic citizenship, new managerial technologies: Miller and O'Leary 1992, Miller 1994; crime control: Feeley and Simon 1992, O'Malley 1992, Stenson 1993, Feeley and Simon 1994; the regulation of unemployment: Walters 1994a, Dean 1995; poverty and insecurity: Dean 1991, Procacci 1991, 1993, 1998; medicine, psychiatry, and the regulation of health: Castel 1988, Castel, Castel and Lovell 1986, Miller and Rose 1986, T. Osborne 1993, Greco

These studies have shown, in their different ways, that the activity of government is inextricably bound up with the activity of thought. It is thus both made possible by and constrained by what can be thought and what cannot be thought at any particular moment in our history. To analyse the history of government, then, requires attention to the conditions under which it becomes possible to consider certain things to be true – and hence to say and do certain things – about human beings and their interrelations as they produce, consume, reproduce, act, infract, live, sicken, die.[8] This insistence on the significance of the formation and transformation of truthful thought differentiates studies of government from most varieties of political sociology.[9] Of course, there are many different ways in which thought has rendered itself truthful and in which authority has linked itself to truth. For many centuries, and in many locales, authority grounded itself in spiritual and theological truth, which has its own particular rules for truth gathering and truth certification, and its own criteria for 'being in truth'. More recently, in many territories and practices, authority has grounded itself in consti-

1993, Rose 1994b; child abuse and sexual offences: Bell 1993, Parton 1995, 1996; alcoholism and addiction: Valverde 1997, 1998a; and new social strategies of empowerment: Baistow 1995, Barron 1996, Cruikshank 1994.

[8] I speak of 'truth' rather than 'meaning' deliberately – that is to say, I am not concerned with the questions that have troubled hermeneutic histories and sociologies – how to discover the social meanings that actions and events held for actors in other times and places– but with the ways in which certain languages of description, explanation, calculation and judgement came to acquire the value of truth and the kinds of actions and techniques that were made possible by such truths. Foucault sets out his own point of view on these issues in his preface to *The Order of Things* and in his inaugural lecture 'Orders of discourse' (Foucault 1970, 1972b). The philosophical issues at stake here are usefully discussed in Herbert Dreyfuss and Paul Rabinow's introduction to the work of Michel Foucault (Dreyfuss and Rabinow 1983).

[9] Of course, this emphasis on political thought is not itself novel: it intersects with, and draws upon, a body of investigation into 'the history of political ideas' which has sought to examine the conventions, presuppositions and values which underpin political argument at different historical moments. Notably, of course, this has been explored in the writings of Pocock (e.g. Pocock 1985) and of Quentin Skinner and his associates (for an introduction to Skinner, see Tully 1988). Some similar arguments have been developed in a more 'Foucauldian' spirit by William Connolly and Michael Shapiro (Connolly 1983, Shapiro 1984). In a slightly different sense, this focus on truthful thought draws attention to the particular procedures through which political argument makes itself convincing, and thus has some affinities with analyses of the rhetoric of political argument (Perelman and Obrechts-Tyteca 1971).

tutional and legal styles of truth telling, which have their own procedures for establishing truth and their own rhetorical devices for
adjudicating and certifying truth claims. But studies of the mentalities
and technologies for the conduct of conduct that have developed in 'the
West' since the nineteenth century have paid particular attention to the
kinds of truthful thought that ground themselves in 'veridical' discourses
about human beings: discourses organized around scientific norms of
truth and hence subject to critical correction.[10]

The kind of work undertaken under the sign of governmentality has
been splendidly varied: it is neither a homogeneous school or a closed
sect. Many researchers who would not place their objects of study under
the sign of 'governmentalities' have nonetheless found these concepts
and approaches of use, for example, in the fields of political philosophy
and social history.[11] And studies of other practices have investigated
analogous relations between the knowledges and expertise of the
human, social and economic sciences and the exercise of political
power.[12] In the various studies that make up this book, I draw upon this
wide literature in order to explicate some of the analytical tools and
concepts that have been developed and to show how these can be set to
work in investigating the strategies that seek to govern us, and the ethics
according to which we have come to govern ourselves. I do not wish to
wrap a general theory of governmentality, power, modernity or post-
modernity around this work. I do not think there is much to be gained
by trying to impose some artificial unity upon it. Nor is this a methodology book, an attempt to draw out a set of generalizable propositions
that can then merely be 'applied' to other problems or issues. Such
methodological formalization would be quite antithetical to the ethos of
these studies. For, I shall suggest, concepts are more important for what
they do than for what they mean. Their value lies in the way in which
they are able to provide a purchase for critical thought upon particular
problems in the present.

The particular set of problems in the present that concern me here

[10] The idea of veridicality in thought is developed in the writings of the French
philosopher and historian of the life sciences Georges Canguilhem. See
the selections collected in Canguilhem 1994, and the series of papers on
Canguilhem collected in T. Osborne and Rose 1997.
[11] For political philosophy see Tully 1989, Hindess 1996a and especially the
work of Duncan Ivison: 1993, 1995, 1997a and 1997b. For social history,
see Joyce 1994.
[12] Notably Ian Hacking's work on the history of statistics (Hacking 1990,
1991) and Theodore Porter's work on statistics, accounting and the invention of objectivity (T. Porter 1986, 1992, 1996).

are questions concerning freedom. I want to consider a number of the ways in which, since the middle of the nineteenth century, and focusing in particular upon the English-speaking world – Britain, the United States, Canada and Australia – the values of freedom have been made real within practices for the government of conduct. I would, therefore, like these studies to be viewed as essays towards a genealogy of freedom. This is not because I want to argue that we should be for freedom or against it. It is not because the freedom we think we have is a sham. Nor is it to assist in the birth of some freer freedom which is to come. It is rather because, in our own times, ideas of freedom have come to define the ground of our ethical systems, our practice of politics and our habits of criticism. Hence it seems relevant to try to analyse the conditions under which these ideas of freedom and these practices in the name of freedom have come into existence, and to try to clarify the lines of power, truth and ethics that are in play within them.

Of course, in choosing the problem of freedom as a pathway into the analysis of the government of our present, I do not contend that coercion, constraint, domination and oppression have ceased to exist or to have significance for us. Nor do I want to deny that certain sectors – certain ethnic groups, inhabitants of particular zones of the inner city, mothers on welfare . . . – are defined, demarcated and delineated such that they can be the legitimate targets of such negative practices of control. But I want to argue that the programmatic and strategic deployment of coercion, whether it be in the name of crime control or the administration of welfare benefits, has been reshaped upon the ground of freedom, so that particular kinds of justification have to be provided for such practices. These might include, for example, the argument that the constraint of the few is a condition for the freedom of the many, that limited coercion is necessary to shape or reform pathological individuals so that they are willing and able to accept the rights and responsibilities of freedom, or that coercion is required to eliminate dependency and enforce the autonomy of the will that is the necessary counterpart of freedom. And I would also suggest that the undoubted persistence and salience of coercive tactics – in the policing of the inner cities and the urban poor, in the surveillance and control of political dissidence, and of course in the various international adventures of advanced liberal nations – must also, today, be justified as the price necessary for the maintenance of freedom. To focus on freedom and its genealogy, then, is not to claim that 'we' – the universal and undifferentiated subjects of the present – have entered the sunny uplands of liberty and human rights. Rather, it is to suggest that certain values and presuppositions about human beings and how they should live, values and presuppositions given the name of freedom and liberty, have come to provide the grounds upon which government must enact its practices for the conduct of conduct. And hence, for that reason alone, it is useful to try to ascertain the costs, as well as the benefits, of organizing our experience, our aspirations, our relations with ourselves and with others, our politics and our ethics in terms of freedom.

Strangely, perhaps, I hope that this book will be viewed as more empirical than theoretical. Much contemporary political and social thought takes the form of a quasi-philosophical meditation upon our present, upon the fragmentation of our ethical systems, the dissolution of old certainties, the waning of an epoch of modernity and the hesitant birth of another, whose name is not yet known. I know that many find such reflections illuminating. I am not among them. Like other historians of the present, I think we would be wise to avoid substantializing either the present or its past. Rather than conceiving of our present as an epoch or a state of affairs, it is more useful, in my own view, to view the present as an array of problems and questions, an actuality to be acted upon and within by genealogical investigation, to be made amenable to action by the action of thought. As an array of questions of this type, the present calls for a style of investigation that is more modest than that adopted by sociological philosophers of history. It encourages an attention to the humble, the mundane, the little shifts in our ways of thinking and understanding, the small and contingent struggles, tensions and negotiations that give rise to something new and unexpected. This is not merely because of a general prejudice that one will learn more about our present and its past by studying the minor and everyday texts and practices, the places where thought is technical, practical, operational, than by attending to the procession of grand thinkers that have usually captivated historians of ideas or philosophers of history. It is also because, so often in our history, events, however major their ramifications, occur at the level of the molecular, the minor, the little and the mundane. So many of the texts which have later become canonical are retrospective attempts to codify such minor shifts. Yet events cannot be identified with these moments of formalization. Things happen through the lines of force that form when a multitude of small shifts, often contingent and independent from one another, get connected up: hence it is these configurations of the minor that seem to me to form the most appropriate object for the work of a historian of the present.

The chapters that make up this book are not linked in a narrative structure or intended as an unfolding exposition of a theory of governmentality or a history of governmentalities. Each stands on its own, as a little map or diagram of a certain set of problems and issues. Together I hope they amount to something like a partial glossary or a selection of entries from an imaginary and always unfinished encyclopaedia. The book itself falls roughly into three parts. In chapters 1 and 2, I am concerned mostly with the development and explanation of some conceptual tools for the analysis of government, in particular those which help investigate the practice of government and those which have been related to the problematics of freedom. In chapters 3, 4 and 5, I examine a number of broad configurations of governmental strategies – which I term 'the social', 'advanced' liberalism, and community – though without intending to suggest that these form a historical series where each time period is characterized by one style of government which is then succeeded by another. In chapters 6 and 7, I focus on two specific 'technological' aspects of government – the significance of numbers and recent inventions in practices of control. In the conclusion to the book I try to address some of the limitations of these 'governmental' styles of analysis and to consider some criticisms that have been directed at them, through an investigation of practices of contestation and political dissidence.

I would like to think that these studies are characterized by a kind of empiricism. This is not an empiricism that would be recognized by those who have codified and criticized the epistemological presuppositions of different 'methodologies' in the social sciences. Rather, it is an empiricism closer to that of Gilles Deleuze when he compares the work of his philosophy in part to a detective novel, in that 'concepts, with their zones of presence, should intervene to resolve local situations. They themselves change along with the problems. They have spheres of influence where, as we shall see, they operate in relation to "dramas" and by means of a certain "cruelty" . . . This is the secret of empiricism.'[13] Empiricism, here, is not a matter of a reaction against concepts, far less an appeal to the primacy of lived experience. It is a method of inventivity, the invention of concepts as objects of an encounter, a here-and-now encounter which produces ever new, ever different 'heres' and 'nows'. It is an attention to all the occasions when a minute modification becomes possible, when difference can be made: 'In all his novels', Deleuze writes, 'Samuel Beckett has traced the inventory of peculiarities pursued with fatigue and passion by larval subjects [that is to say, subjects capable of undergoing a modification, of being a modification]: Molloy's series

---

[13] Deleuze 1994a: xx.

of stones, Murphy's biscuits, Malone's possessions – it is always a question of drawing a small difference, a weak generality, from the repetition of elements or the organization of cases.'[14] Whilst recognizing that the essays that follow are all too often drawn back into the habits of vapid generalization and the search for absolute differences, this Deleuzian empiricism seems closest to the ethos of the most instructive studies of governmentality. In the face of the banal grandiosity of so many sociological proclamations about our 'post'-enlightenment, 'post'-modern, 'post'-traditional epoch, it is this concern with drawing small differences and weak generalities from a respect for the particularities of specific cases that seems to me to be more likely to produce what Deleuze terms, after Nietzsche, an untimely attitude to our present, one that it is capable of 'acting counter to our time and thereby on our time, and, let us hope, for the benefit of a time to come'.[15]

Deleuze utilizes this formulation of Nietzsche elsewhere, in order to characterize Foucault's use of history as a means of acting on the present. Such an untimely use of history was not, thereby, an attempt to predict or to legislate the future, but rather to be attentive to the unknown, to the possibilities of difference that lie within every sameness, to the incidence of the unexpected, the contingent and the encounter with the here-and-now that has produced the apparent given-ness of experience, and to the work of writing that might assist in the ungrounding, the unmaking of the stability of our timely ways of thinking and acting.[16] Foucault once described his works as fictions, which did not thereby weaken the force of the truths that they could make, remake and unmake. Deleuze suggests that a book of philosophy is in part science fiction, because it is a place where one writes 'only at the frontiers of our knowledge, at the border which separates our knowledge from our ignorance and transforms the one into the other . . . To satisfy ignorance is to put off writing until tomorrow, or rather to make it impossible.'[17] If, despite their flaws and gaps, I have thought it worth reframing a number of my previous essays in this book-like form, it is not because I think they say the first or the last word on anything. These pieces are written at that border between what one knows and what one thinks it might be possible to think, between what little one grasps and the great gulf of ignorance which that partial grasp reveals. I present

---

[14] Ibid.: 79.
[15] Nietzsche 1983: 60, quoted in Deleuze 1994a: xxi.
[16] Deleuze 1988: 164–5.
[17] Deleuze 1994a: xxi.

them here with the hope that they may provoke others to do better, for to satisfy the demand that one might write without ignorance would not only make writing impossible; it would also deny that encounter with the unknown that carries with it the possibility, however slim, of contributing to a difference.

1   Governing

How should one analyse political power? For much of the twentieth century in European social and political thought, answers to this question were dominated by the massive spectre of 'the state'. Whilst political theory in the United States up through the 1950s and 1960s was more 'pluralist' in its vision of political power, even there, by the 1970s and 1980s, analysts were advocating the adoption of a 'state-centred' approach. The modern state was analysed in terms of an apparently ineluctable tendency to centralize, control, regulate and manage. Social and political theorists drew attention to this expanding role of the state, discovered the hand of the state even where it appeared absent, criticized prevailing conceptions of political pluralism because they seemed to ignore the structuring role of the state. In short, they wanted to 'bring the state back in' to the analysis of modern society.[1]

Over the last fifteen years, however, many sociologists and political scientists have argued equally vigorously in the opposite direction. They have tried to find ways of thinking about and investigating political power which are not immediately structured in terms of the hegemonic role of the state, which recognize, in different ways, that modern systems of rule have depended upon a complex set of relations between state and non-state authorities, upon infrastructural powers, upon networks of power, upon the activities of authorities who do not form part of the formal or informal state apparatus. One sign of this movement has been the emergence of 'governance' as a new field of social and political analysis. At its most general, the term 'governance' is used as a kind of catch-all to refer to any strategy, tactic, process, procedure or programme for controlling, regulating, shaping, mastering or exercising authority over others in a nation, organization or locality. This wide usage is certainly consistent with the definition provided in the Oxford English Dictionary, which gives examples of use going back to Middle

---

[1] This was the title of the very influential work by Theda Skocpol and others (Evans, Rueschmeyer and Skocpol 1985).

English. Governance directs attention to the nature, problems, means, actions, manners, techniques and objects by which actors place themselves under the control, guidance, sway and mastery of others, or seek to place other actors, organizations, entities or events under their own sway. Used in this way, governance seems a handy and compendious way of pointing to a number of important questions for investigation. Thus texts proliferate on the governance of the universities, of the health service, of the environment, even of cyberspace. The term seems a useful substitute and analogue for regulation, administration, management and the like, precisely because it is not overly burdened with conceptual baggage. But in the more specialized literature on governance, two more specific themes are evoked.

The first is normative.[2] Governance can be good or bad. Governance tends to be judged good when political strategies seek to minimize the role of the state, to encourage non-state mechanisms of regulation, to reduce the size of the political apparatus and civil service, to introduce 'the new public management', to change the role of politics in the management of social and economic affairs. Good governance means less government, politicians exercising power by steering (setting policy) rather than rowing (delivering services). Organizations such as the World Bank have sought to specify 'good governance' in terms of strategies that purport to disperse power relations amongst a whole complex of public service, judicial system and independent auditors of public finances, coupled with respect for the law, human rights, pluralism and a free press. They urge political regimes seeking aid and loans to correspond to this normative image of governance, by privatizing state corporations, encouraging competition, markets and private enterprise, downsizing the political apparatus, splitting up functions and allotting as many as possible to non-state organizations, ensuring budgetary discipline and so forth.

This normative sense of governance links to a second, descriptive, sense. This 'new sociology of governance' tries to characterize the pattern or structure that emerges as the resultant of the interactions of a

---

[2] The classic text here was *Reinventing Government: How the Entrepreneurial Spirit Is Transforming the Public Sector* by David Osborne and Ted Gaebler (D. Osborne and Gaebler 1992). 'Reinventing government' became the slogan for the assault on 'big government' in the United States, and the title of a series of publications of hearings of the United States Congress Committee on Governmental Affairs in the 1990s, examining issues ranging from the use of information technology in government to the restructuring of the public sector to deliver more for less.

range of political actors – of which the state is only one.[3] Governance refers to the *outcome* of all these interactions and interdependencies: the self-organizing networks that arise out of the interactions between a variety of organizations and associations. It is argued that these are of particular significance today because recent political strategies have attempted to govern neither through centrally controlled bureaucracies (hierarchies) nor through competitive interactions between producers and consumers (markets), but through such self-organizing networks.[4] Politics is seen as increasingly involving exchanges and relations amongst a range of public, private and voluntary organizations, without clear sovereign authority. Terms like 'actor networks', 'self-regulatory mechanisms', 'trust', 'habits and conventions', 'gift relations' and 'informal obligations' are utilized to describe the actual operation of the complex exchanges through which governance occurs.

At first sight, it seems that, whilst the approach to political power in terms of 'government' has little in common with normative uses of the notion of governance, it shares much with this new sociology of governance. It is critical of the analytic utility of the classical concepts of political sociology: state and market, public and private, and so forth. It agrees that new concepts are required to investigate the exercise of 'political power beyond the state'. It argues that strategies of political rule, from the earliest moments of the modern nation state, entailed complex and variable relations between the calculations and actions of those seeking to exercise rule over a territory, a population, a nation and a microphysics of power acting at a capillary level within a multitude of practices of control that proliferate across a territory. Like the sociology of governance, it does not to deny the existence of 'states' understood as political apparatuses and their associated devices and techniques of rule. Nor does it ignore the potency of the juridical and constitutional doctrines of state, sovereignty, legitimacy or the specific characteristics of the legal complex in the programming and exercise of rule. But it rejects the view that one must account for the political assemblages of rule *in terms of* the philosophical and constitutional language of the nineteenth century, or that one must underpin this misleading account with a theoretical infrastructure derived from nineteenth-century social and

---

[3] The most developed attempts to conceptualize governance can be found in the work of Jan Kooiman and his colleagues (Kooiman 1993). See also Leftwich 1994.

[4] Rhodes (1994, 1995) has used the phrase 'the hollowing out of the State' to describe this.

political theory which accords 'the state' a quite illusory necessity, functionality and territorialization.

From the perspective of government, the place of the state in specific strategies and practices for governing different zones, sectors or problems becomes a question for empirical investigation. Nonetheless, whatever arguments may have been made by the philosophers of liberalism, the key characteristic of 'actually existing liberalism', as it developed over the second half of the nineteenth century and the first seven decades of the twentieth, was what Michel Foucault termed 'the governmentalization of the State'.[5] That is to say, the invention and assembly of a whole array of technologies that connected up calculations and strategies developed in political centres to those thousands of spatially scattered points where the constitutional, fiscal, organizational and judicial powers of the state connect with endeavours to manage economic life, the health and habits of the population, the civility of the masses and so forth. This governmentalization has allowed the state to survive within contemporary power relations; it is within the field of governmentality that one sees the continual attempts to define and redefine which aspects of government are within the competence of the state and which are not, what is and what is not political, what is public and what is private, and so forth.

From the perspective of government, however, these developments are not best understood in terms of an relentless augmentation of the powers of a centralizing, controlling and regulating state. The thesis, inspired by Jürgen Habermas, that 'the state' has increasingly colonized 'the lifeworld' is misleading, not least because the very nature and meaning of state and lifeworld were transformed in this process.[6] State institutions certainly extend the scope of their operations and the depth of their penetration into the lives of their citizen subjects. But they do so by a complex set of strategies, utilizing and encouraging the new positive knowledges of economy, sociality and the moral order, and harnessing already existing micro-fields of power in order to link their governmental objectives with activities and events far distant in space and time.[7] These links between the political apparatus and the activities of governing are less stable and durable than often suggested: they are tenuous, reversible, heterogeneous, dependent upon a range of 'relatively autonomous' knowledges, knowledgeable persons and technical possibilities.

---

[5] Foucault 1991: 103.

[6] See, for example, John Keane's analysis of the extent to which we are moving towards a 'totally administered society' (Keane 1984, ch. 3).

[7] Cf. Stoler 1995: 28.

Despite these similarities, the ethos of analytics of governmentality is very different from that of sociologies of governance. First, analyses of governmentalities are empirical but not realist. They are not studies of the actual organization and operation of systems of rule, of the relations that obtain amongst political and other actors and organizations at local levels and their connection into actor networks and the like. In these networks, rule is, no doubt, exercised and experienced in manners that are complex, contingent, locally variable and organized by no distinct logic, although exactly how complex etc. they are would be a matter for a certain type of empirical investigation. But studies of governmentality are not sociologies of rule. They are studies of a particular 'stratum' of knowing and acting. Of the emergence of particular 'regimes of truth' concerning the conduct of conduct, ways of speaking truth, persons authorized to speak truths, ways of enacting truths and the costs of so doing. Of the invention and assemblage of particular apparatuses and devices for exercising power and intervening upon particular problems. They are concerned, that is to say, with the conditions of possibility and intelligibility for certain ways of seeking to act upon the conduct of others, or oneself, to achieve certain ends. And their role is diagnostic rather than descriptive: they seek an open and critical relation to strategies for governing, attentive to their presuppositions, their assumptions, their exclusions, their naiveties and their knaveries, their regimes of vision and their spots of blindness.

No doubt, at any one time, one can find a whole variety of different methods in play for acting upon others, linked in a whole variety of ways. Their variety, and their linkages, are empirical matters and worthy of study. But what distinguishes studies of government from histories of administration, historical sociologies of state formation and sociologies of governance is their power to open a space for critical thought. This stems from their preoccupation with a distinctive family of questions, arising from a concern with our own present. How did it become possible to make truths about persons, their conduct, the means of action upon this and the reasons for such action? How did it become possible to make these truths in these ways and in this geographical, temporal and existential space? How were these truths enacted and by whom, in what torsions and tensions with other truths, through what contests, struggles, alliances, briberies, blackmails, promises and threats? What relations of seduction, domination, subordination, allegiance and distinction were thus made possible? And, from the perspective of our own concerns, what is thus made intelligible in our present truths (in a 'cognitive' sense, but also in a bodily sense, in the sense of our habitual modes of being in the world and experiencing the world and ourselves in it, and the ways in which the space of possible actions in that world has been put together) – what do our studies of governmentality make amenable to *our* thought and action, in the sense of us being able to count its cost and think of it being made *otherwise*?

Perspectivism, here, is thus partly a matter of introducing a critical attitude towards those things that are given to our present experience as if they were timeless, natural, unquestionable: to stand against the maxims of one's time, against the spirit of one's age, against the current of received wisdom. It is a matter of introducing a kind of awkwardness into the fabric of one's experience, of interrupting the fluency of the narratives that encode that experience and making them stutter.[8] And the use of history here is to that untimely end – it is a matter of forming a connection or relation between a contemporary question and certain historical events, forming connections that vibrate or resonate, and hence introduce a difference, not only in the present, but also in the historical moments it connects up with and deploys. As Gilles Deleuze puts it, thinking of Nietzsche, things and actions are already interpretations. So to interpret them is to interpret interpretations: in this way it is already to change things, 'to change life', the present – and oneself.

Governmentality

To analyse political power through the analytics of governmentality is not to start from the apparently obvious historical or sociological question: what happened and why? It is to start by asking what authorities of various sorts wanted to happen, in relation to problems defined how, in pursuit of what objectives, through what strategies and techniques. Such investigations do not single out a sector of the real for investigation – ideas rather than events, for example. But they adopt a particular point of view which brings certain questions into focus: that dimension of our history composed by the invention, contestation, operationalization and transformation of more or less rationalized schemes, programmes, techniques and devices which seek to shape conduct so as to achieve certain ends. They distinguish between historically variable domains within which questions of government have been posed: the ways in which certain aspects of the

---

[8] 'Creative stuttering is what makes language grow from the middle, like grass; it is what makes language a rhizome instead of a tree, what puts language in perpetual disequilibrium' (Deleuze, 'He stuttered', in Deleuze 1997: 111). As Deleuze puts it, this stuttering is the moment in which language is strained to the limits that mark its outside, when it is engaged in digging under stories, cracking open opinions, reaching regions without memories, destroying the coherence of 'the self'.

conduct of persons, individually or collectively, have come to be problematized at specific historical moments, the objects and concerns that
appear here, and the forces, events or authorities that have rendered them
problematic. They investigate the ways in which debates and strategies
concerning the exercise of political power have delineated the proper
relations between the activities of political rule and different zones,
dimensions or aspects of this general field of conduct of conduct – for
example, the ways in which the management of virtue and vice has been
contested and divided between theological, pedagogic, medical and political authorities, or the regulation of economic life has been disputed
between attempts at political management and claims made for the virtues of a self-regulating market guided by its own invisible hand. They
concern themselves with the kinds of knowledge, the ideas and beliefs
about economy, society, authority, morality and subjectivity that have
engendered these problematizations and the strategies, tactics and programmes of government.

Governing here should be understood nominalistically: it is neither a
concept nor a theory, but a perspective. For sociologists of governance
such as Kooiman and his colleagues, the object of investigation is understood as an emergent pattern or order of a social system, arising out of
complex negotiations and exchanges between 'intermediate' social
actors, groups, forces, organizations, public and semi-public institutions
in which state organizations are only one – and not necessarily the most
significant – amongst many others seeking to steer or manage these
relations.[9] But the object of analytics of government is different. These
studies do not seek to describe a field of institutions, of structures, of
functional patterns or whatever. They try to diagnose an array of lines
of thought, of will, of invention, of programmes and failures, of acts and
counter-acts. Far from unifying all under a general theory of government, studies undertaken from this perspective draw attention to the
heterogeneity of authorities that have sought to govern conduct, the
heterogeneity of strategies, devices, ends sought, the conflicts between
them, and the ways in which our present has been shaped by such conflicts. Far from reducing all to politics, they draw attention to the complex and contingent histories of the problems around which political
problematizations come to form – cholera epidemics, wars, riots, technological change, the rise of new economic powers and so forth. Such
problematizations may or may not be shaped by previous strategies of
government. In any event, they do not speak for themselves. They must
always be individuated and conceptualized in particular ways. Political

[9] See in particular Kooiman 1993.

thought is thus not auto-effective: in making thought technical, attempts at governing are always limited by the conceptual and practical tools for the regulation of conduct that are available, although they may use them in novel ways and inspire the invention of new techniques. Far from homogenizing discursive space, these studies show how the space of government is always shaped and intersected by other discourses, notably the veridical discourses of science and changing moral rhetorics and ethical vocabularies, which have their own histories, apparatuses and problem spaces, and whose relation to problematics of government is not expression or causation but translation. And far from offering a new theory of power, studies of government offer a perspective which brings into sight a domain of questions to be asked and practices to be analysed. In particular, they seek to interrogate the problems and problematizations through which 'being' has been shaped in a thinkable and manageable form, the sites and locales where these problems formed and the authorities responsible for enunciating upon them, the techniques and devices invented, the modes of authority and subject-ification engendered, and the telos of these ambitions and strategies.

It thus seems to me to be useful to regard the notions of government and governmentality as marking out, in the most general way, the field upon which one might locate all investigations of the modern operations of power/knowledge. The mechanisms and strategies of discipline and normalization that Foucault analysed so provocatively in *Discipline and Punish*[10] may certainly be seen in these terms. The prisoner – or the schoolchild or lunatic – may be constrained and confined. Disciplinary techniques may be embodied in an external regime of structured times, spaces, gazes and hierarchies. But discipline seeks to reshape the ways in which each individual, at some future point, will conduct him- or herself in a space of regulated freedom. Discipline is bound to the emergence and transformation of new knowledges of the human soul. And discipline is constitutively linked to the emergence of new ways of thinking about the tasks of political rule in terms of the government of the conduct of the population, or at least of those sections and zones which have forfeited their claims to be contractual subjects of law or have not yet acquired that right – criminals, paupers, lunatics, children.

Similarly, the technologies of bio-politics and the biologized state that are discussed in the first volume of *The History of Sexuality*[11] can be seen in governmental terms. They are strategies which recognize and act upon the positivity of the domains to be governed – the factors affecting

[10] Foucault 1977.
[11] Foucault 1979a.

rates of reproduction and population growth, the genetic make-up of the race and the like. They seek, with some notable exceptions, to act upon these domains by reshaping the conduct of those who inhabit them without interdicting their formal freedom to conduct their lives as they see fit. And if, in Nazi Germany, the freedom to act, indeed the very existence, of some subjects had to be erased, this was in the name of a greater freedom of the Aryan people and their destiny. Here, without the controls exercised by liberal concerns with limited government and individual freedoms, the despotism of the state that is always an immanent presence in all governmentalities is manifest in all its bloody rationality.

Foucault was far from consistent in his own thinking about the relations between the different ways in which he analysed power. He certainly cautioned against conceiving of a chronology that went from 'sovereignty' – a discontinuous exercise of power through display and spectacle, law as command, sanctions as negative and deductive – to 'discipline' – the continuous exercise of power through surveillance, individualization and normalization – to 'governmentality' focusing on maximizing the forces of the population collectively and individually. At one point he suggested that one could identify a 'triangle' of sovereignty, discipline and governmentality. Elsewhere he argued that it was simplistic to see the societies of normalization of the nineteenth century as disciplinary: rather, in such societies, life was taken in charge by the interplay between the technologies of discipline focused on the individual body and the technologies of bio-politics, which acted on those bodies *en masse*, intervening in the making of life, the manner of living, in how to live.[12] I am happy to leave textual analysis to others.[13] From my point of view, it is most helpful to consider that, in the power regimes that began to take shape in the liberal societies of the nineteenth century, the thematics of sovereignty, of discipline and of bio-power are all relocated within the field of governmentality. Each is reorganized in the context of the general problematics of government, which concerns the best way to exercise powers over conduct individually and en masse so as to secure the good of each and of all. It is not a question of a

[12] See the first volume of *The History of Sexuality* (ibid.), and the discussion of Foucault's 1976 lectures in Stoler 1995, especially pp. 80–8.

[13] It is worth noting, however, that in an interview in 1984, six months before his death, Foucault says: 'I intend this concept of "governmentality" to cover the whole range of practices that constitute, define, organize, and instrumentalize the strategies that individuals in their freedom can use in dealing with each other' (Foucault 1997: 300). I return to this issue of government and freedom in chapter 2.

succession of forms, but of the ways in which the discovery of new problems for government – and the invention of new forms of government –
embraces, recodes, reshapes those that pre-exist them. Reciprocally,
within new styles of government, older forms, for example the claims of
an elected parliament to have assumed the mantle of sovereignty by
virtue of representing the sovereign will of the people, find novel spaces
of deployment and new points of support, and enter new dynamics of
antagonism and conflict.

Rationalities

Of course, even terror can be a calculated instrument of government, as
can naked violence. No complex analysis is required to count the costs
in lies and lives of these ways of exercising power. But the claim of the
analytics of government is that the 'modern' regimes for the conduct of
conduct that have taken shape in the West, and those strategies that
contest them, are ineluctably drawn to rationalize themselves according
to a value of truth. Does it make sense to interrogate strategies of
government in relation to truth? Is not government almost by definition
the realm of the pragmatics of the possible, the territory of the deal-
makers, of corruption, or pork barrelling and the like? Perhaps. But
Foucault's own work on governmentality implied that one could identify
specific political rationalizations emerging in precise sites and at specific
historical moments, and underpinned by coherent systems of thought,
and that one could also show how different kinds of calculations, strategies and tactics were linked to each. Thus Foucault and his co-workers
examined European doctrines of police and argued that these embodied
certain relatively coherent ways of understanding the tasks and objects
of rule, which were codified and rationalized in particular texts and were
linked to a range of regulatory practices which would be hard to understand otherwise. This secular 'science of police' was articulated in the
German-speaking parts of Europe, and also in the Italian states and in
France, in the period from about 1650 to 1800. It saw police not as
a negative activity concerned with the maintenance of order and the
prevention of danger, but as a positive programme (close to our contemporary notions of policy) based upon knowledge, which could act as the
'foundation of the power and happiness of States' (to quote from the
title of von Justi's text of 1760-1).[14] Ian Hunter has suggested that the

---

[14] For discussions, see Knemeyer 1980; Oestreich 1982, esp. ch. 9; Raeff 1983;
and Pasquino 1991. Andrew (1989) has a useful discussion of the arguments
made by eighteenth-century charitable societies in Britain that their efforts

'confessional churches' played a key role in the emergence of this notion of governable populations, developing a particular understanding of their role as one of reshaping the conduct of their subjects in the name of spiritual purity, deploying a range of measures for their spiritual disciplining, and thus uniting those in particular geographical areas in 'moral enclosures'.[15] For present purposes, however, what is significant is that, whether solely secular, solely spiritual or as a conflict ridden hybrid of both, political and religious authorities now understood their powers and obligations in terms of relatively formalized doctrines of rule which made it both necessary and legitimate for them to exercise a calculated power over the conduct of populations of individuals, omnes et singulatim (of each and of all).[16]

Others have shown relatively consistent projects of rationalization at work in nineteenth-century liberal debates about the need to limit the scope of government vis-à-vis a principle of the market or of the rights of the individual: rationalities that make it easier to understand the apparent conflicts between doctrines that seek to delimit political interventions and the proliferation of laws, regulations and apparatuses of government.[17] The same kinds of argument can be made about the New Liberalism that developed in Britain, Australia and the United States in the late nineteenth century in an attempt to transcend the apparently irreconcilable positions of the advocates of individualism on the one hand and collectivism on the other.[18] And a certain attempt at rationalization is at work in the architects of the New Deal in the United States, despite the fact that it is undoubtedly also the case that laws, organizations and devices that it invented were often *ad hoc* attempts to address problems of unemployment, surplus production, farmers' bankruptcy and crises of banking.[19]

It is not only liberal forms of government that operate according to a certain rationality: however barbaric were the murderous strategies of government in Nazi Germany, they were not simply acts of irrational

were an essential part of a good national 'police' to maintain and refine civil order.

[15] Hunter 1998.

[16] See also Foucault's discussion of the idea of 'political reason' in Foucault 1981.

[17] E.g. Dean 1991.

[18] Useful accounts of the New Liberalism, although not formulated in these terms, are Clarke 1978 and Collini 1979; the standard source is Freeden 1978.

[19] On the New Deal, see Eden 1989; S. Fraser and Gerstle 1989; Finegold and Skocpol 1995.

brutality or the institutionalization of resentment. It is true, as Detlev Peukert has pointed out, that 'The social history of the Third Reich was a rank and tangled undergrowth of Nazi projects of reorganization which never got put into practice, rivalries and jurisdictional wrangles between different state, semi-state and non-state organizations, Schweikian stratagems by the oppressed directed against the overweening demands of the bureaucracy, individual and collective acts of freebooting enterprise and clamours for privileges, if necessary at the expense of others, and deliberate self-sacrificing resistance.'.[20] Nonetheless, Nazism fused together a number of distinct elements into a relatively systematic matrix of political thought and action: a eugenic, biologizing and statist racism, prioritizing the management of the population through interventions upon the individual and collective body in order to control lineages, reproduction, health and hygiene; a pastoralized dream of the multiplication of practices for the disciplinary regulation of the body politic in the name of the race; the instrumentalization of the micro-fascisms of everyday life – of the band, the gang, the sect, the family; and a redeployment of an older thematic of race, blood and earth.[21] And, as we know, the actual power of Nazism as a mentality of government was its capacity to render itself technical, to connect itself up with all manner of technologies capable of implementing its nightmarish dreams into everyday existence.

One is not dealing here with a scientific discourse regulated by the apparatus of experiments, proofs, journals, peer review and so forth. Nonetheless, political rationalities are characterized by regularities.[22] They have a distinctive *moral* form, in that they embody conceptions of the nature and scope of legitimate authority, the distribution of authorities across different zones or spheres – political, military, pedagogic, familial and the ideals or principles that should guide the exercise of authority: freedom, justice, equality, responsibility, citizenship, autonomy and the like. They have an *epistemological* character in that, as we shall see in detail later in this chapter, they are articulated in relation to some understanding of the spaces, persons, problems and objects to be gov-

---

[20] Peukert 1987: 24. Other books I have found most helpful on the political rationalities that were at play in Nazi Germany are Mosse 1978 and Proctor 1988.

[21] I am paraphrasing Foucault's remarks in *The History of Sexuality* (Foucault 1979a: 149–50) and Deleuze and Guattari's comments on the relations of macro-fascism and micro-fascism in *A Thousand Plateaus* (Deleuze and Guattari 1987: 214–15). Note that the issue here is one of rationalities in the plural, not of a specific rationality of modernity (cf. Bauman 1989).

[22] I am drawing here upon Rose and Miller 1992: 178–9.

erned. And they have a distinctive *idiom* or language. A certain element of thought, that is to say, is involved in all projects of government. John Maynard Keynes, one of the great thinkers of the social liberalism that took shape in the United Kingdom between the First and Second World Wars, might have been thinking of himself when he wrote, in 1926, 'the next step forward must come, not from political agitation or premature experiments, but from thought'.[23]

The critiques of welfare that have flourished over the past fifty years, in the post-war writings of neo-liberals such as Hayek, through the US critics of the New Deal and the War on Poverty and in contemporary 'post-social' political arguments from left and right, seek to rationalize government in new ways. Such strategic attempts to rationalize the problems of government have effects. For example, the various tactics enacted by the British Conservative government under Margaret Thatcher in the 1980s were not realizations of any philosophy – whether it was Keith Joseph reading Adam Smith or one of his advisers reading Hayek. They were, rather, contingent lash-ups of thought and action, in which various problems of governing were resolved through drawing upon instruments and procedures that happened to be available, in which new ways of governing were invented in a rather *ad hoc* way, as practical attempts to think about and act upon specific problems in particular locales, and various other existing techniques and practices were merely dressed up in new clothes. But, in the course of this process, a certain rationality, call it neo-liberalism, came to provide a way of linking up these various tactics, integrating them *in thought* so that they appeared to partake in a coherent logic. And once they did so, once a kind of rationality could be extracted from them, made to be translatable with them, it could be redirected towards both them and other things, which could now be thought of in the same way – as, for example, in the various deployments of the notion of entrepreneurship. And such rationalities were then embodied in, or came to infuse, a whole variety of practices and assemblages for regulating economic life, medical care, welfare benefits, professional activity and so forth.

It is not that the thought of Hayek, Friedman or anyone else for that matter was realized in neo-liberalism. It is partly that government continually seeks to give itself a form of truth – establish a kind of ethical basis for its actions. We can be cynical about this without, I hope, thinking that this is just legitimization or ideology. To govern, one could say, is to be condemned to seek an authority for one's authority. It is also that, in order to govern, one needs some 'intellectual technology' for

[23] Keynes 1926: 53. I discuss social liberalism in chapter 3.

trying to work out what on earth one should do next – which involves criteria as to what one wants to do, what has succeeded in the past, what is the problem to be addressed and so forth. When studies of governmentality speak of liberalism, of welfare, of neo-liberalism and the like, it is in this sense that these terms should be understood: not as designating epochs, but as individuating a multiplicity of attempts to rationalize the nature, means, ends, limits for the exercise of power and styles of governing, the instruments, techniques and practices to which they become linked. The name merely individuates an assemblage which may have been in existence for a long time before it was named, and which may outlive its naming. But nonetheless, the naming is itself a creative act: it assembles a new individuation of concepts, symptoms, moralities, languages; it confers a kind of mobile and transferable character upon a multiplicity.[24]

At many times and places, and more or less consistently in Europe and the United States since at least the middle of the eighteenth century, those seeking to exercise power have sought to rationalize their authority, and these projects of rationalization have a systematicity, a history and an effectivity. Each such project or strategy of rationalization, in the name of the market, in the name of the social, in the name of the liberty of the individual, is a strategy to intervene, whether in thought or in reality, upon a set of messy, local, regional, practical, political and other struggles in order to rationalize them according to a certain principle. Political rationalities are discursive fields characterized by a shared vocabulary within which disputes can be organized, by ethical principles that can communicate with one another, by mutually intelligible explanatory logics, by commonly accepted facts, by significant agreement on key political problems. Within this zone of intelligible contestation, different political forces infuse the various elements with distinct meanings, link them within distinct thematics, and derive different conclusions as to what should be done, by whom and how.

Intelligibility

It is possible to govern only within a certain regime of intelligibility – to govern is to act under a certain description. Language is not secondary to government; it is constitutive of it. Language not only makes acts of government describable; it also makes them possible. This emphasis on language is not at all novel. In relation to the history of political thought,

---

[24] Cf. Deleuze on the function of the proper name, in Deleuze and Parnet 1987: 120–3.

it is most impressively exemplified in the method of historical critique developed by Quentin Skinner and his colleagues. This 'consists in a survey of the language employed in order to identify the shared conventions (the distinctions, concepts, assumptions, inferences and assertability warrants that are taken for granted in the course of the debate) which render [certain acts] problematic and give rise to the range of solutions' in order to free ourselves from the conventions of our age.[25]

However, analytics of government are not primarily concerned with language as a field of meaning, or with texts embodying authorial intentions which may be recovered and made intelligible in the appropriate historical context. They are concerned with knowledges, or regimes of truth.[26] That is to say, they are concerned with 'historical epistemologies': the reconstruction of 'the epistemological field that allows for the production of what counts for knowledge at any given moment, and which accords salience to particular categories, divisions, classifications, relations and identities'.[27] But perhaps even this 'epistemological' characterization is a little misleading, to the extent that it might imply a somewhat calm and peaceful succession of bodies of knowledge. For it is not a matter of words, of concepts, of epistemologies, but of a whole 'regime of enunciation'. That is to say, an agonistic field, traversed by conflicts over who can speak, according to what criteria of truth, from what places, authorized in what ways, through what media machines, utilizing what forms of rhetoric, symbolism, persuasion, sanction or seduction. It is not so much a question of what a word or a text 'means' – of the meanings of terms such as 'community', 'culture', 'risk', 'social', 'civility', 'citizen' and the like – but of analysing the way a word or a book functions in connection with other things, what it makes possible, the surfaces, networks and circuits around which it flows, the affects and passions that it mobilizes and through which it

---

[25] Tully 1995: 35. A good introduction to the work of Skinner is the collection of essays edited by James Tully (Tully 1988).

[26] It should be noted that I part company with those who have traced a line in Foucault's own writings from 'archaeology' through 'genealogy' to 'ethics'. Analytics of government are concerned with truth, with power and with subjectification. For further discussion of the role of language in the exercise of political power, see the work of William Connolly and Michael Shapiro (Connolly 1983, Shapiro 1984).

[27] Mary Poovey, from whom this quote is drawn, provides a good discussion of this in the context of 'social' history (Poovey 1995: 3). The idea of historical epistemology is derived from the work of French historians of scientific discourse, notably Georges Canguilhem (Canguilhem 1994). The papers collected in T. Osborne and Rose (1998) provide a good introduction to Canguilhem's work. See also the discussion in Daston 1994.

mobilizes. It is thus a matter of analysing what counts as truth, who has the power to define truth, the role of different authorities of truth, and the epistemological, institutional and technical conditions for the production and circulation of truths.

As I have already suggested, one specific characteristic of modern strategies of government is that they harness themselves to practices for the production of particular styles of truth telling: the truth procedures and pronouncements of objective, positive or scientific discourses – what Georges Canguilhem terms 'veridical discourses'. Thus the exercise of government has become enmeshed with regimes of truth concerning the objects, processes and persons governed – economy, society, morality, psychology, pathology. Government has both fostered and depended upon the vocation of 'experts of truth' and the functioning of their concepts of normality and pathology, danger and risk, social order and social control, and the judgements and devices which such concepts have inhabited.

Perhaps there is a methodological point to be made here. A number of historians of political ideas, notably J. G. A. Pocock and Quentin Skinner and his collaborators, have helped us understand that the writings of philosophers – Kant, Hume, Locke and others – can be adequately understood only when located within the context of the problems that concerned the political classes in their time and place, and the field of social and political discourse within which they were engaged. They have also shown how many of those now assimilated into the academic canon were actively involved in inventing and arguing for new ways of governing, whether this be in the form of systems of taxation, practices of education or institutions for the reform of prisoners and paupers.[28] There is no doubt that, in certain times and places, the arguments and activities of philosophers have played a significant role in practices of government. This is a matter for empirical investigation in particular cases. But as significant, certainly since the middle of the nineteenth century, have been the truth claims articulated in texts that have a less elevated character: statistical texts discussing the importance of taking a census; proposals for reform of asylums written by doctors of the insane; medical debates about the nature of cholera and the mechanisms of its spread; economists' arguments for the need for labour exchanges in order to create a true market in labour and to expose the workshy and the unemployable for harsh intervention. This is not the 'appliance of science', in the sense that the truths worked out in the

---

[28] An excellent example is Tully's study of John Locke (Tully 1993); see also the work of Duncan Ivison, especially his book *The Self at Liberty* (1997b).

university study or the laboratory are being applied to specific practical issues. Rather, it is in these pragmatic governmental arguments that the concepts are forged that will later be formalized in theories, experiments, comparative studies and the like. And the methodological point is this: it is, most often, at this vulgar, pragmatic, quotidian and minor level that one can see the languages and techniques being invented that will reshape understandings of the subjects and objects of government, and hence reshape the very presuppositions upon which government rests.

Governable spaces

Governing does not just act on a pre-existing thought world with its natural divisions. To govern is to cut experience in certain ways, to distribute attractions and repulsions, passions and fears across it, to bring new facets and forces, new intensities and relations into being. This is partly a matter of time. Thus, the invention of the factory and work discipline involves novel ways of cutting up time in order to govern productive subjects: we must learn to count our lives by hours, minutes, seconds, the time of work and the time of leisure, the week and the weekend, opening hours and closing time.[29] The bell, the timetable, the whistle at the end of the shift manage time externally, disciplinarily. The beeping wrist watch, the courses in time management and the like inscribe the particular temporalities into the comportment of free citizens as a matter of their self-control.

It is also a matter of space, of the making up of governable spaces: populations, nations, societies, economies, classes, families, schools, factories, individuals. Mary Poovey and Peter Miller have used the term 'abstract spaces' to characterize such governable zones.[30] Poovey used the term 'abstract space' in her examination of the different ways in which space is produced and organized in the exercise of power. She was concerned with the representational assumptions involved, for instance

[29] Mariana Valverde pointed out to me the need to emphasize the role of temporalization in governing (see Valverde 1998c). This point is made classically by Edward Thompson in his analysis of time, work discipline and industrial capitalism (E. P. Thompson 1967). It is also, of course, a key theme in *Discipline and Punish* (Foucault 1977).

[30] Mary Poovey uses this term in her study of the construction of 'the social body' (Poovey 1995); Peter Miller uses it in the context of an analysis of the fabrication of the domains upon which accounting and management will operate (Miller 1994). See also Miller and O'Leary's analysis of the space of the factory (Miller and O'Leary 1994).

whether space is abstract or empty, the ways in which bodies are arranged in space, the metaphors of space such as machines or bodies, the relations of materialization or dematerialization that are involved. This notion of abstract space comes from Henri Lefebvre.[31] For Lefebvre, space becomes abstract only as a result of the crushing of lived experience and its vanquishing by concepts and representations. But these oppositions between the lived and the represented, the experienced and the conceptualized, the abstract and the concrete, seem to me to be misleading. Governable spaces are not fabricated counter to experience; they make new kinds of experience possible, produce new modes of perception, invest percepts with affects, with dangers and opportunities, with saliences and attractions. Through certain technical means, an new way of seeing is constructed which will 'raise lived perceptions to the percept and lived affections to the affect'.[32] They are modalities in which a real and material governable world is composed, terraformed and populated.

I think of these fabricated spaces as 'irreal'. I take this term from Nelson Goodman.[33] We need to use it with caution, lest we concede too much to the realists: reality is irreal; what else could it possible be? Goodman, in his foreword to *Ways of Worldmaking* says his irrealist position is a radical relativism under rigorous restraints. It is a radical relativism because, for Goodman, there is no independent access to one true world against which our versions of it can be compared and evaluated. All we have are different versions of the world, versions constructed out of words, numerals, pictures, sounds or symbols in various media. We take particular versions for real largely as a matter of habit. From my point of view, however, Goodman's irrealism is too psychological. His examples come from such well-worn and psychologically contentious claims as the relativity of the perception of colour, shape and movement. His image of a version of the world is that of a picture. My own irrealism is technical, not psychologistic. It is technical in so far as it asserts that thought constructs its irreal worlds through very material procedures. Thought, that is to say, becomes real by harnessing itself to a practice of inscription, calculation and action.

One should not try to make up a theory of the fabrication of these

---

[31] Notably in Lefebvre 1991.

[32] Gilles Deleuze is here talking about style in writing, music, painting; style in governing may be more mundane but it is no less a process of creative fabulation (Deleuze 1994b: 170).

[33] It is developed most clearly in his *Ways of Worldmaking* (Goodman 1978). Ian Hacking has discussed Goodman's work in a number of important papers (Hacking 1988, 1992).

irreal spaces: they are put together differently in different practices and contexts. But we can make a few general points. The government of a population, a national economy, an enterprise, a family, a child or even oneself becomes possible only through discursive mechanisms that represent the domain to be governed as an intelligible field with specifiable limits and particular characteristics, and whose component parts are linked together in some more or less systematic manner by forces, attractions and coexistences.[34] This is a matter of defining boundaries, rendering that within them visible, assembling information about that which is included and devising techniques to mobilize the forces and entities thus revealed. For example, before one can seek to manage a domain such as an economy it is first necessary to conceptualize a set of bounded processes and relations as an economy which is amenable to management. One could write the genealogy of this 'economy', the ways in which Adam Smith and David Ricardo presuppose that an economy is more or less coincident with the territorial boundaries of a nation state, and that trading relations between countries typically take place between distinct and relatively self-contained national economies.[35] It was thus only in the nineteenth century that we can see the birth of a language of national economy as a domain with its own characteristics which could be spoken about and about which knowledge could be gained. Once such an economy had been delineated, it could become the object and target of political programmes that would seek to evaluate and increase the power of nations by governing and managing 'the economy'. But spaces such as 'the economy' are not brought into existence by theory alone. For example, the strategies of national economic management that were invented in the middle of the twentieth century were made possible not merely by the installation of new sets of concepts to think about 'the economy', but also through the construction of a vast statistical apparatus through which this domain could be inscribed, visualized, tabulated, modelled, calculated, national economies compared, indicators like 'rate of growth' devised and so forth.[36] And today, as the

[34] I am drawing directly here on some formulations in Miller and Rose 1990.

[35] Barry Hindess provides a useful discussion of these issues in the context of an analysis of contemporary arguments concerning the fragmentation of such national economic spaces (Hindess 1998a). Keith Tribe has written a compelling study of the development and transformation of notions of oeconomy and economy (Tribe 1978). The work of Donald Winch is particularly instructive on all these issues: see for example Winch 1969.

[36] Grahame Thompson has analysed the forms of visualization out of which knowledge and sense of the firm and the economy are constructed (G. Thompson 1998).

discourse of globalization implies, this idea of the national economy is beginning to fragment, and we can begin to analyse the shifting forces, conditions and forms of visibility that have allowed the deterritorialization and reterritorialization of economic government, the emergence of a novel conception of economic space.

Elsewhere I consider the formation of a number of governmental fields or governable spaces. Here, however, I would like to make some general remarks on ways in which one might analyse the spatialization of governmental thought.[37] We can make a rough and ready distinction between three dimensions or sets of problems.

Territorializing governmental thought

Governmental thought territorializes itself in different ways. As William Connolly has pointed out, the term 'territory' derives from *terra* – land, earth, soil, nourishment – but also perhaps from *terrere* – to frighten, terrorize, exclude, warn off.[38] It is a matter of marking out a territory in thought and inscribing it in the real, topographizing it, investing it with powers, bounding it by exclusions, defining who or what can rightfully enter. Central to modern governmental thought has been a territorialization of national spaces: states, countries, populations, societies. One can trace the ways in which each of these territorializations takes shape.

Take, for example, 'society'. One can chart how, perhaps beginning with a book like Montesquieu's *Persian Letters* published anonymously in Amsterdam in 1721, a certain way emerges for visualizing the forms of government, religion and habits of a particular country, including one's own, as one of a variety of forms in which human existence can be organized in the shape of a society.[39] Montesquieu's sense of the variety of laws, customs and usages of different peoples is undoubtedly conditional upon the influx of information, speculation and invention 'made possible by the voyages of exploration, trade, missionary activity and colonization that Europeans had begun in the fifteenth century'.[40] This rendered the mores, habits and institutions that are taken for granted by inhabitants of a particular locale simultaneously extraordinary and difficult to understand, and yet intelligible and explicable. This

[37] I am drawing generally on Foucault's suggestions in *The Birth of the Clinic* (Foucault 1973) and more directly on joint work that I have undertaken with Tom Osborne on the history of empirical social thought (T. Osborne and Rose forthcoming).

[38] Connolly 1995: xxii.

[39] Montesquieu [1721] 1971.

[40] Richter 1977: 32.

idea gradually gets linked up to a political understanding of a state as consisting of a differentiated and hierarchical moral order: states and societies become potentially, and indeed ideally, coincident. We know the bloody ways in which this coincidence was often achieved in the process of state-building, by seeking to impose a shared language, values, religious beliefs and habits upon the population living in a territory on the one hand, or by disputing the legitimacy of particular territorializations in terms of their lack of coincidence with the real spatial distribution of the true spirit of a people on the other. And we can also trace the ways in which this space of state/society becomes empirically thinkable and technically governable, as we shall see in chapter 3.[41]

In a related manner, we can analyse the ways in which the idea of a territorially bounded, politically governed nation state under sovereign authority took shape in the religious conflicts that wracked Europe in the early modern period. Whilst populations had been subject to the authority of a variety of religious and secular authorities, the Treaty of Westphalia and the other agreements which ended the Thirty Years War in 1648, 'recognising the existence of irreconcilable religious differences between Lutherans, Calvinists and Catholics within political units . . . nonetheless granted supreme political authority to territorial rulers within their domains, leaving it to rulers and their subjects to come to an accommodation in matters of religion and restricting the right of participating states to intervene in the religious affairs of other participants'.[42] This was an arrangement which, as Barry Hindess points out, had the novel effect of assigning to *states* the government of populations within their territories at the same time as it began to establish an international state system regulating large-scale territorial conflicts in terms of agreements regulating the conduct of states towards one another.

One can trace analogous governmental histories of smaller-scale territorializations: regions, cities, towns, zones, ghettos, edge cities and so forth. And one can also think in these terms about the spaces of enclosure that governmental thought has imagined and penetrated: schools, factories, hospitals, asylums, museums, now even shopping malls, airports and department stores. So, along this dimension of territorialization, we are concerned not merely with describing these various topoi

---

[41] For the later history of the idea of society, see, for example, Melton 1991 and Burke 1991.

[42] Hindess 1998b: 15–16. Ian Hunter has also pointed to the importance of strategies to resolve religious conflicts in the elaboration of novel doctrines of sovereignty and state reason in Europe in this period (Hunter 1998).

and their delimitation and succession, but also with trying to identify
the problematizations within which these particular topoi have emerged:
how it happens, for example, that social thought territorializes itself on
the problem of the slum in the late nineteenth century.

Spatializing the gaze of the governors

A telling picture hangs in the Australian National Art Gallery in Canberra. It shows traces of hills, rivers, trails, borders, overlaid by a vast
eye. It is entitled 'The Governor loves to go mapping.'.[43] Cartography –
the activity of mapping – exemplifies the ways in which spaces are made
presentable and representable in the hope that they might become docile
and amenable to government. To govern, it is necessary to render visible
the space over which government is to be exercised. This is not simply
a matter of looking; it is a practice by which the space is re-presented
in maps, charts, pictures and other inscription devices. It is made visible,
gridded, marked out, placed in two dimensions, scaled, populated with
icons and so forth. In this process, and from the perspective of its
government, salient features are identified and non-salient features
rendered invisible. The construction of such a map is a complex technical achievement. It entails practices such as exploring, surveying, tramp-
ing the streets in order to identify the inhabitants of different dwellings,
collecting statistics from far and wide across the realm, conducting surveys of areas, regions, towns and so on. It involves the invention of
projections, the uses of colour, of symbols, of figures, scales, keys and
much more.

Bruno Latour uses the example of map-making in his discussion of
inscription devices: the modes of objectifying, marking, inscribing and
preserving otherwise ephemeral and subjective visions. It is these
inscriptions which make things stable, mobile, durable, comparable:
maps, charts, diagrams, graphs and so forth.[44] These exemplify what
Latour would call thinking with eyes and hands: they show the ways in
which many of the powers which we tend to attribute to cognition and
reason actually inhere in little material techniques such as drawing a
map, writing a description, making a list or drawing up a table of figures.
Inscriptions are also rhetorical. That is to say that a map, a chart, a

[43] The print, by Christopher Croft, was one of a series of ten commissioned
during the 1980s as a part of the construction of Australia's new Parliament
in Canberra. The phrase comes from a poem entitled 'Sydney Cove 1788'
by Peter Porter (P. Porter 1983).

[44] Latour provide his clearest discussion of this in Latour 1986.

table, a diagram is a little machine for producing conviction in others. Inscriptions thus produce objectivity in a way that is different in its nature and its uses from speech and the bearing of witness. Inscription devices are 'intellectual techniques': material techniques of thought that make possible the extension of authority over that which they seem to depict.

The spatialization of the gaze involves a power relation between knowledge and its subjects (or objects). For example, the maps which Charles Booth drew up of London in the late nineteenth century, depicting the class of inhabitants dwelling in different places street by street and house by house, were definitely practices of a kind of disciplinary expertise whose special concern was to identify and locate dangerous or demeaned subjects.[45] A few decades later, George Gallup's attempts to take 'the pulse of democracy' through his opinion polls embodied a quite different form of authority: the little percentage figures he presented constituted subjects as democratic citizens with a right to a voice in the political decisions that ruled them and producing a quite novel kind of spatial and political object – public opinion.[46] And, in a very different way, the collection and comparison of national economic statistics by the Organization for Economic Co-operation and Development in the period after the Second World War opened up a new vision of competing national economies: the charts and tables stabilized economies in terms of a few simple and elegant figures, and hence rendered them comparable, allowing their strength and health to be measured, followed over time, ranked in terms of such indicators as 'rate of growth'.[47]

Modelling the space of government

I use this notion of modelling to refer to two related processes: first, the ways in which space is modelled in thought through the distributions and relations of concepts that, as it were, open zones of cognition and configure their topography; secondly, the ways in which acts of government re-implant these conceptual models in the spaces of the real and hence remodel space itself. Mary Poovey provides some good ways of thinking about this kind of question. She suggests that, from the

[45] Booth's maps are reproduced and discussed in Martin Bulmer and his colleagues' excellent study of the history of the social survey (Bulmer, Bales and Sklar 1991).
[46] I discuss this in a forthcoming article with Tom Osborne (T. Osborne and Rose forthcoming).
[47] Cf. Miller and Rose 1990.

seventeenth century onwards, one can see the development of a particular idea of space, one in which space is conceptualized as isotropic – everywhere the same – and as reducible to a formal schema or grid: it is a space of 'seriality; repetitious actions; reproducible products; interchangeable places, behaviors and activities'.[48] This geometrical space is dominated by visuality in the sense that it is associated with seeing in a literal or imaginative form, with plans, diagrams, maps and so forth, and because, once produced, these concrete realizations of imaginary space stand in, in thought, for that which they realize. Once grasped through these images or plans, the features of these visualizations take on a life of their own, and are invested with powers which appear to allow the mastery of the phenomena they imagine or model.

Actually, this model of isotropic space needs complicating. In the nineteenth century at least, the governmental modelling of space operated in terms of some denser, more organic conceptual schemas. Space was on the one hand the milieux of activity of human beings as living creatures: populations and peoples. On the other hand, space was the field of action of deeper economic forces and processes: geography formed the 'art whose science is political economy'.[49] The notion of space as isotropic, two-dimensional, a plane upon which the diversity of the world was laid out and could be tabulated, could be termed 'classical' following Foucault's account in *The Order of Things*.[50] Modernity, in the human sciences, is characterized by a bifurcation in which the world of experiences and appearances is cut away from the laws and processes located at a hidden and more fundamental level. It is these deep determinants that shape experience, and it will be the vocation of the human sciences to discover them. Hence the two great underlying thematics that produce the modernity of space: the biological and the economic.

On the one hand, space would be modelled in terms of the laws of population which determine the character of the inhabitants of each territory. Political discourse was transcribed in biological terms and governable space was remodelled in these terms. These biological geographies operated by means of fundamental distinctions between populations, defined and distributed according to a racialized geography. Or rather, as Stoler has pointed out, these geographies modelled space in terms of a distinction between those national spaces of advanced and

[48] Poovey 1995: 29.
[49] Rhein 1982: 229, quoted in Rabinow 1989: 142. My understanding of modernity in geography and government is indebted to Rabinow's account.
[50] Foucault 1970.

civilized populations of citizens – even if their civility was potential – who warranted liberal forms of bio-political and disciplinary adminis- tration – and primitive 'peoples' who were 'regrouped and reconfigured according to somatic, cultural, and psychological criteria that would make . . . administrative interventions necessary and credible'.[51] This was the fecund, organic, sexual space of bio-politics, within which the internal and external racisms of government would operate through the course of the nineteenth century and into the twentieth. Here one would find the sexualization of children, of men and women, of different classes, of the normal and the pervert, of the civilized and the primitive, with all the physical, moral and economic implications for those who would rule. Here, too, one would find the discourses of degeneracy and degeneration, which placed the biology of the population within a dynamic of time and which found degenerate and degenerating individ- uals and sub-populations not only abroad but also in the heart of the great metropolitan cities of Europe. One whole array of political con- flicts, in the colonies and 'at home', would be modelled in terms of the various and conflicting claims to know this space, the diagnoses of its virtuous and vicious dynamics, the technical innovations that would try to shape and govern these biological forces in the interests of good order, national well-being and international competition.

On the other hand, a second great model of space would take shape in the nineteenth century, the model of political economy. This space, once again, is not two-dimensional and isotropic: it has depth and is traversed by natural determinations. The activity of production is no longer distributed upon a smooth plane: its laws have withdrawn into the depth of reality, into the value of goods, the nature of capital, the productivity of labour, the constitutive role of scarcity in the generation of wealth, the laws of supply and demand. In short, one sees a new model of economic space which differentiates between the appearance of things on the surface and their real nature and determinants: the system of production of wealth, which acts as a causal mechanism, has its own natural spatiality and temporality, which cannot be dominated by economic government but to which economic government must defer. These cold laws of economics must moderate compassion and charity and must determine not merely how economic life should be administered, but the administration of life itself: the regulation of flows of 'free' labour, the laws of contract, the freedoms of the employer in the wage relation and so forth. A whole array of conflicts would take shape within and around this model of the space of government, and

[51] Stoler 1995: 39.

between those who would model government in terms of economic space and those who would prioritize the demands of the bio-political space of population. And, as we shall see in later chapters, the history of government can be written, in part, in terms of the vicissitudes of this economic model of political space.

Governable subjects

As Paul Veyne has pointed out, there is no universal object, the governed, in relation to which a body of governors proceeds to act.[52] The governed vary over time; indeed there is no such thing as 'the governed', only multiple objectifications of those over whom government is to be exercised, and whose characteristics government must harness and instrumentalize. In any concrete situation, it appears as if practices of governing are determined by the nature of those who they govern: their character, passions, motivations, wills and interests. But the reverse is the case. Veyne is the author of a great book on bread and circuses.[53] But, he says, he would have written it differently in the light of this understanding.

Take the question of gladiator fighting, which offends our humanist sensibilities but not that of the Romans. Can it be understood in terms of the changing balance of horror and attraction which the spectacle provokes? No. The reason for the changing regulation of this activity has to do with changing ways in which 'the people' – the subjects of government – are politically objectified. Veyne quotes an imaginary Roman senator:

Our politics is limited to keeping the flock together as it moves along its historical trajectory; for the rest, we are well aware that animals are animals. We try not to abandon too many hungry ones along the way, for that would reduce the population of the flock; we feed them if we have to ... We are no more concerned about denying gladiators' blood to the Roman people than a herder of sheep or cattle would be concerned about watching over his animals' mating behavior in order to prevent incestuous unions. We are intransigent on just one point, which is not the animals' morality but their energy: we do not want the flock to weaken, for that would be its loss and ours.[54]

Whereas, if we had been trusted with children instead of sheep, of

---

[52] Veyne makes this point in his illuminating essay 'Foucault revolutionizes history': Veyne 1997. The empirical material collected by Norbert Elias (1969, 1982) remains instructive, as do the problems he addresses, despite the limitations of the form of analysis he uses.

[53] Veyne 1990.

[54] Veyne 1997: 152.

course we could have taken into account their sensitivity and our responsibilities as paternal rulers; if we had been priest-kings, imbued with Christian virtues, we would have led our subjects down the path of virtue towards salvation, whether they liked it or not.

There is a history to be written of the subjects of government. This is not a grand history of the procession of human types which has become a sociological commonplace: from traditional subjects scarcely individuated, through the isolated, self-contained atoms of individualistic capitalism to the fragmented subject of postmodernity.[55] It is a little, variegated, multiple history of the objectifications of human being within the discourses that would govern them, and their subjectification in diverse practices and techniques. Are we to be governed as members of a flock to be led, as children to be coddled and educated, as a human resource to be exploited, as members of a population to be managed, as legal subjects with rights, as responsible citizens of an interdependent society, as autonomous individuals with our own illimitable aspirations, as value-driven members of a moral community . . .

From this kind of perspective, then, how should we understand the objectifications of the subject within liberal governmental thought and technique. Within philosophical discourse, liberal thinkers of the late eighteenth and nineteenth centuries had a rather explicit specification of the subject of liberal rule. This subject was an individual human being with a certain kind of moral relationship with itself. Here, for example, is Adam Smith in the *Theory of Moral Sentiments* in 1759:

When I endeavour to examine my own conduct, when I endeavour to pass sentence upon it, and either to approve or condemn it, it is evident that, in all such cases, I divide myself, as it were, into two persons; and that I, the examiner and judge, represent a different character from that other I, the person whose conduct is examined into and judged of. The first is the spectator, whose sentiments with regard to my own conduct I endeavour to enter into by placing myself in his situation, and by considering how it would appear to me, when seen from that particular point of view. The second is the agent, the person whom I properly call myself, and of whose conduct, under the character of a spectator, I was endeavouring to form some opinion.[56]

Charles Taylor has pointed out the rarity and historical specificity of this kind of subject:

[55] I criticize this kind of story, as it is put forward in the sociologies of Ulrich Beck, Anthony Giddens and Zygmunt Bauman (see Heelas, Lash and Morris 1996), in Rose 1996a and 1996d; see also Rose 1996e.

[56] Adam Smith [1759] 1982: Part III, Ch. 1, para. 6; I owe this quote to Mary Poovey 1995: 33.

The free individual . . . is . . . only possible within a certain kind of civilization; . . . it took a long development of certain institutions and practices, of the rule of law, or rules of equal respect, of habits of common deliberation, of common association, of cultural development and so on, to produce the modern individual.[57]

Human beings can relate to themselves only as subjects of freedom, that is to say, in certain social and cultural conditions.

I will have much more to say about this issue of freedom in chapter 2 and throughout this book. For the moment, let us remain with the particular question: how should we understand the specification of governable subjects in the rationalities of liberalism? Taylor, here as in his magisterial history of the self, ascribes the conditions that make possible certain kinds of subject to the history of culture.[58] But the rather precise formulations used by Adam Smith suggest something a little different: what is involved is not so much 'culture' but the inculcation of particular kinds of relations that the human being has with itself. Steven Greenblatt has used the term 'self-fashioning' to designate these kinds of practices. Self-fashioning entails a self-consciousness about the fashioning of human identity as a manipulable, artful process, embodied in practices of parents, teachers, priests, textbooks of manners etc. And Greenblatt follows Clifford Geertz in ascribing 'self-fashioning' not to customs and traditions, but to 'a set of control mechanisms – plans, recipes, rules, instructions . . . for the governing of behavior'.[59] That is to say, the arts of self-reflection of the moral individual described by Smith did not originate in philosophy, nor was philosophy the most significant locus for their elaboration and dissemination. On the one hand, they were articulated in a whole variety of mundane texts of social reformers, campaigners for domestic hygiene, for urban planning and the like, each of which embodied certain presuppositions about what human subjects were, what mobilized them in different ways and how they could be brought to govern themselves morally. On the other hand they were to be made technical, embodied in a whole series of interventions aimed at producing the human being as a moral creature capable of exercising responsible stewardship and judgement over its own conduct in terms of certain externally prescribed moral principles.

[57] C. Taylor 1955: 200, quoted from Mouffe 1992: 230.
[58] C. Taylor 1989b.
[59] For Greenblatt, see the introduction to his *Renaissance Self-Fashioning* (Greenblatt 1980); the quote from Geertz (1973: 49) comes from Greenblatt 1980: 3.

Foucault terms these kinds of practices 'techniques of the self'.[60] Histories of conduct over the nineteenth century have revealed the ways in
which these techniques – in the form of injunctions to moral government formulated largely in terms of self-control – were instantiated in
architecture, guidance to parents, in the work of pauper schools and the
like. They were embodied in language, in knowledge, in technique, in
the fabrication of spaces and of repertoires of conduct within them.
What was involved here was an exercise of inhibition of the self by the
self, a kind of despotism of the self at the heart of liberalism.[61] These
practices of subjectification have their own history, and it is a history
that is inextricably linked to government and to knowledge. At any one
time human beings are subject to a variety of distinct practices of subjectification in different places and spaces. For example, if one considers
the bourgeoisie of late nineteenth-century Europe, the regimes of subjectification – the relations to the self presupposed and enjoined – on
the sensual subjects of the bedroom are not the same as those for the
self-absorbed subjects of the library, the civilized citizens of the evening
promenade, the disciplined subjects of the schoolroom or the consuming subjects of department stores.[62] We do not need to engage in the
interminable and ultimately fruitless project of constructing a general
history of the human subject, for there is no general history of this type
to be written. Rather, we need to undertake a more modest yet more
practicable task: identifying the ways in which human beings are
individuated and addressed within the various practices that would
govern them, the relations to themselves that they have taken up within
the variety of practices within which they have come to govern
themselves.

One example, taken from studies of self-technologies undertaken by
others, will have to suffice. For much of the nineteenth century, one

---

[60] Foucault's argument is most accessibly set out in his contribution to the
useful edited volume *Technologies of the Self* (Foucault 1988). Ian Hacking
has addressed this issue in a related manner in his analyses of different ways
of 'making up people' which he outlines in Hacking 1986.

[61] I owe the phrase 'despotism of the self' to Mariana Valverde (Valverde
1996a). Roger Smith gives an excellent account of the significance of the
notion of inhibition in nineteenth-century England in the first chapter of his
history of the concept (R. Smith 1992).

[62] I have discussed the conceptual and empirical aspects of these issues in much
more detail in my *Inventing Our Selves* (Rose 1996e). For a wealth of empirical detail, see the successive volumes of *A History of Private Life* (Veyne 1987;
Duby 1988; Chartier 1989; Perrot 1990; Prost and Gerard 1991).

pervasive objectification of the subject of government was as an impulsive, passionate and desiring creature, who was civilized and made amenable to moral order by the action of the will and the inculcation of conscious self-control and habits of responsible self-management. As Mariana Valverde has argued in relation to alcoholism and inebriety, and as Roger Smith has shown in detail in relation to the history of the concept of inhibition, in a wide range of practices and in both academic and popular discourse, issues of self-discipline and, reciprocally, problems of individual and collective pathology were understood in terms of the training of the Will.[63] Civility was understood, here, as the capacity of the self to exercise restraints upon its passions and affections in order to enter into moral intercourse with others. In other words, the problem was one of self-control. In 1842, the physiologist W. B. Carpenter drew conclusions for moral education from his investigations of the role of higher brain functions in controlling the nervous system, and the necessity for moral training to render such controls automatic. 'It is solely by Volitional *direction of the attention*', he wrote, 'that the Will exerts its domination; so that the acquirement of this power . . . should be the primary object of all Mental discipline.'[64] Order, here, as Smith points out, was shaped by potent images of the disorder that seemed to result from the absence of self-control: 'Emotional outbursts, childish behavior, drunkenness, dreams – such common experiences threw into relief the ideal of a rational, conscious and well-regulated life' and the language of neurophysiology was used to describe this loss of control and to provide moral injunctions with a new empirical authority.[65]

The extent of this faculty of control, the degree of consciousness involved, the presence of the force of habit rather than will: all these criteria were also be utilized to differentiate – the child from the adult, the man from the women, the normal person from the lunatic, the civilized man from the primitive. It lay at the foundation of legislation such as the first British Inebriate Act, passed in 1879, which defined the habitual drunkard as one who was, by reason of habitual intemperate drinking of intoxicating liquors, either dangerous or 'incapable of man-

[63] See Valverde's study of alcohol regulation (Valverde 1998a, 1998b) and Smith's social and intellectual history of the concept of inhibition (R. Smith 1992). Valverde's earlier text, *The Age of Light, Soap and Water,* which examined moral reforms in English Canada from 1885 to 1925, contains an excellent discussion of many of these issues and is particularly instructive on the specific practices for the control and reform of 'vicious conduct' in women (Valverde 1991).

[64] In W. B. Carpenter 1842: 25, quoted in R. Smith 1992: 43.

[65] R. Smith 1992: 41–2.

aging himself or herself and his or her affairs'.[66] It underpinned regimes of treatment whose success was, as the Inspector of Inebriate Asylums put it in 1909, based on 'the possibility of awakening dormant self-control, or stimulating, by exercise, weakened self-control'.[67] It was deployed in relation to other vices, and in the techniques utilized by the 'orthopedists of individuality' in reformatories, prisons and schools.[68] Even campaigners for the development of popular education, such as James Kay-Shuttleworth, understood the school as a kind of technology for the formation of individual character, for 'moral training . . . not merely . . . inculcating moral lessons, but forming good moral habits'.[69] As Hunter has pointed out, key elements of the organization of the popular school – from breaks for recreation in the playground super-vised by the teacher as moral exemplar, to the introduction of literary education to inculcate the habits of self-reflection and inwardness – were seen as technologies of moral training, which would ensure that the child acquired the habits of self-observation and self-regulation in every-day existence outside the schoolroom. The aspiration to self-control through ethical training was still at the heart of Thomas Clouston's pro-ject in 1906, when he wrote in *The Hygiene of the Mind*: 'The highest aim of Mental Hygiene should be to increase the powers of mental inhibition amongst all men and women. Control is the basis of all law and the cement of every social system among men and women, without which it would go to pieces.'.[70] This widely dispersed and long-lived notion of the responsibility of the self for governing itself by an act of will was also deployed in wider political discourse. Conceived in these terms, the citizen acquired particular political responsibilities. Thus, Robert Chambers could write in 1861: 'on every man, no matter what his pos-ition, is imposed *Individual Responsibility* . . . from the power of universal self-management and self-reliance . . . must ever spring the chief glory of the State'.[71]

In the chapters that follow, I analyse some of the mutations in concep-tions of subjectivity and technologies of the self from the middle of the nineteenth century onwards. Here, as a rough first approximation, it is possible to trace a series running from the 'thin' moral subject of habits at the start of the nineteenth century, to the individuated normal subject

[66] Quoted in Valverde 1997: 256.
[67] British Inspector of Inebriates 1911, quoted in Valverde 1997: 263.
[68] The phrase 'orthopedists of individuality' comes from Foucault (1977: 294).
[69] James Kay Shuttleworth, Evidence to the Parliamentary Select Committee on the Education of the Poorer Classes 1838, quoted in Hunter 1988: 39.
[70] Clouston 1906, quoted in R. Smith 1992: 27.
[71] Chambers 1861–2: 6; quoted from Poovey 1995: 22.

of constitution, character and condition in the later part of the century, to the collectively understood social subject of solidarity or of alienation and anomie at the turn of the century, through the citizen subject of rights and obligations in regimes of social welfare and social insurance to the autonomous 'deep' subject of choice and self-identity.

However, even this would be to oversimplify. Many of these specifications of subjectivity coexist. Sometimes they are deployed in diverse practices at similar times without being troubled by their discrepancies; at other times they are set off against one another, for example, claims as to the necessity of authenticity are used to dispute regimes of manners and civility. Today, perhaps, the problem is not so much the governability of society as the governability of the passions of self-identified individual and collectivities: individuals and pluralities shaped not by the citizen-forming devices of church, school and public broadcasting, but by commercial consumption regimes and the politics of lifestyle, the individual identified by allegiance with one of a plurality of cultural communities. Hence the problem posed by contemporary neo-conservatives and communitarians alike: how can one govern virtue in a free society? It is here that we can locate our contemporary 'wars of subjectivity'.[72]

Subjectification is simultaneously individualizing and collectivizing. That is to say that the kinds of relations to the self envisaged, the kinds of dispositions and habits inculcated, the very inscription of governmentality into the body and the affects of the governed depend upon an opposition: in identifying with one's proper name as a subject one is simultaneously identifying oneself with a collectivized identity, and differentiating oneself from the kind of being one is not. As William Connolly has put it, 'Identities are always collective and relational: to be white, female, homosexual, Canadian, Atheist and a taxpayer is to participate in a diverse set of collective identifications and to be situated in relation to a series of alter identifications. Hegemonic identities depend on existing definitions of difference to be.'[73]

Studies of the formation of national identity have illustrated these dynamics clearly. For example, Linda Colley's study of the processes involved in forging the British nation from 1707 to 1837 shows how Britishness as a language and a set of self techniques – the distinctive British character, bearing, affective economy and the like – depended crucially on differentiating oneself from those non-British or anti-British

[72] I discuss these in chapter 5; the phrase 'wars of subjectivity' comes from Wendy Brown (W. Brown 1995).
[73] Connolly 1995: xvi.

invaders who threatened this 'essential nationhood': notably opposing Protestants to Catholics who were 'economically inept: wasteful, indolent and oppressive if powerful, poor and exploited if not', to say nothing of their ignorant, credulous and seditious popish affections. Patriotic tracts and numerous other means utilized images of fictive foreigners who threatened the body politic to cultivate attachment to the an ideal of the uniqueness of the British monarchy, the British empire, British military and naval achievements, and government by a virtuous, able and authentically British elite.[74] One can analyse the emergence of the trans-individual identities of class, status, gender and gentility in similar ways: the formation of identifications through the inscription of particular ethical formation, vocabularies of self-description and self-mastery, forms of conduct and body techniques. Thus, for example, nineteenth-century images of the dangerous classes in terms of alien races within the body politic helped form and stabilize bourgeois identities; images of the sexuality of the uncivilized races subject to colonial rule located the ethics and morality of civilized sexuality within a fundamentally racialized opposition; and, as we have seen, practices for the inculcation of civility in terms of self-control were supported by seductive yet horrifying images of forms of 'primitive' life where such controls were absent. The colonial experience and the codes of race were thus constitutively engaged in the formation of governable subjectivities: what Foucault referred to as the kind of racism that a society practises against itself in the name of securing itself against internal dangers, and which will inscribe a whole series of micro-racisms within the government of the population of all 'liberal' societies.[75]

Translation

What makes government possible? Consider the following quote. It comes from an unlikely source, the foreword by Luther Gullick, director of the Institute of Public Administration, to a study of liquor control in the United States published in 1936 – and funded by John D. Rockefeller Jnr – a fact that is not accidental, as us ex-Marxists like to say, for the Rockefeller Foundation played a conscious and very wide-ranging role in trying to invent non-communist forms of government in the first half of the twentieth century. Gullick writes:

With few exceptions all governmental work involves the performance of a service, the exercise of a control, or the execution of a task, not at the center of

[74] Colley 1996; the quotation is from p. 37.
[75] See Stoler 1995, esp. p. 92.

government, but at thousands of points scattered more or less evenly throughout the country or wherever the citizens or their interests may be. The real work of government is not to be found behind the Greek columns of public buildings. It is rather on the land, among the people. It is the postman delivering mail, the policeman walking his beat, the teacher hearing Johnny read, the whitewing sweeping the street, the inspectors – dairy, food, health, tenement, factory – on the farm, in the laboratory, the slaughterhouse, the slum, the mill; it is the playground full of children, the library with its readers, the reservoirs of pure water flowing to the cities; it is street lights at night; it is thousands and thousands of miles of pavements and sidewalks; it is the nurse beside the free bed, the doctor administering serum, and the food, raiment and shelter given to those who have nothing; it is the standard of weight and measure and value in every hamlet. All this is government, and not what men call 'government' in great buildings and capitols; and its symbol is found not in the great flag flown from the dome of the capitol but in the twenty-five million flags in the homes of the people.[76]

Government, as Gullick understands, is exercised in a myriad of micro-locales, where authorities of all types exercise their powers over the conduct of others. But what are the relations between these micro-practices and what 'men call "government" in great buildings and capitals'? How is it possible for the calculations, strategies and programmes formulated within such centres to link themselves to activities in places and activities far distant in space and time, to events in thousands of operating theatres, case conferences, bedrooms, classrooms, prison cells, workplaces and homes? Clearly a plan, policy or programme is not merely 'realized' in each of these locales, nor is it a matter of an order issued centrally being executed locally. What is involved here is something more complex. I term this 'translation'.[77] In the dynamics of translation, alignments are forged between the objectives of authorities wishing to govern and the personal projects of those organizations, groups and individuals who are the subjects of government. It is through translation processes of various sorts that linkages are assembled between political agencies, public bodies, economic, legal, medical, social and technical authorities, and the aspirations, judgements and ambitions of formally autonomous entities, be these firms, factories, pressure groups, families or individuals.

Translation mechanisms are of particular significance in liberal mentalities of government. This is because liberal political rationalities are committed to the twin projects of respecting the autonomy of certain

---

[76] Gullick 1936: xiv. Mariana Valverde drew my attention to this quote.

[77] Once again, I am borrowing a term from the work of Michel Callon and Bruno Latour and using it for my own ends. See especially Callon 1986; Callon and Latour 1981; Callon, Latour and Rip 1986.

'private' zones, and shaping their conduct in ways conducive to particular conceptions of collective and individual well-being. As I discuss in more detail in subsequent chapters, liberalism refers not simply to the canon of liberal political philosophy – Locke, Hume, Ferguson, J. S. Mill – but to a certain way of codifying and delimiting the exercise of sovereign power by identifying a realm of society, with its own economic processes and its own principles of cohesion, and populated by individuals acting according to certain principles of interest. As a diagram of rule, liberalism sought to limit the scope of political authority, and to exercise vigilance over it, delimiting certain 'natural' spheres – markets, citizens, civil society – that were outwith the legitimate scope of political interference. Yet good government would depend upon the well-being of these domains; hence political authorities simultaneously acquired the obligation to foster the self-organizing capacities of those natural spheres. Political rule thus had to concern itself with the procedures for shaping and nurturing those domains that were to provide its counterweight and limit.

Liberal rule is inextricably bound to the activities and calculations of a proliferation of independent authorities – philanthropists, doctors, hygienists, managers, planners, parents and social workers. It is dependent upon the political authorization of the authority of these authorities, upon the forging of alignments between political aims and the strategies of experts, and upon establishing relays between the calculations of authorities and the aspirations of free citizens. I describe their mode of operation as *government at a distance*.[78] Political forces instrumentalize forms of authority other than those of 'the state' in order to 'govern at a distance' in both constitutional and spatial senses – distanced consti-

---

[78] Peter Miller and I adapted this notion from Bruno Latour's suggestion that inscription techniques which brought 'immutable mobiles' from distant places to be accumulated in a centre of calculation and gave rise to interventions allowed 'action at a distance' (Miller and Rose 1990; Latour 1986, 1987: 219–32). For Latour, as a sociologist of science, the notion of 'action at a distance' had a certain irony. Seventeenth-century disputes about the existence of gravity hinged, in part, around whether to posit forces that enabled bodies being able to exert action on other bodies 'at a distance' from them was to invoke occult qualities; Newton's words on this matter at the end of his *Opticks* are know to all historians of science. Engin Isin, who uses the notion of 'government at a distance' in his 1992 study of colonial government, has pointed out to me that Jeremy Bentham's writings on liberal government of the colonies stressed the particular problems of governing distant colonies rather than dominating them: see Bentham's address to the National Convention of France in 1793, published as Bentham 1830. This and related writings are now gathered together in Schofield 1995.

tutionally, in that they operate through the decisions and endeavours of non-political modes of authority; distanced spatially, in that these technologies of government link a multitude of experts in distant sites to the calculations of those at a centre – hence government operates through opening lines of force across a territory spanning space and time. And if translation processes operate without disruption – and they rarely do – the autonomy of the subjects and targets of government is not a threat: autonomy can be allied with, and aligned with, such objectives as economic success, national population policy, conceptions of the desirability of education and training and the like.

There are many strategies of translation. I examine a number of them in detail in subsequent chapters. As Peter Miller and I put it elsewhere:

> To the extent that actors have come to understand their situation according to a similar language and logic, to construe their goals and their fate as in some way inextricable, they are assembled into mobile and loosely affiliated networks. Shared interests are constructed in and through political discourses, persuasions, negotiations and bargains. Common modes of perception are formed, in which certain events and entities come to be visualized according to particular rhetorics of image or speech. Relations are established between the nature, character and causes of problems facing various individuals and groups – producers and shopkeepers, doctors and patients – such that the problems of one and those of another seem intrinsically linked in their basis and their solution.[79]

The literal sense of translation involves a movement from place to place. In the present context, this involves processes which link up the concerns elaborated within rather general and wide-ranging political rationalities with *specific* programmes for government of this or that problematic zone of life. Mobile and 'thixotropic' associations are established between a variety of agents, in which each seeks to enhance their powers by 'translating' the resources provided by the association so that they may function to their own advantage. Loose and flexible linkages are made between those who are separated spatially and temporally, and between events in spheres that remain formally distinct and autonomous. Rule 'at a distance' becomes possible when each can translate the values of others into its own terms, such that they provide norms and standards for their own ambitions, judgements and conduct.

Thus, for example, in the early twentieth century the notion of national efficiency served to ground certain rather abstract problematics of rule: nations rose or fell in international competition because of their relative levels of 'efficiency'; lack of 'efficiency' encapsulated the prob-

---

[79] Rose and Miller 1992: 184. I draw upon this joint paper in the paragraphs that follow.

lems facing politicians; enhancing 'efficiency' was desirable. But this question was translated into arguments about specific issues – the 'physical efficiency' of schoolchildren was to be fostered through attending to their hygiene; the 'mental efficiency' of the race was to be preserved through attention to the feeble-minded; the 'industrial efficiency' of the factory was to be enhanced through programmes of scientific management.[80] In the middle of the twentieth century, the vocabulary of citizenship plays a similar role – at a general level the idea of citizenship encoded certain notions of the mutual rights and responsibilities of subjects and authorities, but could be aligned with the particular programmes of reform and education enacted in schools, asylums and so forth.

Similarly, in the 1980s, in Britain in particular, the notion of enterprise underpinned an abstract political critique of bureaucracy and the welfare state, but was also translated into a variety of specific strategies for reforming economic policy, restructuring social security benefits, reorganizing hospitals and universities, transforming the pedagogic programmes of schools. Translation links the general to the particular, links one place to another, shifts a way of thinking, from a political centre – a cabinet office, a government department – to a multitude of workplaces, hospital wards, classrooms, child guidance centres or homes. Thus national programmes of government can render themselves consonant with the proliferation of procedures for the conduct of conduct at a molecular level across a territory.

Translation is, of course, an imperfect mechanism and one that is subject to innumerable pressures and distortions: it is not a process in which rule extends itself unproblematically across a territory, but a matter of fragile relays, contested locales and fissiparous affiliations. Liberal government, dependent as it is upon the orchestration of the actions of independent entities, is inherently risky – and no more so than in its reliance upon those who are able to mobilize around the power to speak the truth and the capacity to act knowledgeably upon conduct.

Technologies

Thought becomes governmental to the extent that it becomes technical, it attaches itself to a technology for its realization. We are familiar with many uses of the term – high technology, new technology, information

---

[80] On national efficiency in Britain, see Searle 1971. See also the discussions in Rose 1985 and Miller and O'Leary 1989.

technology: here a technology seems to refer to an assembly of forms of knowledge with a variety of mechanical devices and an assortment of little techniques oriented to produce certain practical outcomes. In fact, if we consider any of these, for example information technology, we can see that it entails more than computers, programmes, fibre-optic cables, mobile telephones and so forth. Every technology also requires the inculcation of a form of life, the reshaping of various roles for humans, the little body techniques required to use the devices, new inscription practices, the mental techniques required to think in terms of certain practices of communication, the practices of the self oriented around the mobile telephone, the word processor, the World Wide Web and so forth. Even in its conventional sense, then, technologies require, for their completion, a certain shaping of conduct, and are dependent upon the assembling together of lines of connection amongst a diversity of types of knowledge, forces, capacities, skills, dispositions and types of judgement.[81]

Technologies of government are those technologies imbued with aspirations for the shaping of conduct in the hope of producing certain desired effects and averting certain undesired events. I term these 'human technologies' in that, within these assemblages, it is human capacities that are to be understood and acted upon by technical means. A technology of government, then, is an assemblage of forms of practical knowledge, with modes of perception, practices of calculation, vocabularies, types of authority, forms of judgement, architectural forms, human capacities, non-human objects and devices, inscription techniques and so forth, traversed and transected by aspirations to achieve certain outcomes in terms of the conduct of the governed (which also requires certain forms of conduct on the part of those who would govern). These assemblages are heterogeneous, made up of a diversity of objects and relations linked up through connections and relays of different types. They have no essence. And they are never simply a realization of a programme, strategy or intention: whilst the will to govern traverses them, they are not simply realizations of any simple will.

Two examples may illustrate two rather different assemblings of technologies of government. In the first, the 'scientific management' invented by F. W. Taylor in the early decades of the twentieth century,

[81] These issues have been discussed and analysed in great detail in the sociology of technology and 'actor network theory' which is associated in particular with the work of Thomas Hughes (1983), Michel Callon (1986), Bruno Latour (1988) and John Law (1991). See also Bijker and Law (1992). These issues of technology and government are reviewed in a useful paper by Mitchell Dean (1996).

we can see an explicit attempt to construct a single mechanism for governing the conduct of the working person to produce increased productivity, increased efficiency and increased capacities for management. Taylorism 'entailed assembling and creating a range of practical and intellectual instruments to produce what Taylor termed the "mechanism" of scientific management: standard tools, adjustable scaffolds, methods and implements of time study, books and records, desks for planners to work at, experiments leading to the establishment of formulae to replace the individual judgement of workmen, a differentiation of work into standard tasks, written instructions and instruction cards, bonus and premium payments, the scientific selection of the working man and many more.'[82] Taylorism, then, entailed the calculated construction of a durable set of relations and connections amongst persons, forces and things, under a certain form of knowledge and in relation to very particular objectives. Even as an ideal programme and a calculated strategy, however, Taylorism was clearly dependent on knowledges and techniques that it did not itself bring into existence. The actual networks, connections, relations of force and the like formed through attempts to implant Taylorist technologies involved all manner of translations, alliances and compromises, and seldom approximated to their ideal form. Technologies are not realizations of any single will to govern.

This relation between programme, technology and networks of force is even more evident if one considers a second example: the popular schoolroom that was invented in the nineteenth century.[83] This was an assemblage of pedagogic knowledges, moralizing aspirations, buildings of a certain design, classrooms organized to produce certain types of visibility, techniques such as the timetable for organizing bodies in space and in time, regimes of supervision, little mental exercises in the classroom, playgrounds to allow the observation and moralization of children in something more approaching their natural habitat and much more, assembled and infused with the aim of the government of capacities and habits. As Ian Hunter has pointed out, the popular school first came into existence in European states like Prussia 'as a means of the mass moral training of the population with a view to enhancing the strength and prosperity of the state and thereby the welfare of the people'. But

---

[82] Miller and Rose 1990: 20; cf. Thevenot 1984. See F. W. Taylor 1913 and the discussion in Miller and O'Leary 1994c.
[83] Karen Jones and Kevin Williamson provide a superb analysis in their paper on 'the birth of the schoolroom' (K. Jones and Williamson 1979). See also Hunter 1988.

whilst states may wish to transform their populations 'this does not mean that they can simply whistle the means of moral training into existence'.[84] The European administrative states borrowed these means from attempts by the Christian churches, under the banners of the Reformation and the counter-Reformation, to Christianize the everyday lives of lay people through schooling. Early schooling 'systems' in Europe, England and Australia emerged through a series of exchanges and trade-offs between the administrative apparatus of states that were beginning to governmentalize themselves and religious institutions, practices, knowledges and techniques for the spiritual disciplining of souls. In other words, the technology of schooling was not invented *ab initio*, nor was it implanted through the monotonous implementation of a hegemonic 'will to govern': the technology of schooling – like that of social insurance, child welfare, criminal justice and much more – is hybrid, heterogeneous, traversed by a variety of programmatic aspirations and professional obligations, a complex and mobile resultant to the relations amongst persons, things and forces.

One final point needs to be made about these technologies, assemblages, agencements, dispositifs for the conduct of conduct. To say that they are human technologies is not to subject them to a critique. It is not to imply that technology is somehow antithetical to humanity, and thus a human technology is actually an inhuman technology, a technological rationalization of the human soul or a technological reduction of human subjectivity and creativity to that which can be acted upon in the interests of government. This is certainly the view generally attributed to the writers of the 'Frankfurt School'.[85] Science had mastered the natural world by mathematization and formalization, but the extension of this technological mastery to the human world inescapably distorted human subjectivity, because this subjectivity was of a radically different order, which could not be grasped by the tools, methods or procedures of the natural sciences. The argument of this book is quite different. It is to suggest that all the essential, natural and defining conditions that tend to be ascribed to the human world – modern forms of subjectivity, contemporary conceptions of agency and will, the present-day ethics of freedom itself – are not antithetical to power and technique but actually the resultants of specific configurations of power, certain technological inventions, certain more or less rationalized techniques of relating to ourselves. One cannot counterpose subjectivity to power, because sub-

---

[84] Hunter 1996: 148–9.
[85] The contrasts between Foucault's conception of technology and that of the Frankfurt School are analysed in C. Gordon 1980 and Miller 1987.

jectification occurs in the element of power; one cannot counterpose freedom to technology, because what we have come to understand as our freedom is the mobile outcome of a multitude of human technologies.

Diagnosis

Studies of governmentality practise a certain kind of empiricism. This may sound paradoxical, given that such studies emerge from a tradition of thought that stresses the inescapably constructive nature of all conceptual practice, including description. We are all the wise and weary inhabitants of a time in which there are no such things as Facts, all observations are theory-laden and so forth. But this is not the point. The attention to the empirical undertaken here has nothing at all to do with a valorization of experience, with a denigration of theory and the like. It has to do with a valuation of what one might call the moment of fieldwork in history, the moment when historical thought becomes inventive because it is linked to a practice on its object. We have learnt from a whole tradition of French thought on the history of science that those activities that we know as science entail, in their very nature, a connection between representation and intervention. To say that the inventiveness of social thought requires an empirical moment has nothing at all to do with Anglo-Saxon empiricism, a fetishism of the facts, belief in the pre-theoretic status of observations and so forth. It is to argue for the importance of a kind of experimental moment in thought, a moment when thought tries to realize itself in the real.[86] Gaston Bachelard has argued that those practices we have come to know as the natural sciences are phenomeno-technical.[87] In the moment of the experiment, in the setting of the laboratory, by means of all sorts of apparatus, instrumentation and so forth, these knowledges seek to conjure up in reality the things they have already conjured up in thought. In doing so, they open themselves up to the discovery of error, and hence to a dynamic of critical correction. This is not a matter of claiming that the facts, entities and processes that are created in these complex, artful and highly skilled laboratory processes have a pre-theoretic

[86] Of course the real here is composed in the work of thought itself: a complex of facts, texts, artefacts, persons, statements, pictures, bodies, techniques, buildings and so forth.

[87] See, for example, Bachelard 1951. The most accessible secondary account of Bachelard's notion of phenomeno-technics remains that provided by Stephen Gaukroger (Gaukroger 1976). For a brilliant practical account that illuminates what Bachelard might have in mind, see Latour and Woolgar 1979.

existence. But nonetheless, those forms of knowledge that we have come to call science open themselves up to development in this way. And, through this phenomenotechnical process, science has been inventive: it has created new entities, new forces, new phenomena.[88] It is in this spirit that I would argue that historical work is inventive when – perhaps only when – it is attached to something like the same experimental ethos. That is to say, when the writing of history is the moment of reflection, formalization and abstraction in an empirical, experimental practice on existence, and when this practice is oriented by a norm of truth, attentive to error, and hence open to critical correction.

The kind of empirical analysis that is involved here is not hermeneutic. It is not a question of decoding or interpreting a particular strategy to discover hidden motives, of critiquing a particular alignment of forces to identify class interests or of interpreting a particular ideology to discover the real objectives that lie behind it. Rather, arguments, strategies and tactics are analysed in their own terms, in terms of the identities and identifications which they themselves construct, objectives they set themselves, the enemies they identified, the alliances they sought, the languages and categories they used to describe themselves, the forms of collectivization and division that they enacted. Take, for example, the issue of class. Many sociologists and historians of social control have examined practices of regulation and interpreted them as embodying, sometimes overtly, often covertly, the interests, motives and activities of a dominant social class.[89] The approach to the history of government that I am advocating takes a different view. Of course, many regulatory strategies are articulated, developed and justified explicitly in the interests of increased productivity and the docility or manageability of workers. But the development of a language of class by socialist activists in the nineteenth century to interpret such strategies is itself a historical phenomenon worthy of investigation. To the extent that this language of class sought not only to identify common enemies but also to forge common interests, it sought to obliterate existing identifications in terms of radicalism, Chartism, Owenites, solidarities to particular trades and so forth. And the premise that all control strategies serve the interests of the dominant class is misleading. It is not only bosses and imperialists

[88] I discuss the epistemological implications of this argument in more detail in Rose 1998. For an intriguing and controversial account of science and the invention of phenomena, see Hacking 1983.

[89] From a completely different theoretical and historiographical tradition, Gareth Stedman Jones provides an analysis of the languages of class very close to that suggested here: Stedman Jones 1983.

who have developed racist strategies of segregation, exclusion or exploitation of immigrant labour – organized labour too has engaged in many
racist tactics for the protection of white workers against interlopers seen
as racially inferior and politically dangerous and for the disciplining of
its own members. Similarly, the power relations and ethical imperatives
put in play by strategies such as the social purity movement at the end
of the nineteenth century or feminist mobilizations for birth control –
some emancipatory, some eugenic, some moralistic – need to be examined in their own terms. Against interpretation, then, I advocate super-
ficiality, an empiricism of the surface, of identifying the differences in
what is said, how it is said, and what allows it to be said and to have an
effectivity.

This does not condemn these analyses to the endless redescription
of a technocratic landscape: the rehearsal, in more or less elegant and
convincing ways, of the problem-solutions of our programmers, administrators and managers. Analytics of government are diagnostic. To
diagnose is to discriminate or differentiate. Consider, for a moment,
diagnosis in clinical medicine. In the nineteenth century a new, effectively nominalistic, notion of disease was fabricated, and with it a new
sense of the diagnostic. Disease ceased to be problematized in terms of
species or essences: rather, disease became what the doctor saw in the
fabric of the body; disease, that is to say, became a relation between a
form of visualization or symptomatology (a language of description of
the visual and tactile, a descriptive, probing, educated empiricism of the
medical senses) and a set of procedures for organizing medical statements (the clinical case, the autopsy, the examination, the case
history).[90] To diagnose – the verb form emerged in the middle of the
nineteenth century – was not to locate an essence, but to establish a
singularity or individuation within a whole set of relations by means of
a work on symptoms. In an analogous fashion, genealogies of government seek to establish the singularity of particular strategies within a
field of relations of truth, power and subjectivity by means of a work on
symptoms. The attempt to isolate, group and organize symptoms, to set
forth a symptomatology, undoubtedly involves a certain creativity. The
genealogist of government here takes up the role that Nietzsche ascribed
to artists and philosophers: he suggested that they were physiologists or

---

[90] I am drawing here upon collective work with Tom Osborne (T. Osborne and
Rose 1997). See also the collection of Gilles Deleuze's papers published
under the title *Essays Clinical and Critical* and especially the excellent introduction by Daniel W. Smith (Deleuze 1997, D. W. Smith 1997).

"'physicians of culture", for whom phenomena are signs or symptoms that reflect a certain State of forces'.[91] On the basis of a certain symptomatology, then, genealogies of government seek to reconstruct the problematizations to which programmes, strategies, tactics posed themselves as a solution. If policies, arguments, analyses and prescriptions purport to provide answers, they do so only in relation to a set of questions. Their very status as answers is dependent upon the existence of such questions. If, for example imprisonment, marketization, community care are seen as answers, to what are they answers? And, in reconstructing the problematizations which accord them intelligibility as answers, these grounds become visible, their limits and presuppositions are opened for interrogation in new ways.

Historical investigations are thus used not for knowing but for cutting,[92] as Foucault says in his essay on Nietzsche: to disturb that which forms the very groundwork of our present, to make the given once more strange and to cause us to wonder at how it came to appear so natural. How have we been made up as governable subjects? What kinds of human beings have we come to take ourselves to be? What presuppositions about our nature are operationalized within strategies that seek to act upon our actions? How did human beings become the objects and subjects of government, the subjects of logics of normativity and of practices that made divisions in terms of that normativity – between the mad and the sane, the law-abiding subject and the criminal, the sick and the well, the virtuous and the vicious, the citizen and the marginal?

In stressing the role of thought in making up our present, in making it governable, such studies also suggest that thought has a role in contesting the ways in which it is governed. To this extent, these studies are, to use that much abused word, 'reflexive'. They entail a work of thought on the present that is itself, inescapably, a work of thought. But in order to recognize the effectivity that such investigations may have, it is necessary to discard the last vestiges of those nineteenth-century philosophical disputes between materialism and idealism. These oppositions, which grew out of highly politically charged but very specifically historically located disputes, have a lot to answer for. They have done much to constrain our ways of understanding of the materiality of ideas, and to recognize the embeddedness of thought in the most prosaic aspects of social and economic life. But if human being is always 'being

[91] I am quoting from Daniel Smith's introduction to Deleuze 1997 (D. W. Smith 1997: xvii).
[92] Foucault 1986: 88.

thought' and if human practices are inescapably made up in thought, then thought itself can and does play a role in contesting them. To diagnose the historicity of our contemporary ways for thinking and acting is to enhance their contestability, to point to the need for new experiments in thought which can imagine new ways in which we can be and can act. There have been, there will be other ways of speaking the truth about ourselves and practising upon ourselves and others in the name of that truth. Of course, we can never 'return' to the Greeks, to the Victorians, even to the forms of subjectification that characterized socialism. But, however difficult it is to conceive of this, there will be forms of moral subjectification other than those that we inhabit, which do not valorize the psychologized, interiorized, autonomous individual of choice, self-promotion and familial obligation, other forms of agency, other modes of individuation.

It is often said that such investigations have a problem of normativity: they disguise or deny the normative grounds on which they must rest. This is misleading. As Thomas Osborne has pointed out, whilst they are not critiques, in diagnosing the problem field to which strategies of government purport to offer solutions, they aim to 'sow the seeds of judgement', to help make judgement possible.[93] And in showing the contingency of the arrangements within which we are assembled, in denaturalizing them, in showing the role of thought in holding them together, they also show that thought has a part to play in contesting them. The aim of such studies is thus inescapably ethical. It is ethical in a double sense: first, because questions of ethics lie at the heart of such investigations; secondly, because the destabilizing of our ethical repertoire, its localization within specific historical practices, together with a historical work which shows us that there have been and will be other ways of understanding and acting upon ourselves, is itself an ethical work upon ourselves. This is a work on truth: because we are governed through truth, we need to adopt an irreal attitude to truth itself. And it is also a work on limits, on our limits, a project to disclose limits, to map the horizons of our thought and to enable us perhaps to think beyond them. In particular, what is to be destabilized, what we are to try to think beyond, are all those claims made by others to govern us in the name of our own well-being, to speak for us, to identify our needs, to know us better than we can know ourselves. Perhaps they do, but, to the extent that others claim to speak in our name, we have the right thereby to ask them by what right they claim to know us so well; to the extent that others seek to govern us in our own interests, we have the

[93] Osborne develops this argument in detail in T. Osborne 1998.

right, as governed subjects, to interrogate and even protest those strategies in the name of our own claims to know those interests.

In describing the contingent conditions under which that which is so dear to us has taken shape, such investigations enhance the contestability of regimes of authority that seek to govern us in the name of our own good. Whatever their methodological and conceptual differences, then, these investigations share with Marxism and critical theory a profound unease about the values that pervade our times. They share a suspicious attention to the multitude of petty humiliations and degradations carried out in the name of our own best interests. They do not try to put themselves at the service of those who would govern better. Rather, if they have a political function, it is to strengthen the resources available to those who, because of their constitution as subjects of government, have the right to contest the practices that govern them in the name of their freedom.

2   Freedom

Over the past two decades the value of freedom has become the principle of so many political dreams and projects. We dwell in a historical moment in which 'the free world' has triumphed over its totalitarian adversary, 'the free market' over the command economy and the plan, the freedom-loving authentic individual over the loyal collective subject of traditional moralities and communist ethics alike. Freedom, here, seems to form the foundation of the politics of our present: its presence or absence in particular societies, the struggle to achieve it, the conditions that can make it real. But freedom is not only the touchstone of contemporary liberal politics. As substantive dreams of alternative ways of organizing economic activity, political structures and familial and sexual arrangements lose their allure, an ethic of freedom seems also to suffuse the political imagination of our most radical political thinkers: the search for a new politics of freedom, the attempt to delineate and construct practices of freedom, the idea that we should strive for a style of existence characterized by a certain way of working upon ourselves in the name of freedom.

As the twenty-first century begins, the ethics of freedom have come to underpin our conceptions of how we should be ruled, how our practices of everyday life should be organized, how we should understand ourselves and our predicament. Of course, we are aware of the violence that has, in our recent history, been perpetrated in the name of freedom: the language of freedom provided the flimsy justification for the bloody campaigns and covert wars waged by the United States in Central America in the 1980s; the rhetoric of freedom legitimated the use of all necessary measures to destroy union powers which were considered to be a threat to the freedom of free enterprise. Every reader will have multiple additions to this list of injuries perpetrated under the banner of freedom. As Wendy Brown has pointed out, over this period, other liberal senses of freedom fell into disrepute.[1] The 1960s ideals of ethical,

[1] W. Brown 1995: 9–10.

sexual and personal freedom were characterized as the infantile narcissism of the 'me generation' introducing a moral relativism corrosive to a good society. The celebration of freedom as authenticity and self-expression in child rearing, in pedagogy, in literature and art were seen as having eroded the foundations of social stability, good order, civility, family values and the ethic of work. Yet despite disputes over its definitions and debates over the relative priority of freedom as opposed to other political goals, there is agreement over the belief that human beings are, in their nature, actually, potentially, ideally, subjects of freedom and hence that they must be governed, and must govern themselves, as such.

It is precisely because of the potency of the politics and ethics of freedom that it calls for diagnosis. Can one adopt an 'untimely' attitude to freedom? Can one see the value of freedom itself as a thing of this world, assembled out of a multitude of accidents and contingencies, out of grand strategies of power and control, out of naive gestures of humanitarianism and concern, noble and high-minded philanthropic interventions, out of a thousand petty spites and little manoeuvres? Could we regard the birth of freedom as an achievement of government? In which case, what would it mean to contest government in the name of freedom?

To be governed through our freedom: the very idea seems paradoxical. Freedom appears, almost by definition, to be the antithesis of government: freedom is understood in terms of the act of liberation from bondage or slavery, the condition of existence in liberty, the right of the individual to act in any desired way without restraint, the power to do as one likes. The politics of our present, to the extent that it is defined and delimited by the values of liberalism, is structured by the opposition between freedom and government. As Barry Hindess points out, liberalism 'is commonly understood as a political doctrine or ideology concerned with the maximization of individual liberty and, in particular, with the defence of that liberty against the State'.[2] It is because this dialectic is at the centre of so much of the politics of our present that the problem of freedom lies at the heart of contemporary analytics of governmentality. But the critical force of these investigations does not arise from the familiar paradox that to make humans free it has been necessary to subject them to all manner of compulsion, from the authority of their parents through compulsory schooling to regulations on food hygiene, sewerage and criminal activity. This would make a thin

[2] Hindess 1996a: 65.

and repetitive story. Freedom is an artefact of government, but it is not thereby an illusion.

The problem of freedom is central to a genealogy of contemporary regimes of government because it is a structuring theme of contemporary government itself. Take, for example, a passage from a recent text by Francis Fukuyama. In *Trust: The Social Virtues and the Creation of Prosperity*, Fukuyama writes:

A liberal State is ultimately a limited State, with governmental activity strictly bounded by a sphere of individual liberty. If society is not to become anarchic or otherwise ungovernable, then it must be capable of self-government at levels of organization below the State. Such a system depends ultimately not just on law but on the self-restraint of individuals. If they are not tolerant and respectful of each other, or do not abide by the laws they set for themselves, they will require a strong and coercive State to keep each other in line. If they cannot cohere for common purposes, then they will need an intrusive State to provide the organization they cannot provide for themselves.[3]

Only a certain kind of liberty – a certain way of understanding and exercising freedom, of relating to ourselves individually and collectively as a subjects of freedom – is compatible with liberal arts of rule. And that kind of freedom has a history. We can historicize that which we take for freedom today, and in the name of which we are governed. We can trace the relations between the history of this ethic of freedom and the history of government. We can analyse the practices that gave birth to freedom. And we can begin to understand freedom not simply as an abstract ideal but as material, technical, practical, governmental.

Freedom

Over the final three decades of the twentieth century, the political theorists and philosophers of the 'the right', in particular the 'neo-liberals', provided the most powerful thematization of the project of freedom most powerfully. The most consistent of these thinkers was Friedrich von Hayek. Here is a passage from *Law, Legislation and Liberty*, Hayek's attempt to re-animate the principles that, for liberal thought, are basic to the political order of a free society. It comes from the very end of the third book, *The Political Order of a Free People*:

The only moral principle which has ever made the growth of an advanced civilization possible was the principle of individual freedom . . . No principles of collective conduct which binds the individual can exist in a society of free men.

---

[3] Fukuyama 1996: 357–8.

What we have achieved we owe to securing to the individuals the chance of creating for themselves a protected domain . . . within which they can use their abilities for their own purposes. Socialism lacks any principles of individual conduct yet dreams of a state of affairs which no moral action of free individuals can bring about . . . We ought to have learnt enough to avoid destroying our civilization by smothering the spontaneous process of the interaction of the individuals by placing its direction in the hands of any authority. But to avoid this we must shed the illusion that we can deliberately create 'the future of mankind', as the characteristic hubris of a socialist sociologist has recently expressed it.[4]

Hayek's neo-liberal reflection on the role of freedom in the advance of civilization is uncompromising. But it forms only one pole of a field of political argument linking radicals of the right to conventional liberals, civil libertarians and modern European socialists. Each of these, in their own way, tries to ground the imperatives of government upon the self-activating capacities of free human beings, citizens, subjects. From struggles to overthrow communism in the East to challenges to the welfare State and the public direction of industry in the advanced industrial societies of the West, dreams of freedom are turned against the phantasms of rational and comprehensive planning of economic activity, and deliberate social improvement through educational and social reform that tried to shape 'the future of mankind'. Correlatively, notions of freedom, with the associated celebration of the powers of the individual, of autonomy and choice, underpin attempts to specify and construct new forms of social arrangements. The wealth of nations, the productivity of enterprise, the efficiency of health and welfare provision – all this and more is to be secured by protecting and enhancing the freedom of the citizen – whether as discerning customer, enterprising individual, subject of right or autonomous fellow human.

The demand for freedom is undoubtedly a potent weapon in 'saying no to power'. But if we look at all those nations of the former Soviet bloc that are attempting to turn themselves into societies of freedom, we can perhaps gauge something of the space between freedom as an ideal, as articulated in struggles against particular regimes of power, and freedom as a mode of organizing and regulation: freedom here as a certain way of administering a population that depends upon the capacities of free individuals.[5] Thus, to make up a 'free society' seems to require

---

[4] Hayek 1979: 152–3. Hayek's writings on these issues in English begin with *The Road to Serfdom*, which was published in 1944.

[5] Foucault had something like this in mind when he remarked– although in a rather ambiguous formulation– that the act by which a colonized people liberates itself from its colonizer is not in itself sufficient to establish the practices

one to introduce a whole range of new devices: censuses to provide demographic information on the individuals who compose the nation, public opinion polls to determine the will of the free people. Constructing a 'free market' seems to entail a variety of interventions by accountants, management consultants, lawyers and industrial relations specialists and marketing experts in order to establish the conditions under which the 'laws of supply and demand' can make themselves real, to implant the ways of calculating and managing that will make economic actors think, reckon and behave as competitive, profit-seeking agents, to turn workers into motivated employees who will freely strive to give of their best in the workplace, and to transform people into consumers who can choose between products. Further, the previously unfree subjects of these societies cannot merely be 'freed' – they have to be *made* free in a process that entails the transformation of educational practices to inculcate certain attitudes and values of enterprise, changes in television programmes ranging from soap operas to game shows to implant the desire for wealth creation and personal enterprise, as well as the activities of marriage guidance consultants and a host of other psychological therapists to sort out the difficulties that arise when personal life becomes a matter of freedom of choice.

I think that it is possible, therefore, to distinguish between a number of different formulae of freedom at work in our recent history. In particular, I think we can distinguish freedom as a formula of resistance from freedom as a formula of power. Or rather, to be more circumspect, between freedom as it is deployed in contestation and freedom as it is instantiated in government. I want to suggest some ways of understanding freedom in this second sense: freedom as it has been articulated into norms and principles for organizing our experience of our world and of ourselves; freedom as it is realized in certain ways of exercising power over others; freedom as it has been articulated into certain rationales for practising in relation to ourselves. A genealogy of freedom in this sense would examine the various ways in which the relations between power and freedom have been established. Such critical investigations would not be critical *of* freedom. They would not attempt to reveal freedom as a sham, or to decry the freedom we *think* we have in the name of a truer freedom to come. To adapt a formulation proposed by Michel Foucault, such a genealogy would ask how we have come to define and act towards ourselves in terms of a certain notion of freedom. It would investigate

of freedom necessary to define acceptable forms of individual and collective existence (Foucault 1997: 282–3).

the ways in which what we take to be freedom has been historically put together, the practices which support it, and the techniques, strategies and relations of power that go to make up what we term a free society. And it would try to count the costs, as well as the profits, of organizing our relations with ourselves in terms of freedom.

The history of freedom

Ideals and practices of freedom have a long history. Most authorities agree that for most of human history, and for most of the non-Western world prior to Western contact, values other than freedom were supreme – glory, honour, power, nationalism, imperial grandeur, filial loyalty, hedonism, faith, self-abnegation. Sociologists, especially those writing in the late nineteenth and early twentieth centuries, argued that freedom became an ideal for all, rather than for certain privileged sectors, in the course of the profound transformations in European and American society in which modern individualism was formed. In part, they argued, individual freedom arose from the particular character of economic relations under capitalism. The market depends upon and produces a mode of economic life grounded in a certain freedom – of production, of consumption – but simultaneously related persons only as isolated buyers and sellers of goods: a formal freedom, bought for most at the price of a real economic enslavement.

This economic individuation was linked to a more general fragmentation and pluralization of social values and forms of life. Zygmunt Bauman argues that the heterogeneity and discoordination of social powers, the variety of sources of authority produced the experience, for large sections of the population, of being left without a clear source of guidance, left to one's own motivation, personal discretion and choice: 'the freedom of the modern individual arises . . . from uncertainty; from a certain "under-determination" of external reality, from the intrinsic controversiality of social pressures'.[6] Individuals are forced into a profound inwardness, and cling for comfort to a belief in their own uniqueness, in the process elaborating a complex inner world of self. Hence the fundamental dialectic of modern society – maximum individualization and maximum 'freedom' is developed only at the price of maximum fragmentation, maximum uncertainty, maximum estrangement of individual from fellow individual.

---

[6] Bauman 1988: 41. Bauman provides a useful discussion of many of the issues I raise in this chapter. For an illuminating cultural history of freedom, see Patterson 1991.

Modern freedom certainly entails a novel way of problematizing human conduct with profoundly ambiguous consequences its subjects. But the modes of organizing reality in terms of freedom were not the unintended consequences of changes in social and economic relations; they had to be invented:

> Man has not developed in freedom . . . Freedom is an artefact of civilization . . . Freedom was made possible by the gradual evolution of *the discipline of civilization which is at the same time the discipline of freedom.*[7]

It is not Michel Foucault who is writing in these terms about the discipline of freedom upon which all civilization depends. It is Friedrich von Hayek, in the epilogue to the book I quoted earlier. It is Hayek, the neo-liberal, for whom all 'positive' conceptions of social justice, all attempts to rationally define and produce the 'good citizen', derive from the 'Enlightenment superstition' that human affairs can be improved by the application of reason.

Hayek, characteristically, assigns the inculcation of the discipline of freedom not to conscious human design but to the processes of natural selection upon human groups – in other words, to tradition. But an examination of our history reveals that the disciplines of freedom, the disciplines of civilization, were addressed more directly. Freedom, that is to say, was a central element in government. Strategies and techniques of authority have been regulated by ideals of freedom – of societies, of markets, of individuals – or have sought to produce freedom. Those who administer life, in prisons, asylums, factories and the like, have tried to reconcile the obligation to manage individuals with the requirement that those individuals are not slaves, but free. We have acted upon ourselves, or been acted upon by others, in the wish to be free. Freedom has been an objective of government, freedom has been an instrument or means of government, freedom has inspired the invention of a variety of technologies for governing.

It was this double-edged character of freedom that disturbed Isaiah Berlin.[8] He was critical of those liberal thinkers in the nineteenth century who failed to distinguish 'negative liberty' – in which individuals or groups were to be left alone to do what they wished without interference – from 'positive liberty' – in which authorities sought to 'make people free', to coerce them in the name of justice, rationality or public health to become wiser, healthier, more virtuous than they were, in order to enable them to realize what their freedom was and to exercise

[7] Hayek 1979: 163, emphases in original.
[8] Berlin made this point in his lecture 'Two concepts of liberty' which he gave in 1958 (Berlin [1958] 1969).

it. In the name of positive liberty, argued Berlin, all kinds of despotism – from compulsory education, public health and moral policing – turn out to be identical with freedom. Hence the apparent paradox: that nineteenth-century liberal debates about the limits on power, constitutional doctrines of limited government, liberal principles of the freedom of subjects under the law were accompanied by strategies that sought not only to understand the nature of the market, the public sphere and the individual, but also to intervene in them to enable them to properly bear the demands that were placed upon them. It was not only that a welter of legal and administrative measures had to be taken to establish the conditions for a 'free market'. It was also that, even in what Polanyi calls 'the heroic period of *laissez faire*', a series of administrative inventions appeared to be required to shape and protect the very freedoms upon which liberal government was to depend: from the building of prisons and asylums, through the regulation of hours of and conditions of labour, to legally enforced medical interventions on sanitary reform and compulsory vaccination.[9]

Now it is true that the same people who, in the nineteenth century, celebrated liberty also built the prison.[10] But this link between liberty and discipline was not the outcome of philosophical confusion as Berlin implies. Nor does it demonstrate, as Marxist critics suggest, that the prison was the ignoble truth of the ideology of liberty. Rather, philosophical reflections on freedom, then as now, were always linked to the invention of certain ways of trying to govern persons in accordance with freedom. The value of individuality operated both as a critique of certain ways of exercising power, and as that which certain strategies of power sought to produce. The importance of liberalism is not that it first recognized, defined or defended freedom as a right of all citizens. Rather, its significance is that for the first time the arts of government were systematically linked to the practice of freedom. From this point on, to quote John Rajchman, individuals 'must be willing to do their bit in maintaining the systems that define and delimit them; they must play their parts in a "game" whose intelligibility and limits they take for granted'.[11] Individuals, that is to say, must come to recognize and act upon themselves as both free and responsible, both beings of liberty and members of society, if liberal government is to be possible. And the openness and riskiness of liberal modes of government, both at the level of their rationalities and in the technologies that liberalism has invented

[9] Polanyi 1957: 141.
[10] Foucault makes this comment in *Discipline and Punish* (Foucault 1977).
[11] Rajchman 1991: 101.

in order to govern, lie in the inescapable *quid pro quo* that what individuals are required to give, they may also refuse.

Freedom as discipline

In the middle of the nineteenth century, Pierre-Joseph Proudhon expressed his own views about the relation between government and freedom:

> To be governed is to be kept in sight, inspected, spied upon, directed, law-driven, numbered, enrolled, indoctrinated, preached at, controlled, estimated, valued, censured, commanded . . . at every transaction [to be] noted, registered, enrolled, taxed, stamped, measured, numbered, assessed, licensed, authorized, admonished, forbidden, reformed, corrected, punished.
>
> It is . . . to be placed under contribution, trained, ransomed, exploited, monopolized, extorted, squeezed, mystified, robbed; then at the slightest resistance . . . to be repressed, fined, despised, harassed, tracked, abused, clubbed, disarmed, choked, imprisoned, judged, condemned, shot, deported, sacrificed, sold, betrayed; and to crown all, mocked, ridiculed, outraged, dishonoured.[12]

For Proudhon government was the antithesis of freedom. I take a different view. The achievement of the liberal arts of government was to begin to govern through making people free. People were to be 'freed' in the realms of the market, civil society, the family: they were placed outside the legitimate scope of political authorities, subject only to the limits of the law. Yet the 'freeing' of these zones was accompanied by the invention of a whole series of attempts to shape and manage conduct within them in desirable ways. On the one hand, the 'public' activities of free citizens were to be regulated by codes of civility, reason and orderliness. On the other, the private conduct of free citizens was to be civilized by equipping them with languages and techniques of self-understanding and self-mastery. Freedom thus becomes inextricably linked to a norm of civility; from this moment on, even when freedom is practised as calculated resistance to civility, its exercise entails extrapolating, parodying or inverting its valuations.

Of course, nineteenth-century liberal government was no more a realization of the philosophy of Locke, Hume, Mill and so forth than the programmes and politics of the UK and the United States in the 1980s were a realization of the writings of Hayek or Friedman. Liberalism, rather, relates to a certain style of government, certain ways of problematizing political power, certain presuppositions about the subjects

---

[12] Proudhon's assault here, in his Epilogue to *Idée générale de la révolution au XIX siècle*, is on all who pretend there is any good in government, including democrats, Socialists and proletarians. The translation is quoted from Proudhon [1851] 1923: 294 (emphases removed). See also Oestreich 1982: 272.

and objects of power, certain types of criticism of strategies of power. Foucault himself suggested that liberalism should be seen neither as a historical period nor as a substantive doctrine of how to govern. Rather, liberalism denotes a certain ethos of governing, one which seeks to avoid the twin dangers of governing too much, and thereby distorting or destroying the operation of the natural laws of those zones upon which good government depends – families, markets, society, personal autonomy and responsibility – and governing too little, and thus failing to establish the conditions of civility, order, productivity and national wellbeing which make limited government possible.

As far as the market was concerned, classical economic liberalism of the nineteenth century proscribed direct political interventions into the economic machinery of production and exchange.[13] But this did not mean that liberal styles of government could neglect the economic domain; on the contrary, they had a key role in establishing the conditions under which the laws of political economy might operate to best effect. This was not a matter of direct intervention into the workplace; it was a matter of establishing a free market in labour, and removing all that would hamper or distort the freedom of the labourer to enter into production through the wage contract. As Marx repeatedly pointed out, the worker was to be freed from the land through the removal of longstanding rights which enabled a limited self-subsistence, and freed for exploitation in the labour market through punitive sanctions against gambling, vagrancy and the like which precluded any and all legitimate means of survival other than waged labour. Simultaneously, the worker was to be individualized: freed from collective bonds through laws against combinations and collective action. Once the worker was individualized and wage labour generalized, the dull compulsion of the labour market would combine with the disciplinary organization of time, space and activity in the factory, mill and mine to produce the forms of life and modes of individuality in which docile and utilizable labour would present itself at the workplace 'of its own free will'. The archetypal example here comes from England, in the form of the New Poor Law of 1834. Edwin Chadwick provided this reform of the system of poor relief with its explicit rationale. Mary Poovey points out that the New Poor Law was designed to establish an apparatus for gathering information about the cost of poverty and what Chadwick termed 'a new machinery' which would implement a 'uniform principle of admin-

---

[13] Of course, there were various utopian and socialist projects such as those of Charles Fourier and Robert Owen, which included a transformation of the organization of work in their projects of communal civility.

istration' through the very structure of the workhouse, and through the principle of 'less eligibility': 'the ultimate object of this elaborate machinery was not to deprive poor individuals of their agency, but to ensure that they would act freely – according, that is, to the laws of the market . . . the New Poor Law forced the poor to discipline themselves to that they could rise from an impoverished and dehumanized aggregate to a state of free – that is, self-disciplined – agency . . . the New Poor Law succeeded because it incited in the poor the fear that all freedoms would be abrogated if one acknowledged the need for relief'.[14]

This was merely one of a whole series of experiments motivated by the belief that political rule must be exercised in the form of government. As we shall see in chapter 3, many of these experiments in the conduct of the conduct of those who were the subjects of rule were first tried out in the colonies, where the relations between discipline and freedom were attenuated at best, and frequently absent. 'Nineteenth-century Ireland, W. L. Burn observes, formed "a social laboratory . . . The most conventional of Englishmen were willing to experiment in Ireland on lines with they were not prepared to contemplate or tolerate at home." '[15] Thus writes Oliver MacDonagh, developing the claim that he first made in the 1950s, that nineteenth-century England saw a 'revolution in government'.[16] Few doubt the depth of this transformation in the scope and

[14] Poovey 1995: 106–11. There is a massive literature on the reform of the Poor Laws, but Poovey's account seems to me to be most instructive in relation to the questions that concern me here.

[15] MacDonagh 1977b: 34; he is citing Burn 1949: 68. Amongst the experiments in Ireland in the first half of the nineteenth century were a centralized political administration, a unified police force, paid magistrates, public dispensaries for medicine, state-supported hospitals, a unified and regulated network of lunatic asylums and state-organized elementary schooling; but economic government tended to flow the other way. Thus the implementation of the Poor Law was exported from England, as was support for the land-owning classes. MacDonagh's argument is taken up in Alison Smith's (1997) Ph.D thesis on 'the government of military conduct'. Thanks to Barry Hindess for this reference.

[16] MacDonagh argued that this was generated by a whole series of intolerable social problems that called for amelioration, and that, once begun, the expansion of government acquired its own momentum: a process that could be characterized by a model – exposure of the evil; an inadequate legislative response; further concern leading to the appointment of experts; expert demands for more legislation and better machinery; expert demands for the extension of government; experts taking upon themselves an active governmental role (MacDonagh 1958). MacDonagh's argument is discussed in Roy MacLeod's introduction to *Government and Expertise* (MacLeod 1988). Others argued that this thesis ignored the key role of ideas, in particular

mechanisms for the exercise of political power. Historians debate the 'origins' of this revolution – the respective role of political ideas, political expediency and professional entrepreneurialism – but, from my point of view, it is not origins or causes that are of interest but connections: not 'why' but 'how'. From this perspective, we now have many excellent accounts of the invention and dissemination of the disciplinary assemblages of the nineteenth century: the prison, the workhouse and the lunatic asylum as apparatuses to remodel the character of those citizens who transgressed their part of the contract of civility. But civility was also instituted through strategies which attempted to *construct* well-regulated liberty through creating practices of normality, rationality and sensibility. These practices governed *through* freedom, to the extent that they sought to invent the conditions in which subjects themselves would enact the responsibilities that composed their liberties. Individuals would have to be equipped with a moral agency that would shape their conduct within a space of action that was necessarily indeterminate. These practices of government were thus inescapably bound to certain understandings of what constituted and shaped subjects of this moral agency – whether this be a calculus of pleasure and pain which guided all choices, or an inherited moral character that was both the product and basis of a mode of life. The town, the family and the school were perhaps the most important sites in which the issue of liberty was problematized and technologized. Each can be seen as a kind of 'machine' for assembling civilization.

The government of freedom can first be analysed in terms of the invention of technologies of spaces and gazes, the birth of calculated projects to use space to govern the conduct of individuals at liberty. We may see this in the multitude of programmes for governing urban space that emerged during the nineteenth century.[17] Nineteenth-century thought was haunted by the spectre of the crowd, the mob, the mass, the riot, the multiplication of forces of rebellion which could be brought into being by the concentration of persons in space.[18] These were not the exercise of freedom but its antithesis: the greatest challenge to a

Bentham and utilitarianism, in underpinning the growth of government (e.g. Finer 1972). MacDonagh later produced a synthesis which allotted a role to 'theoretical' factors as well as 'political' and 'technical' ones (MacDonagh 1977a). Mary Poovey's discussion of Edwin Chadwick is usefully located in relation to this debate (Poovey 1995: chs. 5 and 6).

[17] Paul Rabinow provides an excellent analysis of these issues in *French Modern* (Rabinow 1989).

[18] The classic text here is Le Bon 1895. Good accounts of these debates are provided in Moscovici 1988 and Van Ginneken 1994.

public order of liberty. One set of responses sought to use space against space, to transform towns from dangerous and unhygienic aggregations of persons into well-ordered topographies for maintaining morality and public health. This was the start of a series of dreams of the healthy 'liberal' city, in which the spatial forms – buildings, streets, public spaces – that had encouraged the agglomeration of masses outside the gaze of civilization would be reconstructed through town planning in order to produce health, happiness and civility. A whole diversity of inventions were involved which entailed opening space to visibility and locking each 'free' individual into a play of normative gazes. Police forces would patrol, map, inspect, supervise and know the moral character of each district of the town, operating not so much through terror and the certainty of apprehension, but by placing a grid of norms of conduct over urban space and regulating behaviour according to the division of the normal and the pathological. This work would be linked to that of medical practitioners, who would try to turn the town into a multi-faceted apparatus for fighting disease and securing health. Reform of dwelling houses and public institutions, planned patterns of boulevards and streets, public gardens and squares, sewers and running water, street lighting and pavements – this was not just a 'civilized architecture', but the calculated use of architecture in the service of well-regulated liberty. Public peace was to be maintained not through an exhaustive code of sumptuary laws and prescriptions, but through shaping the conduct of free individuals in the direction of civility.

Other spaces of well-regulated liberty were added: museums, exhibitions and department stores which, as Tony Bennett has argued, operated both an explicit and an implicit pedagogy of civility.[19] Their design explicitly sought to discipline and regulate the conduct of the masses they attracted. They were often accompanied by instructions as to proper forms of dress, conduct, cleanliness and deportment and the avoidance of liquor. And, within them, individuals were not only scrutinized by guards and attendants, but were scrutinized by one another, providing the spatial and visual means for self-education. In all these topographical technologies of civilization, persons were to be governed not through imposing duties, but by throwing a web of visibilities, of public codes and private embarrassments over personal conduct: we might term this *government through the calculated administration of shame* Shame here was to entail an anxiety over the exterior deportment of the self, linked to an injunction to care for oneself in the name of the public manifestation of moral character. These strategies govern all the more

[19] Bennett 1988; see also Bennett 1995.

effectively because each individual is to play his or her part in the games of civility. Yet simultaneously they produce new spatial and topographical divisions between those within and those outside civility, and are linked to a whole set of new inventions for disciplining those whose transgressions are now seen as an affront to the order of proper comportment and propriety.

Public space is, of course, a key value for liberal thought. So is the private family, which is celebrated as the essential basis and counter-weight to government. Yet simultaneously, starting perhaps in the eighteenth century, and by different routes for the wealthy and the poor family, a whole range of technologies were invented that would enable the family to do its public duty without destroying its private authority.[20] Throughout the nineteenth century, a variety of strategies sought to medicalize the wealthy family, and to shape the domestic relations of the poor into the form of a private and moral family. These manoeuvres were undertaken by doctors and philanthropists, in schemes of model housing, in feminist campaigns to encourage marriage and to enforce fathers to accept their domestic responsibilities and so forth. They sought to enhance everything that would secure the family as a space for the investment of individual passions, yet to ensure that these passions would be satisfied in a way that would produce public benefits.

The government of freedom, here, may be analysed in terms of the deployment of technologies of *responsibilization*. The home was to be transformed into a purified, cleansed, moralized, domestic space. It was to undertake the moral training of its children. It was to domesticate and familialize the dangerous passions of adults, tearing them away from public vice, the gin palace and the gambling hall, imposing a duty of responsibility to each other, to home and to children, and a wish to better their own condition. The family, from then on, has a key role in strategies for government through freedom. It links public objectives for the good health and good order of the social body with the desire of individuals for personal health and well-being. A 'private' ethic of good health and morality can thus be articulated on to a 'public' ethic of social order and public hygiene, yet without destroying the autonomy of the family – indeed by promising to enhance it.

This liberal strategy of government through the inculcation and shaping of 'private' responsibility assigns a key role to experts. For it is experts – first doctors but later a host of others – who can specify ways

---

[20] The best account here remains Jacques Donzelot's pathbreaking study *The Policing of Families* (Donzelot 1979). See also Valverde 1991; I have addressed some of these issues in Rose 1985 and 1987.

of conducting one's private affairs that are desirable, not because they are required by a moral code dictated by God or the Prince, but because they are rational and true. It is experts who can tell us how we should conduct ourselves, not in airy and vaporous moral nostrums, but as precise technologies for the care of the body, the care of others – the children, the old – and the conduct of our daily routines of life. The notion of normality, the invention of the norm, is the linchpin of this mechanism.[21] In popular discourse, by the middle of the nineteenth century, the term 'normal' had come into common usage to describe things that are regular, usual, typical, ordinary, conventional. But it was the French physiologist Broussais, in 1828, who made the idea of 'the normal state' of an organism or an organ the condition for identifying and explaining pathology as abnormality: normality here already carried both the sense of a state that was usual and one which was desirable. By the time of the publication of his *Système de politique positive* from 1851 to 1854, Auguste Comte had 'raised Broussais's nosological conception to the level of an axiom' applicable equally to biological, moral and social phenomena: each had its normal state, and pathological states were not radically distinct from the normal state but operated through the same laws and differed only in terms of intensity.[22] The ambiguity between the ontological and the empirical, between the average and the desirable, between that which merely is and that which we must strive to achieve, is written into the little word 'normal' from that point onwards.

What was involved here was more than merely semantic; social statisticians over the nineteenth and early twentieth centuries made the notion of the norm technical: norms could be calculated for populations, individuals could be individuated by comparing their characteristics – height, weight, circumference of skull, and later intelligence and moral worth – with those of the population as a whole. The capacity to identify, measure, instil and regulate through the idea of the norm becomes a key technique of government. Georges Canguilhem argued that there was a fundamental distinction between social norms – technological, economic, juridical – and organic norms. 'Between 1759, when the word "normal" appeared, and 1834 when the word "normalized" appeared', Canguilhem argued, 'a normative class had won the power

---

[21] For the genealogy of the emergence of norms in the nineteenth century, the best discussion remains Foucault 1977. See also Hacking's account in *The Taming of Chance* (Hacking 1990: 160–9) and my own discussion in Rose 1985.

[22] Georges Canguilhem has provided the best account of these developments in the life sciences in *On the Normal and the Pathological* (1978: 17). Hacking (1990) provides a good introduction to these issues.

to identify – a beautiful example of ideological illusion – the function of social norms, whose content it determined, with the use that that class made of them.'[23]

But it is misleading to ascribe the rise of normalization to the ideology of a class. It was in the new institutions of government, in the schools, the prisons, the workhouses, the lunatic asylums and the like – all those institutions where individuals were to be governed as citizens, returned to citizenship, reformed because of their lapses from citizenship – that norms of conduct were elaborated that would simultaneously define the capacities and competencies of the normal individual and individualize the miscreant as one who deviated from those norms and could, in some circumstances, be returned to them. From this point on, the norm would that which is socially worthy, statistically average, scientifically healthy *and* personally desirable. Normality was natural, but those who were to be civilized would have to achieve normality through working on themselves, controlling their impulses in their everyday conduct and habits, inculcating norms of conduct into their children, under the guidance of others. Many would aspire to this role as experts of conduct: religious authorities and philanthropists would soon be accompanied by all manner of reformers, child-savers, campaigners for social purity; later they would be joined, but never supplanted, by those who claimed to ground their norms, and their codes of conduct, in objectivity: the proliferating scientific experts of the moral order. In the process, free individuals become governable – in a range of different ways with varying consequences – as normal subjects. To be free, in this modern sense, is to be attached to a polity where certain civilized modes of conducting one's existence are identified as normal, and simultaneously to be bound to those 'engineers of the human soul' who will define the norm and tutor individuals as to the ways of living that will accomplish normality.

The school was a very important locus for the elaboration of the norms of freedom. Ian Hunter and James Donald have shown how the invention of the school was linked to these concerns to produce well-regulated liberty.[24] Schooling of the labouring classes was, of course, partly a matter of security, of the prevention of social danger, of breaking up and supervising inchoate masses of youth in towns. But the child was to be disciplined not merely by supervision, punishment and the learning of the catechism, but through an apparatus that simultaneously individualized and normalized. Through the design of the classroom, in the structuring of lessons, in the emphasis on punctuality and obedience

[23] Canguilhem 1978: 151.
[24] Hunter 1988; Donald 1992.

to authority, the conduct of each child could be ordered, observed, judged and assessed. The normal child was to be produced through this regime of supervision and judgement in relation to norms of scholarly and moral behaviour. Normal individuals were those who were judged, and judged themselves, in relation to a social norm.[25]

But schooling sought also to produce a different relation of the free person to his or her existence: it was a technology of rationality. For example, in the United States, an explicit link was made between democracy and numeracy, especially decimalization.[26] Decimalization, thought Thomas Jefferson in 1790, would introduce a new ease of reckoning to the 'whole mass of people, who would thereby be enabled to compute for themselves whatever they should have occasion to buy, to sell, or measure, which the present complicated and difficult ratios put beyond their computation for the most part'. Decimalization, it was argued, would thus democratize commerce. And George Washington, in a letter to Nicolas Pike, author of one of the earliest elementary arithmetic texts to be published in the republican United States, lauded education in mathematics because it 'accustoms the mind to method and correctness in reasoning' and is 'peculiarly worthy of rational beings'.[27] Mathematics disciplined the mind; it could play its part in the formation of the rational citizen equipped with foresight and a calculative relation to life. Numeracy, that is to say, was an element in an ethical technology whose objective was the production of a certain form of civilized subjectivity.

These technologies were accompanied by a more delicate infiltration of the moral sentiments of the child: a technology of sensibility. This found its basis in the texts of Rousseau, Goethe and Schiller: education was to attempt not simply the formation of the normal citizen, nor the formation of the rational citizen; it also had the vocation of forming the citizen with sensibilities. This was to be accomplished by encouraging a new pastoral relationship between teacher and pupil. As Ian Hunter has shown, David Stow's training manual for the nineteenth-century popular school, first published in 1836, emphasized the role of pedagogy in intensifying the inner life of the child.[28] This was not an airy dream but a technological project. It required a particular, detailed and continual knowledge, not only of the general characteristics of the inner life of

---

[25] Foucault 1977; Rose 1985.

[26] I return to these issues in ch. 6.

[27] Jefferson [1790] 1961: 631 and Washington 1788, quoted from Cline-Cohen 1982: 128 and 132.

[28] Hunter 1988.

children, but also of the specific inner world of each child to be governed. The better the teacher knew each child, the easier it would be to guide him or her. The playground was invented as a space in which the teacher was to build up a relation of sympathy and trust with the pupil, to observe the 'real life of children', to witness their delinquencies, to discover their true character and dispositions. On the return to the schoolroom, events in the playground would be used in training lessons in morality: not only to show the child that he or she was always observed – by God if not by the teacher – but to enable the child to discover his or her own 'superintending eye' as conscience. Subjects such as English were to be introduced into the curriculum, not for purely 'aesthetic' reasons so beloved of those who defend 'liberal education' today, but because they would help the child become aware of these internal states, they would provide a language for speaking about them, they would provide criteria for judging them: in short, they would actually create new civilized sensibilities.

These technologies sought to instil techniques whereby selves would simultaneously practise upon themselves as free individuals and bind them into a civilized polity by means of that freedom and the modes in which it was enacted. They dreamed that one could produce individuals who did not need to be governed by others, who would govern themselves through introspection, foresight, calculation, judgement and according to certain ethical norms. In these ideal individuals the social objective of the good citizen would be fused with the personal aspiration for a civilized life: this would be the state called freedom.

Freedom as solidarity

Towards the end of the nineteenth century, critics, including sociologists, argued that the normalizing, rationalizing and 'pastoral' projects of nineteenth-century liberalism were insufficient.[29] They were powerless in the face of the forces of social fragmentation and individualization in modern society, which social investigation itself appeared to document: rising crime, the disaffection of youth, suicide – all the manifestations of the alienation of the individual in current conditions. Further, critics pointed to the worrying consequences of economic affairs, which had not been ameliorated by rudimentary constraints placed on the powers of bosses – the effects of factory conditions upon health, the effects of low wages and irregular employment – and the dangers of

---

[29] Once more, it is Jacques Donzelot who has analysed this most penetratingly (Donzelot 1984). I return to these issues in more detail in ch. 3.

unrest which these exacerbated by encouraging the growth of unionized and militant labour. The governmental formulae of nineteenth-century liberalism, grounded in the theoretical codes of political economy, had not yet found the ways to mitigate these harmful consequences of economic life whilst preserving the privacy of private enterprise.

There were a number of distinct responses to these perceived difficulties in the early decades of the twentieth century.[30] Some, of course, argued that the sham liberties and freedoms of capitalism should be rejected in the name of full-scale collectivization of social and economic life, although even communist, socialist and social democratic forces proclaimed their allegiance to another, truer form of freedom. Other forces, even those deemed collectivist, sought, in different ways, to reconcile the obligations of liberty with the requirements of sociality. Whilst many radicals in the nineteenth century had sought to regain a lost community, a *Gemeinschaft* which would provide a natural harmony, tranquillity and sure sense of worth for each member, these forces tried to re-invent community governmentally. Their achievement was to see that the bonds of solidarity could be rendered *technical*, that is to say, made amenable to a technique. A variety of competing formulae were proposed, but they had in common the wish to ameliorate the socially dangerous consequences of industrialization and urbanization and to recreate social solidarity. The 'private' family of the labouring classes, cast loose from its traditional moorings, was to be linked back into a community in a whole range of ways. Public housing schemes would seek to create what the Tudor Walters Report of 1918 was to term 'healthy social communities'.[31] Movements such as that for mental hygiene sought to install various kinds of social workers – welfare workers, probation officers, health visitors – who would act as go-betweens, linking public institutions – schools, courts, hospitals, asylums – to domestic life. All the mundane activities of everyday life – the feeding, dress and care of children, the arrangements of kitchen and bathroom, the rituals of washing and tooth cleaning – were to be observed, described and judged by experts in terms of their social costs and consequences. They would be transformed into norms which could be disseminated back into the home. These norms of living were not arbitrary moralities but scientific findings: to follow them was to simultaneously to respect knowledge, to ensure contentment and to assume social responsibility. The normal citizen was to be the social citizen, the citizen adapted *to* society, whose pleasures and aspirations were to be realized *in* society.

[30] I consider these in more detail in ch. 3.
[31] The Tudor Walters Report of 1918 is discussed in Swenarton 1981.

Even more controversial, perhaps, were the challenges posed to the freedom of the free market by economic expertise. Opposing themselves to those socialists who asserted the need for a full socialization of the machinery of production, liberals such as John Maynard Keynes and William Beveridge argued that it was both possible and necessary to act upon the economic machine to produce national wealth and well-being, and that, by so doing, one would not destroy the free market but, on the contrary, save it from those economic and political forces that threatened it.[32] From proposals for labour exchanges to those for countercyclical public works, and from management of exchange rates to attempts to alter the aggregate level of demand, economists tried to develop political programmes and policies that would create the conditions under which the market would prosper, yet without destroying the essential freedom of economic agents – bosses, investors – to conduct their financial affairs according to their own choices and in pursuit of their private profits.

Experts also weakened the boundaries of the workplace: the lines that established the privacy of events within the factory, the mine, the mill or the docks and the inviolability of the wage contract that bound employer to employee.[33] They argued that work would be more productive and less disrupted by inefficiency, accidents and strikes if it was organized in terms of a scientific knowledge of the worker. For proponents of these new interventions upon the workplace, it appeared that work itself could be an answer to fragmentation and social isolation. Individuals, it now seemed, were social creatures who looked to work to provide social satisfactions as much as financial rewards. The contented worker was the productive worker. From C. S. Myers to Elton Mayo, experts would devise all sorts of techniques whereby work, whilst retaining its essentially private character, could cater for the social demands that were placed upon it. This amounted to a gradual socialization of the internal world of the workplace.

For present purposes, the central technological innovation was social insurance. 'If I had to sum up the immediate future of democratic politics in a single word', said Winston Churchill in 1909, 'I should say "Insurance" . . . because I am convinced that by sacrifices which are inconceivably small, which are all within the power of the very poorest man in regular work, families can be secured against catastrophes which

---

[32] Keith Middlemas (1979) provides a good overview of this period. Jose Harris is the best source on Beveridge (Harris 1977). A useful introduction to Keynesianism can be found in Tomlinson 1981a.

[33] I discuss these arguments and strategies further in Rose 1990: pt II.

would otherwise smash them up for ever.'[34] Of course, insurance itself was not new. As Pat O'Malley has pointed out, in Britain, despite suspicion of combinations, successive governments supported the development of friendly societies in providing insurance principally for artisans, which it was thought would foster habits of frugality and diligence.[35] Prudence would instrumentalize existing aspirations for security in this sector of society, with advantages to the state that were both characterological and financial. As commercial industrial life insurance developed, focused not on artisans but on the poorest sections of the working classes, prudentialism took a rather different form: it was a moral technology to discipline the poor in the habits of thrift. A whole variety of criticisms of these prudential arrangements – political, technical, moral – underpinned their displacement by strategies of social insurance over the first half of the twentieth century.

Jacques Donzelot and François Ewald have analysed some of the characteristics of these novel social strategies of insurance.[36] Two aspects are particularly important in relation to our question of freedom. First, strategies of insurance ameliorated the despotism of economic life, in the name of a socially guaranteed right to economic security attaching to each citizen. They thus softened and dissipated the antagonism between employee and boss within the employing firm, in relation to such matters as industrial accidents, industrial disease and dismissal. Hence they reduced the dangers of political action targeted directly at the workplace. Simultaneously, social insurance weakened the boundaries between the family machine, the economic machine and the political machine. These were woven into a complex field of rights, in which the rights of the family were to be secured not merely by individual economic action, but through social provision of pensions and benefits. The riskiness inherent in an industrial system based upon *private* ownership, the employment contract and the pursuit of profit was to be contained by *social* devices which would enable it to deal with its own consequences.

Secondly, insurance domesticated fate by subjecting it to a social calculus of risk. The freedom of the individual or family to conduct its affairs without threat of catastrophe was made possible by taming insecurity with solidarity and the laws of large numbers. In the process the free citizen was locked into a web of social solidarities and

---

[34] Churchill 1909, quoted in Marshall 1975: 66.
[35] O'Malley 1995.
[36] Donzelot 1984, 1991; Ewald 1986, 1991. See also Pat O'Malley's (1995) investigations of prudentialism.

interdependencies – across the individuals' life, across all individuals in a population, across generations. At the same time, insurance accorded a new legitimacy and permanence to the political arrangements that supervised payments and ensured their continuity. Thus social cohesion was enhanced, the dangers of fragmentation reduced, and the threat of a radical challenge to the political order diminished.

Insurance was a governmental formula somewhere between socialism and liberalism, a compact of social and individual responsibility. From Lloyd George to Beveridge, the task for those devising schemes of insurance was to find ways in which security could be combined with responsibility. One needed to safeguard against the individual and collective risks produced by an economic system based upon the private contract of employment, and the dangers inherent in production for profit. Yet, at the same time, individuals must not be excused from their individual responsibility to gain employment in order to provide for themselves and their family. Hence the importance of such matters as the contributory system, requiring the individual to make regular and specific payments into the fund rather than appearing to provide social insurance through general taxation, and the careful construction of a convincing fiction that there was a direct relation between the payments each individual made to the fund and the benefits that he or she received.

Insurance was to be joined, over the course of the twentieth century, by other technologies that operated according to the same diagram of collectivization and individualization of responsibilities. Perhaps the most important, at least in the United Kingdom, was public broadcasting.[37] Lord Reith was not the only one who saw broadcasting explicitly as an 'integrator for democracy', in which the ether would form the invisible medium that would unite the humble highland crofter and the metropolitan city dweller in a single community of citizens. The civilizing message of the public broadcasting services was both universalizing – it was addressed to everyone – and individualizing – it addressed each person as an individual in his or her own home, in relation to his or her own problems, disseminating advice and guidance on domestic duties and household management, child rearing and motherhood – playing its role in installing the little routines of social citizenship and civility

[37] The civilizing governmental role of public broadcasting in the United Kingdom has been discussed by James Donald (Donald 1992). Thomas Osborne and I examine some of the debates involved in the formation of 'public opinion' in the United States in T. Osborne and Rose forthcoming.

into each 'private family', implanting 'social' obligations into the soul of each free citizen.

It was indeed on Reith's own medium, BBC Radio, that one can find this formula of government encapsulated – in one of those minor texts that are nonetheless so telling. In 1944, Donald Winnicott, the child psychoanalyst, gave a radio talk entitled 'Support for Normal Parents':

> The State in England takes pains to leave parents free to choose, and to accept or refuse what the State offers . . . [It] does recognize the fact that a good mother is the right judge of what is good for her own child, provided she is informed as to facts and educated as to needs . . . The State is indeed wise in its policy of education of parents with non-compulsion and the next step is education of those who administer the public services . . . Whatever does not specifically back up the idea that parents are responsible people will in the long run be harmful to the very core of society.[38]

Private individuals were simultaneously assigned their social duties, accorded their rights, assured of their natural capacities, and educated in the fact that they must be educated by experts in order to responsibly assume their freedom within the context of society.

Freedom as autonomy

By the middle of the twentieth century, freedom – strategies and tactics that sought to realize freedom as an operative mode of existence – had apparently assumed an inescapably 'social form'. Freedom, now, would be found within society or it would not be found at all. William Beveridge's report on *Social Insurance and Allied Services*, published in 1942, is sometimes seen as the founding document of the British welfare state. Perhaps, instead, it should be seen as a codification of all these strategies for the government of the social citizen invented over the course of our own century, a codification which emerged not at the dawn of the social but at its dusk. For, over the past fifty years, we have witnessed a series of challenges to this social state. I shall consider them in detail in chapter 4. Most have been couched in what Albert Hirschman terms 'the rhetoric of reaction'.[39] They describe the perverse ways in which well-meaning attempts to recreate community, to ensure equality and to maximize liberty have actually produced the reverse – destroying communities, failing to redistribute wealth, increasing paternalism and interference by authorities and experts. They claim that such attempts are,

---

[38] This talk is reprinted as Winnicott [1944] 1964.
[39] Hirschman 1991.

in any event, futile, for they do not understand the real processes that affect social well-being – the relations of production, the market. And they argue that the activities of the social state put in jeopardy the very things it seeks to defend – democracy, liberty, economic growth.

These challenges have been so potent, in part, because they have been articulated from all parts of the political spectrum. An economic perspective has certainly been central: demands that market relations are re-activated as the guide to economic decision making and risk taking, and for the dismantling of devices that would interfere with freedom of individual economic choice in the name of claims by experts to know what is good for society. But it would be misleading to regard these critiques as merely a revival of an old free-market scepticism over the powers of government or simply as a thinly disguised economic ideology. In particular, they are grounded in the emergence of a new way of understanding and acting upon human beings as subjects of freedom. I term such strategies of governing autonomous individuals through their freedom 'advanced liberal'. In different ways, the problem of freedom now comes to be understood in terms of the capacity of an autonomous individual to establish an identity through shaping a meaningful everyday life. Freedom is seen as autonomy, the capacity to realize one's desires in one's secular life, to fulfil one's potential through one's own endeavours, to determine the course of one's own existence through acts of choice.

No doubt one can find the conditions for shifts in conceptions of the self and their associated ethical regimes within philosophy, literature and aesthetics as well as in the changing explanatory practices of the human sciences.[40] Here, however, we are less concerned with the 'idea of the self' than with the changing ways in which people relate to themselves, the kinds of people we take ourselves to be at particular times, in particular places and contexts, and the ways in which varying presuppositions about the nature of human beings are embodied in technologies that will enable people to be governed, and to govern themselves. Broadly speaking, two interrelated clusters of technologies have taken shape in this century to operate in this space. There are the technologies of consumption that have concerned themselves with the relations between persons and products. And there are psychological technol-

---

[40] There is an extensive literature on 'the history of the self'. Charles Taylor's comprehensive history of the idea of the self is a crucial source (C. Taylor 1989b). Sociologists tend to adopt a rather impoverished linear model in terms of tradition, modernity and detraditionalization (e.g. the papers collected in Heelas, Lash and Morris 1996). I criticize this model in my own contribution to that volume, and in Rose 1996e.

ogies, concerned with the care of the soul. They are interlinked because, on the one hand, consumption technologies have utilized psychological knowledges and techniques – attitude surveys, psychodynamics – to chart the reasons that lie behind the act of consumption for different sectors, ages, sexes, personality types, and to adjust and segment selling techniques accordingly. On the other hand, psychological knowledges and psy experts have disseminated their explanations and techniques through consumption technologies, and a whole variety of types of therapy and counselling now use market mechanisms to generate demand and to link it to supply. And they are also interlinked because of the ways in which they understand the human being in terms of identity, autonomy and the desire for self-actualization through choice.

Consumption

How can the personal practices of consumption be linked to the political problem of the government of conduct? Of course, the relation of humans and goods is 'socially constructed' and in different epochs human beings have used artefacts in various ways to represent, display, augment and distinguish the self in relation to others. The emergence of a mass market for manufactured goods in the eighteenth and nineteenth centuries was linked to new uses for commodities in identifying selves and making distinctions. But the technologies of mass consumption, as they took shape over the course of the twentieth century, established a new relation between the sphere of the self and the world of goods. For the first time, this power of goods to shape identities was utilized in a calculated form, according to rationalities worked out and established, not by politicians, but by salesmen, market researchers, designers and advertisers who increasingly based their calculations upon psychological conceptions of humans and their desires.

By the second half of the twentieth century, many manufacturers and advertisers had become convinced that they could best promote consumption of their products by marketing strategies that played on the aspects of the human personality that were not rational, but which could be made intelligible and practicable by psychology.[41] Psychological and social-psychological techniques – attitude surveys, opinion polling – divided the population by age, sex, status into groups with different tastes, weaknesses, aspirations. Motivation research and in-depth studies of consumption sought to identify the specific insecurities and attachments of these different groups of consumers, to illuminate the non-rational

---

[41] Ewen 1976, 1988; Leiss, Kline and Jhally 1986; cf. Bauman 1988.

gratifications and emotional features of consumption. Advertisements sought to convey the sense of individual satisfaction brought about by the purchase or use of a product. Subsequently a less behavioural or psychodynamic image of the person came to the fore, organized in new research techniques which segmented consumers by lifestyle types and products by their appeal to different market segments. Advertisements now tried to link goods to individual satisfactions placed within a matrix of lifestyle and social activities, and portrayed consumption as locating an individual within a certain form of life. The images they deployed identified persons through the commodities they purchased: commodities appeared to illuminate those who bought them, to have the power to transform purchasers into certain kinds of person living a certain kind of life. Consumption technologies, together with other narrative forms such as soap operas, establish not only a 'public habitat of images' for identification, but also a plurality of pedagogies for living a life that is both pleasurable and respectable, both personally unique and socially normal. They offer new ways for individuals to narrativize their lives, new ethics and techniques for living which do not set self-gratification and civility in opposition – as in the ethical codes of the puritan sects that Weber considered so important in the early moments of capitalism – but align them in a virtuous liaison of happiness and profit. In engaging with these formulae, albeit in creative and innovative ways, individuals play their own part in the games of civilization as they shape a style of life for themselves through acts of choice in the world of goods.

Over the second half of the twentieth century, similar presuppositions about selfhood have infused techniques for the government of conduct far beyond the buying and selling of consumption goods. Marriage and other domestic arrangements are now represented and regulated not as matters of obligation and conformity to a moral norm, but as lifestyle decisions made by autonomous individuals seeking to fulfil themselves and gain personal happiness. Having or not having children is no longer a matter of fate or nature; it too is represented as a matter of lifestyle choice and regulated through voluntary relations between aspiring parents and entrepreneurial doctors.[42] Healthy bodies and hygienic homes may still be political objectives, but they no longer require state bureaucracies inspecting and instructing us in habits of eating, of personal hygiene, of tooth care and the like. In the new modes of regulating health, individuals are addressed on the assumption that they *want to be healthy*, and enjoined to freely seek out the ways of living most likely to

---

[42] Strathern 1992.

promote their own health. Experts instruct us as to how to be healthy, advertisers picture the appropriate actions and fulfilments and entrepreneurs develop this market for health. Individuals are now offered a identity as consumers – offered an image and a set of practical relations to the self and others. In the name of themselves as consumers with rights they take up a different relation with experts, and set up their own forms of 'counter-expertise', not only in relation to food and drink and other 'consumables', but also in relation to the domains that were preeminently 'social' – health, education, housing, insurance and the like.

Through the transformation of all these institutional presuppositions, modern individuals are not merely 'free to choose', but *obliged to be free*, to understand and enact their lives in terms of choice. They must interpret their past and dream their future as outcomes of choices made or choices still to make. Their choices are, in their turn, seen as realizations of the attributes of the choosing person – expressions of personality – and reflect back upon the person who has made them. As these mechanisms of regulation through desire, consumption and the market – civilization through identification – come to extend their sway over larger and larger sectors of the population, earlier bureaucratic and governmental mechanisms of self-formation and self-regulation become less salient and can begin to be dismantled and refocused upon marginalized individuals who through ill will, incompetence or misfortune are outside these webs for 'consuming civility'. Norms of conduct for the civilized are now disseminated by independent experts, no longer explicit agents of a social code of moralizing instructions enjoined by superiors, but concerned professionals seeking to allay the problems, anxieties and uncertainties engendered by the seemingly so perplexing conditions of our present. They operate a regime of the self where competent personhood is thought to depend upon the continual exercise of freedom, and where one is encouraged to understand one's life, actually or potentially, not in terms of fate or social status, but in terms of one's success or failure acquiring the skills and making the choices to actualize oneself.

As this new ethic of self-conduct disseminates across diverse problems and practices, the relations of expertise and politics are further transformed. The embodiment of expertise in centrally directed bureaucracies is criticized as impersonal, demeaning to recipients, crushing choice and imposing arbitrary values. A new relation of individuals to expertise is established, based not upon welfare bureaucracies, social obligations and the inculcation of authoritatively established norms, but upon the mechanisms of the market and the imperatives of self-realization. Abraam de Swaan has proposed the term 'proto-professional' to describe the ways in which lay persons have become experts in redefining their everyday troubles as 'problems amenable to treatment by this or that profession'.[43] Such proto-professionals already organize their everyday world according to the basic stances and vocabularies elaborated by professionals. Hence they readily enter into collaborative work with professionals in their lifestyle choices and the resolution of dilemmas – either indirectly via the mass media or directly through therapeutic encounters. Within these proto-professionalized sectors, the self itself has become the locus of demand for socialization and self-improvement. Disciplinary techniques and moralizing injunctions as to health, hygiene and civility are no longer required; the project of responsible citizenship has been fused with individuals' projects for themselves. What began as a social norm here ends as a personal desire. Individuals act upon themselves and their families in terms of the languages, values and techniques made available to them by professions, disseminated through the apparatuses of the mass media or sought out by the troubled through the market. Thus, in a very significant sense, it has become possible to govern without governing *society* – to govern through the 'responsibilized' and 'educated' anxieties and aspirations of individuals and their families.

It would be a mistake, of course, to think that all procedures for the expert government of conduct now took this form. Rather, strategies for the conduct of conduct increasingly operate in terms of two distinct sectors. For the majority, expertise operated not through social planning, paternalism and bureaucracy, but in terms of a logic of choice, through transforming the ways in which individuals come to think of themselves, through inculcating desires for self-development that expertise itself can guide and through claiming to be able to allay the anxieties generated when the actuality of life fails to live up to its image. Yet a minority remain outside this regime of civility. They are, no doubt, the 'usual suspects' – the lone parent, the delinquent juvenile, the school truant, the drug user, the homeless person, the alcoholic – but their problems are represented in a new way, and are hence amenable to new modes of intervention. The 'urban underclass' becomes a new way of codifying this socially problematic and heterogeneous population of anti-citizens – an amalgam of cultural pathology and personal weakness which is racialized in particular ways, spatialized within the topography of the city, moralized through a link with sexual promiscuity and the 'unmarried mother', criminalized through a propensity to drugs and lawlessness. To this marginal territory are also consigned former psychiatric inmates and others who are expelled from the reformatory insti-

---

[43] de Swaan 1990: 14.

tutions that characterized social government into the imaginary space of 'the community'.

Upon this territory of the marginalized, expertise is integrated in an ambivalent manner into technologies of government that are increasingly punitive. The marginalized, excluded from the regime of choice, no longer embraced within a social politics of solidarity, are allocated to a range of new para-governmental agencies – charities, voluntary organizations supported by grants and foundations. A new territory opens up 'on the margins' – advice bureaux, groups of experts offering services to specific problematic groups, day centres and drop-in centres, concept houses and voluntary homes, as well as a multitude of 'for-profit' organizations receiving funds from both state and private sources. On this new and difficult terrain, deprived of the legitimacy conferred by the rationales of welfare, opposed to the patronizing implications of philanthropy and charity, seeking to do good to others at the same time as they map out a career path for themselves, experts strive to govern their clients according to the new regime of autonomy and choice, utilizing a tool-bag of techniques derived from explanatory systems as distinct as psychoanalysis and behaviourism to attempt to install the capacities for self-determination and self-mastery.

Simultaneously, new lines of possibility are opened up for the enactment of the moral aspirations and social vocations of 'lay persons', so disparaged within the expert regimes of social government. Such lay workers no longer tend to be inspired by the religious motives that fuelled earlier voluntary movements for the disadvantaged. Equipped with counselling skills and psychotherapeutic ethics, a radical politics of rights and empowerment or a commitment arising from personal experience, 'volunteers' come to play a key role in the proliferating agencies operating on the margins, establishing relations with those in distress that are no longer mediated through a complex bureaucracy of care. It is no critique to note that these workers in the twilight world of the marginalized so often deploy the logics of normalization, social skills, self-esteem and so forth in order to 'empower' their clients at the same time as they contest the politics which has made these the organizing principles of 'social' policy. It is indicative, rather, of the ethical complexity of our contemporary politics of life.

Therapeutics

It is against this background that we can locate the emergence of a second cluster of technologies for the government of the autonomous self: those associated with the 'psy' knowledges of human individuals, groups and the determinants of conduct. The significance of psychology within advanced liberal modes of government lies in the elaboration of a know-how of the autonomous individual striving for self-realization. In the nineteenth century, psychological expertise produced a know-how of the normal individual; in the first half of this century it produced a know-how of the social person. Today, psychologists elaborate complex emotional, interpersonal and organizational techniques by which the practices of everyday life can be organized according to the ethic of autonomous selfhood. This know-how has been disseminated by two intertwined routes. The first route works through reshaping the practices of those who exercise authority over others – social workers, managers, teachers, nurses – such that they exercise their powers in order to nurture and direct these individual strivings in the most appropriate and productive fashions. Here one sees the elaboration, in a plethora of self-instruction manuals, training courses and consultancy exercises, of a new set of relational technologies that appear to give professional authority an almost therapeutic character. The second route operates by what one can term the psychotherapies of normality, which promulgate new ways of planning life and approaching predicaments, and disseminate new procedures for understanding oneself and acting upon oneself to overcome dissatisfactions, realize one's potential, gain happiness and achieve autonomy.

We can term this cluster of technologies 'therapeutic', understanding therapy in the broadest sense, as a certain rationality for rendering experience into thought in a way that makes it practicable, amenable to having things done to it.[44] The psychotherapeutic territory is made up of all those practices in which one problematizes one's existence in terms of an interpretation of its inner psychological and psychodynamic meanings and determinants, acts upon one's dilemmas in terms of psychological interpretations of their implications, and intervenes upon oneself (alone or with the assistance of others) in terms of psychological norms and techniques – through self-inspection, self-problematization, self-monitoring and self-transformation. Encounters in a diversity of sites that used to be governed by their own codes and values now take a broadly therapeutic form – not just the client's visit to the counsellor, the patient's encounter in doctor's consulting room or the ward group of the psychiatric hospital, but also the worker's interview with the personnel manager, the parent in debt who visits the Citizens Advice Bureau, the consultation with the lawyer over divorce and child custody.

---

[44] The next two paragraphs draw upon evidence examined in much more detail in Rose 1990.

More fundamentally, perhaps, a number of dimensions of experience have been transformed along psychotherapeutic lines and everyday life has become the object of a kind of clinical reason. Everyday circumstances, such as debt, marriage and divorce, changing jobs, giving birth and so much more have become life events entailing coping and adjustment, spaces within which psychological forces of denial, repression, lack of psychosocial skill are played out, scenarios whose unfolding is dependent upon the level of our self-esteem, affairs whose psychological consequences – neurosis, stress – are as significant as their practical outcomes, occasions for the exercise of interpretation, diagnosis, confession, insight and reformation. Work has become a zone that is as much psychological as economic. We are no longer merely productive or unproductive bodies or even normal or maladjusted workers. We are 'people at work' and we bring to work all our fears, emotions and desires, our sexuality and our pathology. The activity of labour transformed into a matter of self-actualization, in which the cash return is less important than the identity conferred upon the employee. Everyday interactions have been 'neuroticized': our cultural habitat has become saturated with psychological narratives of relationships from the most intense to the most trivial, with lovers, with workmates, with friends. Through the intense focus on biographies, personalities and the minutiae of the lives of the famous and not so famous, in the press, on television and in the cinema, a new culture of the self has taken shape. Confession has moved beyond the consulting room and now forms part of the texture of everyday experience, where today it is more a matter of bearing witness to pain suffered than giving voice to an inner guilt. In all those encounters between two or more people, in relations of love and sex, in the family, in the 'human relations' of the group and the workplace, we discover hidden hurts and abuses that thwart the desire for recognition, for identity, for self-worth and self-actualization. Even in 'the therapeutics of human finitude' we find this ethic of self-fulfilment through relationships. Grief, frustration, disappointment, minor and terminal illness, even death itself have become the subject of intense biographical scrutiny and popular display, thorough personal narratives of coping, grieving, struggling, surviving, dying and much more. Experiences of finitiude have thus become events fraught with pathological possibilities and yet full of therapeutic potentials. Did our culture ever have a 'taboo' on discussion of these issues, as is popularly claimed? Certainly today finitude has found its voice; it is positively garrulous. Of course it is the province of those such as bereavement counsellors, who cluster around events from the illness of a child to the experience of a plane crash or other disaster to the diagnosis of a fatal disease. But above and beyond expertise, in popular discourse each 'life event' has become more than merely a locus of potential personal devastation: it has become the legitimate occasion for public documentation, for the description of the effects on everything from bodily functions and sexuality to feelings of hope and despair, not merely the legitimate object of therapy but also, with or without the benefit of experts, the location of hidden opportunities for personal growth.

We see here that the role of psy professionals cannot be understood through the familiar sociological theme of professional monopolization. Rather, it must be understood in terms of the *generosity* of expertise. The key to the transformations in our present wrought by the expertise of human conduct lies in the way in which certain knowledgeable persons – lawyers, doctors, psychologists, criminologists and so forth – have lent their vocabularies of explanation, procedures of judgement and techniques of remediation 'freely' to others – probation officers, social workers, teachers, managers, nurses, parents, individuals – on the condition that these 'petty engineers of human conduct' think and act a bit like experts. And this includes their subjects. Through such alliances – rather than through exclusivity and monopolization – the expertise of subjectivity has proliferated through our experience at a 'molecular' level. The relation between expertise and its subjects – clients, patients or customers – is not (or not only) one of domination, but one of subjectification, of 'making up' persons whose relations to themselves are configured within a grid of norms and knowledges. The desires, affects and bodily practices of persons get connected up with 'expert' ways of understanding experience, languages of judgement, norms of conduct. Persons become subjects in the same process as they are bound into corporeal and affectual relations with certain truths and authorities. The genealogy of expert knowledge is not a repetitive story of things imposed 'from above' upon a more or less truculent, docile or resistant population. Expertise has been deployed in the service of diverse strategies of control, but it also enters into the passions of individuals and populations and shapes the values and demands of countless contestations 'from below'. There is thus a certain reversibility of relations of expertise. What begins as a norm implanted 'from above', such as the universal obligations of literacy or numeracy, or the adoption of appropriate patterns of conduct in child rearing, can be 'repossessed' as a demand that citizens, consumers, survivors make of authorities in the name of their rights, their autonomy, their freedom.

The proliferation of therapeutic systems and practitioners has often been seen as a sign and effect of more general cultural changes – an index of the narcissism of our age or of the decline of religion.[45] But the territorialization of psychotherapy has a more productive relation to contemporary modes of government. The techne of psychotherapeutics brings the regulation of subjectivity into line with the new rationalities for the government of individuals in terms of their freedom, autonomy and choice: through the regimes of the therapeutic, all manner of social ills from delinquency to marital disharmony can be governed in new ways, and new relations established between the government of others and the government of the self. At a time when the individual is to be free from the imposition of codes of morality by religious, political or legal authorities, we have no authoritative ways of judging conduct other than those founded upon a scientific knowledge of the self. On the one hand, psychotherapeutics provides individuals with new rationales and procedures for living their lives according to a regime of choice, and for governing themselves within an environment that offers a plurality of possible styles of life, and in which individual fate is recast as the outcome of personal acts of choice. On the other, psychotherapeutics elaborates an ethics for which the way to happiness, or at least the conquest of unhappiness, can be specified in terms of apparently rational knowledges of subjectivity and where life conduct is to be shaped according to procedures that have a rational justification in terms of psychological norms of health and contentment. The individual is to adopt a new relation to his or her self in the everyday world, in which the self itself is to be an object of knowledge and autonomy is to be achieved through a continual enterprise of self-improvement through the application of a rational knowledge and a technique. To live as an autonomous individual is to have learned these knowledgeable techniques for understanding and practising upon yourself. Hence the norm of autonomy produces an intense and continuous self-scrutiny, self-dissatisfaction and self-evaluation in terms of the vocabularies and explanations of expertise. In striving to live our autonomous lives, to discover who we really are, to realize our potentials and shape our lifestyles, we become tied to the project of our own identity and bound in new ways into the pedagogies of expertise.

The politics of freedom today

Liberal freedom, today, freedom as autonomy and identity, is understood as freedom of individual right, freedom of employment, freedom

---

[45] Rieff 1966; cf. MacIntyre 1981; Giddens 1991.

of expression, freedom of consumption. As I shall argue in detail in later chapters, such freedoms are not so much ideas or concepts, but operative terms constitutively linked to the four main assemblages of contemporary freedom: the legal complex, the productive machine, the circuits of culture, image and meaning, and the apparatus for promoting and shaping forms of life through relations with the world of goods. As Wendy Brown argues, 'Freedom is neither a philosophical absolute not a tangible entity but a relational and contextual practice that takes shape in opposition to whatever is locally and ideologically conceived as unfreedom ... Rendering either the ancient or liberal formations of freedom as "concepts" abstracts them from the historical practices in which they are rooted, the institutions against which they are oriented, the domination they are designed to contest, the privileges they are designed to protect [and] ... preempts perception of what is denied and suppressed by them, of what kinds of dominations are enacted by particular practices of freedom.'[46]

This recognition of freedom as a set of practices, devices, relations of self to self and self to others, of freedom as always practical, technical, contested, involving relations of subordination and privilege, opens freedom itself to historical analysis and historical criticism. Perhaps today as never before our politics operates over precisely this terrain – battles over freedom, over what it is, what it should be, what purports to be freedom whilst being its opposite. The fact that freedom is technical, infused with relations of power, entails specific modes of subjectification and is necessarily a thing of this world, inescapably sullied by the marks of the mundane, does not make freedom a sham or liberty an illusion; rather it opens up the possibility of freedom as neither a state of being nor a constitutional form but as a politics of life.

If freedom is an object of genealogical investigation it is because it has come to define the problem space within which contemporary rationalities of government compete. The oppositions that concern moral philosophers – such as freedom as moral autonomy versus freedom as substantive capacity – figure in these analyses only as internal elements in disputes about the nature and limits of government and the mandates of different authorities. To analyse these contests over the powers of freedom requires one to discard some of the familiar principles of 'progressive' thought.[47] One must abandon the conventional ways of ascribing ethical value to the opposition between subject and

---

[46] W. Brown 1995: 6.
[47] Colin Gordon pointed to the necessity of these shifts many years ago: C. Gordon 1980: 239.

object, in which subjectivity is privileged as the authentic and natural locus of moral autonomy: we are governed as much through subject-ification as through objectification. One must discard the presupposition that one can criticize regimes of power to the extent that they falsify and distort human subjectivity and utilize the extent of this falsification as a yardstick by which power can be evaluated: regimes of power establish, deploy, promote and intensify the truths of our selves.[48] In short, one must abandon the political calculus of domination and liberation. This is not because we live in some consensual universe. It is because power also acts through practices that 'make up subjects' as free persons.

It might be thought that to approach freedom in this way is to deprive oneself of the opportunity to use the value of freedom as the basis for critical judgement.[49] I am not convinced by this criticism. Foucault certainly maintained the value of freedom not as a state or a quality, but as a way of practising upon oneself – a theme to which I will return. And it was through this way of thinking that he was able to argue for an intrinsic link between power and freedom. Power, he argued, differed from domination in that it presupposed the capacity of the subject of power to act. This argument was not grounded in a universal ontology of the human essence. It was, rather, historical: our history has pro-duced a creature with the capacity to act upon its limits. And we have come to relate to ourselves as creatures of self-responsibility and self-mastery, with the capacity to transform ourselves and make our own lives the object of practices of self-shaping. What does it matter that these ways of relating to ourselves are historical, that they were made through practical, technical and procedural inventions and embodied in ways of thinking, speaking and judging that emerged at a particular time and place and are destined to disappear. They are the values of our own present, they make up our irreality and their 'constructed' nature changes that not at all. How, then, in the light of its genealogy, can we orient ourselves to the value of freedom?

The theoretical anti-humanism that was so significant for radical thought in the 1970s, with its blend of semiotics, psychoanalysis and Marxism, has now had its day. This was a type of thought that sought

---

[48] Peter Miller analyses these issues succinctly in Miller 1987.

[49] For example, this seems to be implied at certain points by Thomas Dumm, in his insightful study *Michel Foucault and the Politics of Freedom* (Dumm 1996); yet at other points Dumm is quite clear that the ethic of freedom is constitutively bound to the practices of discipline and bio-politics, and that any aspiration to freedom in the wake of this insight must recognize that concrete practices of freedom can never take the form of moral autonomy or the absence of government.

to answer questions about the kinds of creatures that human beings are at the level of philosophy: it was as a result of philosophical critique that we were urged to abandon notions of any human essence, of the human being as the centre, originator and principle of history, epistemology, language or politics.[50] But perhaps it is more appropriate to investigate these questions of our materiality as human beings in another way. This would be a kind of materialist humanism, but one that was profoundly anti-romantic. That is to say, it would be an ethic of investigation that would take the materiality and historicity of our human being as central. This would not be a materialism of the body, as in so much recent feminist writing on the body and knowledge. The body does not provide a stable base upon which a materialism can be grounded. Bodies are heterogeneous, linked in to other flows which extend beyond the envelope of the skin, situationally assembled in particular practices through relations with technologies, with spaces, with artefacts and so forth.[51] Hence a new humanism would not pose its concerns in terms of what is inside and what is outside the human, of essence and supplement. It would start from the premise that humans are essentially machinated. And so is the capacity for freedom. Freedom does not arise in the absence of power: it is a mobile historical possibility arising from the lines of force within which human being is assembled, and the relations into which humans are enfolded. Freedom is the name we give today to a kind of power one brings to bear upon oneself, and a mode of bringing power to bear upon others. And freedom is particularly problematic when we demand to be governed in its name.

Human beings have become the kinds of creatures who can and do act upon themselves and against their limits, to increase their capacities and their powers. We do not know what we are capable of, but we do know – and we need no psychological theory to ratify this knowledge – that humans have acquired the capacity to will and to act. Perhaps this is the basis for a minimal normativity. Foucault himself seems sometimes to have been attracted to the Nietzschean opposition between two conceptions of morality and moral obligation.[52] In the first form, which both he and Nietzsche found problematic, morality is obedience to a heteronomous code which we must accept, and to which we are bound by fear and guilt. In the second, morality is an exercise in ascetics, whereby through experimentation, exercise and a permanent work on

---

[50] For a rigorous example of this kind of thinking, see Coward and Ellis 1976.

[51] I develop this argument in the final chapter of *Inventing Our Selves* (Rose 1996e).

[52] This argument has been made by Zwart 1996.

oneself one can make life itself its own telos. Thomas Osborne has suggested that this is what Foucault had in mind when he advocated the transformation of life into a work of art – an ascetics based upon a work of freedom.[53] Freedom, here, was not defined substantively but understood in terms of the constant exercise of detachment from culturally given codes in order to practise a life of constant moral experimentation. These oppositions seem to me to be too sharply drawn. Not only do both Christian and secular moralities draw upon a tradition of ascetics, but experimental ascetics also has its own, scarcely veiled normativities (not least that of ethical activism itself). More significantly, freedom can perhaps also be found within practices, such as the monastic, where the externalities of existence are subject to the highest levels of constraint. If one requires a normativity, it can be derived from a more modest position. This would positively value all stratagems, tactics and practices that enhance human beings' capacities to act; correlatively it would subject all that reduces such capacities to critical scrutiny. Further, it would evaluate practices in terms of the extent to which they accord those caught up within them the capacity to judge, accept or transform the practices that subjectify them.

Genealogical investigations would be active elements within such an ethos, to the extent that they seek to render modes of subjectification intelligible and hence judgeable. They would not be critical because they would mock the shallowness of what we take to be freedom. Rather, genealogy would be critical in its 'untimely' attempt to examine the ways in which freedom was put together historically, and the practices which it entails in our present. It would be critical in that it would ask the price that modern freedom exacts from those who lack the resources to practise it: those 'others' in relation to whom our freedom is always defined. It would ask if there were ways in which we could become experts of ourselves without requiring submission to an image produced by entrepreneurs or a truth produced by authorities. It would ask if there were ways of practising freedom that did not fix us through a hermeneutics of identity, did not entail the forlorn attempt to consume our way out of our dissatisfactions, but were open, inventive and questioning. It would ask if there were ways of organizing our concern for others that did not seek to set them free – relations of obligation, of commitment, perhaps evoking an older sense of care. It would help us to calculate the costs of being what we have become; hence it might allow us to invent ways of becoming other than what we are.

[53] T. Osborne 1996a, 1998.

3   The social

Social insurance, social security, the social services, social welfare, social work . . . the terms are familiar, banal. But what is implied by the term 'social'? This is what I want to explore here. From this perspective, I want to examine some aspects of a phenomenon that is frequently termed 'the crisis of the welfare state'. This 'crisis' can be understood in many different ways. Some suggest that there are, indeed, widespread changes in political ideologies and social arrangements with regard to welfare and security, and these can be understood as inevitable responses to fundamental transformations in political realities: the globalization of economic competition; increased life expectancy; the rise of individualism . . . I find this argument partial: such phenomena may be significant, but they do not in themselves determine how they are responded to.[1] Others doubt the extent to which this so-called crisis of the welfare state exists as an international phenomenon, and suggest that, as ever, politicians, intellectuals and ideologues in the English-speaking world are mistaking their own idiosyncrasies for the tide of world history. I have some sympathy with this view. It would certainly be misleading to consider the British case to be paradigmatic. Many dispute whether developments in the politics and government of security in the United States amounted to even a minimal welfare state. Social states developed in different ways in other European countries and in Canada and Australasia. So let us try not to encroach on the problems that have so exercised students of comparative welfare states and their development. I am happy to concede that there are many differences

---

[1] Of course, the argument that shifts in social policies and welfare arrangements are an effect of real developments in economic organization is familiar to all students of the 'history of the welfare state' in the form of arguments that welfare state development was the inevitable result of economic growth and industrialization and the social changes thus produced. Theda Skocpol has examined the problems with this and other functionalist accounts in her study of the political origins of social policy in the United States *Protecting Soldiers and Mothers* (Skocpol 1992).

even amongst European and Nordic nations in their past and current politics of welfare and security and that it is difficult to accommodate the United States in any general history or theory of the welfare state. This is because I will try to abstain as far as possible from an analysis of 'the welfare state'. We will not be concerned with whether or not there is some set of policies and practices that can be genuinely theorized as welfare. Nor will we ask whether the United States ever had a welfare state, that is to say, whether it has or had a state at all, or whether this state, as proxy for a class, gender or set of social and political interests, did or did not create, organize, animate or benefit from the benign or controlling effects of welfare. Because, whether or not the United States is or was a welfare state, over the course of the late nineteenth and twentieth centuries its cities and regions were subject to the work of philanthropists, labour activists, women' organizations, politicians and others who argued for the implementation of programmes and strategies in the name of their 'social' benefits: it became gridded by institutions and practices that sought to act upon individual and collective conduct in the name of the social. Let us not, then, start with the 'crisis of the welfare state', but with an analysis of the types of thought and action that have, historically, been made possible in terms of this little word 'social'.

In Britain, from about the 1950s to the 1980s, those who were financially supported, in whole or in part, by benefits paid by the state – unemployment benefits, disability benefits, emergency payments, housing benefits and so forth – were often referred to as 'on the social'. But from the 1980s onwards, to be 'on the social' was to be problematized in a particular way. Those who were on the social were not fellow citizens entitled to support to enable them to cope with temporary difficulties brought about by the ups and downs of a life-cycle, or by unexpected ill health or accident. They were spoken about as if they were somehow different, demeaned, dependent: the potentially dangerous inhabitants of marginal territory, the source of fiscal, economic and moral problems, to be feared and condemned or pitied and reformed. Fiscally, they appeared to represent a drain on taxes, recipients of public funds who make no return, sometimes even to be fraudsters working in the 'black economy' or members of organized gangs setting out to defraud the nation or, elsewhere, individuals denied the opportunity to contribute through work. Economically, in addition to their tax cost, they appeared to represent a sector without either the skills or the will to enhance competitiveness, whether this be a result of their own failings or a consequence of social policies and other factors beyond their control. Morally, they were demeaned not merely because of their despair or depravity, but because of their apparent dependence – financial and psychological – upon a system of state hand-outs.

Different terms were used to describe those in this position: a culture of dependency, an underclass, the marginalized, the excluded. Each term was attached to a different politics. But each treated those 'on the social' as inhabiting a form of life that was purely negative: negative for those who inhabit it and for others. There was also a family resemblance to the solutions proffered. Politicians of the right, such as Republicans in the United States and the Conservative regimes that governed Britain in the 1980s and 1990s, proclaimed their intention to 'shut down the something-for-nothing society'.[2] Those of the centre, like Bill Clinton's Democrats in the United States and the 'New Labour' government elected to power in Britain in 1997, spoke in more benign terms of a hand-up, not a hand-out; their mantra is 'from welfare to work'. But the message was the same: the aim was not to be 'on the social' but to be off it.

Could we say that this was a symptom of an event: the death of the social? At the end of the 1970s, Jean Baudrillard was already proclaiming that we had arrived at 'the end of the social'.[3] In his diagnosis, he suggested three possibilities. Perhaps *the social has never existed*, but has always been a kind of simulation of a social relation, and this has now undergone a desimulation: the disintegration of what was, in any event, an imaginary space of reference and play of mirrors. Or perhaps *the social has really existed and now invests everything*, has extended from a process of the rational control of residues – vagrants, lunatics, the sick – to a state in which everyone is completely excluded and taken in charge for a project of functional integration sanctified by the social sciences. Or perhaps *the social has existed in the past but has ceased to do so* – the sociality of the contract, of the relation of state to civil society, of the dialectic of the social and the individual has been destroyed by the fragmentations of the media, information, computer simulation and the rise of the simulacrum. In any event, for Baudrillard, social and socialist thinking was guilty of 'unbelievable naivety . . . for thus having been able to reify as universal and to elevate as ideal of transparency such a totally ambiguous and contradictory – worse, such a residual or imaginary – worse, such an already abolished in its very simulation – "reality": the social'.[4]

---

[2] This phrase was used by Peter Lilley, then Secretary of State for Social Security, at the Conservative Party conference in Blackpool, September 1996.
[3] Baudrillard 1983.
[4] Ibid.: 86.

Baudrillard's diagnosis is couched in characteristically apocalyptic tone and its field of reference is typically opaque. But it can serve to remind us that 'the social' is not an inevitable horizon for our thought or our political judgement. As Gilles Deleuze points out, we are not talking here merely of the adjective 'social' that has come to be applied to all those phenomena with which sociology deals: '*the* social refers to a *particular sector* in which quite diverse problems and special cases can be grouped together, a sector comprising specific institutions and an entire body of qualified personnel'.[5] From this perspective, 'the social' does not refer to an inescapable fact about human beings – that they are social creatures – but to a way in which human intellectual, political and moral authorities, within a limited geographical territory, thought about and acted upon their collective experience for about a century.

The moral technologies of discipline

In European thought from at least the eighteenth century, one can trace a variety of reflections on the special characteristics of discrete 'nations' and 'peoples', the possibility of writing the history of different peoples, anatomizing their differences, demonstrating how each participates in a shared tradition of customs, a shared descent, a shared language; how each has a set of habits, beliefs, mores, systems of law, morality and politics which partake in this common spirit.[6] Over the course of the nineteenth century, a mutation occurred in this way of apprehending the collective existence of a people. Nations were now seen as populations of individuals with particular characteristics, integrated through a certain moral order. But more significantly, this way of understanding the subjects of rule as subjects of morality was linked to a plethora of interventions into the economy, the family, the private firm and the conduct of the individual person which sought to shape them in beneficial ways whilst safeguarding their autonomy. I have outlined many of these in chapter 2. The very notions of economy, family, firm, individual were invented in the course of these events. These modes of intervention did not answer to a single logic or form part of a coherent programme of 'state intervention'.[7] Rather, they were deployed around particular issues: epidemics and disease, theft and criminality, dangerous and

---

[5] Deleuze 1979: ix.
[6] For example, in the writings of Montesquieu [1748] 1900, Godwin [1793] 1976, Condorcet [1794] 1795.
[7] Foucault 1980b; see also Rose 1993.

endangered children, pauperism and indigence, insanity and imbecility, the breakdown of marital relations, overcrowding in the towns and so forth. And it was largely through the endeavours of independent reformers that these frictions and disturbances were recoded as moral problems which had consequences for national well-being. These were linked to a new perception that the conduct of individual citizens must be governed in the interests of the nation and that, despite all their hesitancies, even a liberal state must take some steps to actively govern the moral order of its citizens, to create citizens who would govern themselves.

The emergence of a notion of 'the economy' in economic and social thought in the early nineteenth century was an essential part of these shifts.[8] Classical political economy effected a separation of a domain of 'economic' events with their own laws and processes from a 'moral' domain. Economic events were territorialized within a national space, seen as governed by laws and relations whose scope and limits seemed to map on to the territory of political rule. As they crystallized within nineteenth-century thought, 'economies' were organized within nations, limited by borders, customs and other restrictions on imports and exports, unified through a single supply of money, characterized by a set of functional relations between their components; and these unities were located in a wider space within which they could engage in 'foreign trade' with other national economies. The responsibility of the political authorities for the security of a nation, a state and a people, came to be understood in terms of their capacity to ensure the security of its national economic well-being.[9] Further, over the course of the nineteenth century and into the twentieth, the solidity of these national economies was increased by the regular publication of various national indicators of economic performance, and by the gradual tracing out of a plane of 'economic policy', which concerned itself with the proper ways in which the strengths of such an economic system could be enhanced: action on the money supply, on the labour market, together with tariffs and restrictions on imports and so forth, especially as national wealth came to be understood in terms of competition between discrete economies and their struggle to gain access to sources of cheap raw materials, cheap labour or lucrative markets outside their own territorial bounds.

As this economic order came to be identified and delineated in the

---

[8] This has been spelled out in more detail by Barry Hindess (1994) and I have drawn upon his argument here.

[9] The best discussion of this remains Tribe 1978. See also Meuret 1988.

first half of the nineteenth century, it was both *related to* and *distinguished from* a 'moral' dimension of collective existence. The term 'moral' here referred to a set of phenomena that seem confused to our eyes but which once had a characteristic unity. The moral was a kind of plane of intersection between experience, inheritance, conscience, character and conduct, located within a wider space of the character of a people as a whole. The economy was to be understood in terms of its own laws and causalities, and political interventions upon it were to be limited in the light of these. But the moral domain was construed as a proper territory for action by politicians, the churches, philanthropists and others – although exactly what was to be regulated, how and by whom was a matter of contestation.

As we saw in chapter 2, the middle decades of the nineteenth century saw the invention of a whole variety of 'moral technologies' designed to shape the character and conscience of those who were to be moral subjects and hence to mould their conduct – pauper schools, reformatory prisons, lunatic asylums, public baths and washhouses.[10] The great 'machines of morality' invented in the nineteenth century took the characteristic form of enclosed sites for the manufacture of character. Thomas Markus quoted Coleridge's description of the monitorial school: 'An incomparable machine – a vast moral steam engine'.[11] For Coleridge, the steam engine functioned as something like a weaving together of imagination, knowledge, myth and technique in a figure of heat, water, pipes, pressures, conduits and cogs. This mechanical model, as Michel Serres has shown us, is more than metaphor. It exemplifies the multiple points of exchange between the exact sciences, the sciences of the human being, the rationalities of government and the concern for the self.[12] Markus has given us a number of compelling images of such disciplinary machines.[13] They operated through the spatial organization of human beings, through the instrumentalization of institutional time, through the practical collection, classification and division of persons, through materializing relations of authority in the physical relations of foreman and worker, teacher and pupil, gaoler and prisoner, asylum superintendent and inmate. As has often been pointed out, neither the architectural forms nor the organizational techniques were new – monasteries, barracks, Sunday schools, pauper schools had

---

[10] I have adapted the following four paragraphs from Rose 1996e. See also Riley 1988, Joyce 1995 and 1996.

[11] Markus 1993: 41.

[12] Serres 1982.

[13] Markus 1993. The classical analyses remain Foucault's study of the asylum (1972a) and the prison (1977).

all tested out such arrangements. But in the course of the nineteenth century these exemplars were to be widely emulated. Schools for infants and for older children were to be the site of a variety of different programmes for the shaping of character *en masse* with the aim that the corporeal and moral habits of industriousness and obedience would be inculcated into the members of the labouring classes, to fit them 'to become good servants – good tradesmen – good fathers – good mothers, and respectable citizens. The intellectually cultivated Christian mechanic is the best safeguard of our nation, and his moral worth is the very salt and leaven of civil society.'[14] New regimes of the body – its purity, its hygiene, its sexual continence – were to address problems posed in terms of sexuality, disease and virtue. New regimes of the intellect – numeracy, literacy, calculation – were to install foresight, prudence and a planful relation to the future. Social danger was recast as a violation of norms of respectable citizenship and a new way was invented 'for collecting and confining those who in one way or another could introduce chaos into the social order', [15] for reforming moral character by confining and regulating the person of the transgressor: the criminal, the lunatic, the workshy, the alcoholic, the vagrant and all those others who suffered from defects of character that would later be codified, by the psy disciplines, as defects of personality.

Analogous spaces were invented for requalifying those whom disease had disqualified – hospitals, sanatoria and infirmaries – and for cleansing and purifying the soul through the medium of the body – bathhouses, washhouses. Recreation was also to be spatially organized – no longer in the rowdy and transgressive hurly-burly of the market, the fair, the baiting of bears – but in new moral habitats – public parks, municipal swimming pools. Knowledge was to be civilized, ordered and embodied as a means of popular instruction – in zoos, botanical gardens, libraries, museums, panoramas, dioramas, exhibitions – spaces which enjoin civility and the control of the outward signs of character at the same time as they instruct in order. The space of labour itself, the manufactory, was to be problematized not only in terms of its immediate economy of wealth, but also in terms of its consequences for the habits of labour – temperance, diligence, sexual propriety. And the space of the labourer outside work was to be subject to a statistical and literary mapping that rendered the town intelligible as a spatial distribution. Figures, charts, maps, vivid descriptions of social explorers showed how coextensive

[14] Stow 1834, quoted in Markus 1993: 84; cf. K. Jones and Williamson 1979; Hunter 1994.
[15] Markus 1993: 95.

were the topographies of class, occupation, morality, criminality and disease.[16] Thus the space of the town became intelligible in new ways, in the spatial imagination produced by all those who thought that in order to govern relations between people more effectively one had first to inscribe them. One sees, in short, a multiplication of 'laboratories of conduct' in which were performed a whole variety of ethical experiments on human beings.

In the middle of the nineteenth century, the language of character established a set of mobile and productive links between political problematizations of conduct and the spatial fixing and regulation of the person. As Bernard Bosanquet, the key thinker of the Charity Organisation Society, put it in 1895, 'character is the condition of conditions'.[17] Diverse forces argued that the development of the virtues of character – self-reliance, sobriety, independence, self-restraint, respectability, self-improvement – should be a positive function of the state: an end that statesmen should keep constantly in view in programmes of legislation and reform.[18] Problems of human conduct were articulated as expressions of moral character, character was construed as an outcome of the interaction between constitution or stock and habits of conduct learned by example or inculcation, and good character was to be promoted through the organization of human beings in certain relations of proximity, hierarchy, visibility and so forth. As innumerable theological, physiological and educational texts spelled out, the need was for the will to exercise dominance over conduct: a matter of moral control which could be inculcated in calculated, controlled and ordered regimes for the management of conduct.

Mariana Valverde has referred to this as the 'despotism over the self' which lies at the heart of the ethical formation of the citizen of liberal freedom in the nineteenth century.[19] The will is to be trained to master the lower passions – hence, civilization required a constant despotism over oneself. But also, those who are civilized must accept the responsibility set out for them by that philosopher of liberal freedom, John Stuart Mill: they must become 'good despots' and so long as they are 'full of the spirit of improvement' they are warranted in the use of any expedients to procure the improvement of those who cannot improve

[16] For three very different projects of inscription, see Engels [1844] 1976; Mayhew [1851] 1969; and Booth 1892–7.

[17] Bosanquet 1895: vii–viii, quoted in Clarke 1978: 17.

[18] See the work of Stefan Collini, especially Collini 1979: 29–32, and 1991: ch. 3.

[19] Valverde 1996a.

themselves.[20] For Mill, this had particular implications for the exercise of power in relation to primitive, backward or degenerate races: I will say a little more about this presently in relation to the government of the colonies. But it also justified a kind of despotism over the child. Hence education for the children of the labouring classes was to be a means of saving them from their state of slavery to prejudice, vice and momentary passion, enhancing the possibility of control exercised by the reflective mind over bodily nature.[21] The mechanism of control, as Valverde points out, was through the inculcation of virtuous habits, especially in childhood – patterns of conduct and self-control over the baser passions that would ideally retain their influence throughout life. But the struggle for control was a lifelong task: lack of this control was the explanation for all sorts of pathologies of conduct, from madness to assaults on political order to the woman question. New divisions and classifications of persons – by others, and by themselves – emerged here: divisions between classes of persons embodied in forms of life that both realize and produce certain forms of character. Charles Booth exemplifies this in his classification of the population into eight classes, each of which was an amalgam of a mode of employment, a moral character and a form of life.[22] From this moment on, the political problem of the relation between authority and its subjects was to be redefined; it was to be achieved through enmeshing subjects in spatially organized practices for the formation of moral character, and in enclosures where those who lacked or refused this moral character could be reformed.

The new arts of government were certainly debated in terms of 'liberal' concerns about the principle of individual liberty and the inviolability of the moral person. Nevertheless, over a relatively short period, the conduct of individual members of the population became the object of philanthropic, medical, architectural and hygienic programmes, and the moral domain became traversed by innumerable interventions from industrial schools to sewers, from police forces to lady missionaries, from friendly societies to model housing schemes. These interventions took diverse technical forms, in particular differentiating themselves according to whether their targets were the wealthier classes, the labouring poor or paupers. Thus, for example, in the medical reform of child rearing in wealthy families in the nineteenth century, doctors problematized such issues as wet nursing and childhood masturbation from the

[20] Mill [1859] 1975, quoted by Valverde 1996a: 360–1.
[21] More on this can be found in Roger Smith's study of *Inhibition* which I discussed in ch. 1 (R. Smith 1992: 27–65).
[22] Booth 1892–7; see the discussion in Rose 1985.

perspective of the future of the family line, promoted new forms of anxiety amongst parents and entered into voluntary relations that offered medical help in the self-promotion of the family.[23] In the emergence of juvenile delinquency in the same period, one sees the elaboration of a division between the respectable classes of the poor – honest and diligent labourers governing their lives with tolerable decency according to the rules of conduct disseminated in church, law, education and example – and those who lived a life that posed a constant threat to the moral order of society. Children provided a potent source for the renewal of this class of paupers or unemployables. The child offender, children without homes, on the streets or in houses of ill-repute were problematized by doctors, philanthropists, social statisticians, churchmen and educationalists in terms of the moral danger they were in and the future criminality and vice that they represented. They were to be removed from their vicious milieux and placed in remoralizing institutions.[24] Paradoxically, such enclosures for reconstructing character were often referred to as 'colonies'.

Disciplining the colonies

Whilst in the metropolitan polities liberal concerns halted the tendency for disciplinary technologies to be utilized directly in the name of 'reason of state', many of these technologies were deployed in colonial government. There was nothing essentially liberal in disciplinary techniques, and in the colonies their use was seldom troubled by liberal concerns. In Australia and the Americas, over the course of the nineteenth century, a liberal transformation would occur; in India, Egypt and 'the Orient' colonial subjects were seldom thought even potentially competent to take up the burdens of freedom.

A few examples must suffice.[25]

Engin Isin has shown that in colonial America as early as the middle of the seventeenth century, towns were the sites of experiments in

[23] Donzelot 1979.

[24] David Garland (1985) provides an excellent introduction to the wealth of empirical material available on these issues. For one classic study, see Platt 1969.

[25] I am particularly grateful to members of the *History of the Present* Research Network for helping me with references to this material. My account is regrettably brief (note also the brief comments on the government of Ireland in ch. 2, n. 15). The secondary material tends to be specific to particular national contexts, and it is not possible to refer the reader to a single source that brings together material on 'governing the colonies'.

pre-liberal government. Ordinances were passed with regard to the good
order of roads, bridges, houses and streets, the care and discipline of the
poor, the maintenance of the peace, the moral and religious character of
those admitted to residence, schools to train 'the Children of the Town
in religion, learning and Civility', watchmen 'to see to the regulating of
other men's actions as manners' and the like.[26]

Eric Stokes has argued that, in colonial rule in India in the early nineteenth century, the pragmatic and defensive strategies of the earlier
period, which sought merely to safeguard the extraction of wealth, were
reshaped by a governmental project 'consciously directed upon Indian
society itself'.[27] This would first of all seek to evangelize the Indian, a
member of 'a race of men lamentably degenerate and base; retaining
but a feeble sense of moral obligation; yet obstinate in their disregard of
what they know to be right, governed by malevolent and licentious passions . . . and sunk in misery by their vices, in a country peculiarly calculated by its natural advantages, to promote the prosperity of its inhabitants'.[28] Later it would seek to educate the Indian, not only for the same
ends but also to create a wealthy and orderly society. And under the
influence of 'utilitarian' thought, notably that of James Mill, it would
seek to create a form of political education, through government and
laws, that would not only render India governable, but would save it
from the political and religious despotism of native rule. But such
government was a rather hybrid affair of law and norm, rational administration and spectacle. Bernard Cohn has shown that strategies for the
government of India after the period of military and civil unrest in the
late 1850s included a whole series of pre-disciplinary rituals for the spec-
tacular display of the might of the Empire: ceremonial representations
of imperial history were used to provide authority with a secure and
usable past; British notables toured India and sought to recruit Indian
rulers to their cause by ceremonial displays and the dispensation of hon-
ours; public ceremonies were staged to mark occasions such as the
laying of foundation stones for public buildings to display the power
and legitimacy of the British sovereign, her respect for India's own traditions and her beneficence for her subjects.[29]

---

[26] Isin 1992: 72–3.
[27] Stokes 1959: 27. This point is emphasized and developed in Scott 1995.
[28] Charles Grant, *Observations on the State of Society among the Asiatic Subjects of
Great Britain, particularly with respect to Morals and on the Means of Improving
It. Written chiefly in the Year 1792*, privately printed in 1797, p. 71, quoted in
Stokes 1959: 31.
[29] 'Representing authority in Victorian India', in Cohn 1990.

Where classical disciplinary technologies were deployed in colonial government, this was usually in the service of order and docility rather than self-regulated liberty. Timothy Mitchell has analysed the export of technologies of discipline to nineteenth-century Egypt: the introduction into the Egyptian military in the 1830s of techniques to regulate soldiers through relations of hierarchy and subordination, continual surveillance, corporeal training and calculated punishment; attempts in the 1840s to form a parallel system of rural discipline and surveillance in particular through the design and construction of model villages and the relocation of families within them; a strategy developed from the late 1840s to spread this disciplinary order across the population as a whole through the introduction of a schooling system modelled on Joseph Lancaster's Central School in London, with its minutely calculated orchestration of the activities and comportment of pupils under constant supervision through a hierarchy of monitors; and a series of other 'civilizing innovations' concerning hygiene and public health, the redesign of urban space and the introduction of pavements and street lighting to open towns and thoroughfares to continuous inspection and orderly conduct and the organization of a system of criminal courts, prisons and insane asylums.[30] As for the technologies of the colonial prison, for example, whilst arguments for the disciplinary reform of the Indian prison had been made since the 1830s, reform was not instituted until the late nineteenth century and always ran up against what Arnold terms 'its Orientalizing other': arguments for the futility of attempts to reform the Indian soul.[31] Panoptic measures – surveillance, separation, silence – proved hard to achieve. But nonetheless, the prison, in India as in Britain, served as a fertile site for medical observation and experimentation, the calculation of statistics of health, information on the progress of cholera, experiments with prophylaxis including vaccination and quinine, research on diet and on physiological differences between the

---

[30] Mitchell 1988: these disciplinary innovations are summarized on pp. 174–6. Mitchell quotes Lord Cromer's summing up of the achievements of the British occupation in *Modern Egypt* published in 1908: 'The waters of the Nile are now utilized in an intelligent manner . . . The soldier has acquired some pride in the uniform which he wears. He has fought as never before. The lunatic is no longer treated like a wild beast. The punishment awarded to the worst criminal is no longer barbarous. Lastly, the schoolmaster is abroad, with results which are as yet uncertain, but which cannot fail to be important' (Cromer 1908, vol. II: 556–7, quoted from Mitchell 1988: 175).
[31] Arnold 1994: 163, on which I have drawn for these few sentences on the Indian prison.

races – as well as providing a supply of corpses for medical dissection.[32]

In North America and Australia the majority of the indigenous inhabitants were murderously eliminated and the survivors governed – or ungoverned – by spatial exclusion.[33] Those concerned with the government of settlers, including those once transported and now freed, sought to transform their language, methods and techniques in a liberal direction and thereby to limit the direct deployment of disciplinary technologies in the service of colonial domination, pacification and exploitation. Alan Atkinson has suggested that the disputes over the form and legitimacy of government following the French revolution of 1789 led to 'profoundly new experiments in public order', and Gavin Kendall has suggested that, in the same period, Australia was something of a laboratory for the liberal deployment of techniques of person formation.[34] Engin Isin has shown how, from the 1780s to the 1840s, debates about the government of British North America came to prioritize the city as a key instrument for techniques of government infused with a liberal ethos, through trying to incorporate subjects into their own government.[35] Other innovations linking discipline with liberty also took shape in North America.[36] In sum, then, it is clear that there were complex interdependencies between metropolitan liberal government and its colonial experiments, and that these colonial experiences provided a rich store of examples, salutary lessons, metaphors and techniques for governing 'at home'. This was not least because, in a kind of internal

[32] Despite these differences, reformers in the metropolitan countries often drew lessons from colonial institutions. Mary Carpenter, for example, campaigning in England for the establishment of reformatory and industrial schools for dangerous and endangered juveniles, drew on the experience of the Irish convict prisons in her proposals for reformatory prison discipline in 1870 (M. Carpenter 1872: I am grateful to Eoin O'Sullivan for this reference). Stoler points out that the development of juvenile reformatories, orphanages and agrarian colonies in the Dutch East Indies was simultaneous with their proliferation as technologies for the government of the urban poor in Holland itself (Stoler 1995: 121). On colonial psychiatry, see the account in McCulloch 1995.

[33] See O'Malley 1996a.

[34] A. Atkinson 1997: 7; Kendall 1997.

[35] As Isin shows, the city was eventually to be provided with a constitutional and legal form through the re-invention of the instrument of the corporation (Isin 1992, especially chs. 4 and 5).

[36] For example, as early as 1830 in Lower Canada, John Roebuck was arguing for the centrality of the survey for a colonial government which must base itself upon a knowledge of the territory and population to be governed: see Isin 1992: 159.

racism, the problem of governing the urban poor, slum children, the dangerous classes, the degenerates and the unemployables in the metropolitan countries was often considered to be analogous to that of governing the uncivilized, or only potentially civilized, inhabitants of the colonies.[37]

As important, perhaps, for the new arts of government were the ways in which colonial government problematized those who would rule, and invented strategies for the ethical formation of the colonizer; these would shape the very nature of expert administration and the moral formation of civil servants and experts in the centres of empire themselves. Given the geographical distance between the colonies and the metropolitan European centres, government was inescapably 'at a distance' in a rather literal sense.[38] That is to say, to govern the colonies it was necessary to shape and regulate the practices of self-government of those who would govern: the colonial administrators and the colonists themselves. India, of course, was the prime case here because, in India, a small British ruling group had to govern about a quarter of a billion Indians. Thus, as Osborne has shown, James Mill's *History of British India* published in 1818 was the first of a whole series of works that 'was to make India a key target for elaborations of the ideal "science of the legislator" ', and which sought to adjust the nature of the exercise of rule to the level of moral development of the subjects who were to be ruled, and to make rule itself a means of bringing that subjectivity to an appropriate level of maturity.[39] Not least, here, was the development of a certain idea of the moral formation of the administrators themselves such that they were able to take on the task of 'governing at a distance'. Further, as Stoler has argued, the management of the home environments, child-rearing practices and sexual arrangements of those European colonists formed a key focus of anxiety and was the target of a 'vast compendium of health manuals and housekeeping guides that threatened ill health, ruin, and even death, if certain moral prescriptions and modes of conduct were not met'.[40] In the process, the very character of Europeanness was being defined; so too were the characteristics of a new style of governing.

[37] On metaphors of the colonies in Victorian government of the metropolitan slums, see Valverde 1996b.

[38] See ch. 1, n. 78.

[39] T. Osborne 1994: 300. See also Bernard Cohn's analyses of colonizing India, especially his essays on 'The recruitment and training of British civil servants in India' and 'Representing authority in Victorian India', both collected in Cohn 1990.

[40] Stoler 1995: 102.

The invention of the social

In Britain and many other European states over the second half of the nineteenth century a cascade of measures for the government of the physical and moral competences and capacities of individuals were given a legal form. These were the apparently illiberal acts of legislation that concern critics of the philosophical coherence of nineteenth-century liberalism: restrictions on child labour; the establishment of prisons, asylums, reformatories and workhouses; measures for compulsory education of paupers and, later, of all; enforced vaccination of pauper children; regulation on the sale and quality of pharmaceuticals and food; even interventions into 'freedom' in the economic domain itself such as factory inspection and workman's compensation.[41]

In the United States, such enactments usually occurred at the level of individual state legislatures. Individual states set up systems of almshouses with mandatory work for the able-bodied poor, custodial institutions for the wayward, lunatic asylums, asylums for the deaf and dumb and the like, often funded through a combination of charity, endowment and subsidies from the state. It is undoubtedly the case that the variability and lability of these arrangements were ensured by their dependence upon party patronage and legislative idiosyncrasies.[42] But we should not be diverted by these differences, however significant they may be for those who wish to theorize 'the history of the welfare state'. For our present purposes, however institutionally organized, in the United States too, human beings were discovered to be creatures whose conduct was to be subject to investigation, classification and normalization in the interests of order and civility: in the process, in the United States too, new classes of dependent, dangerous and delinquent persons were distinguished on the grounds of their abnormality. These were new classes of individuals unified by their make-up and character, and hence requiring government.

By the start of the twentieth century, however – the date is simply a convenient marker for a threshold achieved through a whole variety of different shifts occurring in different places at different times over the second half of the nineteenth century – the targets and objectives of intervention had begun to change, as had the site or space in which they were located. We can term this shift 'the invention of the social'. Urbanization and immigration into the town, crime, war, disease and so forth clearly played a role in the reframing of the moral domain in

[41] For an instructive list, see Polanyi 1957: 147.
[42] This is argued by Skocpol 1992: ch. 1.

social terms. But the status of these events was focal rather than causal. As I have already suggested, events themselves do not determine how they are to be understood and responded to. The reframing of thought arose, in part, out of a labour of documentation. Statistical investigations, which were initially concerned with estimating and comparing the wealth of nations and examining the relation of national wealth to population size, division into different trades and issues of taxation, gradually revealed the population as a domain with its own specificity and irreducibility.[43] Investigations by various independent inquirers during the nineteenth century inscribed the nation in terms of a set of aggregated statistics with their regular fluctuations, and as knowable processes with their laws and cycles.[44] Inscriptions of this sort rendered these as phenomena which were thinkable and calculable by knowledgeable persons. They could thus become the object of proposals and strategies for reform or prevention by expertise. The quotidian lives of the masses became gridded by regulatory codes demanding, for example, the registration and recording of births, marriages, illnesses, numbers and causes of death, types of crime and their geographical location.[45] The work of doctors, teachers, philanthropists and police, especially in the towns, gave rise to further detailed statistical mapping of urban space: moral topographies which inscribed the city as a domain with its own specific characteristics and consequences for its inhabitants.[46] Poverty and pauperism, illness, crime, suicide and so forth were the subjects of a whole labour of documentation: written down in evidence, counted, tabulated, graphed, drawn. Statistics, censuses, surveys and a new genre of explorations of the lives of the poor attempted to render moral events knowable and calculable.[47] Theorists of the moral order sought to delineate regularities in conduct that would enable it to be understood in the same way as the natural world, and argued that the moral domain, like

[43] Foucault 1991.

[44] Procacci 1989 provides an excellent overview. Philip Abrams' history of British empirical sociology remains an invaluable source (Abrams 1968).

[45] Hacking 1990 provides the best introduction to this material. Quetelet [1835] 1842 is the best-known statement of the argument that moral laws can be grasped by statistics; for an analogous British example, see Rawson 1839. Economic life was also a key focus of these early investigations: see, for example, the project for a study of strikes proposed by the Statistical Society of London (1838).

[46] The best account is given by Paul Rabinow (Rabinow 1989). The work of statisticians of disease and death was particularly significant; see, for one British example, Farr 1895.

[47] I examine this in more detail in current work with Tom Osborne (see T. Osborne and Rose forthcoming).

nature itself, was governed by its own intrinsic laws. The moral order, once a zone where diverse opinions competed and contested, justified by reference to extrinsic ethical or theological principles, came to be accorded a specific 'positivity'. That is to say, it mutated into a reality with its own regularities, laws and characteristics. It was these character-istics that gradually came to be termed 'social'.

One begins to see the emergence of a new 'social' language: 'social' novels, the 'social evil', the National Association for the Promotion of Social Science. A new breed of experts of the social was born – the doctors, the charity workers, the investigators of the 'dark continent of the poor' – who spoke 'in the name of the social'. This social gaze focused, in particular, upon the conditions of life of the labouring poor and paupers, with a particular eye for issues of domestic squalor, immorality, child mortality, household budgeting and the conditions and actions of the working-class woman.[48] Gradually 'social' came to be accorded something like the sense it was to have for the next hundred years. It was a plane or dimension of a national territory, which formed, shaped and even determined the characteristics and character of the individual. And it was the problem space within which one must pose a range of questions and struggles about matters of life, of conduct, of powers and authority, questions and struggles that lay outside the formal scope of the political apparatus but were to become intensely 'political'.

The social was not to remain merely an empirical amalgam of these diverse problems, investigations of the lives, labours, crimes, diseases, madness and domestic habits of the poor, a space of polemics, pam-phlets and philanthropies. It was to be formalized. This was to occur in a number of distinct, but interrelated ways, each of which would have consequences for government. The two that are of most significance here are *population* and *society*.

In the organic language of population that took shape in the late nine-teenth century, the inhabitants of a territory were more than merely a 'people' with certain attributes, habits, customs, physical characteristics and the like. The population that had been revealed by statistics cer-tainly had 'its own regularities, its own rate of deaths and diseases, its cycles of scarcity, etc. [involving] a range of intrinsic, aggregate effects, phenomena that are irreducible to those of the family, such as epi-demics, endemic levels of morality, ascending spirals of labour and wealth . . . [and exhibiting] through its shifts, customs, activities, etc.,

---

[48] Riley 1988: 49. Of course, women themselves were not passive spectators of this process but active participants: see L. Gordon 1989.

... specific economic effects'.[49] But the population was now understood organically. In this organic perception, which owed as much to Malthus as it did to Darwin and Wallace, the inhabitants of a nation were regarded as a kind of living, breeding unity composed of individuals with varying characteristics reproducing themselves across the generations.[50] The characteristics and destiny of the population as a whole, its physical characteristics, moral propensities, aesthetic qualities and intellectual capacities were shaped by the laws of evolutionary biology. This organic and evolutionary perception of the social order linked up an older form of racial classification of humankind with a novel biological and constitutional basis. The fitness of the race could improve or deteriorate, and external and internal conditions which affected the rates of breeding from different sectors of the race would shape the fitness of the race overall, and hence its ability to survive and prosper, and to succeed in the struggle between nations. The various social pathologies could now be reconceptualized as flowing from the character of the race and the effects of external and internal conditions upon that character. A nation could be understood as a race, with particular characteristics, which conferred upon it a greater or lesser degree of fitness: what would degenerate now was not an individual or a lineage but the population as a whole. Here one finds a whole discourse on the deterioration, later the degeneration, of the British race as a consequence of migration from the country to the towns, the deleterious effects of modern forms of life, the differential rates of reproduction of the fittest and the less fit. Or alternatively, a nation could be seen as mixture of races, whose differential rates of breeding, in relation to their differential characters, would determine the overall quality of the population as a whole: here one finds the emergence of various forms of internal racism. Or, alternatively, the world could be populated with a small number of distinct races – some superior, some inferior – in a deadly battle for survival and superiority within each nation: here one finds the racism that will lead, in German National Socialism, towards the 'final solution'.[51]

This naturalized and racialized conception of the social would exist in complex relationships with an idea of 'society' that was no less organic and law-governed, but whose laws were not primarily or solely those of

[49] Foucault 1991: 99.
[50] François Jacob gives an excellent account of the conceptual regime involved in *The Logic of Living Systems* (Jacob 1974). I discuss this myself in Rose 1985: ch. 3.
[51] Of the many analyses, I have found the work of George Mosse particularly instructive: see in particular Mosse 1978.

biology and population but were peculiar to society itself. Society was to become the domain that sociology would define as a reality *sui generis*: hence one that could be known by a social science. The social question would now become a sociological question. By the end of the century, Durkheim, in the opening pages of his *Rules of Sociological Method*, was deploring the fact that 'the designation "social" is used with little precision. It is currently employed for practically all phenomena generally diffused within society, however small their significance. But in reality there is in every society a certain group of phenomena which may be differentiated from those studied by the other natural sciences . . . They constitute, thus, a new variety of phenomena; and it is to them that the term "social" ought to be applied.'[52] Despite Durkheim's disagreements with Spencer, the role of biology in early sociology was not restricted to the advocates of 'social Darwinism'.[53] French sociology remained bound to organic conceptions of society as population, and its problems, concepts and arguments were still marked by the themes of social decadence and degenerescence that culminated in Morel's *Traité des dégénérescences* published in 1857.[54] The British sociology of J. A. Hobson and L. T. Hobhouse was not only organized in terms of evolutionary arguments, but was open to the idea of stern repression of the unfit, plus positive eugenic measures for environmental and hygienic improvements in the interest of social progress. As Hobson put it in *The Social Problem*, published in 1901, 'Selection of the fittest, or at least, rejection of the unfittest, is essential to all progress in life and character . . . To abandon the production of children to unrestricted private enterprise is the most dangerous abnegation of its functions which any government can propose.'[55] On the basis of such a knowledge of the dynamics of society, the unruly complex of the social could be organized, disciplined and governed. Sociologists and other 'social scientists' would begin to stake their claim as experts of the social, uniquely able to speak and act in its name. They would claim to be engineers of society itself.

The invention of the social had a direct political status. The transformation of the British Labour Party over the early years of the 1990s provoked a rather ignorant debate over whether it was a 'Socialist' party, a 'Social-ist' party, a 'Social Democratic' Party, or perhaps, not a 'social'

[52] Durkheim [1895] 1964: 1–3.
[53] The best source on these disputes is Steven Lukes' (1973) biography of Durkheim.
[54] See Pick 1989: pt I. See also Rabinow 1989.
[55] Hobson 1901: 214, quoted in Freeden 1978: 178.

party at all, but a 'liberal' party. It was in the middle of the nineteenth century that political parties started identifying themselves through the term 'social'. This is not the place for a history of socialism. We know that the word was first used in France and Britain in the 1820s and was adopted by workers' movements on both sides of the Channel in the 1830s. By the middle decades of the nineteenth century, the social question and the political question existed in an uneasy relation. Fears throughout Europe were not only of political revolution but also of social revolution. In Germany at the time of the Revolution of 1848: 'Prince Metternich acknowledged despairingly that the crisis "was no longer about politics (*Politik*) but the social question". In Berlin, the radical republican Rudolf Virchow concurred: "This revolution is not simply political: it is at heart social in character." '[56] Alongside the designation 'socialist' – indeed often opposing it – the term 'social' became the indicator of a certain kind of politics: one that could be directed against the claims of the state on the one hand and demands for the freedom of the market and the autonomy of the individual on the other. The social question referred to all that had to do with this 'social order': a sphere of the collective activities and arrangements of the lives of individuals, families and groups within a nation. The German Social Democratic Party polled nearly half a million votes in 1877 and won thirteen seats in the Reichstag; in 1881 the Social Democratic Federation was formed in England. [57]

By the early decades of the twentieth century, politicians in many different national contexts were under increasing pressure to accept that government of at least some aspects of this social domain should be added to the responsibilities of the political apparatus and its officials. European political parties increasingly rejected the claims of political economy to prescribe and delimit the legitimate means to be used for the government of economic life. Simultaneously, it appeared that law alone was no longer the sufficient legitimate political means for achieving order and security; indeed law itself must answer to the demands of social government. The political rationalities that played so great a part in our own century – socialism, social democracy, social liberalism – differed on many things, but they had one thing in common: the belief that the question of how to govern must be posed from 'the social point of view'.[58]

---

[56] Melton 1995: 199.
[57] Although it did not add the 'Social' to its title until 1884: see Pelling 1965.
[58] Cf. Procacci 1989. For France, see Donzelot 1984; for England, see Collini 1979 and Clarke 1978.

Some still argued that to govern from the social point of view was to govern too much. If society had its own natural laws, the laws of evolution, competition and survival of the fittest, government overrode or ignored these at the cost of the health of society itself.[59] This argument, most associated in Britain with Herbert Spencer, deployed its own version of Darwin's thesis to assert the primacy of competition in social development: as *The Encyclopaedia of Social Reform* put it, 'probably the chief arguments raised today to show the impracticability of Socialism are . . . biologic'.[60] But this was not a question of socialism versus the rest. Most political forces, whatever their disagreements, agreed that politics would have to become social if political order was to be maintained. In France, Durkheim was intimately involved in the French politics of solidarism. In England the political struggles were not fought in terms of social right; rather, they were structured by the opposition between individualists and collectivists which focused upon the role of the state.[61] Social politics was debated in terms of the rights and obligations of the state to extend itself into zones outside those marked out by the rule of law. Factory legislation, educational compulsion, regulation of highways and foodstuffs and so forth had already become matters of dispute over the course of the late nineteenth century. In the face of rising political unrest and evidence of the malign effects of irregular employment, poor living conditions and squalor, socialists and social liberals were now demanding more extensive social intervention to mitigate what were now seen as the inevitable social consequences of capitalist economic arrangements. Whatever their differences, in each case the term 'social' implied a kind of anti-individualism: the need to conceive of human beings as citizens of a wider collectivity who did not merely confront one another as buyers and sellers on a competitive market. Hence at least some aspects of the economy required to be politically governed in the name of the social, in order to dispel a whole range of conflicts – between the rights of property and those of the property-less, between liberals and communists, between revolutionists and reformists – and to ensure social order, social tranquillity, perhaps even social justice.

It is undoubtedly the case that, in the United States, this govern-

---

[59] Spencer 1884.
[60] Quoted in Collini 1979: 26. Collini (ibid.) quotes further from this source: 'The leadership in the application of the doctrine of evolution to social science belongs undoubtedly to Herbert Spencer . . . [who] makes biology teach the folly of state intervention and the necessity of industrial competition.'
[61] Clarke 1978; Collini 1979.

mentalization of politics took a different form.[62] This was, no doubt, because of longstanding differences in the organization of political institutions, with national, state and local governments in a non-hierarchical matrix of associations, with political parties of great importance in the organization of powers and privileges, with the courts playing a key role in striking down attempts at legislation that appeared to interfere with constitutionally protected freedoms, and with jurisdiction over industrial and social policies largely held by the forty-eight individual states. The United States in the nineteenth century developed, in Skocpol's phrase, as a federal state of 'courts and parties', and even through the first half of the twentieth century its governmentalization was limited: 'because of its limited fiscal and bureaucratic capacities, the US national government has often relied for policy implementation on subsidies and activities channeled through business enterprises, state or local governments, or "private" voluntary associations'.[63] Hence, Skocpol argues, when new agencies were established to administer social legislation, 'they were typically islands of expertise within local, state, and federal governments, limited by ongoing jurisdictional disputes among legislatures, executives, and courts . . . [and initially] limited to information gathering and regulation'.[64] But, as we shall see, despite these differences in political organization, in the United States too, new ways of thinking and acting emerged in which the conduct of human beings, individually and collectively, was to be governed in the name of the social.

Government from the social point of view

Government of the social, during the second half of the nineteenth century, was embodied in a haphazard array of devices, addressed to this or that specific problematic sector or issue; only a minority of these

---

[62] There is a considerable literature on American exceptionalism from the point of view of state-building from the 1880s to the 1960s. Badie and Birnbaum argue that over this period the American state remained backward compared with states in Germany and France, with a relatively low level of state autonomy and institutionalization and a larger role played by the business community and the market (Badie and Birnbaum 1983). Stephen Skowronek, in *Building a New American State*, concludes that the early 'weak state' was not transcended in the twentieth century, and that the national administrative state in the United States remained diffuse in purpose, relatively decentralized in structure and operationally weak (Skowronek 1982).

[63] Skocpol 1992: 45.

[64] Ibid.: 46.

devices of government were linked into the formal political apparatus. Over the course of the twentieth century, in most European nations, these forms of expert government 'at a distance' became linked to the political field in a new way, and expertise acquired a new constitutional status and new technical and bureaucratic forms. Diverse political forces and social commentators, from the end of the nineteenth century, argued that these unsystematic and dispersed interventions were insufficient to stem the forces of fragmentation and individualization which social change was producing and which social science appeared to document – suicide, crime, anomie, the alienation of the individual.[65] In particular, economic exigencies – want of employment, industrial injury and poor factory conditions – had damaging social consequences, and the disaffection produced was provoking a worrying rise of labour unrest. The problem was to devise a way of ameliorating these problems caused by the imperatives of profit whilst maintaining the principle of private ownership.

As it took shape in the early decades of the twentieth century, the idea of 'social rights' shifted the claim for distributive justice from the conflicts over the state itself towards questions concerning the functioning of its administrative agencies.[66] Through these agencies, the state would fulfil its responsibilities by acting to reduce the risks to individuals and families that were entailed in the irrationality of economic cycles and shifts of fortune, would mitigate the worst effects of unbridled economic activity by intervening directly into the terms and conditions of employment, and would act so as to enhance the opportunities for the social promotion of individuals through their own action. The state would no longer be the stake in social conflicts: it would now stand outside such conflicts as the guarantor of social progress for all.

A new liberalism would take shape, both in Britain and to a lesser extent in the United States, that tried to overcome in thought the classical liberal opposition to state intervention. In *Liberalism*, his classic text of 1911, Hobhouse argued that there was no opposition between liberty and control, every liberty resting instead on a corresponding act of control. Further, aspects of current social and economic arrangements could themselves be seen as coercive to whole classes of individuals, and hence it was legitimate for the state to seek to combat these in order to allow citizens to develop their personalities freely.[67] And, for Hobson,

---

[65] Donzelot 1984.
[66] Procacci 1998: 21.
[67] The standard text on British new liberalism is Freeden 1978. See also Collini 1979. May O. Furner provides a good introduction to new liberalism in the United States: Furner 1993.

sociology was to be the servant of these political and ethical programmes of social reform. The state had a moral function to re-assert
the quality of human life in the face of industrialization. Government
must conserve individual rights because 'an area of individual liberty
is conducive to the health of the collective life'.[68] Freedom required
the re-affirming of the rights, and the development of the capabilities
of the individual, but this could only occur through the action of the
state and the development of communal responsibility and citizenship,
guided by social science. The social reform policies of the Liberal
administrations of 1905-14 operated according to this diagram: workmen's compensation, benefits for industrial disease, old-age pensions,
labour exchanges, minimum wage boards and unemployment and
health insurance for those in certain industries all indexed a new
reciprocity between state and citizen in the service of individual development and social progress.

In the United States, alongside this new liberalism, a rather different
notion of social control was taking shape in which 'the state' played a
minimal role. In the words of Hamilton and Sutton, 'progressive American thinkers responded to a perceived crisis of political authority by
articulating an original and widely influential ideology of social control
that implied a subtle, but decisive shift in the nature of political domination in America ... [the foundation of] the emergent Progressive
strategy of institutional reform was laid by American intellectuals who
struggled to rethink the fundamental principles of obedience and ethical
obligation ... [These were] no longer rooted in an innate human nature,
but came to rest instead on principles of social responsibility.'[69] William
James, Lester Ward and George Herbert Mead and many others argued
that ethical conduct had its origins in social groups, and hence rules of
right conduct properly arose from within this social space. This did not
lead to a conflict between the values of individualism and those of collectivism, for in the process of child rearing, in the family, the workplace, the peer group and the school, social control is internalized and
becomes self control. 'Organizations in American sociology ranged from
play groups and communities to government and industrial adminis-

---

[68] Hobson 1914: 304, quoted in Freeden 1978: 110.
[69] Hamilton and Sutton 1989: 6. I draw on this instructive analysis of 'the problem of control in the weak state' in the paragraphs that follow, despite
my unease with the notion of the weak state upon which it is predicated.
I also draw upon the excellent discussion contained in chapter 1 of *The
Molecular Vision of Life*, Lily Kay's superb account of the role of the Rockefeller Foundation in the development of the new molecular biology (Kay
1993).

trations, and ideally they all possessed the same two purposes, as locations in which social goals could be accomplished and individual selves could be realized . . . the act of organization was intrinsically an ethical act, vital to human nature and society.'[70] Social control, that is to say, must arise from the natural processes of society, to the extent that they produce social roles which ascribe both individual selfhood and ethical responsibility. E. A. Ross had initiated this line of thought on social control when, in 1894, he 'jotted down 33 ways in which society exercised social control . . . [and then] proceeded to develop these preliminary thoughts into the organizing principles of sociology'. Ross concluded that the success of social control depended upon the professional sociologist 'who will address himself to those who administer the moral capital of society – to teachers, clergymen, editors, lawmakers and judges, who wield the instruments of control; to poets, artists, thinkers and educators, who guide the human caravans across the waste'.[71]

This conception of the social control that could and should be inscribed within the very processes and relations of organizational life itself was, of course, crucial to American sociology right through its structural-functionalist heyday after the Second World War. By the 1920s, it had become dominant in the human sciences in the United States. In 1925, E. A. Lumley synthesized the received view thus:

Social control has usually meant that kind of life patterns, which a government, through its officers, imposes upon the citizen. But we have seen that social control means vastly more than that. We might speak of it as the practice of putting forward directive stimuli or wish patterns, their accurate transmission to, and adoption by, others, whether voluntarily or involuntarily. In short, it is effective will-transference . . . A little reflection will show that all social problems are ultimately problems of social control – capital and labor, prostitution, taxes, crimes, international relations.[72]

In the United States, this idea of the instrumentalization of social control within the practices of everyday life under the guidance of expertise was the key to the philanthropic programmes of the Rockefeller Foundation and other institutions and corporations of the Progressive Era animated by the twin fears of social revolution on the one hand and the

---

[70] Hamilton and Sutton 1989: 14–15.
[71] Ross 1901. I quote both this and the previous description from Kay 1993: 22–3.
[72] Lumley 1925: 12–14, quoted from Kay 1993: 36.

social and biological decay of the race on the other. In Britain and Europe, the idea of the social state played an equivalent role in relation to equivalent fears. Despite the real differences that would arise in each case, it nonetheless appeared that an alternative to attempts to control and shape the destiny of society through whole-scale collectivism could be found. Rather than one overarching 'social problem' located in the opposition between Labour and Capital, the One and the Many, Freedom and Co-operation, the social problem was to fragment into a whole array of distinct 'social problems' – the health and safety of workers, the education of paupers, the regulation of hygiene.[73] Each of these problems could be addressed and ameliorated discretely, administratively. Experts of the social, increasingly integrated into the state machine, would play their part in formulating the problems in a soluble way, developing appropriate responses to them, and in the ramifying assemblages through which these responses would be enacted. Philanthropists and feminists would deploy the social in the name of the rights of women and the protection of domesticity. Mass schooling would be proclaimed as the mechanism sought to promote social citizenship and compulsory education would be construed not merely in terms of a pedagogy of habits of conduct and thought, but as the means to produce social civility and social peace. Concerns about poverty and inequality would be shifted from the political to the social sphere, tamed by the language of statistics and the pragmatic activities of reformers. Upon this imagined territory of the social, upon the presupposition of its existence, its relations with the economy and the machinery of production, its necessity, its value, its inescapability, welfare states, in their different forms and with their different specific histories, took shape.

This entailed, in particular, a transformation of the divisions and relations between the territory of 'politics', on the one hand, and those of family and economy on the other. As far as the economy is concerned, different paths would be followed in Europe and in the United States for the first three decades of the twentieth century at least. In Europe, a variety of strategies sought to transform the working-class family into a unit of economic government: social insurance and the tax and benefit system would safeguard it against the economic exigencies that would cast it into poverty with all the demoralizing and dangerous consequences that were held to follow. Over the course of the twentieth century, economic activity, in the form of wage labour, was given a new set of *social* responsibilities, seen as a mechanism which would link males

[73] Schwartz 1997.

into the social order, and which would establish a proper relationship between the familial, the social and the economic orders. Simultaneously, the privacy of the wage contract was weakened, as politicians came to accept that conditions of labour and pay should be regulated in the name of social peace. This was an element in the reshaping of the divisions between 'the social' and 'the economic' as employment itself came to be seen as a phenomenon that had consequences that were as much social as economic. A new alliance came to be forged between what Denis Meuret has termed the 'economic machine' and the 'social machine'.[74] The rights of workers outside work were addressed through unemployment insurance and the like; the enclosure of the workplace was penetrated through regulations on contracts, hours, safety and conditions of work; the labour exchange and allied inventions were to make the labour market visible as a social domain of transactions between the demand and supply of labour, regularizing employment and rendering individual idleness into a socio-economic phenomenon of unemployment.[75] The aleatory and contingent encounter of work – exemplified in particular by the problems of casual labourer – would thus be organized over a territory – striated, as Deleuze and Guattari would have it.[76] The mobility of the economic encounter, the nomadism of the individualized labourer, would be captured and located in a circuit of flows amenable to individual and collective social government.[77]

In the United States, a different path was followed. Many progressives advocated the development of social insurance to replace the very extensive regime of social protection that had developed under the rubric of Civil War pensions, often arguing in the terms of the 'New Liberalism'.[78] But compared with their British counterparts, American campaigners had little success. Many were certain that the United States would follow the 'universal tendency' in the industrial world 'toward a complete and connected system of insurance ... under which workingmen would be insured against all contingencies where support

[74] Meuret 1981.
[75] Donzelot 1981; Ewald 1991.
[76] Deleuze and Guattari 1987.
[77] For an illuminating discussion, see Walters 1994b.
[78] I have drawn freely on Skocpol's account (Skocpol 1992) in this paragraph. As she points out, apart from the claims of corruption in administration, a key difficulty in any attempt to generalize the system of Civil War pensions lay in the fact that they were not conceived as 'social' benefits, but as arising from the moral duty of the nation to support those who had earned aid for themselves, their dependants and their communities by their patriotic efforts.

from wages is lost or interrupted by any cause other than voluntary cessation of labor'.[79] For Isaac Max Rubinow, this would be an expression of 'ethical statism'; social insurance would be 'a powerful object lesson of the reality of the new concept of the stare as an instrument of organized collective action, rather than of class oppression, the concept of the future state in the making, rather than of the state in the past'.[80] But proposals for social insurance schemes for working men found little support from the political classes and were largely defeated. Labour laws, with the exception of provisions for industrial accidents, were struck down by the courts which saw then as infringements of the constitutionally protected 'freedom of contract'. Proposals for old-age pensions were perceived as plans for government hand-outs and led to fears of a repetition of the patronage and corruption that had surrounded the schemes of Civil War pensions and outdoor relief; Skocpol argues that this was largely responsible for their failure to gather the broad coalitions necessary for political success.

However, in the period leading up to the First World War, and in the decades after the war, the productive machine in the United States was socialized in a different way: through a range of amendments, additions and modifications to the nature of employment itself.[81] F. W. Taylor's attempts to render the productive body calculable and manageable in the name of industrial efficiency were formulated in terms of an improvement of the welfare of both the corporation and the worker. They were linked to a whole raft of measures aimed at identifying the particular characteristics of individuals through psychological testing, notably developed in the armed forces during the First World War, and hence eliminating 'misfits' and allocating the right individual to the right position. But, more generally, the introduction of 'scientific management' went some way to providing a democratic legitimacy to the private workplace, by enabling managerial authority to be depicted as rational and objective. Whilst Taylor's system was resisted by both organized and unorganized workers because it allowed employers to set arbitrary standards of performance and was seen as dehumanizing, corporate reformers found more acceptable solutions in the introduction of programmes of 'industrial relations' and 'personnel management', which understood the worker as a human being, and overlaid the workplace

[79] This is from L. K. Frankel and M. M. Dawson's 1910 survey *Workingmen's Insurance in Europe*: 395, quoted from Skocpol 1992: 173.

[80] This is from Rubinow's 1913 book *Social Insurance, With Special Reference to American Conditions*, quoted from Skocpol 1992: 175.

[81] Peter Miller and I discuss some of these in our paper 'Production, identity and democracy' (Miller and Rose 1995b).

with a grid of subjectivity. Initially the subjectivity of the worker was individualized – notably in the identification of industrial problems with emotional maladjustment amongst workers, within a growing movement which sought to resolve industrial problems and increase industrial efficiency by improving the mental hygiene of the worker.[82] By the time of Elton Mayo's studies between 1923 and 1932, the workplace had become a social environment, suffused with meanings, beliefs and attitudes, and, crucially, a matter of group relations.[83] For Mayo, work had a social function in two senses: it could satisfy the needs of the individual for human association and hence, if properly organized, could contribute both to productivity and efficiency and to mental health. And, on the other hand, the working group was a crucial mechanism for dragging individuals who had been increasingly isolated by the division of labour into the 'general torrent of social life'.[84] The workplace became a 'social domain', although this sociality was construed as a field of psychological relations amongst workers.

Hesitant steps towards industrial democracy had been made in the United States during the First World War, but these were largely dismantled in the next decade. But in their place came a growing management recognition of the 'human factor', consultative machinery on workplace conditions, the development of personnel management and 'welfare provisions' such as health facilities, wholesome meals, provision for healthy recreation, advice and support for investment, savings and loans and so forth. These measures did not merely address many of the points of antagonism between workers and employers, they actually made work an apparatus for reshaping the ways in which workers would live their lives in a socialized direction. Further, the development of workmen's compensation schemes, by corporate and legislative initiative, reduced 'the vicious antagonism and dramatic courtroom battles between employers and workers over the question of responsibility for industrial ills' and repositioned them in a realm where political conflicts were replaced by social and technical questions about the distribution of risks and the prevention of accidents. By the 1930s, as Keith Gandall and Stephen Kotkin put it, work was 'situated in a social field of risks, accidents, preventative measures and social burdens; new "social" agents such as psychologists were brought into the workplace to govern it, and a new type of worker populated this social field, a worker with a

[82] See for example National Committee for Mental Hygiene 1929.
[83] Mayo's experiments and arguments have been exhaustively discussed: I analyse them myself in chapter 6 of *Governing the Soul* (Rose 1990).
[84] Mayo 1933, quoted from Miller 1986: 152.

personality or a psychology that was a factor in a calculus of social hazards and social costs'.[85]

As is well known, in the 1930s, the paths of the United States and Europe came together again. New Deal measures, such as the Social Security Act of 1935 and the utilizing of deficit financing to pay for public works and relief efforts to combat unemployment, acknowledged that the economy was not inviolable, but was a system whose inherent rationality was limited and partial; 'it must be brought to its social optimum with the help of State intervention'.[86] Even the labour market itself was seen as in need of optimization through political action, as embodied in devices ranging from labour exchanges to vocational training. Gradually, over the next six decades, new indexes of economic activity were invented that would render the economy amenable to social management, and new technologies of macro-economic regulations were brought into being. In these strategies of government, the domains of the economic and the social were distinguished, but governed according to a principle of joint optimization. The name of John Maynard Keynes came to index this new conception, not merely particular measures such as deficit spending by national governments to counter unemployment, but the reformulation of the role of national governments entailing an obligation to play an active part in reshaping economic conditions for social ends, advised by disinterested social scientific and economic experts and effected through a rational administration.[87] Through mechanisms of social insurance – unemployment

[85] Keith Gandall and Stephen Kotkin's pathbreaking paper 'Governing work and social life in the USA and the USSR' (1985) came out of the work that students at the University of California, Berkeley, did with Michel Foucault with the aim of writing a collective book on welfare practices in Western societies; Gandall and Kotkin took up research for this book themselves, but, as far as I am aware, neither the book nor the paper was published, although the paper achieved some circulation through the original *History of the Present* group at Berkeley. These two quotes are from pp. 19 and 20 of this manuscript.

[86] Meuret 1981: 29. Weir and Skocpol suggest that there was never full-hearted acknowledgement or acceptance of deficit financing, and that the goal of a 'balanced budget' was held up as the measure of New Deal success (Weir and Skocpol 1985: 134).

[87] See, for example, Keynes' 1926 lecture 'The end of laissez-faire' (Keynes 1926) for a programmatic argument along these lines. Of course, there is much debate about whether there was ever a 'Keynesian' revolution in economic policy in Britain (see Tomlinson 1981b and Schott 1982). Weir and Skocpol have argued that, between the wars, Sweden and the United States show much clearer, if different, evidence of 'Keynesian' thinking in the

benefit, accident insurance, health and safety legislation and so forth – and through an array of forms of economic government – tax regimes, interest rates and other techniques of 'demand management' – the state assumed responsibility for the management of a whole variety of risks – to individuals, to employers, to the state itself – in the name of society.

The family was a second key site for social government. As far as the bourgeois family is concerned, there is much truth in Foucault's suggestion that the socio-political role of the family had already, in the nineteenth century, shifted from one centred on alliances, the transmission of wealth, privilege and status, to one centred on sexuality, and the maintenance and reproduction of healthy and normal offspring whose intellectual abilities, constitution and moral fibre were not compromised.[88] The bourgeois family was problematized in terms of the sexuality of children and adolescents; the bourgeois mother was assigned new conjugal and domestic responsibilities accompanied by a widespread psychiatrization of the female condition. It required a further small shift for this deployment of health, hygiene, sexuality and reproduction to be incorporated into a hereditary and eugenic framework. As far as the working class was concerned, however, it was now, within this social field, that the family came to be recoded as a living unity – in terms of its biology, its bodies, its sexuality, its reproduction – and hence subjected to medico-hygienic scrutiny focused upon the contribution which it could make to the fitness of the population. The family of the labouring classes was not merely a deployment for the moralization of adults and children, subject to exhortation from the church or political leaders, and threatened with sanctions if it failed in its moral responsibilities. It was now an organic component of a society and a population, with its own internal living processes, to be shaped, educated and solicited into a relation with the state if it was to fulfil the role of producing healthy, responsible, adjusted social citizens. The political task was to devise mechanisms that would support the family in its 'normal' functioning and enable it to fulfil its social obligations most effectively without destroying its identity and responsibility. The technical details of the internal regime of the working-class family would become the object of new forms of pedagogy, for example through medical inspection of schoolchildren and the invention of 'health visitors', to instil norms of personal hygiene and standards of child care. Whilst the mothers of the wealthier classes had been solicited into

economic policies of their respective 'new deals' in the face of recession and mass unemployment (Weir and Skocpol 1985).

[88] Foucault 1979a: 120–1.

alliances with medics in the nineteenth century – acquiring new powers and obligations in the household in relation to child rearing and domesticity in the process – one sees a new specification of the role of the working-class mother as one who was to be educated by educationalists, health visitors and doctors into the skills of responsible government of domestic relations. A revised ethic of womanhood, of the respectable and educated woman who was best suited to staff the devices that would relay government into the household, of the decent and educable woman who was to enact government within the domestic space, of the feckless and irresponsible woman whose character was impermeable to education, would be central to a new mode of social government.

Indeed, Skocpol has argued convincingly that, although the paternalistic model of social policy, based around the protection of the rights of the workingman, and organized around the security of the male wage earner, would make limited progress in the United States in the first three decades of the twentieth century, a different form of social protection did make progress, mobilized by the campaigns of women reformers and organized around the protection of the mothers and children of the race.[89] As the president of the National Congress of Mothers put it in 1906:

When the birds have flown from the nest, the mother-work may still go on, reaching out to better conditions for other children. It may be in providing day nurseries, vacations schools, playgrounds, and kindergartens, manual and domestic science . . . It may be in working for laws regulating child labor, juvenile courts and probation, pure food, divorce and marriage, compulsory education . . . It may be in providing wholesome, hygienic homes through tenement house inspection, visiting nurses, schools for the defective and backward, homes for the homeless, help for the erring. It may be in fighting against any evil that menaces the security and sacredness of the home and undermines the moral tone of society.[90]

Female social reformers were leaders in campaigns for such 'maternalist' social policies: restrictions on women's working hours to safeguard the 'mothers of the race', child labour reform, campaigns to establish a US Children's Bureau to look after the needs of American infants and mothers and after its inauguration in 1912 to expand its mission to include health education for all American mothers, campaigns to improve child hygiene under the motto 'better mothers, better babies, and better homes'. Unlike their paternalist counterparts, these endeavours often succeeded, although with ambiguous results. Thus the

---

[89] Skocpol 1992: chs. 6–9.
[90] Quoted ibid.: 336.

campaign to establish mothers' pensions, so that the United States could make 'full use of the love of mothers' and keep children out of institutions, was largely successful. But the provisions of inspection that went along with it, to ensure that funds went only to those mothers deemed to be able and willing to keep good homes, imposed a whole variety of moral injunctions upon potential recipients. Whilst these varied from state to state, in general recipients had to show that they were fit and capable to bring up their children: drunkards and those who had been deserted by their partners or were unmarried were excluded; recipients were subject to constant inspection as a condition for receiving aid; immigrant women were required to apply for citizenship and judged using culturally specific criteria, penalized for using a language other than English in the home, for refusing to remove relatives deemed unsavoury from their homes, for living in improper houses or neighbourhoods and for failing to maintain the home in a clean and orderly condition. Women in receipt of aid were also required to swap full-time for part-time work in order to remain at home with their children: all this, as the *Second Annual Report of the State Public Welfare Commission* in Rhode Island put it in 1925, 'in an effort to build for the State the best possible type of citizen'.[91]

It is not, then, a case of whether or to what extent various countries developed 'the welfare state'. Rather, it is more useful to understand this as *government from the social point of view*.[92] Organized attempts to govern conduct, in particular but not exclusively the conduct of the poor, proliferated in Britain, Europe and the United States around a variety of different problems, but underpinned by the same socializing rationale. In the United States, the prohibition movement saw its problem not merely as alcohol but as the saloon, which not only promoted drunkenness but increased poverty, degradation, violence and crime: prohibition was thus seen as a part of the struggle to create safe and healthy social lives for normal individuals: an element of a social politics. During the First World War, a campaign was waged against prostitution in order to protect citizens from 'social disease': states passed legislation for compulsory medical examination of prostitutes on the basis of which infected women could be imprisoned without trial; social workers tried to set up centres to reclaim them as socially responsible citizens and workers. The United States had the dubious privilege of pioneering eugenic legislation to safeguard the race from threats to its well-being: civic organizations argued for welfare measures for immigrants in the

---

[91] Quoted ibid.: 469.
[92] I take this term from Procacci 1989, but use it slightly differently.

interests of social defence, in the attempt to create Americans out of immigrants and socialize them to increase their resistance to radical politics. In the name of eugenics, legislation was enacted in the 1920s restricting immigration from the lower races of Southern and Southeastern Europe, and sterilization laws were passed in many states to protect the race from the dangers posed by the breeding of the feeble-minded, the mentally defective and unfit. In both the United States and Britain, alongside these negative and deductive campaigns of eugenics and racial improvement, wide-ranging campaigns for mental hygiene sought to turn not merely the home and the factory but also the school and the city into machinery for producing adjustment and thus promoting individual contentment, familial stability and social adjustment, seen as the adjustment of individual instincts to the necessities of civility and social life.[93]

In Britain and most European nations, this array of social devices for the government of insecurity, poverty, employment, health, education and so forth would increasingly be connected up and governed from a centre. New links, relays and pathways were to be established to connect political aspirations, calculations and decisions to events at a multitude of local points – in households, educational establishments, health clinics, courtrooms, benefit offices, workplaces and the like. Further, government from the social point of view aimed to connect the 'prophylactic' dimensions of social government – those concerned with preventing possible social risk and danger by pre-emptive means ranging from social insurance through the promotion of full employment and measures to ensure social hygiene to the inculcation of norms of child rearing – with the 'reactive' elements of social government. Thus labour exchanges, courts, child guidance clinics, schools and factories all provide institutional loci for identifying pathological men, women and children, classifying and judging them, not only prescribing measures of individual reformation but tracking them out again, through the activities of social workers and others, into a web of social relations which can be made visible and subject to normalizing intervention.[94] But what was at stake here, overarching the different institutional forms taken in different national contexts, was the endeavour to construct a new kind of human being, social citizens taking responsibility for their own physical and mental health and that of their family, and enwrapped in a range of other practices that actively promoted the values of a social way of life.

[93] I discuss the mental hygiene movement in detail in Rose 1985.
[94] Rose 1985: 200–5; cf. Walters 1994a and Armstrong 1983: ch. 2

Expert authority would flourish in these social assemblages and would elaborate new bodies of mundane, practical social knowledge of the habits, conducts, capacities, dreams and desires of citizens, and of their errors, deviations, inconstancies and pathologies, of the ways in which these might be calibrated, classified, ordered, shaped and moulded by doctors, social workers, probation officers, welfare workers and all the other minor doctors of conduct. Experts would enter into a kind of double alliance. They would ally themselves with political authorities, focusing upon their problems and problematizing new issues, translating political concerns about economic productivity, innovation, industrial unrest, social stability, law and order, normality and pathology and so forth into the vocabulary of management, accounting, medicine, social science and psychology. They would attach themselves to practices that previously secreted their own truths: even the law itself would no longer find its justification in an abstract theory of justice but in the positive truths of expertise. Experts would also seek alliances with individuals themselves, translating their daily worries and decisions over investment, child rearing, factory organization or diet into a language claiming the power of truth, and offering to teach them the techniques by which they might manage better, earn more, bring up healthier or happier children and much more besides. Around the problem family, experts would seek to mobilize the powers of the state in order to realize the dream of a rationalized and comprehensive system of services exercising a continuous educational scrutiny over the potentially dangerous household. Eileen Younghusband, a key figure in these strategies in Britain, put it thus: ' "You can't give children love by Act of Parliament", said Margery Fry when the 1948 Children Act was passed. But love [can] . . . be refined by knowledge and supported materially and by clinical judgement. So it also proved true that . . . you cannot give some children love without Act of Parliament.'[95] Only the 'constitutionalization' of the pedagogy of love, it appeared, could combine prevention in the form of education and instruction of parents with re-education of miscreants through reformatory interventions into the failing family.

Government from the social point of view thus entailed an array of strategies and devices, themselves shaped and administered in the light of expert truth claims, that supported the powers of experts with laws and regulations and socially distributed funds, which promoted the dissemination of expert knowledge to the responsible citizen through radio, television and the advice of all those who would surround individuals at potentially troublesome moments (childbirth, illness, marriage, school-

[95] Younghusband 1978: 51; cf. G. Burchell 1981.

ing, career choice, unemployment and so on) and accorded experts the powers to assess and allocate troubled or troublesome individuals to specialized reformatory institutions (old people's homes, professional social work agencies and so on). Benign education of the normal citizen, enlightened use of discretion, the professional calculus of risks and benefits, the expert deployment of compulsory powers in the best interest of the child, the mental patient, the old person or the handicapped were the order of the day. Professional knowledge, training, expert skills and knowledgeable judgements animated and legitimated a complex social bureaucracy of pedagogy and care. Within these assemblages – with their own logics, criteria of judgement, professional codes and values, notions of autonomy and specialism – enclosures of expert power were formed which were largely insulated from political control, from market logics and from the pressures exerted by their subjects.[96]

The social citizen

The nineteenth century saw the invention of the calculable individual, with the birth of techniques of individualization and classification: the individual whose personal adjustment or maladjustment was to be judged in relation to a norm. But in the middle decades of the twentieth century, one sees the invention of the social individual, whose character was shaped by social influences, who found his or her satisfaction within the social relations of the group. This was not an abstract event in knowledge or a cultural shift in meaning. The new images of the individual were elaborated within specific institutional sites – notably the juvenile court, the school and the factory – in relation to specific problematizations of conduct – delinquency, maladjustment, labour problems – and through the new systems of visibility, identification, classification, assessment and judgement that they established. This new image of the individual, as was so often noted, embodied an 'environmental' account of the causes of personal success or failure, and was linked to a certain 'positivism' in the underlying rationale of regulatory practices. Thus the administration of criminal justice came to presuppose that penal measures must be based upon an 'understanding' of the pressures that led to transgression and should be directed towards reform through the application of a quasi-therapeutic penal regime – especially in the case of the juvenile offender.[97] Childhood problems within and outside school were understood in terms of the influences of family environment upon

[96] Rose and Miller 1992.
[97] See Garland 1985.

individual constitution, and child guidance clinics organized programmes of advice, instruction and therapy for reform.[98] Maladjustment in the factory – industrial accidents, absenteeism, inefficiency – came to be understood in terms of the social relations of the workplace and to be managed by acting upon the social bonds that produced contentment or discontent – as in the famous arguments of Elton Mayo.[99]

The person also became social in an ethical sense, enjoined by feminists, social liberals, Fabians and many others to construe him- or herself – whether worker, mother, neighbour – as a citizen with social obligations, and to steer a path through the world by a constant normative social evaluation of duties and responsibilities.[100] Thus Eva Hubback, in *The Population of Britain*, argued that citizenship should be diffused through all educational levels, embodied in marriage guidance clinics, adult education classes and a new school curriculum which would teach 'hygiene, family relationships, child management and the domestic crafts' and 'education in family living'.[101] Evidence from the Fabian Society to the 1945 Royal Commission on Population argued for education in citizenship: every woman must be educated to recognize not only that motherhood was an important job, for her family, her community and a democratic society at large, but also that the duties of citizenship were such that marriage alone was no justification for abstention for work – 'what is really involved is a new set of values which allow women to take their proper place in society, as mothers, workers and citizens'.[102] The 1942 report on *Social Insurance and Allied Services* written by William Beveridge envisaged that the technology of social insurance would not destroy but encourage the sense of personal responsibility and mutual obligation on the part of each citizen.[103] And T. H. Marshall's famous lecture of 1949 on the 'development of citizenship' in the West is best understood as a programme to rationalize and render coherent this diverse set of strategies that specified the individual as a citizen who had not only acquired civil, political and social rights, but also the ethical obligations that accompanied them.[104]

[98] Rose 1985.
[99] See Miller 1986; Rose 1990: chs. 6–8.
[100] I draw the examples that follow from Denise Riley 1983: 168–88.
[101] Hubback 1947, quoted in Riley 1983: 168.
[102] Fabian Society 1946: 21, quoted in Riley 1983: 177.
[103] Beveridge 1942.
[104] Marshall [1949] 1992.

Beyond the social state

As Robert Castel points out, the idea of the social state was grounded in the presupposition that the gradual betterment of the conditions of all forces and blocs within society – employers, labourers, managers, professionals – could be achieved.[105] Political strategies could be devised that would ameliorate the hardship of the worst-off and maintain the principle of productive labour, whilst cushioning its harshness within the workplace and lessening the fear of unemployment by supporting those outside the labour market. One could thus contain the dangers posed by the worst-off and reinforce the security and individual freedoms of the better-off. Simultaneously, this would provide the legitimacy for a range of projects to sequester and reform those who refused this social contract or were unable to give assent to it – the mad, the criminals, the delinquent, the workshy, the socially inadequate. It thus seemed possible to bind all strata and classes into an agreement for social progress of which the state was, to a greater or less extent (this would be the political territory fought over for some fifty years), the guarantor. This image of social progress through gradual amelioration of hardship and improvement of conditions of life won out over the image of social revolution on the one hand and the image of unfettered competition on the other. The social state would have the role of shaping and co-ordinating the strategies which would oblige all partners, no longer antagonists, to work towards and facilitate social progress.

For perhaps fifty years, the social imperative for government remained relatively uncontested. Today, however, it is mutating. This is not a resurgence of unbridled individualism. We can begin to observe a reshaping of the very territory of government: a kind of 'detotalization' of society. The continuous (if not homogeneous) 'thought-space' of the social is fragmented, as indexed in the rise of concerns in terms of 'multi-culturalism', and political controversies over the implications of 'pluralism' – of ethnicity, of religion, of sexuality, of ability and disability – together with conflicts over the competing and mutually exclusive 'rights' and 'values' of different communities. Subjects of government are understood as individuals with 'identities' which not only identify them, but do so through their allegiance to a particular set of community values, beliefs and commitments. Communities of identity may be defined by locality (neighbourhood), by ethnicity (the Asian community), by lifestyle (as in the segmentation of lifestyle operated by advertisers, manufacturers and the media), by sexuality (the gay

---

[105] Castel 1995: 387.

community) or by political or moral allegiance (environmentalists, vegetarians). But however defined, the individual is no isolate – he or she has 'natural' emotional bonds of affinity to a circumscribed 'network' of other individuals.

In this 'advanced' diagram of community, which I will consider in more detail in chapter 5, individual conduct no longer appears to be 'socially determined': individual choices are shaped by values which themselves arise from ties of community identification. Community thus emerges as the ideal territory for the administration of individual and collective existence, the plane or surface upon which micro-moral relations amongst persons are conceptualized and administered. Collective existence is made intelligible and calculable in terms of community, and this 'advanced' vocabulary of community places collective existence under a new description, making it amenable to intervention and administration in novel ways. Issues are problematized *in terms of* features of communities and their strengths, cultures, pathologies. Strategies address such problems by seeking to *act upon* the dynamics of communities, enhancing the bonds that link individuals to their community, rebuilding shattered communities and so forth. Community constitutes a new spatialization of government: the territory for political programmes, both at the micro-level and at the macro-level, for *government through community*.[106] In such programmes 'society' still exists but not in a 'social' form: society is to be regenerated, and social justice to be maximized, through the building of responsible communities, prepared to invest in themselves.[107] And in the name of community, a whole variety of groups and forces make their demands, wage their campaigns, stand up for their rights and enact their resistances.

It is, of course, not a question of the replacement of 'the social' by 'the community'. But the hold of 'the social' over our political imagination is weakening. While social government has been failing since its inception, the solution proposed for these failures is no longer the re-invention of the social. As 'society' dissociates into a variety of ethical and cultural communities with incompatible allegiances and incommensurable obligations, a new set of political rationalities, governmental technologies and opportunities for contestation begin to take shape.

---

[106] E.g. Etzioni 1993; Gray 1996. I shall examine these in detail in chapter 5.
[107] Commission on Social Justice 1994.

4   Advanced liberalism

Reflecting on fascism and Nazism in the immediate aftermath of the Second World War, a number of intellectuals began to challenge the rationale of any social state. In *The Road to Serfdom*, published in 1944, Friedrich von Hayek argued that those who advocated planning by politicians and experts in the interests of society were unwittingly embarking upon a road that could only lead to totalitarianism in socialist or national socialist form. When the state takes on itself the role of planning society, planning production, housing, transport, welfare, it becomes an instrument for imposing a morality. It inescapably violates the requirements for formality and generality required by the rule of law, in favour of substantive decisions about worthy activities and worthy persons. These then have to be rendered acceptable to 'the people' through all sorts of propagandist means. Intellectuals may claim to be able to take judgements about right and wrong ways of acting and behaving, and so to direct society, but such intellectual hubris is specious and self-serving: it subordinates the necessary pluralism of reason to the totalitarian claim to eternal truth. The only principles upon which true freedom can be based are those of classical liberalism, 'freedom to order our own conduct in the sphere where material circumstances force a choice upon us, and responsibility for the arrangement of our own life according to our own conscience'.[1]

For Alexander Rüstow and the group of jurists and economists known as *Ordoliberalen* (from their association with the journal *Ordo*), a return to classic liberalism was not the answer. What was required was a neo-liberalism that had nothing to do with the revival of the old ideology of *laissez faire*.[2] The market was not a quasi-natural reality to be freed;

---

[1] Hayek 1944: 157.
[2] For my remarks on the *Ordoliberalen* I am drawing on Colin Gordon's discussion of Foucault's 1979 lecture on neo-liberalism in West Germany, the United States and France: C. Gordon 1987, 1991. Rüstow's project is framed in world historic terms in *Freedom and Domination: A Historical Critique of Civilization* (1980), commenced in 1937 and written whilst he was a political

rather it was 'incumbent on government to conduct a policy towards society such that it is possible for a market to exist and function'.[3] The market economy had become degenerate, penetrated by monopolies, subsidies and government regulations brought about by the interventionist, protectionist and monopoly-fostering measures of the state. A framework of institutional and legal forms had to be assembled to free the market from these public and private distortions. But this was not enough. The historical transformation of labour into a commodity had made the worker dependent, and made work a monotonous and meaningless curse. This had facilitated the rise of barbarism, domination and violence, the eternal threats to freedom most recently incarnated in Nazism. Within a *Vitalpolitik* designed to create a life worth living, a new set of ethical and cultural values had to be created, not least within work itself, which would accord individuals and families the power to shape their own lives. If the powers of self-actualization were enhanced, individuals would defend freedom itself. In order to achieve this, as Gordon puts it, 'the whole ensemble of individual life is to be structured as the pursuit of a range of different enterprises', a person's relation to all his or her activities, and indeed to his or her self, is to be given 'the ethos and structure of the enterprise form'.[4]

It took some three decades for themes from these and other intellectual critiques to be taken up in Britain, Europe and the United States within political programmes that sought to overturn the logics of social government. The problem of government was, first of all, articulated in terms of the anti-competitive and anti-entrepreneurial consequences of government itself or, rather, of that form of government that had associated the optimization of social and economic life with the augmentation of the powers of the state. Shortly after her election in 1979, at the start of what was to be eighteen years of Conservative government in Britain, Prime Minister Margaret Thatcher posed this in terms of an antagonism between the powers of the state and the responsibilities of the people: 'the first principle of this government . . . is to revive a sense of individual responsibility. It is to reinvigorate not just the economy and industry but the whole body of voluntary associations, loyalties and activities which give society its richness and diversity, and hence its real strength . . . [We] need a strong State to preserve both liberty and order . . . [But we] should not expect the State to appear in the guise of an extravagant

refugee in Atatürk's Turkey; it originally appeared in three volumes in 1950, 1952 and 1957.

[3] C. Gordon 1991: 41.
[4] Ibid.: 42.

good fairy at every christening, a loquacious and tedious companion at every stage of life's journey, the unknown mourner at every funeral.[5] No longer was the state to accompany the citizen 'from cradle to grave', in the familiar slogan of welfare.[6] The relation of the state and the people was to take a different form: the former would maintain the infrastructure of law and order; the latter would promote individual and national well-being by their responsibility and enterprise.

Of course, there was an economic rationale to this reconceptualization of the role of the state: the state had grown too large; it was undertaking projects that could better be accomplished by the private sector; its Keynesian attempts to sustain aggregate demand by deficit spending were inflating the money supply to fund public sector deficits and hence fuelling inflation; it was raising taxes to a level that penalized industry in order to fund a welfare system that sapped incentives to work.[7] To govern better, the state must govern less; to optimize the economy, one must govern through the entrepreneurship of autonomous actors – individuals and families, firms and corporations. Once responsibilized and entrepreneurialized, they would govern themselves within a state-secured framework of law and order. The state can never have the information to enable it to judge and plan each micro-event in a free-market society. Only individual economic actors possess the information to enable them to make the best judgements on risks and potentials in order to guide their conduct; they must be freed to choose according to the natural laws of the free market on the one hand and human nature on the other.

The first responses to these changes in political rationality from those who placed themselves on the progressive side of politics were uniformly hostile. But over the closing two decades of the twentieth century, beyond the politics of the right, a new way of thinking about the objects, targets, mechanism and limits of government has taken shape which shares many of the premises of neo-liberalism. It entails a new conception of the inherent rationality of the different domains to which government must address itself – the market, the family, the community, the individual – and new ways of allocating the tasks of government between the political apparatus, 'intermediate associations', professionals,

[5] Margaret Thatcher (1980): 10–11, quoted from Hall 1986: 127.
[6] *Free to Choose*, Milton and Rose Friedman's (1970) attack on welfare state arguments, contained a chapter entitled 'Cradle to grave' that elaborated many of these arguments and suggested that the efforts of well-meaning reformers did not actually help the poor but benefited middle- and upper-income groups.
[7] These arguments are examined in detail in Hall 1986.

economic actors, communities and private citizens. I term this new diagram of government 'advanced liberal'.

Some suggest that the contemporary reconstruction of government is an inevitable response to a transformation of the conditions that made social government and the welfare state possible. It is claimed, for example, that such solidarism had its economic basis in the kinds of collectivization of consciousness, identity and shared fate that were produced by 'Fordist' methods of production. As these have been dismantled in former welfare societies, the industrial working class has shrunk and the political base of support for a social state has disintegrated. And it is suggested that other changes, such as globalization, the information revolution, the end of the Cold War, the rise of ecological risks, the ageing of the population, the rise of individualism and active models of identity and the like, have also contributed to the necessity to rethink social government.[8] But which factors are given salience, where and how? And how are they conceptualized and their consequences calculated? Government, as I have argued throughout this book, is a work of thought. And it was through thought, not through brute reality, that rationalities of social government began to crumble.

Already in the 1970s, both left and right were arguing that the increasing levels of taxation and public expenditure that were required to sustain what Marxists like James O'Connor termed the 'legitimation function' of the state – social, health and welfare services, education and the like – were a threat to the 'accumulation function', because they required penal rates of tax on private profit. What the left termed 'the fiscal crisis of the state' was formulated from the right in terms of the contradiction between the growth of an 'unproductive' welfare sector – which created no wealth – at the expense of the 'productive' private sector in which all national wealth was actually produced.[9]

In the United States, neo-liberals criticized the excessive government that had been developing since the New Deal and through the Great Society and the War on Poverty, with its large bureaucracies, its welfare programmes, its interventionist social engineering and the like. Big government interfered with the market, produced expensive and inefficient bureaucracies, led to excessive taxes and produced a bloated and corrupt political class and political apparatus. Welfare was also perverse in its effects, futile in its ambitions and jeopardized the very accomplishments on which it depended.[10] There were attacks on the arrogance of

[8] For one British example, see Giddens 1998.

[9] O'Connor 1972; Bacon and Eltis 1976.

[10] Perversity, futility and jeopardy are the three theses that together Albert O. Hirschman (1991) terms 'the rhetoric of reaction'.

government overreach and warnings of imminent government overload. There were diatribes against the inefficiencies of planning in picking winners counterposed to the efficiency of markets. There were, as we have seen, claims that Keynesian demand management stimulated inflationary expectations and the debasement of the currency. Both the Marxist left and the neo-liberal right argued that the social state had actually achieved little in the way of maximizing equality and minimizing poverty, insecurity and ill health. Indeed, many on the left agreed with the arguments put forward by neo-liberal critics of welfare, that public expenditure on health, housing and security were largely paid for by the poor and largely benefited the middle classes, that measures intended to decrease poverty had actually increased it and that attempts to advantage the deprived actually locked them further into disadvantage. Left liberal civil libertarians tended to agree with their neo-liberal opponents that the discretionary powers of welfare bureaucrats were incompatible with the rights of their clients, that welfare bureaucracies sought to further their own interests by making repeated demands for funding to extend their own empires, that they actually destroyed other forms of social support such as church, community and family and created not social responsibility and citizenship but dependency and a client mentality.[11] Whatever their other differences, all agreed that the belief in a social state guaranteeing steady and incremental progress for all citizens must be rejected.

Gradually, a new diagram of the relation between government, expertise and subjectivity would take shape. This would not be a 'return' to the liberalism of the nineteenth century, or, finally, government by *laissez faire* It was not a matter of 'freeing' an existing set of market relations from their social shackles, but of organizing all features of one's national policy to enable a market to exist, and to provide what it needs to function. Social government must be restructured in the name of an economic logic, and economic government must create and sustain the central elements of economic well-being such as the enterprise form and competition. As this advanced liberal diagram develops, the relation of the social and the economic is rethought. All aspects of *social* behaviour are now reconceptualized along economic lines – as calculative actions undertaken through the universal human faculty of choice.[12] Choice is to be seen as dependent upon a relative assessment of costs and benefits

[11] These themes were elaborated by liberals and libertarians, by left-wing critics of state-inspired social control of deviance, and by right-wing radicals and neo-liberals: Murray 1984; Friedman and Friedman 1980; Adler and Asquith 1981. See, for an earlier version of some of these criticisms, C. Reich 1964.

[12] This view is given its clearest intellectual articulation in the work of the Chicago school of economists, notably Gary Becker (e.g. Becker 1976).

of 'investment' in the light of environmental contingencies. All manner of social undertakings – health, welfare, education, insurance – can be reconstrued in terms of their contribution to the development of human capital. Their internal organization can be reshaped in enterprise form. And the paths chosen by rational and enterprising individuals can be shaped by acting upon the external contingencies that are factored into calculations. The notion of enterprise thus entails a distinct conception of the human actor – no longer the nineteenth-century economic subject of interests but an entrepreneur of his or her self.[13] The human beings who were to be governed – men and women, rich and poor – were now conceived as individuals who were *active* in making choices in order to further their own interests and those of their family: they were thus potentially active in their own government. The powers of the state thus had to be directed to empowering the entrepreneurial subjects of choice in their quest for self-realization.

We need to avoid thinking in terms of a simple succession in which one style of government supersedes and effaces its predecessor.[14] Rather, we can see a complexification, the opening up of new lines of power and truth, the invention and hybridization of techniques. But nevertheless, the ideal of the 'social state' gives way to that of the 'enabling state'. The state is no longer to be required to answer all society's needs for order, security, health and productivity. Individuals, firms, organizations, localities, schools, parents, hospitals, housing estates must take on themselves – as 'partners' – a portion of the responsibility for their own well-being.

Marketizing economic life

Classical political economy effected a separation of a domain of 'economic' events with their own laws and processes from a 'moral' domain. Economic events were territorialized within a national space, seen as

---

[13] Colin Gordon (1991: 44) puts it thus: 'The idea of one's life as the enterprise of oneself implies that there is a sense in which one remains always continuously employed in (at least) that one enterprise, and that it is a part of the continuous business of living to make adequate provision for the preservation, reproduction and reconstruction of one's own human capital. This is the "care of the self" which government commends as the corrective to collective greed.' For discussion of the idea of enterprise in British politics in the 1980s, see Keat and Abercrombie 1991 and Heelas and Morris 1992; I develop this argument myself in Rose 1992a.

[14] This point has been made strongly by Pat O'Malley: see O'Malley, Weir and Shearing 1997; cf. my own discussion in Rose 1996c.

governed by laws and relations whose scope and limits seemed to map on to the territory of political rule. As they crystallized within nineteenth-century thought, 'economies' were organized within nations, limited by borders, customs and other restrictions on imports and exports, unified through a single supply of money, characterized by a set of functional relations between their components; and these unities were located in an external space within which they could engage in 'foreign trade' with other national economies. The responsibility of the political authorities for the security of a nation, a state and a people, came to be understood in terms of their capacity to nurture natural economic processes to ensure national economic well-being. Further, over the course of the nineteenth century and into the twentieth, the solidity of these national economies was increased by the regular publication of various national indicators of economic performance, and by the gradual tracing out of a plane of 'economic policy', which concerned itself with the proper ways in which the strengths of such an economic system could be enhanced: action on the money supply, on the labour market, together with tariffs and restrictions on imports and so forth, especially as national wealth came to be understood in terms of competition between discrete economies and their struggle to gain access to sources of cheap raw materials, cheap labour or lucrative markets outside their own territorial bounds.

The perception of 'the economy' which underpinned such endeavours is now undergoing a mutation.[15] 'An economy' is no longer so easily imagined as naturally coextensive with the realm of a nation state, with different 'national economies' inhabiting a wider common field in which they traded, competed, exploited one another. Theorists and practitioners alike now construe economic relations as 'globalized', and this new spatialization of the economy is coupled with arguments to the effect that flexible economic relations need to be established in particular localities. There is a dispersal of the apparent unity of 'the national economy' on the one hand to supra-national, international networks of finance, investment, employment and trade, and, on the other, to infra-national, local and regional economic relations. New global institutions of economic governance such as the World Bank, the OECD and the European Union are seen as constraining or even supplanting

---

[15] I have drawn on arguments developed by Barry Hindess (1994, 1998b) who develops this point in much more detail. For one influential US example, see R. Reich 1992. Of course, there are good arguments to show that the discourse of globalization vastly overstates the case: see Hirst and Thompson 1992.

the possibilities of national economic governance. The mobility of finance capitalism is perceived as weakening the possibility of political action shaping, let alone resisting, the pressures of markets. Overlaying this 'dialectic of the global and the local' are other trans-national spatializations of economic relations, such as the argument that there is a 'global economy' of 'world cities', in which Birmingham, Sydney, Baltimore, Budapest compete amongst one another for the economic benefit of company location, conferences, sporting events, tourism.[16]

Irrespective of the accuracy with which these trends are portrayed, the economic problems of government are rethought in terms of a revised image of economic space and the means by which it can be acted upon. It appears that, while national governments still have to manage the affairs of a country, the economic well-being of the nation and of its population can no longer be so easily mapped upon one another. Nor does it appear that they can be governed according to principles of mutual optimization in which a Beveridgean programme of welfare and security will provide the necessary instruments for the Keynesian management of the national economy. Government of the social in the name of the national economy gives way to government of particular zones – regions, towns, sectors, communities – in the interests of economic circuits which flow between regions and across national boundaries. In significant ways, the economic fates of citizens within a national territory are uncoupled from one another.

The social and the economic are now seen as antagonistic: economic government is to be desocialized in the name of maximizing the entrepreneurial comportment of the individual. This is not a politics of economic abstentionism: on the contrary, it is a politics of economic activism. Politics must actively intervene in order to create the organizational and subjective conditions for entrepreneurship. The organizational conditions: de-nationalization of publicly owned enterprises; minimization of rigidities in the labour market; ensuring ample availability of skilled labour; acting against all that which seeks to inhibit the freedom of the market. The subjective conditions: restructure the provision of security to remove as many as possible of the incitements to passivity and dependency; make the residual social support conditional, wherever possible, upon demonstration of the attitudes and aspirations necessary to become an entrepreneur of oneself; incite the will to self-actualize through labour through exhortation on the one hand and sanctions on the other.

[16] Zukin 1991, Lash and Urry 1994.

The first version of these arguments was crudely but accurately paraphrased by Denis Meuret: 'If the economy is doing badly, it is because you are no longer up to taking risks – businessmen afraid to export, the unemployed who sit and wait for the dole instead of starting new businesses, cosseted state employees; we need to get the market to work again, to send schoolchildren on placement to industry so that they learn what their work is all about; above all, we need to stop thinking the State owes us a living.'[17] But this neo-liberal argument was soon joined by a neo-social version: 'Look, we care about all our people and don't want anyone to suffer; we'll help the needy because we are concerned about them, but we must recognize the realities – we live in a global competitive market; only countries with flexible labour markets will be able to succeed. You cannot rely upon the state to provide you with unconditional security against risks and to protect you from the consequences of your own actions. If your business goes to the wall we can teach you the skills to manage a new business better; if you are unemployed it is because you lack the skills to make yourself employable; work is in any event the best way in which you can improve your own situation. It is not that we can't afford benefits but honestly they aren't doing you any good; they are just keeping you in poverty and sapping your self-confidence; have pride in yourself, get yourself trained, learn to present yourself to employers, appreciate the values of work and you and your country will both benefit. Our political responsibility is to provide you with training, combat discrimination, help with child care for lone parents, even to improve your rights and protections as a worker and at work. But your political responsibility as a citizen is to improve your own lot through selling your labour on the market.'

No longer is there a conflict between the self-interest of the economic subject and the patriotic duty of the citizen: it now appears that one can best fulfil one's obligations to one's nation by most effectively pursuing the enhancement of the economic well-being of oneself, one's family, one's firm, business or organization.[18] Freedom, here, is redefined: it is no longer freedom from want, which might be provided by a cosseted life on benefits: it is the capacity for self-realization which can be obtained only through individual activity. Hence an economic politics which enjoins work on all citizens is one which provides mutual benefit for the individual and the collective: it enhances national economic health at the same time as it generates individual freedom.

---

[17] Meuret 1981: 35.
[18] Cf. Procacci 1991.

Fragmenting the social into a multitude of markets

By the 1970s, neo-liberalism took as its target not just an economy but society itself. All kinds of practices – health, security, welfare and more – were to be restructured according to a particular image of the economic – the market. Markets were seen as the ideal mechanisms for the automatic co-ordination of the decisions of a multitude of individual actors in the best interest of all. Hence these styles of governing sought to create simulacra of markets governed by economic or para-economic criteria of judgement in arenas previously governed by bureaucratic and social logics: the new techniques were those of budgets, contracts, performance-related pay, competition, quasi-markets and end-user empowerment.

In British 'personal social services', for example, the so-called purchaser–provider split separated the responsibility for identifying need and working out of a care plan, which was still to be undertaken by a social worker, from the provision of the required care. This was to be purchased in a quasi-market within which different 'providers' compete: state-funded operations, not-for-profit organizations and private profit-making enterprises. Other welfare provision was restructured in the form of quasi-autonomous 'agencies': the child support agency to chase errant fathers for contributions to their children's upkeep, the pensions agency, even a 'prison service agency' to take on a function which Althusserian Marxists had considered essential to the repressive state apparatus. These processes were not to be regulated by intervening directly upon organizational processes or by relying upon professional or bureaucratic expertise. Government was to act indirectly upon the actions of these autonomous entities, by focusing upon results: setting targets, promulgating standards, monitoring outputs, allocating budgets, undertaking audits. Thus agencies are set targets – numbers of errant fathers to catch each week, number of fraudulent claims to detect and so forth – and their payment by government depends upon their meeting these targets. In the case of private prisons, the Prison Service acts as a customer, buying a certain number of daily places from suppliers, with places defined not merely as cells, but in terms of a standard of staffing levels, health care, catering and so forth – a whole 'custodial service package' managed by making the supplier accountable for performance and delivery.[19]

[19] See Tonkiss forthcoming.

Through such techniques, advanced liberal strategies of governing seek to attack intermediate enclaves of power: fiefdoms of local government, enclosures of professional expertise, the rigidities imposed on labour markets by trades unions. This certainly autonomizes agencies and makes them responsive in different ways to those now constituted as their consumers. But it also tries to put in place new techniques of control, strengthening the powers of centres of calculation who set the budgetary regimes, the output targets and the like, reinstating the state in the collective body in a new way and limiting the forms and possibilities of resistance.

In this new dispensation, experts, as knowledge workers, no longer merely manage disciplinary individualization or act as functionaries of the social state. They provide information – for example, risk assessments – that enables these quasi-autonomous entities to steer themselves. They tutor them in the techniques of self-government – as in the burgeoning of private consultancies and training operations. They provide the information that will allow the state, the consumer or other parties – such as regulatory agencies – to assess the performance of these quasi-autonomous agencies, and hence to govern them – evaluation, audit. They identify those individuals unable to self-govern, and either attempt to re-attach them – training, welfare-to-work – or to manage their exclusion – incarceration, residualization of welfare. In short, 'free individuals', 'partners' and stakeholders are enwrapped in webs of knowledge and circuits of communication through which their actions can be shaped and steered and by means of which they can steer themselves.

Experts and bureaucrats

It is worth saying a little more about some of these advanced liberal strategies for governing the powers of experts and bureaucrats. For many centuries, one recurrent way in which the authority of authority was authorized was through the ethical formation of those who would wield such authority. Reciprocally, where the authority of authority was problematized, the answer was thought to lie in the reshaping of the ethical comportment of those who are in authority. In one formula, those who would wield power over others were required to demonstrate that they could first wield it over themselves in the form of self-regulation and self-mastery. Thus Peter Brown has examined the self-formation of privileged males in Rome in the second century AD and has shown that, amongst other practices upon the self, they were obliged to free themselves of any attributes that might imply or embody a 'womanish' lack of self-restraint.[20] Gerhard Oestreich has described the rise of neo-stoic ethics in Europe in the sixteenth and seventeenth centuries, stressing the cultivation of the inner qualities of self-mastery and self-control amongst those who would hold high office.[21] With the rise of bureaucracy, as Max Weber argued, a novel ethos for the bureaucrat took shape. This was a certain ethic of office entailing delimitation of spheres of jurisdiction, impartiality, subordination to rules, hierarchy, documentation, decisions 'without regard for persons' and so forth.[22] Along the same lines, Ian Hunter has argued that the governmental 'bureaux' that emerged in the context of state-building, especially where the legitimacy of the expansion of the powers and capacities of the state was subject to dispute, entailed a particular 'technology of existence': 'strict adherence to procedure, dedication to a special expertise, a "service" mentality, and the subordination of the "person" to the "office" are positive abilities only acquired through the mastery of specific ethical practices'.[23] Bureaucracy, that is to say, entailed a particular way in which authority and morality were fused in a particular vocation, an ethical mode of life conduct.

As we have seen, in chapter 2, the problem of 'government at a distance' in the nineteenth century led to an intense problematization of the ethical comportment of those who would govern, and the attempt to inculcate these ethical technologies through systems of training. Nonetheless, it is undoubtedly true that the practical ethic of the bureaucrat, the government agent and the civil servant often fell short of the ideals sketched out by Weber and Hunter. For the whole of this period, bureaucracy has been ridiculed, parodied and subject to criticism on the grounds of its pedantry, obsession with rule-following, dedication to the preservation of itself rather than to its practical outcomes for those who are dependent on it, its denial of democracy and much more. These criticisms were intensified because of the ways in which, over the course of the twentieth century, governmental bureaucracies and departments managed to enclose themselves, run themselves according to their own customs and logics, and make themselves resistant to being governed by others, not least to direction from political centres.[24] The machinery of social government in Britain, Europe and

---

[20] P. Brown 1989: 11.
[21] Oestreich 1982.
[22] Weber 1978: 956–1005.
[23] Hunter 1993: 262.
[24] This is discussed, using the specific example of the British National Health Service, in Rose and Miller 1992. I have drawn directly on this paper in the discussion that follows.

the United States was affected by these difficulties, which were made even more complex by the linking together of departments of central government, often at war with one another, and a whole variety of more or less peripheral and *ad hoc* agencies, associated in complex, fragile and mobile relationships and dependencies, and involving struggles, alliances and competitions between different groups for resources, recognition and power.[25] Those who staffed these assemblages of government claimed their rights to make decisions not on the basis of an externally imposed plan, or according to criteria reaching them from elsewhere, but according to professional codes, training, habit, moral allegiances and institutional demands. How were these bureaucrats and civil servants to be governed?

The nineteenth-century governmentalization of the state was accompanied not only by the growth in bureaucratic administration; as we have seen, it was also accompanied by the incorporation of experts into the machinery of political government. The devices of 'the welfare state' opened a multitude of new locales for the operation of expert judgements about investment in this or that ailing or up-and-coming branch of the economy, about interest rates and regional policy, about housing regimes and planning, about the best interests of the child and much more. The powers of experts were based on beliefs about the competence provided by knowledge and training, and also about the ethical values imparted by professional identity. Their deliberations were undertaken in obscurity in thousands of locales – bureaux of various types, benefit, social security and unemployment offices, case conferences and tribunals – and involved esoteric knowledges, references to research findings, professional rules and conventions, specialist interpretations of complex data. Experts were vital relays for social government, linking political objectives and personal conduct. But they too had enormous capacities to 'enclose' themselves and their judgements, to render themselves almost ungovernable. How were these experts to be governed?

Beyond planning

By the 1960s in Britain, the technological questions of how the machinery of government could itself be governed were already being sharply posed. The notion that efficiency and rationality could be achieved through mechanisms of planning crossed the boundaries of economic and social policy and the bounds of political party. The Plowden Report

[25] For Britain, for example, see Bulpitt 1986: 24.

of 1961 called for the use of public expenditure control as a means to stable long-term planning, with greater emphasis on the 'wider application of mathematical techniques, statistics and accountancy'.[26] A range of new techniques were invented by which civil servants and administrators might calculate and hence control public expenditure: the Public Expenditure Survey Committee (PESC), the use of cost-benefit analysis, of PPB (Planning, Programming, Budgeting) and PAR (Programme Analysis Review). Official documents like the Fulton Report envisaged these as gaining their hold upon the machinery of government through their inculcation into a professional corps of administrative experts, specialists both in techniques of management and those of numeracy.[27] Management, mathematics and monetarization were to render governable a bureaucratic complex in danger of running out of control.

But for neo-liberal strategies, these solutions were in danger of re-inventing the very systems of professional power that had produced the problems in the first place. The solution was not to seek to govern bureaucracy better, but to transform the very organization of the governmental bureaucracy itself and, in doing so, transform its ethos from one of bureaucracy to one of business, from one of planning to one of competition, from one dictated by the logics of the system to one dictated by the logics of the market and the demands of customers. These neo-liberal arguments were, however, just one factor in an international trend which became known as 'the new public management'.[28] In the new public management, the focus is upon accountability, explicit standards and measures of performance, emphasis on outputs, not inputs, with rewards linked to performance, desegregation of functions into corporatized units operating with their own budgets and trading with one another, contracts and competition, and insistence on parsimony maintained by budget discipline. This required a shift from an ethic of public service to one of private management. As Hood points out, the new public management, in various guises and to various degrees, was not an exclusive dogma of the neo-liberals: 'From Denmark to New Zealand, from education to health care, from central to local government and quangos, from rich North to poor South similar remedies were prescribed.'[29]

---

[26] Chancellor of the Exchequer 1961, quoted in Klein 1983: 65.
[27] Committee on the Civil Service 1968.
[28] I have drawn upon Christopher Hood's work (especially Hood 1991) in my discussion here. See also the useful discussion in du Gay 1996.
[29] Ibid.: 8.

A series of experiments in governing were inaugurated that would radically reshape the assemblages of the social state in the interests of rendering them governable. Thus, in the 1980s in Britain, the 'Next Steps' programme of civil service reform replaced the Financial Management Initiative which had sought to govern through installing a hierarchical managerial structure, delegating management responsibilities within it, establishing clear lines of responsibility and inculcating a concern with the achievement of 'value for money' and the control of costs and subjecting the whole process to repeated evaluation.[30] In the Next Steps, monetarization and managerialism were to be replaced with privatization and marketization. The civil service would be reduced to a core, its functions would be privatized or hived off, the new agencies would compete in a market which would impose its own disciplines upon them. No longer would bureaucracy authorize itself through its ethical claims: it would focus on the delivery of services, and be judged according to its capacity to produce results. It would be governed indirectly, through contracts, targets, performance measures monitoring and audit. In the process, the subjectivity of the civil servant, the administrator and the bureaucrat would itself be transformed. They would be rendered accountable: but to whom?

Accounting and accountability

The new forms of accountability that were to breach the enclosures of expertise were strikingly similar to those which were used in the reconfiguration of the state apparatus.[31] In the new regimes for managing universities, hospitals, social services and the like, and whether in the residual public sector, in quangos, quasi-private organizations or private providers of services, the fulcrum of governability was financial. Modes of financial calculation were imposed upon areas which were previously governed according to bureaucratic, professional or other norms. In this way, they would remake the relation between the political and the non-political in a new way, by translating 'public' objectives such as value-for-money, efficiency, transparency, competitiveness, responsiveness to the customer into 'private' norms, judgements, calculations and aspirations. The university department, the hospital speciality, the 'not-for-profit' organization delivering home care to the elderly were each

---

[30] On these changes, see ibid. and Zifcak 1994.
[31] Peter Miller provides a series of extended analyses of many of these aspects of accountability, which I have glossed here: see for example Miller 1990, 1992 and 1994.

obliged to organize their activities as if they were little businesses. Their activities were recoded in a new vocabulary of incomes, allocations, costs, savings, even profits. A new financial rationality was thus thrown over the organizational life of these institutions and those who worked within them. Accounting was to prove a powerful technology for acting at a distance upon the actions of others.

This overlaying of financial rationality did not leave the organizations as they found them. Organizations had to be rendered accountable, and the terms of that accountability were not professional but those of accounting. They were reorganized, transformed into aggregations of accountable spaces, reshaped into cost-centres and the like, rendered calculable in financial terms. As Peter Miller points out, these abstract spaces were made material through physical redesign of organizational space, inscribed in new budget headings and divisions, instantiated in the structure of communication networks, built into organization flow diagrams, used to configure managerial responsibilities and so forth. The construction of calculable spaces 'makes it possible for the organization to be represented as a series of financial flows, enables the evaluation of these spaces according to a financial rationale and allows particular forms of action upon the component parts of the organization'.[32] Each of these new calculable spaces required its inhabitants to calculate for themselves, to translate their activities into financial terms, to seek to maximize productivity for a given income, to cut out waste, to restructure activities that were not cost-effective, to choose between priorities in terms of their relative costs and benefits, to become more or less like a financial manager of their own professional activities. In this way, the technologies of accounting link political aspirations with individual actions and judgements 'by transforming . . . organizations into a complex of incessant calculations'.[33] The allocation of budgetary responsibilities to professionals requires them to calculate their actions not in the esoteric languages of their own expertise but by translating them into costs and benefits that can be given an accounting value. Accounting discourse gained a wholly new power in the management of expertise. In the process, experts and bureaucrats are subjectified in two ways: as *objects* of calculations and as *relays* for calculations: 'As object, calculations from a central point can be made of workers, managers, doctors, or teachers in attempts to assess their performance in relation to a specified standard. And as relay . . . individuals can be encouraged or required to evaluate their own activities and those of others through the calculative routines of accountancy . . . Calculative technologies

[32] Miller 1992: 76.
[33] Ibid.: 67.

make it possible to render visible both the near and the distant activities of individuals, to calculate the extent to which they depart from a norm of performance, and to accumulate such calculations in computers and files and compare them.'[34]

In the context of the raft of other elements of 'the new public management', this transformed the governability of professional activity. Whilst apparently devolving more decisional power to those actually involved in devising and delivering services in local sites, it renders those activities governable in new ways. The enclosures within which expertise could insulate themselves from 'political interference' in the name of 'professional autonomy' are punctured. New grids of visibility have been established, which render activities visible in terms of the relative cost of the same operation at different hospitals, the relative cost of street cleaning in different cities, the relative costs of producing one economics undergraduate at different universities. Each such decision is no longer unique: they have been made inscribable and comparable in numerical form, in figures that can be transported to centres of calculation, aggregated, related, plotted over time, presented in league tables, judged against national averages, and utilized for future decisions about the allocation of contracts and budgets. Arbitrary power appears to have been tamed and liberalized through the neutrality and objectivity of accounting. But if experts have, in the process, been rendered governable, this has changed expertise itself: financial vocabularies, grammars and judgements have infiltrated the very terms in which experts calculate and enact their expertise. And the apparent transformation of the subjective into the objective, the esoteric into the factual masks somewhat the weak knowledge base – the uncertain status, inescapably partial vision, lack of evidential support, history of failure, vulnerability to changes in fashion and convention and much more – of the new forms of expertise granted the power to objectify: that of accountants and managers.

The audit explosion

Audit has a key role within this complex of methods for the government of bureaucratic and professional expertise.[35] Indeed Michael Power has suggested that it would only be a slight overstatement to deem ours an

---

[34] Ibid.: 67–8.

[35] In this section I have drawn heavily on the lucid account developed by Michael Power, in particular on a paper presented to the London *History of the Present* Research Network in 1992, and later developed and published as Power 1994a and 1994b, and in a much extended form as Power 1997.

'audit society': a society organized to observe itself through the mechanisms of audit in the service of programmes for control. Audit – academic audit, medical audit, environmental audit, financial audit: the varieties proliferate – utilizes a rather mundane set of routines that purport to enable judgements to be made about the activities of professionals, managers, businesspeople, politicians and many others. Whilst audits of various sorts have been around for many years, within the new rationalities of advanced liberal government, audit, as Power points out, is transformed from a relatively marginal instrument in the battery of control technologies to a central mechanism for governing at a distance. In particular, its power derives from its capacity to act upon systems of control themselves as, for example, in the ways in which financial audits examine the control systems that organizations use to govern transactions, rather than the transactions themselves. Audit, as Power puts it, is the control of control.

As with the practices of accountability discussed above, government by audit transforms that which is to be governed. Rendering something auditable shapes the process that is to be audited: setting objectives, proliferating standardized forms, generating new systems of record-keeping and accounting, governing paper trails. The logics and technical requirements of audit displace the internal logics of expertise. The emphasis on defined and measurable goals and targets in the work that professionals do with their clients is an element within a much wider reconfiguration of methods for the government of specialist activities. As Power points our, these methods do not so much hold persons to account as create patterns of accountability. They create accountability to one set of norms – transparency, observability, standardization and the like – at the expense of accountability to other sets of norms. Indeed, accountability in itself becomes a criterion of organizational health. These arrangements retain the formal independence of the professional whilst utilizing new techniques to render their decisions visible and amenable to evaluation. They are entirely consonant with one key vector of the strategic diagram of advanced liberal styles of governing: autonomization plus responsibilization.

Audits of various sorts have come to replace the trust that social government invested in professional wisdom and the decisions and actions of specialists. In a whole variety of practices – educational, medical, economic, organizational – audits hold out the promise – however specious – of new distantiated forms of control between political centres of decision and the autonomized loci – schools, hospitals, firms – which now have the responsibility for the government of health, wealth and happiness. Power suggests that audit is a technology of mistrust, designed in the hope of restoring trust in organizational and professional competence. Yet it appears that the very technologies of mistrust perpetually fail to immunize the assemblages they govern from doubt. Mistrust is generated not only by the organizations and individuals pronounced unhealthy by audit, but also by those pronounced healthy that nonetheless fail. Hence the proliferation of audit serves only to amplify and multiply the points at which doubt and suspicion can be generated. Whilst audits have become key fidelity techniques in new strategies of government, they generate an expanding spiral of distrust of professional competence, and one that feeds the demand for more radical measures which will hold experts to account.

The shadow of the law

The United States has long utilized legal powers to regulate professional judgement and the fear of the law to pre-emptively shape their decisions and actions. The courts have created all sorts of duties for professionals: for example, the duty for a mental health professional to protect third parties against patients' violence was created in the California Supreme Court in 1976, and obliged those working in this area to reshape their calculations – and the documentation of these calculations – so that they were in a position to demonstrate to a court of law that they had taken into account the risk that their clients might harm members of the 'general public' or family members in recommendations as to confinement or release. In Britain these mechanisms have, historically, been less favoured: the courts themselves have tended to defer to professional expertise and political decision making, except in cases of sexual or financial misconduct. But we are now seeing a renewed emphasis upon the potential of a variety of legal and quasi-legal mechanisms to meet political obligations to address 'problems' – from discharged psychiatric patients to insider dealing – whilst refusing an extension of the politico-administrative machinery of the state.

The mechanisms of legal regulation are heterogeneous and fragmented. Politicians, professionals and consumer groups organize around the production of codes of professional conduct which specify various rights for users and clients. Struggles over the regulation of expertise occur not only in the courts, but also in campus sexual harassment offices, human rights committees and commissions, review bodies for appealing welfare decisions and in many new and diverse forums. Most of these legal procedures are not in themselves new. Nonetheless, in the current regime of distrust, they render the actions and judgements of professionals governable in new ways – and change the terms in which they are construed, prioritized, justified, documented and enacted.

I am thinking here partly of the use of such statutorily specified and legally enforceable criteria as those governing minimum service standards and contracts specifying performance targets and outputs – numbers of patients to be treated, length of time a case must wait until dealt with, obligations for the relations between case managers, their clients and the providing organization and so forth. But I am also thinking of the ways in which professional activity in a whole range of fields has become structured by the obligation to documentation – the maintenance of information systems, registers, notes of all meetings, written statements of grounds for decision and the like – in the hope of making judgements defensible in an imagined future court case. Professionals must now act in such a way that that action might be, at some future moment, defensible in terms of the criteria and evidentiary requirements of another profession and body of expert knowledge, that of the law. The spread of this 'litigious mentality' ensures that 'the shadow of the law' itself acts as a means of managing professional activity. Professionals begin to add the possibility of legal action to the factors entering their judgements, decisions and recommendations. The impetus to defensibility shapes the actions of professionals, responsibilizing them in new ways, in new practices and according to new criteria.

Employees into entrepreneurs

For about 100 years, the labour contract and wage were central mechanisms for linking labour of individual into productive apparatus. Full-time, lifelong employment was the regulative ideal, although it was far from the universal form of work. This ideal, with its way of dividing employment and unemployment, of full-time work and the full-time wage, is currently under question. It is not simply that, across Europe, employment has become a precarious activity for many, and lack of employment a long-term reality for many more.[36] Nor is it only that an increasing number of people are employed part-time, and there has been a return to casualization, short-term contracts, zero-hours contacts, the growth of the 'black economy' and much more. Perhaps more significant is the fact that such economic insecurity is now given a positive value in economic strategies from a whole variety of political perspec-

---

[36] See Castel 1995. See, for one example, the way in which the OECD posed the problem of the labour market politics required for the 1990s (OECD 1990).

tives. Flexibilization is the name for this arrangement of labour when it becomes an explicit political strategy of economic government. It has a 'macro-economic' moment, consisting of contests over how much it is possible to minimize or dismantle everything that can be construed as 'rigidities' in the labour market. And it has a 'micro-economic' moment, in terms of struggles over the appropriate tactics to increase the flexibility of relations between the individual and the workplace.

The disciplinary space of the factory and the discipline of the wage and the labour relation were key junction points between the economic, the social and the subjective. Within this nexus, the labour of individual subjects was linked into economic flows, conduct was regularized, access was provided to all kinds of social benefits as a *quid pro quo* for regularity of employment. Labour, through the wage contract, regularized, individualized and disciplined the labourer. And labour linked the 'family machine' into the 'productive machine' by means of the male family wage and all that went with it. Hence a whole series of strategies were adopted, over the last fifty years of the nineteenth century and into the first half of the twentieth, to instil the norm of the working day and the working week, to effect decasualization of work, to draw a clear line between employment, with all the values and benefits that it commanded, and unemployment. Unemployment was to become the site of a whole new range of policies at the junction of the economic and the social domains.[37] These would seek to maintain the financial situation of those genuinely seeking work and to re-attach them to the productive machine through the labour exchange. And, simultaneously, these devices would act as classificatory machines, identifying those who were able to work but not willing to work, and opening them up for reformation or punishment. Regulations on the contract, on hours of employment, on conditions of work, on dismissal, on accidents at work and so forth made the labour relation a primary site of social governance: regulation operated through this 'assemblage' of labour, in the name of a joint optimization of the economic and the social. And, of course, wage discipline makes labour social in another sense, providing the conditions for struggles and resistances of all sorts.

The very image of work as regular, continuous and durable was forged in these processes. It may be the case that precarious employment is now on the rise. But, equally significant, such employment is no longer judged against the same the *ideal* of permanent, lifelong work. One great objective of techniques for the regulation of labour from the start of this century was to establish a clear division – spatial, moral, economic –

---

[37] On the history of the idea of unemployment, see Harris 1972.

between employment and unemployment. This division of work and life has not only become blurred at the level of reality, it has also become permeable at the level of images and strategies. The segmentation of time and space introduced by industrial capitalism with the disciplines of the clock and the factory is giving way to a more dispersed, but more intensive, inscription of the obligation to work into the soul of the citizen, not a reduction of the principle or ethic of work but, in many ways, its intensification. At the 'positive' pole of this shift lie the dreams of the integration of life and work made possible by new technologies of communication. At the 'negative' pole, which is undoubtedly more significant, the working relationship has become saturated with insecurity. Whilst the workplace once functioned as a secure site for inclusion, in the form of the lifelong career, the permanent job and so forth, the space of work can no longer be regarded as an automatic mechanism for the promotion of security. Rather, work itself has become a vulnerable zone, one in which continued employment must ceaselessly be earned, the employment of each individual constantly assessed in the light of evaluations, appraisals, achievement of targets and so forth – under the constant threat of 'down-sizing', efficiency gains and the like. Perpetual insecurity becomes the normal form of labour.

As the twentieth century draws to a close, politicians and experts of most political persuasions agree that lifelong 'social' labour cannot be re-activated as the primary mechanism for the social integration of individuals and families, and hence also that the promise of lifelong social support for those outside the labour market cannot be sustained. The political and economic problem, then, is understood in terms of the need to devise strategies that will retain the apparent economic benefits of flexibilization whilst minimizing their costs to individuals, families and communities and guard against the potential threats to public order without recreating the obligation for the state to support all those outside the labour market in perpetuity. These economic parameters shape the space within which residual 'social' policy will have to operate.

A new prudentialism

Genealogies of social insurance have traced the ways in which, over the course of the twentieth century, *security* against risk was socialized. I have examined some aspects of this in previous chapters. In the late nineteenth century, the respectable working man was urged to be *prudent*, an obligation which required him to take a range of active steps to secure himself, his family and his dependants against future misfortune: joining insurance schemes provided by trade associations or friendly societies; later, contracting into private insurance schemes run for profit.[38] At the turn of the century, in most European countries, these voluntary relations of prudence – mutual or commercial – were further transformed with the implementation of national schemes of compulsory social insurance.[39] As European societies come to secure their security through a generalized technology of risk, the individual becomes a social citizen, a member of a collectivity, pooling his or her own risks across a lifetime.

Of course, the injunction to personal prudence on the behalf of oneself and one's dependants did not disappear over the twentieth century. But nonetheless, today, a strategic shift is occurring in the politics of security. Within the economic rationalities of advanced liberalism, social insurance is no longer seen as a socializing and responsibilizing principle of solidarity: not only does it not provide adequate security; not only does it represent a drain on individual incomes and on national finances; it also stifles responsibility, inhibits risk taking, induces dependency. Hence it actually exacerbates, rather than reducing, the division between the included and the excluded: it is not an agent of cohesion but of divisiveness on the one hand and passivity, indolence and idleness on the other. In this context, it appears, those who can provide for their own security will choose to do so by the application of their own funds to private health insurance, private pension schemes, investment and the like. Those who cannot will be subject to all the psychologically deleterious and financially inadequate consequences of the benefit culture. Hence all individuals, not just the well-off, would benefit if they took *upon themselves* the responsibility for their own security and that of their families. Individuals and families should insure against the costs of ill health through private medical insurance, should make provisions for their future through private pensions, should take an active role in securing themselves against all that could possibly threaten the security of their chosen style of life. Pat O'Malley has termed this 'the new prudentialism'.[40] It uses the technologies of consumption – advertising, market research, niche marketing and so forth – to exacerbate anxieties about one's own future and that of one's loved ones, to encourage each of us to invest in order to master our fate by purchasing insurance designed especially for us and our individual situation. There is obviously an industry of risk here, seeking out and creating markets for products in the interests of its own profit. But this is linked to a politics of risk, as

[38] Defert 1991, O'Malley 1995.
[39] Ewald 1991.
[40] O'Malley 1992. See also O'Malley 1996b.

politicians warn about the future of social pension and insurance schemes, and exhort responsible individuals to take primary responsibility for the management of their own security and that of their families by disposing of their current income in the interests of their own future contentment. The person who is to be made prudent is no longer mutualized but autonomized. Thrift is recast as investment in a future lifestyle of freedom. In this new configuration, taxation for the purposes of welfare becomes the minimum price that respectable individuals and communities are prepared to pay for insuring themselves against the riskiness now seen to be concentrated within certain problematic sectors.

Insurantial expertise is no longer a matter of actuarial wisdom, the assurance of stability and probity, and the personal relation with the contributions collector, but works through amplifying the very anxieties against which security is to protect, and promoting the dreams of tranquillity and a golden future which insurance can provide, through the use of all the techniques of advertising and marketing. Further, insurance agents now offer themselves as versatile advisers in the techniques of risk reduction and risk management. The ethics of lifestyle maximization, coupled with a logic in which someone must be held to blame for any event that threatens an individual's 'quality of life', generate a relentless imperative of risk management not simply in relation to contracting for insurance, but also through daily lifestyle management, choices of where to live and shop, what to eat and drink, stress management, exercise and so forth. These new logics of risk management fragment the social space of welfare into a multitude of diverse pockets, zones, folds of riskiness each comprising a linking of specific current activities and conducts and general probabilities of their consequences. This inaugurates a virtually endless spiral of amplification of risk – as risk is managed in certain zones and forms of conduct (e.g. shopping in malls scanned by security cameras; foetal monitoring; low-fat diets to combat the risk of heart disease), the perceived riskiness of other unprotected zones is exacerbated (high streets; unsupervised pregnancies; the uneducated dietary habits of children and the poor). The culture of risk is characterized by uncertainly, plurality and anxiety, and is thus continually open to the construction of new problems and the marketing of new solutions.

From disciplinary pedagogy to perpetual training

Education is no longer confined to 'schooling', with its specialized institutional sites and discrete biographical locus. The disciplinary individualization and normalization of the school sought to install, once and for all, the capacities and competencies for social citizenship. But a new set of educational obligations are emerging that are not confined in space and time in the same ways. The new citizen is required to engage in a ceaseless work of training and retraining, skilling and reskilling, enhancement of credentials and preparation for a life of incessant job seeking: life is to become a continuous economic capitalization of the self.

The idea of lifelong learning goes back to the 1970s.[41] In its earliest formulations, its leitmotif was 'change'. On the one hand it was formulated in terms of the need to make every individual capable of adapting to the pace of technological change, and hence to be able to avoid the individual and social consequences of being left behind by the tide of change, unable to find work, unable to cope psychologically, condemned to an existence of premature redundancy or retirement. Here we see one set of pressures for a transformation in the attitude of individuals, employers, educators and politicians: there must be opportunities for 'a continuous process of retraining, from the cradle to the grave, designed to provide the individual with a feeling of autonomy in relation to work, and at work . . . [This might also help alter] the paradoxical situation where society is obliged to support a still able-bodied worker for whom active life has become unbearable.'[42] On the other hand, there were pressures from employers' organizations, and from international economic organizations such as the OECD, concerned about the industrial and economic consequences of the rapid changes in technology for the labour force, and the need to produce workers who were able to accept the need for permanent reskilling and continual change in their working skills. Employers, unions and educators invested hope in the development of such policies of lifelong learning; industrial psychologists, consultants, training organizations, enthusiasts for universities of the third age and a whole host of psychological entrepreneurs invented, developed and marketed the technical and organizational forms that it would take; employers enjoined, and sometimes compelled, participation by their workforce.

These developments in the 1960s and 1970s were just one element in a whole slate of programmes and proposals in Europe and North

---

[41] I draw here, once more, on the work of Jacques Donzelot (1981). Donzelot is writing specifically about France and the response of the OECD, but the situation – both problematization and solution – was much the same in other national economies.

[42] Ibid.: 22.

America, including work reform and the humanization of work, that saw
the transformation of the subjectivity of the worker as necessary in order
to cope with the new challenges faced by the 'turbulent environment'
of labour in the new economic conditions of technological change, competition from the newly emerging dynamic economies of the Third
World and Japan and so forth. These combined with 'socio-political
demands that production take as central the values of adaptability, innovation, flexibility, excellence, sensitivity to consumer pressures and the
demands of the market'.[43] Whilst the new demands placed upon the
labourer in the closing decades of the twentieth century continued these
concerns with the reconstruction of the subjectivity of actual and potential workers, they were articulated in novel ways. In particular, they were
organized around a different set of questions concerning the government
of unemployment. Unemployment now was conceptualized as a
phenomenon to be governed – both at the macro-economic level and at
the level of the individual who is without work – through acting on
the conduct of the unemployed person, obliging him or her to improve
'employability' by acquiring skills, both substantive skills and skills in
acquiring work, and obliging the individual to engage in a constant and
active search for employment. The general problem of unemployment
is reconceived in terms of the respective competitiveness of different
labour forces. National and international competitiveness was recoded,
at least in part, in terms of the psychological, dispositional and aspir-
ational capacities of those that make up the labour force. Thus each
individual is solicited as a potential ally of economic success. Personal
employment and macro-economic health is to be ensured by encouraging individuals to 'capitalize' themselves, to invest in the management,
presentation, promotion and enhancement of their own economic capital as a capacity of their selves and as a lifelong project.

These understandings are not merely abstract or programmatic; they
are embodied in the so-called active unemployment policies emerging
in Europe, Australia and the United States. These stress 'active job
search', maintaining 'job readiness' and avoiding the 'risk of dependence'; experts happily promote a whole range of little pedagogic techniques, training schemes, skills packs and so forth to seek to implant
these aspirations in the unemployed self.[44] In the UK, the focus of argu-

---

[43] Miller and Rose 1995b: 449. Peter Miller and I discuss these programmes in
   more detail in this paper, where we argue that work has been, and remains,
   a crucial site for the problematization and reconstruction of identity in industrial democracies.
[44] Mitchell Dean has provided an illuminating discussion of these programmes:
   Dean 1995. See also Walters 1996 and 1997.

ment around unemployment came to be directed towards a question of 'skills' which was linked to conception of employment policy through the idea of an 'active labour market'. Activity now became an obligation of the labouring individual and an objective of policy. In the policies of the Conservative regime that held political office in Britain from 1979 to 1997, the final manifestation of this was the Jobseeker's Allowance. Unemployment benefits encouraged dependency, did nothing to encourage unemployed persons to change their conditions and actually served to reinforce the apparently ridiculous situation where the state actually supported people in their location outside the civilizing and motivating forces of work. The Jobseeker's Allowance which would replace it would 'improve . . . the operation of the labour market by helping people in their search for work, while ensuring that they understand and fulfil the conditions for receipt of benefit . . . All unemployed people will sign an individually tailored Agreement as a basic condition for receipt of benefit. This will help the jobseeker and the Employment Service to identify together the appropriate steps to get the jobseeker back to work and will provide the basis for further guidance and reviews of the jobseeker's efforts . . . the test of "actively seeking work" . . . will be broadened so as to encourage unemployed people to explore other ways of making their job search more effective (for example, preparing CVs).'[45]

These emphases do not merely come from the political parties of the right. From the social democratic left, too, work was now seen as the principle mode of inclusion, and absence from the labour market the most potent source of exclusion. In Britain, the Commission on Social Justice established by the Labour Party argued that 'paid work remains the best pathway out of poverty, as well as the only way in which most people can hope to achieve a decent standard of living'.[46] The Commission of the European Community asserted that 'income maintenance can no longer be the only objective of social policy . . . social policies now have to take on the more ambitious objective of helping people to find a place in society. The main route, but not the only one, is paid work.'[47] Thus a pamphlet issued by a British movement against the Jobseeker's Allowance, which called itself 'the Job Shirkers Alliance', was headed with the infamous words on the entrance to the concentration camp at Auschwitz 'Arbeit macht frei.'

[45] UK Department of Trade and Industry 1995.
[46] Commission on Social Justice 1994: 151.
[47] Commission of the European Community 1993; see the discussion in Walters 1997.

Training here became the major technology of re-attachment of the unemployed individual to the inclusory lines of control immanent in the activity of paid labour, and the labour market became the principle machine for inclusion. Labour becomes a switch point of the economic and the psychological: unemployment must become as much like work as possible if it too is to connect the excluded individual with the modalities of control which have come to be termed 'freedom' and 'choice'. Indeed it would not be too much to claim that, in the countries of the European Union, 'social' policy has come to be understood as policy around work: the regulation of working hours and working conditions, the rights and responsibilities of workers and employers, the creation of work and the promotion of policies of inclusion through work. Assistance, in the form of unemployment benefit, was perhaps the central 'right' of welfare states; now it is no longer a right of citizenship but an allowance which must be earned by the performance of certain duties, and labour alone is to be the means by which the poor can acquire the status of citizen – a status which is itself now increasingly a matter of consumption rights.

Making citizens consumers

In the styles of government that I have termed 'advanced liberal', the conception of the citizen is transformed. It became commonplace in the 1980s to hear talk of the 'active citizen' who was to be counterposed to the 'passive citizen' or the social state – the citizen of rights and duties, of obligations and expectations. The active citizen was not, in this version, the republican citizen, who would become so significant within later discourses of communitarianism, which I discuss in chapter 5. It was not a question here of active involvement in public affairs, in local democracy, in the conduct of politics. Rather, the model of the active citizen was one who was an entrepreneur of him- or herself. This was not simply a re-activation of values of self-reliance, autonomy and independence as the underpinning of self-respect, self-esteem, self-worth and self-advancement. It is rather that the individual was to conduct his or her life, and that of his or her family, as a kind of enterprise, seeking to enhance and capitalize on existence itself through calculated acts and investments. These shifts were located within a cultural field that I have outlined in chapter 2. This is marked by the proliferation of new apparatuses, devices and mechanisms for the government of conduct and forms of life: new forms of consumption, a public habitat of images, the regulation of habits, dispositions, styles of existence in the name of identity and lifestyle. In this new field, the citizen is to become a consumer, and his or her activity is to be understood in terms of the activation of the rights of the consumer in the marketplace.

Consider, for example, the transformations in the relations of experts and clients. Whilst social rule was characterized by discretionary authority, advanced liberal rule is characterized by the politics of the contract, in which the subject of the contract is not a patient or a case but a customer or consumer. Parents (or children – the issue is contested) are consumers of education, patients are consumers of health care, residents of old people's homes are in a contractual relation with those who provide care, and even those occupying demeaned categories (discharged prisoners shifted to halfway houses, drug users in rehabilitation centres) have their expectations, rights and responsibilities contractualized. Of course, these contracts are of many different types. Few are like the contracts between buyer and seller in the market. But, in their different ways, they shift the power relations inscribed in relations of expertise. This is especially so when they are accompanied by new methods of regulation and control such as audit and evaluation. Some contractualization enhances the possibilities of political control over activities previously insulated by claims to professional autonomy and the necessity of trust – as, for example, when contracts specify the delivery of a certain quantum of medical care or a certain volume of completed cases. Some contractual forms provide new opportunities for users and clients of professionals who are able to contest 'patrimonial powers' by insisting on specified services and agreed standards, and having new sanctions if they are not provided.[48] Some, like the contracts used for clients in psychiatric wards and other residential establishments, shift responsibilities to users for their own condition and for the personal comportment and behaviour necessary to receive care, and thus bind them into professional powers and expert norms in new ways. The politics of the contract becomes central to contests between political strategies concerning the 'reform of welfare', and to strategies of user demand and user resistance to professional powers.

Active citizenship?

If neo-liberal political rationalities began the process of challenging and transforming social government in the late twentieth century, it was in part because of their consonance with the new regime of the self that I outlined in chapter 2. For it was, initially, the right, and not the left, that managed to render this regime technical, that is to say, to find ways

---

[48] Yeatman 1995.

to govern in accordance with the new ethics of the subject. But as the twentieth century draws to a close, political reason from all quarters no longer phrases itself in the language of obligation, duty and social citizenship. It now justifies itself by arguing over the political forms that are adequate to the existence of persons as essentially, naturally, creatures striving to actualize themselves in their everyday, secular lives. Within such rationalities, it appears that individuals can best fulfil their political obligations in relation to the wealth, health and happiness of the nation not when they are bound into relations of dependency and obligation, but when they seek to *fulfil themselves* as free individuals. Individuals are now to be linked into a society through acts of socially sanctioned consumption and responsible choice, through the shaping of a lifestyle according to grammars of living that are widely disseminated, yet do not depend upon political calculations and strategies for their rationales or their techniques.

Advanced liberal forms of government thus rest, in new ways, upon the activation of the powers of the citizen. Citizenship is no longer primarily realized in a relation with the state, or in a single 'public sphere', but in a variety of private, corporate and quasi-public practices from working to shopping. The citizen as consumer is to become an active agent in the regulation of professional expertise; the citizen as prudent is to become an active agent in the provision of security; the citizen as employee is to become an active agent in the regeneration of industry and much more. Even in politics, through new techniques such as focus groups and attitude research, the citizen is to enact his or her democratic obligations as a form of consumption. But this citizen was not to remain the isolated and selfish atom of the free market, the single-minded pursuer of purely personal interest and advantage. The citizen was to be located in a nexus of ties and affinities that were not those of the social, but appeared to have a more powerful, and yet more natural, existence: community.

5   Community

Community emerged as a rather unexpected theme in debates about
the governability of liberal, democratic and market-based societies in
the closing decades of the end of the twentieth century.[1] Some predicted
that the collapse of state socialism in the Soviet Union and its allies
would lead to an uncritical acceptance of neo-liberal individualism: of
the economic arrangements, social institutions and political mechanisms
espoused by the regimes of Margaret Thatcher and Ronald Reagan.
These solutions have been adopted and promoted by the know-how
funds and financial institutions of the West. But this hegemony has not
been uncontested. The arts of welfare government in the West have
certainly come under sustained attack. Yet those who advocate individualistic, market-based solutions to all the ills that welfare addressed have
also been judged to be mistaken in their premises, inaccurate in their
analyses and deficient in their strategies of government. Freed from the
necessity to repeat the old battles between left and right, there has been
a flowering of arguments which attempt to identify a 'third way' of governing. This is associated with the powers of a territory between the
authority of the state, the free and amoral exchange of the market and
the liberty of the autonomous, 'rights-bearing' individual subject. Whilst
it begs many questions, let us call this space of semantic and programmatic concerns 'community'.

There are different and competing versions of this 'third space'. Yet
all have one paradoxical feature in common. On the one hand, the third
space they identify appears as a kind of natural, extra-political zone of

[1] My analysis in this chapter is largely confined to the English-speaking world.
However, developments in a number of Nordic countries have some parallel
with these. And, programmatically at least, some intellectuals and politicians
are beginning to suggest that the 'third way' discussed here should be a model
for continental Europe. Others, of course, see these proposals as based on a
peculiarly Anglo-American assessment of the failure of welfare, not shared in
other welfare states, and view the 'third way' as a Trojan horse for the introduction of the kinds of control mechanisms I discuss in chapter 7.

167

human relations; and this 'natural-ness' is not merely an ontological claim but implies affirmation, a positive evaluation. On the other, this zone is identified as a crucial element in particular styles of political government, for it is on its properties and on activities within it that the success of such political aspirations and programmes depend. This third space must, thus, become the object and target for the exercise of political power whilst remaining, somehow, external to politics and a counterweight to it.

In this vein, recent economic writings have turned away from neoclassical models of free competition amongst rational economic actors: instead they emphasize that successful economic government must recognize the significance of relations of interpersonal trust, local and community-based trading networks, collaboration amongst enterprises sharing a commitment to their particular geographical region.[2] Political scientists, as we have seen in earlier chapters, have turned away from themes of state power, state autonomy, state capacities; instead they emphasize governance: good governance must recognize the political importance of the patterns that arise out of complex interactions, negotiations and exchanges between intermediate' social actors, groups, forces, organizations, public and semi-public institutions.[3]

Left intellectuals, during the crisis and collapse of state socialism, rejected the classical themes of central planning and the authority of the party, and placed their faith in a politics of 'civil society': 'an aggregate of institutions whose members are engaged primarily in a complex of non-state activities – economic and cultural production, household life and voluntary associations – and who in this way preserve and transform their identity by exercising all sorts of pressures and controls upon State institutions'.[4] This idea of civil society is particularly instructive. As Graham Burchell has pointed out, civil society was not a kind of aboriginal reality or natural given, but the correlate of a political technology of government – a transactional reality existing at the mutable and contestable interface between political power and that which is outwith its reach.[5] Civil society, conceptually and historically, was linked to the

---

[2] Grahame Thompson gives an excellent account of these in G. Thompson 1997. See, for example, Piore and Sabel 1984; Hirst and Zeitlin 1988; Fukuyama 1996.
[3] For example, a journal simply entitled *Governance* published its first issue in 1988. Other examples include Kooiman 1993 and Hirst 1994; for European governance, Hooghe 1996; and for the governance of international relations, Rosenau 1997.
[4] Keane 1988: 14.
[5] G. Burchell 1991: 141.

state within a particular schema for the exercise of political power. So
it is not surprising that, when left intellectuals hailed civil society as
the antidote *both* to the state and its bureaucratic apparatus of political
administration and control, *and* to the free market celebrated by liberal
individualists and neo-conservatives, their analyses were linked to calls
for conscious political action to recreate this zone of natural liberties
and associations.

At around the same time, a revived civic republicanism came to the
fore in political philosophy. In their different ways, Charles Taylor,
Michael Sandel, Michael Walzer, Alistair MacIntyre and others contributed to a critical evaluation of the passive, privatized, individuated citizen of contemporary liberal democracies, and the view that this isolated
individual was the image of the citizen legitimated by liberal theorists of
'negative liberty' and individual rights.[6] This civic republicanism counterposed a different image, that of the active republican citizen, guided
by common virtues and a commitment to the common good, whose
active engagement in the life of the *polis* and the affairs of the community
would revitalize civil society. Such a form of citizenship was justified by
a 'positive view of liberty' which entailed the active exercise of good
citizenship within a political community in defence of freedom.

As David Burchell points out, this radical civic republican literature
on citizenship adopts a tragic tone: the key features of this state of affairs
have existed, but only in the distant past, and the citizenship we have
today is merely a hollow shell of this real and authentic form.[7] Alistair
MacIntyre put this at its starkest. Our age has parallels with the descent
of the Roman empire into the dark age, except that the barbarians are no
longer waiting beyond the frontiers: they have already been governing us
for some time. For MacIntyre, what is required is a return to a single
authoritative moral conception of the good: 'the crucial moral opposition', he argued, 'is between liberal individualism in some version or
other and the Aristotelian tradition in some version or other'.[8] The name
of Aristotle, here, denotes the possibility that individual human actions
should be guided towards the good through the exercise of a set of
interrelated qualities – virtues – agreed upon and exercised within a
moral community or *polis* which can provide the standards against which
the goodness of each of its citizen members can be judged. This neo-
Aristotelianism does not necessarily urge a return to the kinds of virtues

[6] These positions are usefully discussed in Mulhall and Swift 1997. See, for
example, C. Taylor 1989a; Sandel 1982; Walzer 1983; MacIntyre 1981.
[7] D. Burchell 1995: 542.
[8] MacIntyre 1981: 243.

identified by Aristotle – justice, prudence, temperance, fortitude and associated qualities such as courage, magnanimity, munificence, liberality, fidelity and gentleness. But it does suggest the need for some equally select, authoritative and agreed table of virtues to be promulgated, acquired and lived out within a unified moral community. MacIntyre's damning judgement on our present is not, for him, a message of political pessimism and inactivity. Quite the opposite – it is a call, once more, for action: 'What matters at this stage is the construction of local forms of community within which civility and the intellectual and moral life can be sustained through the new dark ages which are already upon us.'[9] A politics of virtue thus takes the paradoxical form of an attempt to create, by political action, that which is to be the counterweight and antidote to political power itself.

More recently such a politics of virtue has run into difficulties. It has seemed impossible to reconcile the civic republican idea that there must be common and agreed cultural and political virtues for all citizens with the diverse qualities of character and conduct that are valued by different sectors and groups of citizens within our contemporary multicultural, multi-racial and multi-religious polities. Communitarian and associationalist arguments have responded to these difficulties by seeking to affirm the moral codes of diverse 'cultural' communities. They have argued that the apparently different values of such communities actually operate around a shared common core, and that this can be embraced and empowered within a common constitutional framework.[10] This core can thus form the basis of an ethico-politics which overcomes the contradiction between the need to respect autonomy and diversity on the one hand, and the need for some basis for authoritative judgements of good and bad, right and wrong, on the other. I shall discuss this literature and its governmental aspirations in more detail presently.

Policy debates in the 1990s also appealed to this third space as a solution to problems of government. Since perhaps the mid-1960s, the community was proclaimed to be the appropriate locus for crime control, punishment, psychiatric services, social welfare and much more: community care, community correction, community architecture, community policing, community safety . . . As is now well known, whatever images of spontaneity of care it conjured up, this community was actu-

---

[9] Ibid.: 245.

[10] Etzioni 1993, 1997; Hirst 1994. This also seems to be implied in the writings of John Gray (1995, 1997) on pluralism and community in what he terms the 'late modern' period or 'the close of the modern age'.

ally a diagram for the reorganization of publicly provided, bureau-cratically organized and professionally staffed services. In the political programmes of Clinton and Blair, references to community have a dif-ferent resonance: they are infused with notions of voluntarism, of chari-table works, of self-organized care, of unpaid service to one's fellows. The space appealed to here has been made increasingly real and given its own name: the third sector.[11] In 1995, a widely discussed book by Jeremy Rifkin gave a boost to these arguments. He suggested that the problem of structural underemployment generated by technological advances in the labour process could be overcome by creating millions of new jobs in the 'third sector' between market and government. This would empower all those voluntary and not-for-profit organizations, through which many people already devote their time to their neigh-bourhoods and communities: volunteers who assist the elderly and handicapped, refurbish apartments, work in hospitals and clinics, deliver meals to the poor, act as volunteer firefighters, assist in day-care centres, work for advocacy organizations and participate in local theatre groups, choirs and orchestras. '[T]he commercial and public sectors are no longer capable of securing some of the fundamental needs of the people, the public has little choice but to begin looking out for itself, once again, by re-establishing viable communities as a buffer against both the impersonal forces of the global market and increasingly weak and incompetent central governing authorities.'[12] But, whilst, for Rifkin, the third sector was distinct from both the market and government, its revi-talization was nonetheless a key element in government. Like the politi-cal objectification of civil society in the early phase of liberalism, this third sector was 'a fertile ground for experimentation in the develop-ment of political technologies of government': it was a space in which one could observe the hybridization of political power and other non-political forms of authority in a variety of attempts to enframe and instrumentalize the forces of individuals and groups in the name of the public good.[13]

Of course, communitarianism is one of the traditional themes of con-stitutional thought: liberal political discourse always tempered the ideal of individual liberties and rights with claims made in the interests of communities. The idea that communities could take upon themselves responsibility for governing themselves would not have been foreign to many philanthropists and reformers in eighteenth-century Britain, nor

[11] E.g. Van Til 1988; Drucker 1995.
[12] Rifkin 1995: 238.
[13] G. Burchell 1991: 141.

to many who tried to define a federal politics for the United States based on the idea of self-rule.[14] The theme of loss of community, and the need to remake community or substitute something for its benefits, emerges with remarkable regularity in critical reflections on the state of the nation from the nineteenth century onwards. From the familiar nineteenth-century tales of the loss of tradition and the rise of individualism in the shift from *Gemeinschaft* to *Gesellschaft*, through the analyses of the damaging effects of metropolitan life in the 1920s and 1930s, to the community studies of the 1950s, sociologists, moralists, politicians and pamphleteers rehearse similar themes. But this similarity is a little misleading. The community appealed to is different in different cases: differently spatialized and differently temporized. When social and political theorists in the late nineteenth and early twentieth centuries claimed that there had been a shift from community to society, they located this within a metaphysics of history: community was that set of moral bonds among individuals fragmented by the division of labour and capitalist production, to be re-assembled in a 'social' form through a politics of solidarism and social right. The community of 'community studies' in the UK in the period after the Second World War was associated with the apparent anomie created by the disturbance of 'settled' working-class urban communities. This was community as the 'traditional' order of neighbourhood – a localized space of habitation – eroded by the bureaucratic incompetence of well-intentioned but patronizing planners, the bonds of mutuality destroyed by the very welfare regime that sought to support them. The community of welfare reformers of the 1960s and 1970s was different again: it was a network of professional institutions and services for social citizens that was spread across the territory of their everyday lives.

The community of the third sector, the third space, the third way of governing is not primarily a geographical space, a social space, a sociological space or a space of services, although it may attach itself to any or all such spatializations. It is a moral field binding persons into durable relations. It is a space of *emotional relationships* through which *individual identities* are constructed through their bonds to *micro-cultures* of values and meanings. 'Community', says Etzioni, 'is defined by two characteristics: first, a web of affect-laden relationships among a group of individuals, relationships that often criss-cross and reinforce one another ... and second, a measure of commitment to a set of shared values, norms, and meanings, and a shared history and identity – in short, to a particular culture.'[15] And it is through the political objectification and instru-

[14] Tully 1995; Hindess 1996c. For England, see, for example, Andrew 1989.
[15] Etzioni 1997: 127.

mentalization of *this* community and its 'culture' that government is to
be re-invented.

Diagnosis

In a discussion of 'the crisis of the welfare State', Jacques Donzelot
points out that some arguments are difficult to evaluate because they
present themselves simultaneously as diagnosis and as cure.[16] This is
undoubtedly the case with the new discourses of community. They present themselves simultaneously as a description of certain social and
economic ills, a diagnosis of the causes of these ills and a solution to
them. One way round this normative problem is to ask ourselves this: if
community, in so many guises and forms, is proposed as a solution,
what is it in our welfare democracies that it is seen as a solution *to*? If
there is an answer, there must be a question.

Some might suggest that we can best approach these issues in 'epochal' terms: that we have moved into an age of 'late modernity', for
example, of post-history and detraditionalization, where the stable historical, cultural and institutional markers that used to provide the bear-
ings for living a life have been eroded or subverted. From this perspective, what I have termed 'ethico-politics' would appear as merely one
aspect of the more general rise of 'life politics' in an age of risk, self-
reflexivity and the dethroning of traditional authority. Community here
would appear as an essentially nostalgic wish for a solution to the per-
plexities of the autonomous self, condemned to search for meaning in
a fragmented world resistant to stable sense-making procedures. I am
sceptical about approaches of this 'epochal' sort. I prefer to examine
changes at a more modest level, not in terms of cultural shifts but as
empirically identifiable differences in ways of thinking and acting. It is
not a question of claiming that the older ways have been erased or consigned to history, but of identifying something new taking shape within
and alongside the old arrangements, something different threatening or
promising to be born. Its birth is slow, complex; it is conceived out of
the intersection of heterogeneous social, political, discursive and technological shifts, often in apparently unconnected fields. But in this process,
and despite its family resemblance to now deceased relatives, a novel
sense of community is emerging both as a means of problematization
and as a means of solution.

Barry Hindess has drawn our attention to the rise of 'anti-political
motifs' within political discourse.[17] These motifs stress some ancient

[16] Donzelot 1991: 169.
[17] Hindess 1997.

themes concerning the corruption and ineffectiveness of the political classes. More fundamentally, they are informed by a sense of the limits of any politics that sees itself as omni-competent, any politics that expresses itself in overarching political programmes or that suggests that politicians and their organizations have either the resources or the ability to answer the problems that beset individual citizens. Jonathon Simon, writing in another context, provides a small but telling example. In popular and political discourse in the United States, certain laws have come to be known by the names of the politicians or legislators who framed them. But what, then, of Megan's Law?[18] Megan's Law in the United States is named for a child who was the victim of a sexual attack. The law requires the registration of convicted 'sex offenders' and the release of information on them to community groups. It is not a law formed in the interests of the state or the general will. Rather it is formed in the image of the victim, the parent, the family and the community. And the practices mandated by Megan's Law bypass, or at least supplement, the traditional powers of the agencies of law enforcement. They open a new circuit of power between the demands of communities and the penal authorities.

This is a small symptom of the wider rethinking of the political role of the state that I discussed in chapter 4. As the image of the social state gives way to that of the facilitating state, the enabling state or the state as animator, political government is to be relieved of its powers and obligations to know, plan, calculate and steer from the centre.[19] The state is no longer to be required to answer all society's needs for order, security, health and productivity. Individuals, firms, organizations, localities, schools, parents, hospitals, housing estates must take on themselves – as 'partners' – a portion of the responsibility for resolving these issues – whether this be by permanent retraining for the worker, or neighbourhood watch for the community. This involves a double movement of autonomization and responsibilization. Organizations and other actors that were once enmeshed in the complex and bureaucratic lines of force of the social state are to be set free to find their own destiny. Yet, at the same time, they are to be made responsible for that destiny, and for the destiny of society as a whole, in new ways. Politics is to be returned to society itself, but no longer in a social form: in

---

[18] Under the name 'Megan's Law' the New Jersey legislature in 1994 actually adopted ten separate measures against sex offenders; by 1995 the registration and notification mechanism under the name 'Megan's Law' had been adopted by more than a dozen states, and many others have followed since (Simon 1996, forthcoming). I take up these issues again in chapter 7.

[19] Donzelot and Estebe 1994.

the form of individual morality, organizational responsibility and ethical community.

Whilst the term 'community' has long been salient in political thought, it becomes governmental when it is made technical. By the 1960s, community was already being invoked by sociologists as a possible antidote to the loneliness and isolation of the individual generated by 'mass society'. In social politics, this idea of community as lost authenticity and common belonging was initially deployed as part of the language of critique and opposition directed against remote bureaucracy. Community activists were to identify not with a welfare system that they saw as degrading, policing and controlling, but with those who were the subjects of that system – the inhabitants of the housing estates, projects and ghettos. More or less simultaneously, the language of community was utilized by authorities such as police to comprehend the problems they encountered in dealing with difficult zones – 'the West Indian community', the criminal community. Community here was a point of penetration of a kind of ethnographic sociology into the vocabularies and classifications of authorities. Reciprocally, sociology itself intensified its investigations of collective life in terms of community: it anatomized the bonds of culture and the ties of locality that were thought to be essential conditions for the moral order of society and for individual and familial well-being. Within a rather short period, what began as a language of resistance and critique was transformed, no doubt for the best of motives, into an expert discourse and a professional vocation – community is now something to be programmed by Community Development Programmes, developed by Community Development Officers, policed by Community Police, guarded by Community Safety Programmes and rendered knowable by sociologists pursuing 'community studies'. Communities became zones to be investigated, mapped, classified, documented, interpreted, their vectors explained to enlightened professionals-to-be in countless college courses and to be taken into account in numberless encounters between professionals and their clients, whose individual conduct is now to be made intelligible in terms of the beliefs and values of 'their community'.

No doubt a whole range of other local shifts in vocabulary in diverse sites contributed to the emergence of community as a valorized alternative, antidote or even cure to the ills that the social had not been able to address – or even to the ills of the social itself. In the 1980s, in the midst of this shift, sociologists were already seeking to diagnose what was occurring in terms of power. Most notable here was the suggestion that, at least as far as deviance was concerned, the space of community was being colonized by agents, institutions and practices of control.[20] This argument remains valuable and insightful. But I would frame it slightly differently. For what is happening here is not the colonization of a previous space of freedom by control practices; community is actually instituted in its contemporary form as a sector for government. And this is not a process of social control if this be understood in the sense of mechanisms to ensure that members of a society conform to expectations. Rather, in the institution of community, a sector is brought into existence whose vectors and forces can be mobilized, enrolled, deployed in novel programmes and techniques which encourage and harness active practices of self-management and identity construction, of personal ethics and collective allegiances. I term this *government through community*.

Political subjectivity

In part, what was involved here was a remaking of political subjectivity. Whilst the policies and programmes of the social accorded individuals personal responsibility for their conduct, this individual responsibility was always traversed by external determinations: the advantages or disadvantages conferred by family background, social class, life history, located within a wider array of social and economic forces such as changes in the labour market, booms, slumps, industrial cycles, the exigencies of urban environments, problems of housing supply. Of course, the extent to which such external determinants could or should mitigate personal responsibility was subject to continual dispute, as was the extent to which they could or should be compensated for in education, in the decisions of the criminal court and so forth. Nevertheless, this configuration of ethical vectors is reorganized under the sign of community. The subject is addressed as a moral individual with bonds of obligation and responsibilities for conduct that are assembled in a new way – the individual in his or her community is both self-responsible and subject to certain emotional bonds of affinity to a circumscribed 'network' of other individuals – unified by family ties, by locality, by

---

[20] This argument was made brilliantly by Cohen in his (1985) book *Visions of Social Control*. His argument is much more complex than this, and I cannot do it justice here. But I think it remains true to say that he envisions control as a dispersal of the techniques of disciplinary individualization and normalization across the territory of everyday life and that he understands these disciplinary techniques as essentially negative and constraining in their intentions and effects.

moral commitment to environmental protection or animal welfare. Conduct is retrieved from a social order of determination into a new ethical perception of the individualized and autonomized actor, each of whom has unique, localized and specific ties to his or her particular family and to a particular moral community.

The regulative ideal of universal and uniform social citizenship is called into question by these new collectivizations of political subjectivity. The practices that assembled the social certainly entailed 'identification projects': programmes of mass schooling, of public housing, of public broadcasting, of social insurance and so forth had at their heart an image and a goal of the socially identified citizen, the person who, above all, understood him- or herself to be a member of a single integrated national society. The vocabulary of community also implicates a psychology of identification. To imagine oneself, or to imagine another, as a member of a community is to posit its actual or potential existence as a fulcrum of personal identity. Yet these lines of identification are configured differently. Community proposes a relation that appears less 'remote', more 'direct', one which occurs not in the 'artificial' political space of society, but in matrices of affinity that appear more natural. One's communities are nothing more – or less – than those networks of allegiance with which one identifies existentially, traditionally, emotionally or spontaneously, seemingly beyond and above any calculated assessment of self-interest.

Hence, like so many other similar loci of allegiance – class, civil society, ethnicity – arguments about community employ a Janus-faced logic.[21] Each assertion of community refers itself to something that already exists and has a claim on us – our common fate as gay men, as women of colour, as people with AIDS, as members of an ethnic group, as residents in a village or a suburb, as people with a disability. Yet our allegiance to each of these particular communities is something that we have to be made aware of, requiring the work of educators, campaigns, activists, manipulators of symbols, narratives and identifications. Within such a style of thought, community is to be achieved, yet the achievement is nothing more than the birth-to-presence of a form of being which pre-exists.

This new relation between community, identity and political subjectivity is exemplified in debates over 'multi-culturalism' or the rights of indigenous peoples, and in political controversies over the implications of 'pluralism' – of ethnicity, religion, of sexuality, of ability and

[21] Cf. Hindess 1996b.

disability – and the recognition to be accorded to the 'rights' and 'values' of different communities.[22] The shift from the image of the 'melting pot' to that of the 'rainbow' illustrates the way that the politics of recognition stresses the existence and legitimacy of incommensurable – or at least distinct – domains of culture, values, mores. These are not unified across a nation but localized, fragmented, hybrid, multiple, overlapping, activated differently in different arenas and practices. The uniform social citizenship that was the objective of the citizen-forming and nation-building strategies of the nineteenth and twentieth centuries is challenged by a diversity of forms of identity and allegiance no longer deferential to such an image of national and territorialized civic culture. As I argued in chapter 4, individuals no longer inhabit a single 'public sphere', nor is their citizenship conferred upon them through a singular relationship with the state. Rather, citizenship is multiplied and non-cumulative: it appears to inhere in and derive from active engagement with each of a number of specific zones of identity – lifestyle sectors, neighbourhoods, ethnic groups – some private, some corporate, some quasi-public. The political problem of citizenship is reposed: it is no longer a question of national character but of the way in which multiple identities receive equal recognition in a single constitutional form. We have moved from 'culture' to 'cultures'.

This multiplication of the forms of political subjectivity is linked to new practices of identity formation. These fuse the aim of manu-facturers to sell products and increase market share with the identity experiments of consumers. They are mediated by highly developed techniques of market research and finely calibrated attempts to seg-ment and target specific consumer markets. Advertising images and television programmes interpenetrate in the promulgation of images of lifestyle, narratives of identity choice and the highlighting of the ethical aspects of adopting one or other way of conducting one's life. Practices and styles of aestheticized life-choice that were previously the monopoly of cultural elites have been generalized in this new habitat of subjectification: that is to say, the belief that individuals can shape an autonomous identity for themselves through choices in taste, music, goods, styles and habitus.[23] This embodies a shift away from emphasis upon morality – obedience to an externally imposed code of conduct and values in the name of the collective good – and towards ethics – the active and practical shaping by individuals of the

[22] The best discussions of these issues are to be found in Tully 1995, Connolly 1995, especially ch. 6, and Shapiro 1997.
[23] See T. Osborne 1998.

daily practices of their own lives in the name of their own pleasures, contentments or fulfilments.

As Cindy Patten has suggested, within such a regime, the spaces of lifestyle and culture are no longer integrated in a total governmental field.[24] They are spaces of territorial competition and ethical dispute. Within these spaces, it is possible for subjects to distance themselves from the cohesive discourses and strategies of the social state – schooling, public service broadcasting, municipal architecture and the like. They can now access a whole range of resources and techniques of subject formation in order to invent themselves, individually and collectively, as new kinds of political actors. This fragmentation of the social by the new technologies of images and identities, of lifestyles and choices, of consumption, marketing and the mass media has thus produced new collectivizations of 'habitus' outside the control of coherent discourses of civility or the technologies of political government. The commercialization of lifestyle formation thus allows the possibility of 'other subjectivities' – novel modes of individuality and allegiance and their public legitimation. The politics of conduct is faced with a new set of problems: governing subject formation in this new plural field. Our current 'wars of subjectivity' emerge here.

Communitarianism

Nowhere are these wars of subjectivity better exemplified than in debates around communitarianism in the United States. The arguments of American communitarians take a characteristic socio-ethical form. They claim to identify a significant deterioration of *social* order in the United States in the period from 1960 to 1990, and they locate this in an *ethical* field. Thus Etzioni seems to be both describing and explaining when he paints his picture of a weakening of the moral infrastructure:

strong consensus on *core values* of the 1950s was increasingly undermined . . . The rise of the counterculture in the 1960s further weakened the country's values of hard work and thrift, as well as compliance with most rules of conduct, from dress codes to table manners, from tastes in music to cuisine . . . followed in the 1970s and especially in the 1980s by a different, instrumental brand of individualism [which] provided a normative seal of approval to a focus on the self rather than on responsibilities to the community and saw in self-interest the best bast for social order and virtue . . . Traditional virtues lost much of their power, and no strong new shared values arose. The notion that one should not be judgmental gained currency; various social and psychological theories that blamed the system for the misconduct of its 'victims' caught on . . .

[24] Patten 1995: 226; cf. Hardt 1995.

Permissiveness was much extended, especially in areas such as sexual conduct and lack of achievement in schools. Even etiquette . . . declined.[25]

As autonomy increased in a whole range of areas, notions of deviance were relaxed, commitment to marriage weakened, respect for authority waned, voter turnout declined and alienation rose. These 'cultural' changes were underpinned by 'socio-economic' changes: job instability increased, dependency in welfare grew, the family declined, divorce rates rose, ethnic diversity increasingly produced ethnic tension. Whilst the 1970s and 1980s saw a return to coercion as a means of seeking to restore order, Etzioni argues that this was paralleled by an increase in social disorder and anti-social behaviour. Autonomy was enhanced, but anarchy rose: crime, drugs, family breakdown, violence, lack of respect for authority, decline of commitment to work, isolation, individualism, anomie, democratic deficit, political alienation, not to mention reduced economic competitiveness in a globalized economy.

This literature thus encourages us to look on our present and our past with a certain ethical gaze. Alexis de Tocqueville's observations on the United States in the 1830s, in his *Democracy in America*, are a key source for these American analysts.[26] Robert Bellah and his colleagues suggest that the 'habits of the heart' of which Tocqueville wrote had undergone a profoundly individualist shift.[27] History had borne out Tocqueville's prophesies that Americans were prone to isolation and increasing individualism, 'which disposes each citizen to isolate himself from the mass of his fellows and withdraw into the circle of family and friends; with this little society formed to his taste; he gladly leaves the greater society to look after itself'.[28] Robert Putnam, in his influential article 'Bowling alone: America's declining social capital', also starts with Tocqueville: ' "Americans of all ages, all stations in life, and all types of disposition", Tocqueville observed, "are forever forming associations. These are not only commercial and industrial associations in which all take part, but others of a thousand different types – religious, moral, serious, futile, very general and very limited, immensely large and very minute." ' For Putnam, this propensity for civic association impressed Tocqueville as 'the key to [Americans'] unprecedented ability to make democracy work'.[29] When Putnam directs this ethical gaze at the recent history of

[25] Etzioni 1997: 64–5, 69.
[26] Tocqueville [1835, 1840] 1969; cf. Shapiro 1997.
[27] Bellah et al. 1985. Tocqueville discussed these habits of the heart in [1835, 1840] 1969: 287.
[28] Bellah et al. 1985: 37; cf. Tocqueville [1835, 1840] 1969.
[29] Putnam 1995a: 65–6; see Tocqueville [1835, 1840] 1969: 513–17.

American society, he discovers 'the strange disappearance' of this range of social connections, norms and trust relations – what he terms, after James Coleman, 'social capital'.[30] Nearly 80 million Americans went bowling in 1993, he claims, about the same number as attended church regularly. But these Americans are no longer bowling in organized leagues – they are bowling alone. And this is only one example of the decline, perhaps even the collapse, of civic engagement. Political participation is down; religious sentiment is no longer institutional but tends to be self-defined; labour union membership is falling; volunteering for civic and fraternal institutions from the Boy Scouts to the Masons is on a steep downward trend. While there are apparent countertrends, such as membership in environmental organizations, membership here frequently consists only of paying dues, and has nothing to do with social connectedness. And the growing fashion for support groups and self-help organizations hardly fosters community: for Putnam, as for Wuthnow, such groups 'merely provide occasions for individuals to focus on themselves in the presence of others'.[31] Whilst Putnam considers the causes of this process to be multiple and uncertain, he paints a familiar image of the plight of the United States – drugs, crime, alienation, family breakdown, loss of good neighbourliness and the like – visualized in terms of the decay of these ethico-cultural networks of civic trust.

This ethico-cultural problematization is mirrored by the proposed solutions. The values of society must be rebuilt, in order to restore the ethical relations of trust and reciprocity upon which good government must depend. For Bellah and his colleagues, isolation and individualism can best be overcome by encouraging citizens to actively involve themselves in associational life. For, as Tocqueville suggested, 'Citizens who . . . take part in public affairs must turn from the private interests and occasionally look at something other than themselves.'[32] Associational life provides 'forums in which opinion can be publicly and intelligently shaped and the subtle habits of public initiative and responsibility learned and passed on'.[33] For Putnam, social science has demonstrated that 'the quality of public life and the performance of social institutions (and not only in America) are indeed powerfully influenced by norms and networks of civic engagement', and that 'successful outcomes in education, urban poverty, unemployment, the control of crime and drug

[30] Putnam 1995b; Coleman 1990.
[31] Wuthnow 1994: 3, quoted in Putnam 1995a: 72.
[32] Tocqueville, quoted in Bellah et al. 1985: 38.
[33] Bellah et al. 1985: 38.

abuse, and even health ... are more likely in civically engaged communities'.[34] The attainment of ethnic groups is related to the strength of social bonds, the success of capitalism is dependent upon networks of collaboration amongst workers and entrepreneurs, the performance of representative government is determined by traditions of civic engagement and much more. Thus, however difficult it may be, it is necessary to seek to re-invent community by conscious political action. This is what I meant when I suggested that community names a 'transactional' reality: it is the objectification of a plane formed at the unstable and uncomfortable intersections between politics and that which should and must remain beyond its reach.

Etzioni quotes approvingly from Gertrude Himmelfarb's article 'Beyond social policy: remoralizing America': 'It is not enough, then, to revitalize civil society. The more urgent and difficult task is to remoralize civil society.'[35] However, this apparent ethico-political consensus is misleading. Is there one set of virtues or many acceptable values? What is to be governed and how is it to be governed? What are the respective roles and functions of laws, exhortations, codes, pedagogy, religion? Is it a matter of the re-invention of an external, prescriptive and authoritative morality of the code, with fixed norms of proper personal, familial and sexual conduct, or is it a matter of encouraging a practical ethics of everyday life? There are many different ways of re-introducing ethical and moral concerns into political practice, and they have different implications for politics itself.

In the USA, the religious right called for a return to tradition and to organized religion and obedience to the biblical moral codes. Neoconservatives such as Himmelfarb similarly sought for an authoritative moral code. They were dubious about whether one could legislate for morality. But, nonetheless, they argued that the state inescapably does govern morality, for example through its allocation of benefits to different types of household or different categories of personal troubles, and its legitimation of certain kinds of relations as marriages. The problem is that it has fallen victim to the ethos of value pluralism. Hence, what is required is a programme of reform of legislation in areas from crime control to the welfare system in order to penalize undesirable forms of conduct – lone parents, use of illegal drugs, homosexual 'marriages' – and to reward those whose conduct is virtuous. The law and the state must combat the relativization and pluralization of 'values' to rebuild the moral and spiritual ethos of society around an abiding sense of moral

---

[34] Putnam 1995a: 66.
[35] Himmelfarb 1995a, quoted in Etzioni 1997: 96.

and civic virtues. Indeed it must reject the relativism that is built in to
the very term 'values'. For values, in the plural, are merely the beliefs,
attitudes, feelings or opinions that an individual, group or society happens to value at a particular time. But virtues are the fixed certain standards which allow conduct to be judged in moral terms, not as misguided, undesirable, inappropriate, but as bad, wrong or evil. The
remoralization of society would not be paternalistic or impose moral
tutelage. The reverse is true: it is the trendy proponents of 'political
correctness' who are moral authoritarians. A politics of the virtues, in
contrast, will sustain the 'traditional' and 'commonplace' values of
everyday life – responsibility, respectability, sobriety, independence.
These not only encourage each individual to be virtuous, but they can
also be readily applied to public affairs.[36]

Communitarians occupy a different position on these dimensions of
virtue versus value, and morality versus ethics. Their question is something like this: how can virtue be governed in a multi-cultural and multi-
faith society in accordance with the liberal presuppositions of individual
freedom and personal autonomy? Thus Etzioni argues that 'strong individual rights (autonomy) presumed strong personal and social responsibilities' rather than a return to an order based upon imposed duties.[37]
Moral order rests not on laws enforced and upheld by guardians, but
on a core of values shared by the members of all communities and
embodied in the rituals of everyday life. Beliefs do not get their legitimacy through the freely given agreement of autonomous individuals:
this is a mistaken assumption of both classical and contemporary liberals. 'Community provides [individuals] with history, traditions, culture, all deeply imbued with values.'[38] And whilst religion is undoubtedly important, the religious basis of ethics is a community matter, not
a state matter: ethics may be based in Christianity, Judaism, Islam or
secular humanism. Remoralization does not seek to unify all values, but
rather, it seeks to recognize and strengthen a single core set of moral
values that is compatible with a range of religious and cultural beliefs.
'[T]he main fault line', writes Etzioni, 'does not separate those whose
commitment to core values is a matter of religious considerations from
those whose reasons are secular; instead, it separates those who are truly
committed to a core of shared values from those who have lost theirs,
have not affirmed any new ones, or deny the existence of virtues, or
worship self-interest, cynicism or post-modern or old-fashioned

[36] Himmelfarb 1995b.
[37] Etzioni 1997: 74.
[38] Ibid.

nihilism.'[39] We should not look to law, information, reason or deliberative democracy to regenerate society, but to moral dialogue amongst community members and between moral communities. The moral voice of the community 'is the main way that individuals and groups in a good society encourage one another to adhere to behavior that reflects shared values and to avoid behavior that offends or violates them'.[40]

Etzioni refers to a recent speech by Tony Blair – the leader of the British Labour Party, who became British prime minister in 1997 – on the stakeholder society to support his view that 'for a society to be communitarian, much of the social conduct must be "regulated" by reliance on the moral voice rather than on the law, and *the scope of the law itself must be limited largely to that which is supported by the moral voice*'.[41] In the Thatcher years, the government of the United Kingdom frequently condemned the Church of England for failing to assert its traditional moral authority. In fact, the Church was pursuing a different, perhaps communitarian path, for example in its influential 1986 report *Faith in the City* And Tony Blair chose to mark the tenth anniversary of this report in a newspaper article entitled 'Battle for Britain' written a year before his election victory: 'the search is on to reinvent community for a modern age, true to core values of fairness, co-operation and responsibility'.[42]

Between security and autonomy

Since the end of the Second World War, it had been thought that politicians could invent and manage technologies of government – from social insurance to personal social services – that would secure the security of each individual citizen without diminishing their personal autonomy and responsibility for their fate. Increasingly, however, politicians, policy makers and propagandists speak of a conflict between the maintenance and promotion of individual autonomy and the social guarantees of individual security.[43] How can the security of individuals be promoted without encouraging dependency, and without corroding the self-reliance which is required of the contemporary citizen by a modern, competitive and entrepreneurial nation?

The neo-liberal strategy in these 'culture wars' relied upon traditional

---

[39] Ibid.: 255.
[40] Ibid.: 124.
[41] Ibid.: 139, emphasis in original.
[42] Blair 1996. For a further British example of this period, see D. Atkinson 1994.
[43] N. Fraser and Gordon 1994.

agencies of moral authority – church, school, public figures – whose teachings and preachings would denounce bad or inferior forms of life conduct and set out authoritative guidance on the correct ways to live a life. But these traditional modes of authorization for a politics of conduct were exactly those that welfare regimes had themselves weakened. Welfare strategies – for example, promoting health, hygiene, sexual and personal fulfilment in the family as matters of positive knowledge (psychology and the like), individual choice and personal fulfilment – placed the authority of received morality over matters of life conduct in question in favour of the voices of expertise and objectivity. Further, demands for the revival of the traditional agencies of moral authority threaten the very basis of the economic development of the West since the 1960s: the commercialization of lifestyle and the demands of the free market which had vested so much in the unstoppable enhancement of the commodification of sex, pleasure, leisure and desire. A strategy of moral reform which relies upon the re-introduction of responsibility in problematic sectors – youth, the poor and so forth – through attempts to impose and inculcate external and binding moral codes grounded by reference to tradition or theology seems bound to fail in its attempts to re-invent the past.[44]

In the United States, the neo-conservative programme of Newt Gingrich and his allies pursued a slightly different route. This was to use the state itself and its legislative powers to fight the culture wars. To quote Barbara Cruikshank, 'To restore civil society back to a state of natural liberty and self-reproduction, neoconservatives argue that it is necessary to inculcate civic virtue in the citizenry, if necessary, by force.'[45] As the 'Contract With America' states, schools are graduating illiterates, families are in disrepair, prisons are coddling repeat offenders, government programmes have bred illegitimacy, crime, illiteracy and more poverty. And, in the view of Gertrude Himmelfarb, a strange alliance has formed between the irresponsible elites seeking liberation from the moral restraints of bourgeois values and the underclass who have rejected such values; together they have almost managed to make illegitimate the traditional commitments to hard work, respectability, self-help, self-control and personal responsibility.[46] Intellectuals have relativized virtue in the

---

[44] Not that this dissuades many from adopting such a strategy, but trying to adapt it to the individualized values of personal autonomy and free choice: for example, the Promise Keepers in the United States, an exclusively male organization, seek to re-activate such codes by making each man pledge himself to them as a personal act of allegiance and commitment.

[45] Cruikshank 1998: 146.

[46] Himmelfarb 1994: 221–57.

'Nietzschean' form of 'cultural values' without transcendental foundation. Government itself is the only force powerful enough to carry out the culture war necessary to remoralize the United States and to recreate that responsible autonomy and civic virtue upon which republican government must rely. Hence the Contract relies upon law to renew the republic. A counter-counter-culture war must be waged, using illiberal measures, in order to attack the corruption of the American people themselves, to renew civilization and reconstruct the proud muscular autonomy of the citizens of the original American republic.

Neo-conservatives were thus forced into a paradoxical position: the legislative machinery of the state was to be used to enforce particular forms of morality, at the very same time that the capacity and legitimacy of central political institutions were in question. How can enhanced liberty and enhanced security be achieved without requiring the dangerous enhancement of the powers of the state?

Communitarianism draws its power from its way of answering this question: its promise of a new moral contract, a new partnership between an enabling state and responsible citizens, based upon the strengthening of the natural bonds of community. But communitarian thought gives civility a definite shape. The problems to be addressed are rendered understandable in the ethical terms of dependency, licence, idleness, irresponsibility. The virtues espoused to combat them are those of a 'civil religion', a secular and civic Christianity of respectability, moderation, charity, giving, probity, fidelity and the like. But crucially, this complex of virtues is not to be imposed from above. It is to be organized and sustained through the bonds of community, to receive its authority from the moral voice of community, and hence to be integral to the belonging-ness and the self-government of each citizen of a community. In this way, bonds between individuals are rendered visible in a moral form, and made governable in ways compatible with the autonomy of the individual and the reproduction of the collective: the self must govern itself communally in the service of its own liberty, autonomy and responsibility. This is well illustrated by the Responsible Communitarian Platform issued by the Communitarian Network:

A communitarian perspective recognises that the preservation of individual liberty depends on the active maintenance of the institutions of civil society where citizens learn respect for others as well as self-respect; where we acquire a lively sense of our personal and civic responsibilities, along with an appreciation of our own rights and the rights of others; where we develop the skills of self-government as well as the habit of governing ourselves, and learn to serve others – not just self.[47]

47 Communitarian Network 1996: 1.

What is at issue here is the relation of liberty to authority. Authority – though the word itself is not used – is the inescapable other side of responsible liberty. Liberty is not merely the active exercise by each individual of authority over themselves, but, at the same time, the voluntary acceptance of the authority of particular moral code as the basis for the government of our own conduct, and hence a willed subordination to the authority of particular authorities of conduct. Who are these authorities? From where does their authority derive? How are these authorities to govern?

The community-civility game

Reading Bellah, Coleman, Putnam, Etzioni, Fukuyama and the others, I am reminded of Jeremy Bentham's preface to his *Panopticon*, and the list of benefits that were to be obtained from his 'inspection house':

Morals reformed – health preserved – industry invigorated – instruction diffused – public burthens lightened – Economy seated, as it were, upon a rock – the Gordian knot of the Poor-Laws not cut, but untied – all by a simple idea in architecture![48]

Now perhaps, one would write:

virtue regenerated – crime reduced – public safety enhanced – institutionalization banished – dependency transformed to activity – underclass included – democratic deficit overcome – idle set to work – political alienation reduced – responsive services assured – economy reinvigorated by seating it, as it were, within networks of trust and honour – the Gordian knot of State versus individual not cut but untied, all by a simple idea in politics: community.

Almost a quarter of a century ago, Michel Foucault notoriously took Bentham's inspection house as the model for a certain type of power which he termed 'discipline': a versatile and productive micro-physics of power 'comprising a whole set of instruments, techniques, procedures, levels of application, targets'.[49] The Panopticon was the diagram of a political technology, one that was individualizing, normalizing, based on perpetual surveillance, classification, a kind of uninterrupted and continuous judgement enabling the government of multiplicities, reducing the resistant powers of human bodies at the same time as it maximized their economic and social utility. Foucault argued that the forms of individual civility and docile citizenship set in place by the minute web of panoptic techniques and disciplinary norms was to be the real foundation of the formal political liberties of the

[48] Bentham 1843: 39, quoted in Foucault 1977: 207, italics in original.
[49] Foucault 1977: 215.

abstract juridical subject of law and the rational economic individual of contract and exchange.

Suppose, then, that instead of considering all these debates about communities, associations, networks and the like as descriptions of states of affairs, we thought of them in terms of government. Could one say that these programmatics of communities, associations and so forth are related to a new diagram of power? I am tempted to answer this in the affirmative. That is to say, I suggest that one can discern here the emergence of a new 'game of power'. We could call this the 'community-civility' game. It involves new conceptions of those who are to be governed, and of the proper relations between the governors and the governed. It puts new questions into play about the kinds of people we are, the kinds of problems we face, the kinds of relations of truth and power through which we are governed and through which we should govern ourselves.

I have suggested that this new game of power operates in a field one could term *ethico-politics* Foucault, of course, identified the rise of *disciplinary power*, focusing upon maximizing the utility and docility of individuals, and *bio-power*, focusing upon maximizing the health and welfare of the population. Ethico-politics reworks the government of souls in the context of the increasing role that culture and consumption mechanisms play in the regulation of forms of life and identity and self-techniques. If discipline *individualizes and normalizes*, and bio-power *collectivizes and socializes*, ethico-politics concerns itself with the *self-techniques necessary for responsible self-government* and the *relations between one's obligation to oneself and one's obligations to others* Ethico-politics has a particular salience at the close of the twentieth century. For it appears that somehow 'we' – the subjects of advanced liberal democracies – in the absence of any objective guarantees for politics or our values, have become obliged to think ethically. Hence it is likely to be on the terrain of ethics that our most important political disputes will have to be fought for the foreseeable future. If this is the case, it would be pointless to condemn this ethical mutation in our ways of thinking about politics. More usefully, we would need to find ways of evaluating the new technologies and the new authorities that seek to find a way of governing us, as free individuals, through ethics.

Technologies of community

For those who advocate an anti-politics of community, civil society or the third sector, part of the political attraction of these zones lies in their apparent naturalness: their non-political or pre-political status. But like the social before them, these 'third spaces' of thought and action have to be made up.[50] Boundaries and distinctions have to be emplaced; these spaces have to be visualized, mapped, surveyed and mobilized. And, perhaps, what distinguishes the contemporary spaces of community from those references to community in the social philosophies of the late nineteenth and early twentieth centuries is precisely this – that communities have been objectified by positive knowledges, subject to truth claims by expertise and hence can become the object of political technologies for governing through community. And these political technologies involve the constitution of new forms of authority of this new space of natural associations, and the instrumentalization of new forces in the government of conduct.

Over the second half of the twentieth century, a whole array of little devices and techniques have been invented to make communities real. Surveys of attitudes and values, market research, opinion polls, focus groups, citizens' juries and much more have mapped out these new spaces of culture, brought these values and virtues into visibility and injected them into the deliberations of authorities. The techniques that have been used to segment consumption communities are related, in complex and interesting ways, to those used to chart the values of electors in opinion polls and those used to chart the pathological values of the anti-communities of the depraved or the poor. New 'experts of community' have been born, who not only invent, operate and market these techniques to advertising agencies, producers, political parties and pressure groups, but who have also formalized their findings into theories and concepts. These experts are now on hand to advise on how communities and citizens might be governed in terms of their values, and how their values shape the ways they govern themselves. As community becomes a valorized political zone, a new political status has been given to the 'indigenous' authorities of community. For to govern communities, it seems one must first of all link oneself up with those who have, or claim, moral authority in 'the black community' or 'the local community'. Ethnographers have charted the disputed and problematic ways in which this authority is claimed and identified. And they have also shown that, in this apparently natural space, the authority of community authorities, precisely because it is governed by no explicit codes and rules of conduct, is often even more difficult to contest than that of experts and professionals. Other techniques are also used to mobilize territories in the name of community self-management. Programmes of community policing, community safety and community

[50] T. Osborne and Rose 1997.

development grid these territories with circuits of communication. They develop new expert knowledges of these new irreal spaces of government. In the name of community, political programmes, both at the micro-level and at the macro-level, disperse the tasks of knowing and governing through a myriad of micro-centres of knowledge and power.[51]

The relations of translation between political rationalities and governmental technologies are complex. Technologies of government are heterogeneous and hybrid assemblages. They do not, cannot, merely be *expressions* of moral principles. And they must frequently rely upon techniques for the conduct of conduct that are present at hand, rather than invent them *ab initio*. Some recent initiatives in the area of juvenile justice, for example, are certainly consistent with communitarian principles. In Britain, for example, soon after it came to power in May 1997, the Labour administration sought to introduce the fining of *parents* for the juvenile delinquency of their *children* as a means of inculcating a practical ethic of responsibility and obligation between members of a household. Similarly, in the UK and in the USA, there are programmes of juvenile justice that are based upon 'restorative principles' of naming, blaming and shaming: bringing the offender face to face with the victim, in the presence of the offender's family and loved ones, and exploring in depth the consequences of the act for others and hence seeking to inscribe awareness of the dire personal consequences of illegal acts for others directly into the ethical make-up of the offender. But in neither case were the techniques themselves new, or developed within this particular rationale. Here, as elsewhere, government is not a matter of the realization of a programme so much as of the complex construction of assemblages that will link up rather general ethical rationalities to very specific, local and technical devices for the government of conduct.

As the examples that I have cited show, governing through communities involves establishing relations between the moral values of communities and those of individual citizens. Of course, practices of citizen formation are not themselves new, but what is perhaps novel is the attention paid to citizens as autonomous individuals who must actively construct a life through the practical choices they make about their conduct, and who must bear individual responsibility for the nature and consequences of those choices. I have suggested in earlier chapters that leading a life in the contemporary world is a matter of the fabrication of identities within personal projects of self-actualization in a whole variety of practices and sites: lifestyle shopping, the shaping of a habitus, the choice of faith and the like. Within this culture of the self, techniques

[51] Ericson and Haggerty 1997: I return to this issue in chapter 7.

of citizen formation – in schools and colleges, in the little pedagogies of confessional talk shows and soap operas – are no longer about the inculcation of externally validated morals and obligations. They address themselves to the practices, techniques and styles of self-reflection and self-management necessary for the active construction of an ethical life. As we have seen, the closure of the twentieth century is no more exempt than any other time from lofty pronouncements of moral decline. But, in fact, one can perhaps see just the opposite: the proliferation of sites and practices for ethical self-formation. Many of these sites and practices are organized in the service of other objectives – marketing and the maximization of consumption, the promotion of particular styles of music, the generation of television audiences through appeals to prurience and the search for titillation. Nonetheless, these practices use techniques that take up and disseminate the idea that the consumer is an ethical citizen; consumers can and should consciously seek to manage themselves and their conduct in an ethical fashion according to principles that they have chosen for themselves.

In the face of such developments, a whole range of more mundane practices and techniques of citizen formation are being developed that seek to cope with this new multiple and fragmented field of identity and allegiance. As Jeffrey Minson and Denise Meredyth point out, this practical work of government is especially focused on schooling, where a variety of programmes try to modify older techniques of citizen formation to shape the cultural capacities and interests of these new multicultural citizens.[52] But these attempts to programme ethics in the service of political objectives are caught in powerful tensions. These are tensions between the imperatives of common norms and the demands for recognition of cultural diversity. And they are tensions between the moral high ground of communitarian thought and the mundane practicalities of policy formation. Can an active ethics of self-fabrication through choice be governmentalized, or are any such attempts doomed to slide into moralism?

Morality or ethics?

The language of ethics is proliferating. In Britain one hears of an ethical foreign policy, ethical banking, ethical investment, ethical agriculture, ethical business, ethical politicians, the ethic of public service, ethical shopping, as well as the increasing salience of more traditional ethical disputes in the areas of medicine, genetic technologies and the rights to

[52] Minson and Meredyth forthcoming.

life and death. How should one begin to weigh up the costs and benefits of this new ethico-politics? I do not think that it is sufficient to dismiss all this talk of ethics as ideology, mystification, a guise for new and more subtle modes of control, domination and economic exploitation.[53] Indeed, as I have already hinted, I think one should welcome the infusion of ethical discourse into politics. One should welcome it because it can be counterposed to all those attempts to translate ethical judgements into apparently more 'objective', scientific', rational or uncontestable terms: normal/pathological; social/anti-social; natural/ unnatural; productive/unproductive; progressive/reactionary; feminist/ patriarchal; oppression/liberation. Whilst each of these oppositions derives from a different account of conduct and its evaluation, each nonetheless seeks to close off ethical debate by appealing to the authority of a true discourse and, hence, inescapably, to the authority of those who are experts of this truth. To the extent that it escapes this will to truth, this will to closure, ethico-politics thus allows the possibility of opening up the evaluation of forms of life and self-conduct to the difficult and interminable business of debate and contestation.

But one also needs to try to identify the switch points where an opening turns into a closure. That is to say, when the vocabulary of ethics actually operates to impose a different but no less motivated and directive politics of conduct.[54] It is all too easy for all this talk about ethics to become merely a recoding of strategies of social discipline and morality. That is to say, political strategies which prioritize the ethical reconstruction of the citizen seem almost inescapably to try to propagate a code which once again justifies itself by reference to something natural, given, obvious, uncontestable: the virtues of work, the importance of family, the need for individual responsibility to be shown by respect for the basic contours of the existing state of affairs.

Apart from its other difficulties, such a moralizing ethico-politics tends to incite a 'will to govern' which imposes no limits upon itself. Here one can identify the threat of governing too much which characterized the moralizing politics of the administrations of Bill Clinton and Tony Blair in the 1990s. Take, as a trivial example, the following insignificant little text which appeared on the front page of the British newspaper the *Guardian* three months into the term of the New Labour government headed by Tony Blair:

Parents told to sign reading pledge
Primary school parents will be asked to sign an undertaking to read with their

[53] This seems to be Michael Hardt's (1995) view.
[54] T. Osborne 1998.

children at home for at least 20 minutes a day under government proposals for improving literacy published yesterday. The parental reading pledge will be included in home-school contracts setting out teachers' responsibilities and parents' contribution towards the good behaviour, attendance and punctuality which will be expected of the children.[55]

In what other politics would elected politicians seek to use the apparatus of the law to require parents to read to their children for a fixed period each day? This is an ethico-politics that operates, as it were, at the pole of morality. It seeks to govern a polity through the micro-management of the self-steering practices of its citizens. Rather than endeavouring to make forms of life open to explicit political debate, it attempts to technically manage the way in which each individual should conduct him- or herself and his or her relations to others in order to produce politically desired ends. Ethico-politics operates at the pole of morality to the extent that it seeks to inculcate a fixed and uncontestable code of conduct, merely shifting the loci of authority, decision and control in order to govern better.

Against such closure, one could seek to develop an ethico-politics that operates closer to the pole of ethics. This would be a politics whose ethos is a reluctance to govern too much, that minimizes codification and maximizes debate, that seeks to increase the opportunities for each individual to construct and transform his or her own forms of life, that validates diverse ethical criteria and encourages all to develop and refine their practical and experimental arts of existence. It would be a politics which would value the conscious fabrication of particular styles or arts of living.

One community or many?

Can 'multi-culturalism' coexist with a single political community? Increasingly, politicians of the right answer this question in the negative. Michael Shapiro has argued that the neo-Tocquevillian vision, as expressed in particular by Robert Putnam, is blind to the fragmentation of territory in post-liberal societies and that, despite its avowed commitment to pluralism, it seeks to expunge contestability, and to set in place a unitary social order.[56] To the extent that this is the case, communitarian thought reproduces the problems of civic republicanism and neo-conservatism. Shapiro's view is that communitarianism, in these versions, fails to recognize the variety of incommensurable spaces of

[55] *Guardian* 29 July 1997: 1.
[56] Shapiro 1997.

community and identity constitutive of the present. It is blind to the new locally situated and technologically mediated networks of association that have taken shape in our present. And it cannot comprehend the diverse types of political enactment occurring within these different spaces.

The communitarian thought of Putnam, and indeed of Etzioni, does indeed appear to wish to re-invent community in a disciplinary and normalizing form. For example, in attempting to deal with the various compelling criticisms of a 'community-based relativism' that would argue for the legitimacy of any set of values which had majority support within a community – criticisms which show how this might lead to the support of anti-semitism or the suppression of the rights of minorities – Etzioni elaborates his 'new golden rule': 'The basic social virtues are a voluntary moral order and a strong measure of bounded individual and subgroup autonomy held in careful equilibrium.'[57] This rule, for Etzioni, allows judgements to be made about those moral voices that sound genuine enough but are actually *errant*: whether they be the values of the mafiosi or of those who are besotted with consumer goods or caught in religious fanaticism. These arguments serve as proxies for the same values of civic religion as those favoured by the social conservatives: as elaborated by its authorities, communitarian thinking certainly does seem to foreclose debate on the legitimacy of certain values. Hence it fails to diagnose the power relations created in the struggles over cultural diversity and the validity of certain forms of life. But beyond its own particular valuations, I think that contemporary discourses of ethico-politics do open new spaces for contestation and the recognition of diversity. At the rhetorical level, even normalizing communitarianism does recognize that 'America's diverse communities of memory and mutual aid are rich resources of moral voices.'[58] Hence it recognizes that the pluralization of cultures that provokes the culture warriors is an inescapable aspect of our present. Whatever closure it may itself seek to impose, it seems to me that this inescapably plural field invites an agonistic politics of ethics, one that argues for the powers of 'other communities' and 'other subjectivities', for an experimental ethical politics of life itself.

Fixing identities or unworking identities?

It is true that the analyses of the communitarians value community, in part because of a myth that it is a natural space where individuals' ident-

[57] Etzioni 1997: 244.
[58] Communitarian Platform 1996: 1.

ities are fixed in the spontaneous emotional relations of everyday life: community as a realm of intersubjective transparency and self-presence. But against this view of community as a space for the fixing of identities, one can counterpose a different view of community. In this different view, community is not fixed and given but locally and situationally constructed. From this perspective, communities can be imagined and enacted as mobile collectivities, as spaces of indeterminacy, of becoming. To community as essence, origin, fixity, one can thus counterpose community as a constructed form for the collective unworking of identities and moralities. Once more, this is to suggest the possibility of an explicit and agonistic ethico-politics, where the values of different forms of life would be directly at stake.

There are undoubtedly signs of such a politics, in the emergence on to the political stage of all those communities standing up for 'their' values, waging their campaigns, demanding their rights and enacting their resistance in the name of their values. As Michael Hardt and Michael Shapiro point out, control societies produce their own forms of dissent and dissidence: within their circuits there are 'networks of sociality and forms of co-operation embedded in contemporary social practices' which 'constitute the germs for new movements, with new forms of contestation and new conceptions of liberation'.[59] Not, of course, that those who campaign against new roads, nuclear reprocessing plants, hostels for discharged psychiatric patients and the like are radical; the reverse is often the case. But they operate on the same political territory as those who Risto Eräsaari terms 'non-conventional communities'.[60] I am thinking here of the communities of 'survivors' of anything from incest to psychiatry, and of the politics of lifestyle enacted by gays and lesbians, ecofreaks, New Age travellers and the like: the contemporary inheritors of a long history of what Shapiro terms 'insurgent community building'.[61] These radical movements seek to turn community against itself, to resist communization in the name of the bonds of community themselves. For, as Barbara Cruikshank argues, if the communitarian and neo-conservatives are right in their assessment of the dangers posed by counter-cultures to the authority of god, family and nation perhaps the counter-culture can win – perhaps it has already won – the culture war.[62]

In our plural present, it may be impossible, even if one should wish

---

[59] Hardt 1995: 41, quoted in Shapiro 1997: 12.
[60] Eräsaari 1993.
[61] Shapiro 1997: 7.
[62] Cruikshank 1998.

to, to re-activate the politics of equality and justice based on principles of solidarity amongst all citizens of a common political community. Radical culture warriors displace such a politics just as much as those who advocate a cultural politics of identity and recognition.[63] But leftist versions of the politics of identity are merely the mirror image of communitarianism and are traversed by analogous moralisms and analogous practices of inclusion and exclusion. They are tied to a hermeneutics of depth: a therapeutic version of subjectivity in which health depends upon the discovery, acceptance and assertion by oneself of who one really is, upon bonding with those who really are the same, upon the claim that one has the natural right to be recognized individually and collectively in the name of one's truth. The radical potential of those 'becoming communities' – conceptually elaborated by Jean-Luc Nancy and Giorgio Agamben, and practically enacted in all those hybridized, queer, subaltern and non-essentialized communities – lies in the extent that they reject such principles in favour of an ethic of creativity.[64] Within such an ethic, it is not a question of the discovery of one's truth, of a commitment to the project of one's individual and collective identity, but of the active, material, technical, creative assembling of one's existence, one's relation to oneself, even one's corporeality. Community here would be the name for the forms of collectivization that create such new types of non-individuated subjectivity and bring new mobile forces into existence. Whilst it is too early to tell what future there may be for such a radical ethico-politics, perhaps one can find, in the emergence of these creative ways of thinking and acting, some limited grounds for optimism.

[63] See N. Fraser 1995.
[64] See, for example, Nancy 1991; Agamben 1993. These issues require a much more extensive discussion than I am able to provide here: once again, William Connolly's (1995) reflections on pluralization are particularly instructive.

6   Numbers

Numbers have achieved an unmistakable political power within technologies of government. An initial inventory might distinguish four sorts of political numbers.

First, numbers determine who holds power, and whose claim to power is justified. Electoral districts apportion persons according to numerical criteria. Elections and referenda count votes. Executive powers are related to numerical calculations of majorities and minorities. The fate of a nation can depend upon a percentage point or less; the character of an assembly can depend upon a complex mathematical calculation of proportionality. Numbers, here, are part of the mechanism of conferring legitimacy on political leaders, authorities and institutions.

Secondly, numbers operate as diagnostic instruments within liberal political reason. Opinion polls calibrate and quantify public feelings; as George Gallup put it, they 'take the pulse of democracy'.[1] Social surveys and market research try to transform the lives and views of individuals into numerical scales and percentages. Numbers here promise to align the exercise of 'public' authority with the values and beliefs of 'private' citizens. And this promise becomes even more alluring as democratic citizens themselves come to be understood as consumers with preferences which politicians ignore at their peril.

Thirdly, numbers make modern modes of government both possible and judgeable. Possible, because they help make up the object domains upon which government is required to operate. They map the boundaries and the internal characteristics of the spaces of population, economy and society. And other locales – the organization, the hospital, the university, the factory and so on – are made intelligible, calculable and practicable through representations that are, at least in part, numerical. Judgeable, because rates, tables, graphs, trends, numerical comparisons have become essential to the critical

---

[1] *The Pulse of Democracy* is the title of Gallup and Rae's book of 1940.

scrutiny of authority in contemporary society. Liberal political thought has long been characterized by sceptical vigilance over government. This vigilance is increasingly conducted in the language of numbers.

Fourthly, numbers are crucial techniques for modern government. They have become indispensable to the complex technologies through which government is exercised. Tax returns enable an administration over individuals and private enterprises in the light of a knowledge of their financial affairs. Counts of population, of birth, death and morbidity have become intrinsic to the formulation and justification of governmental programmes. Grants to local authorities and health agencies are distributed on the basis of complex numerical formulae applied to arrays of numbers claiming to represent states of affairs in this or that part of the realm. The rates at which pensions or social security benefits are paid, and when or if they are to rise, are calculated according to complex numerical indices.

I would make three initial points about these political numbers.

First, the relation between numbers and politics is reciprocal and mutually constitutive. As Alonso and Starr point out, acts of social quantification are 'politicized' not in the sense that the numbers they use are somehow corrupt – although they may be – but because 'political judgements are implicit in the choice of what to measure, how to measure it, how often to measure it and how to present and interpret the results'.[2]

Secondly, our images of political life are shaped by the realities of our society that numerical technologies appear to disclose: statistics, population counts, accountancy, economic forecasts, budgets and the like. It is not simply that political debate deploys numbers, or that so many political decisions affecting our lives entail the deployment of numbers in their calculation and legitimation. Numbers, like other 'inscription devices', actually constitute the domains they appear to represent; they render them representable in a docile form – a form amenable to the application of calculation and deliberation. Hence it is not just that the domain of numbers is politically composed, but also that the domain of politics is made up numerically.

Thirdly, whilst numbers seem indispensable to politics, they also appear to depoliticize whole areas of political judgement. They redraw the boundaries between politics and objectivity by purporting to act as automatic technical mechanisms for making judgements, prioritizing problems and allocating scarce resources. As Anthony Hopwood puts it, numbers, and the specialist knowledges and professional techniques

[2] Alonso and Starr 1987: 3.

associated with them, become 'implicated in the creation of a domain where technical expertise can come to dominate political debate'.[3] A spiral of 'technicization of politics' emerges between the new visibility of 'the facts' and the imperative of increased technical expertise to gather and interpret them. Numbers are not just 'used' in politics. The apparent objectivity of numbers, and of those who fabricate and manipulate them, helps configure the respective boundaries of the political and the technical. Numbers are part of the techniques of objectivity that establish what it is for a decision to be 'disinterested'.

Of course there has long been a politics of numbers: a politics of accuracy – for example, in Britain there was a protracted wrangle about the 'fudging' of the statistics on unemployment under Margaret Thatcher's governments; a politics of adequacy, about which numbers are best for what purpose – for example, which numbers should be used to determine the rate of inflation or of economic growth; a politics of use and abuse, for example, should questions concerning ethnicity be included in the census; a politics of privacy, seeking to place a limit on the public collection of numbers on private persons, and their utilization in making decisions about individuals. And there is a politics of ethics, perhaps best illustrated in debates about whether decisions about giving or withholding medical treatment should be made in terms of numbers – calculations of cost, risk and so forth.

However, in this chapter, drawing on the empirical work of others, I want to propose a more general argument about politics, or rather government, and numbers.[4] The organization of political life in the form of the modern 'governmental' state has been intrinsically linked to the composition of networks of numbers connecting those exercising political power with the persons, processes and problems that they seek to govern. Numbers are integral to the problematizations that shape what is to be governed, to the programmes that seek to give effect to government and to the unrelenting evaluation of the performance of government that characterizes modern political culture.

Further, I want to suggest a more specific hypothesis: that there is a constitutive interrelationship between quantification and democratic government. This is not, of course, to say that numbers have been unimportant in non-democratic regimes: for example, in Nazi Germany the

---

[3] Hopwood 1988: 263.

[4] I draw, in particular, upon Patricia Cline-Cohen's (1982) study *A Calculating People: The Spread of Numeracy in Early America,* and upon the papers collected in William Alonso and Paul Starr's (1987) study of the 1980 US census *The Politics of Numbers.*

policy of killing those whose lives were deemed not worth living was justified by detailed calculations about the costs to the German Reich of maintaining the mentally ill and others deemed socially unfit.[5] Nonetheless, numbers have a characteristic role in democracies. Democratic power is calculated power, and numbers are intrinsic to the forms of justification that give legitimacy to political power in democracies. Democratic power is calculating power, and numbers are integral to the technologies that seek to give effect to democracy as a particular set of mechanisms of rule. Democratic power requires citizens who calculate about power, and numeracy and a numericized space of public discourse are essential for making up self-controlling democratic citizens.

The social history of numbers

Most social historians of numbers suggest that the earliest relations between numbers and politics were anything but democratic. They point out that the term 'censor' dates from Roman times: the censor was one who censed, who counted adult male citizens and their property for purposes of taxation and to determine military obligations and political status, and one who censured, who was charged with the control of manners. Patricia Cline-Cohen cites Jean Bodin arguing in similar terms in 1606. It was expedient to enrol and number the subjects of a commonwealth because, from the numbers, ages and quality of persons, a government could learn the military and colonizing potential of a country and plan for adequate food at time of siege or famine. But also, as he enrolled the subjects, the censor would be inspecting, exposing and judging them, serving thereby 'to expell all drones out of a commonweale, which sucke the honey from the Bees, and to banish vagabonds, idle persons, thieves, cooseners, & ruffians ... who although

---

[5] In his study of medicine under the Nazis, Robert Proctor gives a number of chilling examples. One depiction from a 1933 edition of *Volk und Rasse* pictures the burden of maintaining the social unfit in terms of four sacks of unequal sizes each labelled with a number: 125, 573, 950, 1,500. The caption reads 'The Prussian Government provides annually the following funds for: a Normal Schoolchild (125 RM); a Slow Learner (573 RM); the Educable Mentally Ill (950 RM); and Blind or Deaf Born Schoolchildren (1,500 RM)' (Proctor 1988: 183). A problem from a German high school mathematics textbook of the same period requires the schoolchildren to calculate the cost to the state of mentally ill people in receipt of state support or various sorts of institutional care, and then to work out how this cost varies depending on the length of stay. A further problem is simpler: 'The construction of an insane asylum requires 6 million RM. How many housing units at 15,000 RM could be built for the amount spent on insane asylums?' (ibid.: 184).

they walke in darkness, yet hereby they should bee seene, noted and known'.[6]

In the science of police that was formulated in Europe in the seventeenth and eighteenth centuries, this link between numbering, surveillance and censure was maintained. But it was combined in the notion that the power of the prince could and should be exercised in a rational way, dependent upon a knowledge of and a calculation about those over whom government was to be exercised. Indeed, the term 'statistics' derives from the seventeenth-century German notion of a science of states: in Herman Conring's notion of *Staatenkunde*, and in Gottfried Aschenwall's conception of *Statistik*, the systematic study of states required the collection and tabulation of significant facts, although these facts did not consist exclusively of numbers.[7] Statistics, the census and statecraft were intrinsically related.

Dreams of democratic potential that numbers held for politics probably date from the French revolution. Condorcet's proposal for a 'social mathematics' was set out in his unfinished essay *Tableau général de la science qui a pour objet l'application du calcul aux sciences politiques et morales*.[8] This was published in the short-lived *Journal d'instruction sociale*, in the revolutionary year of 1793, and just before his death in jail after his denunciation of the Jacobin constitution. Condorcet's aim was to free the people from the ignorance and error upon which political despotism depended: scientific reasoning in human affairs would enable citizens to decide social and political questions on the authority of their own reason. Social mathematics would be a unified science embracing the application of all branches of the arts of mathematics to social phenomena in order to provide reason with its methods: 'without the application of rigorous methods of calculation and the science of combinations, one would soon come to the limit beyond which all progress becomes impossible and the advance of the moral and political sciences (as that of the physical sciences) would soon be halted'.[9] A few years earlier Condorcet seems to have urged the Commissioners of the National Treasury to set up a public bureau for this purpose, to assemble a large enough body of facts to enable conclusions to be drawn about the laws governing human affairs from observations about births,

[6] Bodin [1606] 1962: 537-46, quoted in Cline-Cohen 1982: 37.
[7] On the German pedigree of statistics in the eighteenth century, see Hacking 1990: 22-4. See also the discussion in Cullen 1975.
[8] The best account of Condorcet's life and work is in Keith Michael Baker's compelling book *Condorcet: From Natural Philosophy to Social Mathematics* (Baker 1975), which I have relied upon here.
[9] Condorcet, quoted from Baker 1975: 333.

marriages and deaths, the strength and stature of individuals, even their moral qualities and behaviour. All the data relating to population, commerce, territorial production collected in different parts of the administration would be gathered together in such a bureau. But social mathematics was not envisaged as a technocratic social science: as Baker puts it 'social mathematics . . . was intended not to replace parliamentary government but to produce the conditions necessary for its preservation and rational operation'.[10]

A century earlier, William Petty had attempted a rather more technocratic version of the numericization of politics, although one that also dreamed of resolving political controversy through arguments of sense and the science of numbers. Petty's project was inspired by John Graunt's use of the bills of mortality kept by the City of London from 1603, which listed the numbers of children christened each week and the numbers of deaths classified by disease.[11] On the basis of this he examined 'The course of various diseases across the decades, the numbers of inhabitants, the ratio of males to females, the proportion of people dying at several ages, the number of men fit to bear arms, the emigration from city to county in times of fever, the influence of the plague upon birth rates, and the projected growth of London', and drew practical conclusions for government such as the advantages of a guaranteed annual wage. Petty transformed Graunt's speculative musings into a project for a political arithmetic that would introduce reliable political argument based on the facts of the natural world into the tumult of theological controversy. Political arithmetic was 'uncontaminated by "passion, interest and party"' and it provided 'an answer to the problem of how to create a science of policy "free from the distorting effects of controversy and conflict"'.[12] It would be 'a science which could be expressed purely "in terms of *Number*, *Weight* or *Measure*", and which would use "only Arguments of Sense" rather than "those that depend on the mutable Minds, Opinions, Appetites and passions of particular Men"'.[13] And his arguments appear to have born fruit. An Act of 1694 ordered what was effectively a complete enumeration of the inhabitants of England and Wales, which was to lead to an attempt to tax births, deaths and marriages and to levy annual fines on bachelors over twenty-five and childless widows. The act lapsed a decade later,

---

[10] Baker 1975: 340.
[11] Graunt 1662. Hacking 1975: ch. 12 gives a lucid account which I have drawn upon here. The following quote is from p. 106.
[12] Petty 1648: 157, quoted from D. Burchell 1998: 199.
[13] D. Burchell 1998: 199.

but in 1696 it led to the creation of the first special statistical department successfully established by any Western European state.[14]

Paul Starr suggests that Petty's political arithmetic sought 'the application of rational calculation to the understanding, exercise, and enhancement of State power'.[15] But historical accounts tend to stress that political numbers were to play a key role in liberal political thought. Thus Peter Buck argued that, in the second half of the eighteenth century, a broad ideological shift transformed political arithmetic from 'a scientific prospectus for the exercise of State power' into 'a program for reversing the growth of government and reducing its influence on English social and economic life'. For Buck, this was a matter of conceiving of people not as subjects but as citizens, and of freeing political arithmetic from state power, 'allowing it to reenter the domain of public controversy on new terms'.[16]

From this point forward it is possible to provide a rough and ready division into two sorts of histories of politics and numbers – a benign American history and a less optimistic European history. Thus, for example, Paul Starr concludes that, in modern societies, numbers have become a means for reducing the fear of unchecked power:

> To subordinate ourselves under an impersonal rule is the fundamental reason why we have laws and constitutions. However imperfect, a rule of law tends to restrain the use of powers and thereby enlarges liberty. Statistical systems help to accomplish similar purposes, and, despite their imperfections, they may also contribute to our freedom.[17]

On the other hand, Ian Hacking concludes that the collection of statistics is enmeshed in the formation of a great bureaucratic state machine, part of the technology of power of the modern state. Statistics, in enabling the taming of chance, in turning a qualitative world into information and rendering it amenable to control, in establishing the classifications by which people come to think of themselves and their choices, appears to be bound up with an apparatus of domination.[18]

Let me first say a few words about the benign and optimistic analysis of the links between statistics and government proposed by American social historians. It is true that Otis Dudley Duncan claimed that social and economic statistics, like other forms of measurement, are developed, promoted and imposed at particular historical moments because

[14] Cline-Cohen 1982: 34; D. Burchell 1998: 202.
[15] Starr 1987: 14.
[16] Buck 1982: 28, 35, quoted by Starr 1987: 15.
[17] Starr 1987: 57.
[18] Hacking 1981: 15.

they serve particular interests, including a state interest in co-ordination and control.[19] But in the American writings, this interest in control and co-ordination is not construed in terms of surveillance and discipline. Rather, it is analysed in a pluralist manner, in terms of the means whereby private entities may co-ordinate one with another; in terms of the defeat of superstition by the belief in quantitative control; in terms of the replacement of old relations of status, rank and dependence by those of objectivity and truth.

Thus Paul Starr, whilst recognizing that the key issue to be explored concerns 'the demands of the modern State for social and economic intelligence' distinguishes the pre-modern census – 'used explicitly for keeping people under surveillance and control' – from the modern census, which, he claims, 'has as its primary and manifest function the production of quantitative information'.[20] Within this kind of analysis, power is construed in terms of surveillance, control and suppression. Hence, when analysts cannot find evidence of domination by numbers, they conclude that power too is absent. But if we are really to appreciate the links of government and numbers in advanced liberal democracies we are going to have to discard this naïve calculus of power and think in other terms.

Many of these American accounts argue that there is something *intrinsic* to numbers, and it is in terms of this intrinsic property that their social history should be written. For Starr, for example, this intrinsic power lies in the reduction of complexity. 'Social conditions and the characteristics of people are myriad and subtly varied; statistical inquiries must be limited to particular items and categories of response. Yet the raw data thereby collected can be combined and analyzed in sundry ways; scarce cognitive as well as economic resources dictate that only some routes be followed.[21] The possibility of a social history of numbers arises from the fact that such reduction of complexity can be neither ideologically nor theoretically innocent: hence the social enters the statistical through the 'interests' of those who undertake this task.[22] The processes of simplification embody the expectations and beliefs of the responsible technicians and officials. The discretion that they inevitably exercise is dissimulated by the claim that their expertise, whilst indispensable, is 'merely technical'. Expectations and beliefs are embodied

---

[19] Duncan 1984: 12-38, cited by Starr 1987: 9.

[20] Starr 1987: 15, 11.

[21] Ibid.: 40.

[22] An analogous interest-based history of statistics in Britain is developed in Mackenzie 1981.

in the framing of statistical enquiry, for example, in the form of explicit or implicit theories shaping what is counted and how it is to be counted. They are embedded in the systems of classification adopted, for example, ethnicity rather than race, nationality, ancestry, caste or religion. They are embodied in how the measurement is done, and what forces have their concerns embedded in numbers. They are bound up with questions as to how often to measure and how to deal with change; for example, data on the money supply are published monthly, but estimates of poverty are annual, and the census is taken every ten years. And they are embodied in the ways in which bureaucrats choose to shape and present the data – for example, the 'specious accuracy', to use Morgenstern's term,[23] in which figures are reported to several decimal places.

When such numbers are used as 'automatic pilots' in decision making they transform the thing being measured – segregation, hunger, poverty – into its statistical indicator and displace political disputes into technical disputes about methods. As Kevin Prewitt has put it, 'Arguments about numerical quotas, availability pools and demographic imbalance become a substitute for democratic discussion of the principles of equity and justice.[24] And Starr notes that the ultimate reduction of complexity in official statistics is the choice of the single number that will figure in the briefings and speeches of politicians and in the headlines. Others have also highlighted the 'power of the single figure', drawing attention to the particular potency of those numerical technologies that can reduce the complexity of experience to a single comparable, quotable, calculable number: a score on an IQ test, a rate of inflation, the percentage growth in GDP . . .'[25]

Patricia Cline-Cohen also suggests that the power of numbers in modern societies has something to do with their intrinsic qualities.[26] She suggests that the power of numbers arises, in large part, from their 'ordering capacity'. Numbers are 'ordering', she claims, for four basic reasons. First, enumeration creates a 'bond of uniformity' around the objects counted – one *can* add oranges and apples if one wants to know how much fruit there is. Secondly, numbers enable unlike orders of magnitude to be brought into a relation with one another – distances over oceans with altitudes of mountains, the volume of a barrel of ale and that of a tub of lard, the climate of Massachusetts and that of

[23] Morgenstern 1963: 62.
[24] Prewitt 1987: 272.
[25] Miller 1992; cf. Hopwood 1986.
[26] Cline-Cohen 1982: 43-4.

London. Thirdly, numbers can sort out the combined effects of several components and hence stabilize a process that is in flux: velocity can be decomposed into time and distance, population growth into fertility and mortality. And numbers can be utilized in matters of probability, to convey a notion of risk.

Cline-Cohen argues that these cognitive features of numbers prove attractive and are drawn upon in certain cultural conditions. The ordering qualities of numbers, she suggests, help explain why quantification emerges in the seventeenth century: this is in response to major political, economic and cosmological shifts marked by disorder and even chaos. Whilst political and economic changes are both important to her argument, most significant is cosmology. This is not the familiar Weberian link between Calvinism and calculation, but the inability of the Aristotelian system of scientific classification to make sense of a world newly teeming with activities cutting across the classic categories. Given that all the 'ordering qualities' of numbers existed in the seventeenth century; in those 'turbulent and disorderly years, quantification must have seemed an alluring way to impose order on a world in flux'.[27] This account is attractive but inadequate. Turbulent circumstances cannot in themselves lead to a desire to quantify. The relation between numbers and the reduction of turbulence has itself to be forged conceptually. It is as unsatisfactory to seek to explain new modes of cognition by pointing to 'social conditions' as it is to point to 'economic needs' or 'political functions'. 'Social conditions' are never active in human affairs as 'raw experiences' but only in and through certain regimes of language and value. Ideas are constitutively social in that they are formed and circulated within very material apparatuses for the production, delimitation and authorization of truth. It is not very helpful to artificially distinguish the intellectual from the social and then to perplex ourselves with the conundrum of how they are related.

The most rigorous attempt to conceptualize the link between statistics and standardization is to be found in the work of Theodore Porter.[28] Porter argues that standardization is not just a matter of the imposition of a system of bureaucratic regulation. Rather, it is a condition for interaction in diversified societies with an expanded division of labour, requiring a common means of 'trading' between different sectors – that is to say, requiring something that will provide a certain 'translatability'. Stable standards thus enable the co-ordination of commercial activities

[27] Ibid.: 44.
[28] T. Porter 1986, 1990.

across wide time-space zones, producing a means by which widely dispersed activities can be made commensurable one with another.

For Porter, quantification is significant because it standardizes both its object and its subject. It standardizes the object in that it establishes in univocal terms what is a yard, a bushel, a kilometre, the exchangeable worth of a piece of coin. Witold Kula has documented a range of practices up to the end of the eighteenth century where measures of land or grain were inextricably bound up with locally established customary practices.[29] Thus in the measure of land, for example, its square dimensions were frequently less significant than local judgements about its quality, the time taken to cultivate it, the harvest it was capable of yielding. And in the measure of grain, which was arrived at through the filling of a container such as a bushel, not only did the actual volume of the container vary according to precisely how it was made – unseasoned wood, for example, would dry out and diminish the measure – but how much it contained depended on the height from which the grain was poured, whether it was heaped or flattened and so forth. Quantification standardizes the object, but it also standardizes the subject of measurement: the act of exchange is no longer dependent on the personalities or statuses of those involved. The lord can no longer require that his bushel be measured out in grain poured from a greater height into the container – thus packing it more densely – or in a wide, shallow container that will gather a greater quantity in the heaping. Hence, while quantification is certainly bound up with the emergence of a specialist elite who calculate in terms of numbers, this is not simply a matter of the rise of technocracy. The officials who use these statistical and calculative methods are themselves constrained by the calculative apparatus they use. And this means that quantification produces a certain type of objectivity. As Anthony Hopwood has remarked, a network of the apparently precise, specific and quantitative emerges out of, and is superimposed upon, the contentious and the uncertain.[30]

For Porter, the objectivity imposed by standardization and quantification is not merely a matter of epistemology. The establishment of a domain of objectivity is linked to those social transformations that increase mobility of populations, and expand the domain of trading into new markets and locales. The old bonds that assured the mutuality of persons entering into trade no longer figure: a new objectivity is a substitute for that lost trust. In that it attempts to externalize the individual

---

[29] Kula 1986.
[30] Hopwood 1988: 261.

from the calculation, the objectivity conferred by calculation establishes a potential domain of 'fairness' of that which is above party and peculiar interests. And to the extent that decisions are transformed from acts of judgement to the outcome of rule-following, the opportunity for discretion and the imposition of partiality is reduced. Thus numerical rules constrain: impersonality rather than status, wisdom or experience becomes the measure of truth. In a democratic society with an elaborated sphere of 'civil society' and a plurality of interest groups, numbers produce a public rhetoric of disinterest in situations of contestation.

But this rhetoric of disinterest has to be interrogated. Why is it – or when is it – that scientific and technical experts have recourse to quantification? For Porter, this is not a sign of their weakness but of their strength.[31] When the authority of authority is secure, when authoritative judgements carry inherent authority, when the legitimacy of their authority is not subject to sceptical scrutiny and challenge, experts have little need of numbers. But where mistrust of authority flourishes, where experts are the target of suspicion and their claims are greeted with scepticism by politicians, disputed by professional rivals, distrusted by public opinion, where decisions are contested and discretion is criticized, the allure of numbers increases. It is in these circumstances that professionals and experts try to justify their judgements on the ground of objectivity, and frequently frame this objectivity in numerical form. Numbers are resorted to in order to settle or diminish conflicts in a contested space of weak authority. And the 'power of the single figure' is here a rhetorical technique for 'black boxing' – that is to say, rendering invisible and hence incontestable – the complex array of judgements and decisions that go into a measurement, a scale, a number. The apparent facticity of the figure obscures the complex technical work that is required to *produce* objectivity.[32]

These American considerations of the politics of numeracy and quantification echo themes common to much American sociology and political science. They raise points about why particular numerical indi-

---

[31] T. Porter 1996.

[32] Porter gives the example of the complex process of decisions involved in ascertaining even such an apparently simple number as the population of a country: how to count tourists, aliens, military personnel, persons with multiple residences or citizenship, how to deal with known undercounting of the poor and homeless, how much effort to put in to reaching people who are difficult to find at home, how to actually collect the data (door-to-door questions, postal methods), how to aggregate it, which tables to present in the report and so forth (T. Porter 1996: ch. 2). We will meet these issues again in this chapter, in the discussion of the US census of 1980.

ces are salient rather than others, about why this is counted rather than that, about the accuracy of the figures or about the disputes between different forces, locales, interests about what should be counted and by whom. They demonstrate that political numbers are bound up with struggles and contestations amongst interest groups and sectional lobbies. They illuminate the clashing cultures, values and objectives of the academics who theorize the figures, the statisticians who calculate them, the technocrats who utilize them and the politicians who calculate or pontificate in terms of them. They contribute to what one might term the 'political sociology' of numbers. But I think it is also fruitful to approach the history of numbers from another direction.

Undemocratic and democratic numbers

Like these American studies, I am interested in the relations between numbers and democracy. But my starting point is different – it is in the tradition of European considerations of numbers and politics which have placed this relation within a different kind of analysis of power. I would like to draw out five significant themes from previous studies.

The first is the role of numbers in the link between government and knowledge. In his consideration of the mentalities of government that characterize all contemporary modes of exercise of political power in the West, Foucault argues that rule becomes understood as the exercise of power over domains that have their own internal laws and conditions: for these to be acted upon, they must be known.[33] Knowledge was not just a matter of numbers – but numbers were an essential feature of the new positive knowledges of political economy, sociology, public health and medicine, psychology and so forth. In the nineteenth century, statistics thus becomes one of the key modalities for the production of the knowledge necessary to govern. The statistics of crime, of trade and industrial disputes, of morbidity and mortality, of population size and growth, render the objects of government into thought as domains with their own inherent density and vitality. And one can trace the reciprocal and symbiotic relations between numericization of such disciplines of economics, accountancy, sociology, psychology and health and their relations with the practical domains of their deployment within human technologies.[34]

The second theme is the link between government and information.

---

[33] Foucault 1977.

[34] Danziger (1990) examines this in relation to psychology; T. Porter (1996) examines it in relation to economics, accountancy and engineering.

This is emphasized, for example, in the work of Pasquale Pasquino.[35] In the eighteenth-century German writings of von Justi, Sonnenfels, Obrecht and other theorists of 'police', a vital link is constructed between a politics of calculated administration of the population – with the ends of wealth, public order, virtue and happiness – and information. There can be no well-ordered political machinery or enlightened administration, they argue, without a knowledge of the state of the population, and the numbering of persons, goods, activities, births, crimes, deaths and much else provides the material upon which administrative calculation can operate. Nineteenth-century arguments from social statisticians in Britain and the USA, and arguments in favour of the census, maintain this link in a more liberal form – judicious legislation and wise government must be founded upon statistical knowledge of the matters and persons to be governed if problems are to be ameliorated, economy advanced and the condition of the people improved and civilized. But there was no necessary political complexion to these arguments. The link between government and information was central to political concerns with degeneration and eugenics in the latter decades of the nineteenth century and the early decades of the twentieth. A quantification of the problem spaces of crime and degeneracy through moral topographies of populations was central to statistical arguments about the decline of the quality of the race that found their apotheosis in eugenics.[36] But the numericization of the population was also crucial to democratic and republican arguments in the United States that the effective and acceptable exercise of political and organizational authority needed to be guided by information on attitudes and beliefs provided by attitude surveys and opinion polling.

The third theme concerns the role of numbers in the formation of centres of government. Some ways of thinking about this can be derived from the work of Bruno Latour.[37] Traditionally, conceptions of politics see the state as a centre of power that monopolizes force and legitimate rule over a zone of space and time. The state has power and exercises it. But how does it become possible to extend government over events and things that are distant? This is a very empirical and material matter. It entails establishing links, networks, alliances and conduits that in various ways allow 'action at a distance'. Only to the extent that it is possible

---

[35] Pasquino 1991. For further discussions of 'police', see Knemeyer 1980; Oestreich 1982; Andrew 1989.

[36] On moral topographies, see K. Jones and Williamson 1979. On the charting of the population in its eugenic and pre-eugenic forms see Haller 1963; Hofstadter 1955; Kevles 1985; Proctor 1988; Searle 1971.

[37] Latour 1987.

to do so can a centre be constituted. There are two reciprocal aspects to this, and numbers have been important to both.

The first aspect has to do with calculation. The formation of a centre of calculation requires the assembly together of what Latour calls immutable mobiles, traces that will, when transported to a particular locale, literally re-present that which is distant in a single plane, visible, cognizable, amenable to deliberation and decision. To put together a network that will enable power to be exercised over events and processes distant from oneself, it is necessary to turn these into traces that can be mobilized and accumulated. Events must be inscribed in standardized forms, the inscriptions must be transported from far and wide and accumulated in a central locale, where they can be aggregated, compared, compiled and the subject of calculation. Through the development of such complex relays of inscription and accumulation, new conduits of power are brought into being between those who wish to exercise power and those over whom they wish to exercise it. As Ian Hacking has pointed out, over the past two centuries in Europe, political attempts at the calculated administration of life have been accompanied by a veritable 'avalanche' of printed numbers.[38] Figures from parish registers, censuses, surveys, enquiries have been collected, compiled extracted, mobilized to travel across space and time to come together in an office – of a colonial governor, a cabinet minister, a general, a religious organization, a tax office. These did not merely connect centres of calculation to other locales – they enabled the centre to act as a centre by means of its centrality in the flows of information that 're-present' that over which it is to calculate and seek to programme. Indeed, drawing on the innovations in accounting practices in France in the late seventeenth century, associated in particular with the name of Colbert, who was Louis XIV's Superintendent of Commerce and Controller of Finances as well as Superintendent of Buildings and Secretary of State for Marine, Peter Miller has argued that the earliest kinds of numerical relations between the political apparatus and those whom it would govern – relations of accounting – actually constituted the possibility of 'the state'. Merchants were required to keep and produce books of account and educated in the proper procedures for accomplishing this. An array of inquiries were set up in which 'Intendants' located in each province would be responsible for investigating surveillance over Huguenots, the provision of military supplies, the allocation and collection of taxes, the distribution of wealth among the population, the condition of roads, rivers and bridges, the levying of local tools and duties, the

[38] Hacking 1981: 19.

integrity of local officials and much more. These Intendants would submit information to Colbert's office in response to a stream of questionnaires and requests for information. Tables, registers and accounts were drawn up to enable judgements to be made based on detailed reporting of the facts. The vast project of information gathering set out by Colbert was not to be fully achieved. But, for Miller, 'According a visibility to the minutiae of the activities of the nation, devising the calculative techniques through which this visibility is to be made operable, and representing the nation by means of a variety of knowledges . . . [were crucial steps] in the very construction of "the state" viewed as a complex of practices of government.[39] Turning the objects of government into numericized inscriptions, then, enables a machinery of government to operate from centres that calculate.

The second aspect is that numbers function in these governmental relays as powerful 'fidelity techniques', means for ensuring the allegiance of those who are distant to decisions in a centre – budgets, tax returns, figures concerning levels of business or trade, crime figures and so forth all allow a centre to maintain its hold over the actions of those who are distant from it. For example, in the case of the regulation of economic life, to quote Peter Miller, 'the calculative technologies of accountancy act as the "civilizing medium", by transforming the management of private firms and public sector organizations into a complex of incessant calculations'.[40] In chapter 4 I examined some ways in which these means of 'government at a distance' through numbers have been central to the innovations in governmental regimes associated with advanced liberalism, whether it be in the form of the numericization of the activities of schools, hospitals and universities or in the extension of the mechanisms of audit as a means of ensuring the fidelity of professionals and experts in a whole host of different fields.

Fourthly and arising from this, it is clear that such numbers do not merely inscribe a pre-existing reality. They constitute it. Techniques of inscription and accumulation of facts about 'the population', 'the national economy', 'poverty' render visible a domain with a certain internal homogeneity and external boundaries. In each case, the collection and aggregation of numbers participate in the fabrication of a 'clearing' within which thought and action can occur. Numbers here help to delineate 'irreal spaces' for the operation of government, and to mark them out by a grid of norms allowing evaluation and judgement.[41] These

[39] Miller 1990: 323.
[40] Miller 1992: 67.
[41] Miller and O'Leary 1987; Rose 1988; Miller and Rose 1990.

'calculable spaces' have made up the fields of government at both macro- and micro-levels. At the macro-level, one can consider the way in which such innovations as national income accounting, and the activities of the OECD, made up 'the national economy' as a domain which could be measured, calculated, compared, assessed over time, acted upon in the name of its optimization through the kinds of technologies we now term 'Keynesian'. At the micro-level one can consider the ways in which the calculative technologies of accountancy brought into existence the space of the factory, of the cost centre, of the profit centre, of the division, fabricating these in terms of budgets and the hierarchical regimes and responsibilities for their administration. 'The "division" that a manager controls, the "cost center" or "profit center" that one is responsible for, and the "budget" that the individual administers are calculable spaces that accountancy fabricates . . . These abstract spaces are objects to be known and regulated in terms of their performance and to be brought into relation with other abstract spaces. The loose assemblage of practices that goes under the name of management accounting constructs the boundaries that define these spaces, endows them with content, and links them together in variable relations of dependency.[42] They may be 'abstract spaces' but they are very material: for they are made up of inscriptions, acted upon by techniques, utilized as the basis of organization architecture and divisions of managerial responsibility, and utilized as a grid to 'realize' the real in the form in which it may be thought. And, of course, as these accountancy-shaped spaces are thrown over a whole range of other institutions, from the civil service to the child support agency, a whole variety of new calculable spaces are brought into existence, spaces which must calculate *about themselves* in certain ways because they are calculated about in certain ways *by others*.

Fifthly, one can point to the rise of the calculable person, the person rendered calculable to others and to him- or herself in terms of numbers. There are a whole array of practices and locales where this occurred. In the twentieth century, the workplace has been one crucial site and the military has been another. But it was in the nineteenth century that, as Foucault put it, we can first observe a reversal of the axis of political individualization, where those who were most individualized were no longer the sovereign, the lord, the mighty, but the criminal, the mad person, the patient, the child.[43] This simultaneous individualization and

---

[42] Miller 1992: 75: the omitted reference within this quote is Hopwood 1986.
[43] This is, of course, one of the central arguments of Foucault's *Discipline and Punish* (1977).

normalization occurred within the apparatuses of rule that proliferated in the nineteenth century – the prison, the factory, the asylum, the school and later in the military – all those places where individuals were gathered together and their conduct made visible by being judged against institutional norms. We are familiar with the account of the rise of notions of intelligence, personality and so forth in these locales, their invention in the same process as the development of the technical devices to assess them, and the organizational procedures to distribute individuals in the light of them – once more, the power of the single number becomes apparent.[44] The history of all those programmes that acted upon each in the name of all reveals a profound ambiguity in the status of numbers – IQ testing was crucial to the 'democratic' eugenic programmes in Britain and the United States, but virtually irrelevant to the murderous politics of racial hygiene in Nazi Germany. Numbers, then, are neither necessary nor sufficient to particular regimes of government; they take their character from the complex of values, agents, concepts and strategies within which they are linked in loose assemblages.

But we should not think of these practices that make individuals calculable purely as technologies of domination, for they can also be technologies of autonomization and responsibilization. Numbers, and the techniques of calculation in terms of numbers, have a role in subjectification – they turn the individual into a calculating self endowed with a range of ways of thinking about, calculating about, predicting and judging their own activities and those of others. The inculcation of calculating mentalities has been key to the practices of schooling since the nineteenth century – calculation engenders foresight and prudence. It is key to the regulation of economic action both for the worker and for the manager. This is not merely a matter of a 'psychological' transformation, although it does change the way in which the individual relates to him- or herself. It is also a matter of the enmeshing of the calculating self 'in networks of calculation, as objects and as active participants'.[45] The manager may calculate the performance of the worker, even as the worker is trying to maximize her achievement in terms of the norms that have been laid down within the organization, and as the manager herself is assessing the performance of her section and being assessed by her superiors. The inculcation of calculative practices was central to a whole

---

[44] I discuss the rise of IQ testing from this perspective in Rose 1985 and discuss the significance of the workplace and the army in Rose 1990. See also Danziger 1990. Peter Miller and Ted O'Leary consider the role of accounting and calculation in Miller and O'Leary 1987.

[45] Miller 1992: 75.

variety of interventions upon the lives of women, to render them prudent, and to the pedagogies of domestic science in the first half of the twentieth century – as well as in the practices of social workers and Citizens Advice Bureaux today. And, in recent transformations in government, each individual and his or her family are to be transformed into a little calculative locale, planning the present in terms of the future through share ownership, investment, pensions, insurance plans, linking the individual and family into a web of expert advisers and suffusing it with expert calculative technologies in the name of maximizing their human capital and their lifestyle.

If we start from these five themes, European approaches to the social history of quantification seem to suggest that this 'statisticalization' of politics was bound up with attempts by the state to control and subordinate individuals and populations. But this emphasis on surveillance, inspection, centralization and subordination is too limited. I would like, instead, to emphasize the links between the numericization of political argument and democracy as a mentality of government and a technology of rule. This is not a question of the intrinsic capacity of numbers. As I have already suggested, I do not think there is any essential unity to the relations of numbers and politics. Rather, it is a question of the 'what' and the 'where' of the deployment of numbers, and the 'how' of their alignment within rationalities and technologies for the conduct of conduct. Let me illustrate this by three examples: democracy and the census; democracy and citizenship; democracy and economy.

Calculating authorities: the census

At first sight, the modern deployment of numbers in the form of the census of population has little to do with democracy. For whilst each country has its own history, by and large the first to be enumerated were the most dominated – the inhabitants of the colonies. Ian Hacking provides a lucid summary:

The Spanish had a census of Peru in 1548, and of their North American possessions in 1576. Virginia had censuses in 1642-5 and a decade later. Regular repeated modern censuses were perhaps first held in Acadie and Canada (now the provinces of Nova Scotia and Quebec) in the 1660s. Colbert, the French minister of finance, had instructed all regions to do this, but only New France came through systematically and on time. Ireland was completely surveyed for land, buildings, people and cattle under the directorship of William Petty, in order to facilitate the rape of that nation by the English in 1679. The sugar islands of the Caribbean reported populations and exports to their French, Spanish or English Overlords. New York made a census in 1698, Connecticut in 1756, Massachusetts in 1764 . . . The British took the same pains to count their subject peoples. India evolved one of the great statistical bureaucracies, and later became a major centre for theoretical as well as practical statistics.[46]

By the eighteenth century, the demand for numbering the population had reached back from the colonies to the colonizers. In Britain and the United States, as in France, Spain, Germany and Italy, many felt that the advance of civilization itself was leading to a decline in their population with potentially damaging consequences for national strength. In his *Estimate of the Manners and Principles of the Times* – the times being 1757 – the Reverend John Brown followed a path that would have been familiar to his readers. 'Commerce, in its most advanced stages "brings in Superfluity and vast Wealth; begets Avarice, gross Luxury, or effeminate Refinement among the higher Ranks, together with general Loss of Principle" ... "Vanity and Effeminacy" reduce the desire for marriage; the "lower Ranks" in the large cities are rendered partly impotent by "Intemperance and Disease"; and "this Debility is always attended with a Shortness of Life, both in the Parents and the Offspring; and therefore a still further Diminution of Numbers follows on the whole".[47] David Glass, in his account of the population controversy in eighteenth-century England, remarks that there is nothing new in this analysis of the relation of civilization and population. 'What is new is the specific suggestion that England was, on the whole, "less populous that it was fifty Years ago", and the statement that "it appears by the Registers of some Country Parishes, which I have looked into, that from the Year 1550 to 1710, the Number of Inhabitants increased gradually ... and that from 1710 to the present Time, the Number has been at a Stand, if not rather diminished" ... the population controversy had begun.[48]

Arguments for and against enumeration in Britain had occurred throughout the second half of the eighteenth century, for example, in relation to a Bill of 1753 entitled 'An Act for Taking and Registering an Annual Account of the Total Number of People and the Total Number of Marriages, Births and Deaths; and also the Total Number of Poor receiving Alms from every Parish and Extraparochial Place in Great Britain'. The Bill was defeated. The *Gentleman's Magazine* for November 1753 listed the advantages put forward by its proponents: 'to show the total numbers and their distribution; offer a basis for deciding whether a general naturalization was desirable; make it possible to estimate how large an army could be raised in time of need; provide evidence as to the desirability of emigration to the colonies; give a much

[46] Hacking 1990: 17.
[47] J. Brown 1757, quoted from Glass 1973: 26.
[48] Glass 1973: 26.

firmer basis for local government; and for the first time show correctly
the burden of the poor to the kingdom and enable new enquiries about,
and proper provision for, them to be made'.[49] But opponents of the Bill,
such as Mathew Ridley, argued that the people regarded the very act of
numbering with fear and superstition and, if it were to be required by
law, 'there is great reason to fear, they will in many places oppose the
execution of it in a riotous manner'. And, for William Thornton, the
results of an enumeration would be increased tyranny: the Bill was 'totally subversive of the last remnants of English liberty'.

But was there a danger of underpopulation or of overpopulation?
Whilst some tried to calculate that Bills of Mortality and tax statistics
showed the population declining, and thought the trend to be a dangerous one, Malthus' famous *Essay on Population* weighed in on the other
side – the danger was not that civilization was leading to a decline in
population numbers, but the reverse, that it was removing the natural
checks that held population size in check with potentially disastrous
results.[50] In the face of continuing controversy, by the turn of the century, the argument for enumeration won out. As John Rickman argued,
'if *some* knowledge of a country be more than useful, be even absolutely
necessary, it cannot be denied that, with the accuracy of such knowledge, legislation and politics must make proportional steps towards per-
fection – that, without the increase of it, they must be stationary – without its continuance, possibly even retrograde'. Rickman thus considered
it most regrettable that there was no accurate knowledge of the numbers
of the persons in the population which was vital for purposes of ascertaining the appropriate number to be employed in national defence, the
increase or decrease in the numbers of marriages, the relationship
between sizes of the English, French, Irish and Scottish populations and
much more.[51]

The first British census was in 1801 and it was repeated every ten
years, although established in its modern form only with the founding of the General Register Office in 1841. But the regular census was
only a part of the establishment, in the first half of the nineteenth
century, of a whole variety of offices and bureaux for the keeping of the
official numbers without which it had become impossible to govern.
And, as we know, over the course of the nineteenth century, the statistics themselves led in two directions – an empirical direction of social

[49] Quoted ibid.: 19. The following quotes come from pp. 19 and 20 of Glass's
account.
[50] Malthus [1798] 1970.
[51] Rickman 1800, quoted in Glass 1973: 106-13.

investigation and social ameliorism and a theoretical direction through the argument that there were laws of the moral order as much as laws of the natural order, in other words to the discipline of sociology. In Britain and Europe, numericization was crucial to liberal government.

Democracy

The American case is more helpful than the British in understanding the link with democracy. In the United States, from the late eighteenth century and throughout the first half of the nineteenth century, a host of individuals carried out enquiries into the civil condition of the people and compiled these into gazetteers. These diverse quantifiers first made the link between number, fact and good government. To govern legitimately was not to govern at the mercy of opinion and prejudice, but to govern in the light of the facts. On the one hand, government needed more facts. On the other, government could be pressed to adjust its policies – in relation to the miseries of the public prisons, the suppression of intemperance, the availability of educational facilities – in the light of the facts. The formation of a numericized public discourse is not only a resource for government; as Kenneth Prewitt points out, it is also a resource whereby various forces may seek to mobilize government by challenging its claims to efficacy. Indeed information, 'facts and figures', 'may give an advantage to the weak, whose case, if strong and technical, can count for something'.[52] In modern democratic discourse, numbers are thus not univocal tools of domination, but mobile and polyvocal resources.

New Politics

But statistics in the United States were to have a second democratic vocation. They were to be deployed in a problem space peculiar to an ethic of democratic authority – that of constituting a public domain that unifies individual wills, of governing diversity in the name of the common good. As Cline-Cohen puts it: 'proponents of statistics claimed that a comprehensive knowledge of general social facts could be the foundation of a new politics. Knowing the exact dimensions of heterogeneity would compensate for the lack of homogeneity in the diverse United States . . . Facts would dispel the factious spirit.[53] Facts, being above factions, would illuminate that overarching realm within which the nation was to be unified in a single moral universe. And, indeed, proponents of the census in the United States stressed its role as a ritual for the formation of national identity. The census, argued members of Congress in 1879, was 'the great picture of our physical and social freedom . . . displayed for the judgement of mankind' from which not only

[52] Wilensky 1967, cited by Prewitt 1987: 271.
[53] Cline-Cohen 1982: 155.

foreigners but also 'our own people' were to learn 'what we really are'.[54]

If facts are necessary for good government, then it makes sense for the facts to be governmentalized. Herein lay the argument for an expanded census. The requirement for a census was built in to the Constitution: a periodic count of free and enslaved persons was necessary to determine the numerical basis for representation in the lower House of Congress. In the early nineteenth century, many agreed with James Madison that an expanded census was desirable because, 'in order to accommodate our laws to the real situation of our constituents, we ought to be acquainted with that situation'.[55] Yet proposals for anything other than a simple head count proved controversial.

One problem concerned the content of counting – what was it legitimate to count and why. But a second problem concerned the nature of the polity in a democracy. As Cline-Cohen argues, this was a controversy over the existence of peculiar interests as opposed to the common good – should democratic government be based upon the premise of a single common good embracing the whole community, or should it seek to adjust itself to the several classes of persons with their various – principally economic – interests. Some viewed society as an organic whole. For them, as Prewitt points out, the object of government was the pursuit of a public good that could not be divided. Others, notably Madison, 'viewed society as consisting in multiple and diverse interests. To govern such a society in democratic fashion required complex information about the composition of the public.[56] By 1820, the 'Madisonian' ideal of democracy, as a nicely calculated exercise of power, had prevailed. The polity was now to be broken into its several classes; the census was to require each household to be allotted to one, and only one, sector of the economy. As Cline-Cohen puts it, 'The common good was being broken into constituent parts, and the social order could now be comprehended through arithmetic.[57]

In the preface to the 1838 edition of his almanac, Joseph Worcester wrote: 'all intelligent and judicious legislation must be founded, in great measure, on statistical knowledge'; if statistics on population, manufactures and agriculture, crime and pauperism, education and religion were collected regularly, it would 'greatly increase the ability of the national and State governments, as well as of societies and individuals

---

[54] Kelman 1987: 287-8.
[55] Quoted in Cline-Cohen 1982: 160.
[56] Prewitt 1987: 268.
[57] Cline-Cohen 1982: 164.

to promote the interest, and advance the moral civilization and improvement, of the people'.[58] President Martin Van Buren demanded that the 1840 census should 'embrace authentic statistical returns of the great interests specially entrusted to, or necessarily affected by, the legislation of Congress'.[59] Some had hoped that the 1840 census would be a 'full dress inventory of the greatness of America'. In fact, this census led to a new scepticism over the reliability of numbers. This scepticism arose around the potent mixture of race, slavery and insanity.

Amongst those who had become objects of government, and hence objects of statisticalization, by 1840 were the mad. The 1840 census added a count of the insane and idiots, distinguished by race and by mode of support, to the counts of the blind, deaf and dumb, that had been included in 1830. When the results of the census were published in 1841, the total number of those reported as insane or feeble-minded in the United States was over 17,000. More to the point, perhaps, nearly 3,000 were black, and the rate of insanity amongst free blacks was eleven times higher than that of slaves and six times higher than that of the white population. For those who opposed abolition, like US vice president John C. Calhoun, these census figures proved that blacks were congenitally unfit for freedom. Abolition, far from improving the condition of 'the African', worsened it: where 'the ancient relations' between the races had been retained, the condition of the slaves had improved 'in every respect – in number, comfort, intelligence and morals'.[60] Gilman quotes an essay in the *American Journal of Insanity* as late as 1851 citing the 1840 census as proof of the inferiority of the black population. Cline-Cohen argues that the public and ill-tempered wrangle between the various officials and Congressmen took a novel form, a questioning of the facticity of numerical facts: it marks the moment of loss of innocence for political statistics – the recognition that statistics could lie, and that statistics can be challenged by other statistics. But from this point on political controversy and numerical controversy were inseparably intertwined: political disputes would now be waged in the language of number.

The key argument for the expansion of the census in the USA from the 1840s to the present was put succinctly in 1849: 'the American statesman', argued Senator Hunter, must 'obtain a full and accurate view of all the parts of that vast society whose machinery he directs'.[61]

---

58 Worcester 1838, quoted by Kelman 1987: 281-2.
59 Kelman 1987: 282.
60 Quoted in Gilman 1985: 137.
61 Quoted by Kelman 1987: 282.

By 1880, few would dissent from Representative Cox's assertion that 'a country without a census cannot be well-governed'.[62]

Three themes emerge clearly from the genealogy of the American census in the nineteenth century.

First, numbers are linked to specific problematizations. To problematize drunkenness, idleness or insanity requires it to be counted. Reciprocally, what is counted – slavery, pauperism, insanity – is what is problematized. To count a problem is to define it and make it amenable to government. To govern a problem requires that it be counted. As Kelman points out:

> The introduction of questions on manufacturers in the 1810 census reflected a new interest in the industries of the industrial revolution and demands for legislative action to aid them. The dramatic expansion of statistics about social problems such as illiteracy, ill health, insanity, pauperism, crime and so forth, that began in an important way with the censuses of 1840 and 1850, mirrored a growing concern that the large wave of immigration of poor people was creating social problems. The collection of wage statistics and detailed information about the railroad and insurance industries, introduced after the Civil War, was a sign of the growing legislative interest in labor relations and big business.[63]

Secondly, numbers are linked to evaluation of government. To count is bound up with a new critical numeracy of government; to measure the success of government is to measure quantitative changes in that which it seeks to govern. As George Tucker put it in his 1847 prospectus for a nationwide General Statistical Society, statistics alone enable us to trace the success of government in relation to 'a nation's moral and religious improvement; its health, wealth, strength and safety'.[64]

Thirdly, numbers are essential to authority's claim that it is legitimate because it is representative. Numbers figure out the continual adjustment between those who have power and those over whom they claim the right to exercise it. Again, the American case is exemplary in making the links between numbers, citizenship and democracy.

Counting subjects: representation and democracy

Democracy as an ethico-political governmental rationality is based upon the legitimacy apparently conferred upon political power by a quantitative relation between those holding political authority and those subject to it. But who is a subject and how are they to be counted? The debates

---

[62] Quoted ibid.: 283.
[63] Ibid.
[64] Cline-Cohen 1982: 221.

in the United States over the apportionment of delegates to Congress and the Senate illustrate the complex relationship between democratic political rationalities based upon the ideal of an electoral mandate and the technologies of government which claim to be able to operationalize democracy. Prior to the Constitutional Convention of 1787, each state had equal power within the Confederation. However, at that convention, the delegates from the larger states wanted to give equal weight to each person, and thus most power to the states with the biggest populations. As William Petersen explains, 'The compromise effected was to balance power by establishing a bicameral Congress; in the Senate, with equal representation from each member of the Union, the less populous states had relatively more weight; and in the House, with representation proportional to the population, those with more inhabitants dominated. To maintain this balance the number in the lower house had to be adjusted periodically to population growth, and the first link between politics and enumeration was thus inscribed in the Constitution itself.[65] But, of course, the delegates from North and South were divided, above all, on the question of slavery; the compromise on this was precisely numerical: apportionment was based on all free persons except Indians 'not taxed' (that is, not living in the general population), plus three-fifths of 'all other persons'. For each hundred slaves in a congressional district, that is to say, it received representation equivalent to that for sixty free persons.

From the time the Constitution was written, the census was bound up with both the spatial and the racial distribution of political power. By the end of the nineteenth century, this was taking the form of a new politics of blood and race, problematizing not the rate of increase of the population of free white men and coloured slaves but immigration. Francis Amaso Walker, 'the intellectual founder of the immigration restriction movement, ... warned native Americans that they were being overrun by hordes of "degraded" immigrants from Southern and Eastern Europe: "beaten men from beaten races"'.[66] And Francis Walker was none other than director of the 1870 and 1880 census.

Walker's statistical argument that new immigrants were breeding faster than old immigrants was materialized through the new techniques he introduced for monitoring changes in the population and representing these in population maps and population density maps. They proved crucial in the passage of the legislation that restricted immigration to the United States on racial lines. A range of events – the

[65] Petersen 1987: 192.
[66] Walker 1899, quoted by Conk 1987: 162.

effects of mobilization for the war on perceptions of immigrants from the Central Power nations, the 1919 strike wave – led many to see the cities and their polyglot population as destroying the fabric of American democracy. Congress balked at passing the re-apportionment legislation that was indicated by the 1920 census, for population growth would add representatives to those urban industrial states with large foreign-born populations. But if the census produced and demonstrated the problem, it could also promise to resolve it.

A study of the 'national origins' of the population showed that, though immigrants were one of the fastest-growing groups in the population in the early twentieth century, the 'descendants of persons enumerated at the Second Census' actually made up over half the 1900 white population. The grounds for this characterization of the composition of the American population in 1790 was W. S. Rossiter's rather speculative estimate made on the basis of the surnames listed in the enumeration. Nonetheless, it enabled the restrictionists to argue that, since the majority of Americans in 1800 came from Northern Europe, the majority of twentieth-century immigrants would have to come from Northern Europe in order to preserve the exiting 'racial' balance of the nation. The National Origins Act of 1924 called for a calculation of 'the number of inhabitants in the continental United States in 1920 whose origin by birth or ancestry is attributable to [each] geographical area'.[67] The Act operationalized the numericization of the population through immigration quotas, cut immigration to 150,000 per annum and allocated 71 per cent of the quotas to Great Britain, Germany and Ireland.

As the related events of the next two decades in Europe were to show, such a numericization of a politics of the population founded on blood, race and territory was to have global implications; indeed, eugenicists in Germany in the 1920s and 1930s were full of admiration for the steps that had been taken by the United States to address their own problem of racial degeneration. As Stefan Khl points out, the 1924 Act was applauded by German racial hygienists, and in an article in 1932 entitled 'The Nordic ideal' the Bavarian health inspector Walter Schulz took the Act 'as evidence that "racial policy and thinking has become much more popular [in the United States] than in other countries". One other important German figure, in a famous book from 1924, was full of praise for the fact that the Immigration Restriction Act excluded "undesirables" on the basis of hereditary illness and race. His name was Adolph Hitler; the book was *Mein Kampf*.'[68]

---

[67] Quoted by Petersen 1987: 220.
[68] Kühl 1994: 26.

The numerical inscription of race in the first half of the twentieth century was two-faced. It grounded both a politics of racial purity and a politics of racial identity. As Petersen points out:

those departing from the multi-ethnic pre-1914 empires of Central and Eastern Europe had little or no consciousness of belonging to a nationality. He was the subject of a particular State, for example Russia; he spoke a particular language, for example Lithuanian, he was an adherent of one or another religion, and he regarded a certain province or village as home . . . The technical requirement that the question on ethnicity be put in a simple form – 'What was your country of birth?' or something equivalent . . . helped solidify new ethnic groups. Having learned that they belonged to a nation, some of the immigrants submerged their provincialisms into a broader patriotism, their local dialects into a language.[69]

Hence it is not paradoxical that the first Lithuanian newspaper was published in the United States; that the Erse revival began in Boston; that the Czechoslovak nation was launched at a meeting in Pittsburgh. Identity, here – as in the case of the contemporary fabrication of Hispanic identity in the United States – is literally a matter of being counted as identical. And counting, and being counted, as I have said, is not merely 'objectifying': it enjoins a certain identity upon human beings as a way in which they will relate to themselves.

The controversies that surrounded the 1980 census included fifty-four lawsuits filed by cities, states, private citizens and lobbying groups against the Census Bureau claiming that it inadequately or improperly counted the population.[70] Much was now at stake, including not only the re-apportionment of seats in Congress in the light of population movements, but also the use of population numbers in attempts by minorities to press their case for social justice. But if the census has become an arena of political struggle, this has a significance that goes beyond the bargaining of interest groups: it reveals the intrinsic dependence of the problematics of democratic politics upon technologies for numbering of the population.

Calculating citizens: numbers and subjectivity

It was in the nineteenth century, argues Cline-Cohen, that numbers established the basis for their modern hold on the American political imagination. 'The commercial revolution stimulated reckoning skills as it pulled more people into a market economy. The political revolution that mandated the pursuit of happiness as an important end of govern-

[69] Petersen 1987: 218.
[70] Conk 1987: 155-6.

ment found its proof of the public's happiness in statistics of growth and progress. And the proliferation of public schools, designed to ensure an educated electorate, provided a vehicle for transmitting numerical skills to many more people.'[71] It is at this point that we can trace out most clearly the relation between disciplined subjectivity, numeracy and democracy. Arithmetic was to cease being commercial – it was to become republican. For Protestants like Benjamin Franklin, numbers were linked to personal conduct. Numbers were bound up with a certain way of approaching the world. They conferred certainty, they contributed to knowledge, they revealed regularities, they created regularities. And, in doing so, numbers could be thought of as fostering detachment from feeling, passions and tumults. The promulgation of numbers was thus inseparably bound up with the valorization of a certain type of ethical system. Numeracy was an element in the ethical technologies that would, it was hoped, produce a certain kind of disciplined subjectivity.

Take, for example, decimal money. Decimals had been studied for two hundred years by mathematicians, but the United States in the nineteenth century was the first country to put them to practical use. Jefferson, in 1790, had argued for the superior ease of reckoning in decimals in these terms:

The facility which this would introduce into the vulgar arithmetic would, unquestionably, be soon and sensibly felt by the whole mass of people, who would thereby be enabled to compute for themselves whatever they should have occasion to buy, to sell, or measure, which the present complicated and difficult ratios put beyond their computation for the most part.[72]

Proponents of the new federal money based on the decimal system took up these concerns, and claimed 'that they were democratizing commerce by putting computation within the reach of nearly all. At the same time, the self-consciously utilitarian spirit of the new nation invaded education and elevated arithmetic to the status of a basic skill along with reading and writing. Decimal money and arithmetic education were justified as fruits of republican ideology; numeracy was hailed as a cornerstone of free markets and a free society.'[73]

The pedagogy of numbers was republican not only because it generalized the competence to calculate; it was republican because it was a pedagogy of reason itself. As the investigation of mathematical truths accustomed the mind to method and correctness in reasoning, it was

[71] Cline-Cohen 1982: 117.
[72] Jefferson [1790] 1961: 631, quoted in Cline-Cohen 1982: 128.
[73] Cline-Cohen 1982: 127.

thus an activity that was peculiarly worthy of rational beings. The object in studying arithmetic, declared Catherine Beecher in 1874, 'is to discipline the mind'.[74]

Cline-Cohen puts it thus:

numeracy spread in the early nineteenth century under the influence of two powerful attitudinal changes: the extension of the commercial, or marketplace, frame of mind and the growing dominance of certain ideas associated with the fostering of democracy, especially the notion that rationality in the greatest possible number of people was desirable. As commerce invaded everyday life, more people had somehow to acquire the mental equipment to participate in it. As widespread rational thinking came to be perceived as necessary to the workings of democracy, educators looked to mathematics as the ideal way to prepare a republican citizenry.[75]

Of course, there are innumerable philosophical writings debating the meaning of citizenship and its moral basis. No doubt these texts are significant. But this significance is not that usually accorded to them by historians of ideas. It is not that either the roots or the evidence of citizenship are to be found in them; rather they can be seen as intellectual problematizations of, and philosophical commentaries upon, their own times. To understand the genealogy of citizenship as a sociohistorical phenomenon we should lower our eyes from these grand and airy deliberations and examine also the mundane, the small-scale, the technical. Citizenship should be studied at the level of the practices, technologies and mentalities within which citizens were to be formed, not simply as the moral subjects that philosophical deliberation seeks to equip with abstract rights and freedom, but as the subjects of governmental technologies, ethicalized individuals capable of exercising self-mastery, discipline, foresight, reason and self-control.

Ian Hunter has shown the ways in which pedagogic discourses and techniques in the nineteenth century took such a 'responsibilizing' role upon themselves, seeking to utilize practices ranging from playground supervision, through teaching style to curriculum content in the service of the production of a regulated subjectivity.[76] Such a genealogy linking democratic mentalities of government, pedagogy and regulated subjectivity gains support from Cline-Cohen's account of republican arithmetic. Democracy requires citizens who calculate about their lives as well as their commerce. Henceforth, the pedagogy of numeracy was an essential part of the constitution of subjects of a democratic polity. If

[74] Quoted ibid.: 145.
[75] Ibid.: 148-9.
[76] Hunter 1988.

government was to be legitimate to the extent that it was articulated in
a discourse of calculation, it was to be democratic to the extent that it
required and sought to produce responsible citizens, with a subjectivity
disciplined by an imperative to calculate.

An economy of numbers

Census numbers are not only politicized; they are also monetarized. In
the United States, complex allocative mechanisms have been built into
legislation that tie grants of government funds to population statistics.
Grant programmes from federal to state and local governments in the
pre-Depression period already used numerical formulae in making their
allocative decisions, based on such measures as population, area or road
mileage. With the New Deal programmes of the 1930s, in which large
sums of federal money was allocated to state and local agencies for social
welfare programmes, new measures were introduced based on such
numbers as per capita income, maternal mortality rates or population
density. The census, that is to say, became enmeshed in national income
redistribution. As Margo Conk points out, 'A new set of census
apportionment mechanisms – this time designed to distribute economic
power – was being born.'[77]

Margo Conk argues that Congress and the public had looked to the
census in the early years of the Depression for a description as to what
was happening and clues as to why. The census could not even provide
a credible count of the unemployed. Hence the Roosevelt administration and the New Deal put the experts to work in upgrading the
statistical system. More people were employed in counting and in analysing numbers; more things were counted; more numbers were published. The bureau and its statisticians dreamed of further advances in
statisticalizing national reality. Amongst their products over the next
decade were the Current Population Survey, monthly unemployment
statistics and the National Income and Product Accounts.

The case of national income accounting is revealing.[78] Like the other
examples that I have discussed, national income accounting demon-
strates the relations between the formation of political problematizations
and the attempt to render them calculable through numerical technologies. Prior to the 1930s, attempts to estimate the distribution of American income and wealth were bound up with issues of social distribution,
with which social classes bore the costs and reaped the benefits of the

---

[77] Conk 1987: 169.
[78] I have drawn on Perlman 1987 here.

incidence of taxation, of seasonality in employment, of the growth in manufacturing output. By the 1930s, Simon Kuznets was pointing out that the play of economic forces could be measured at a number of levels – that of production, distribution or consumption – the level of measurement being determined by the question to be asked. Kuznets was concerned about the social importance of the distribution of family income, and the roles played by banking and by government in stimulating growth. He concluded that the best measures of welfare and growth were to be found at the level of income received by individuals 'after it leaves the productive units proper and before it has been diverted into the various channels of consumption'.[79]

During the 1930s statisticians helped to shape a new problematization to which national income accounts would be the solution. The arguments put forward by those who advocated an increased governmental role in the preparation of such accounts sought to enrol a variety of allies in support of accurate and adequately classified national income data. The administration needed them in order to design appropriate welfare and economic recovery programmes. The Internal Revenue Service needed them for making projections of the effects of tax changes. Business needed them for market analysis. But only the federal government had the resources to provide them in a form that was untainted by accusations of unreliability and bias. 'Thus developed an identifiable new objective for national income accounting, namely an equitable, efficient, reliable, and speedy numbers supply, essential to the experimental functions associated with economic reform through legislative action.'[80] A new plane of reality was to be composed in the process, a public habitat of numbers encompassing business activity, purchasing power, demand for employment, government action, social welfare and economic recovery, and within which businessmen, politicians, economists and scholars could calculate their way to their objectives.

One might regard this public habitat of numbers, in the 1930s and 1940s, as 'Keynesian'. This was not in the sense that it was originated or inspired by Keynes, but in that Keynesian macro-economic theory came to provide the intellectual medium within which measures of economic activity could be seen as vital relays between socio-economic problematizations – fears of economic stagnation and large-scale unemployment – and political programmes – calculated attempts at economic management by government. Indeed, as Perlman points out, this 'Keynesianism' was embedded in the way in which the whole national

[79] Kuznets 1933: 205, quoted in Perlman 1987: 137.
[80] Perlman 1987: 139.

accounting system focused on measuring consumer purchasing powers as a key to economic recovery.

Wartime was to provide a key test and a key triumph for these projects of 'accounting for government'. Roosevelt demanded far more in the way of tanks and planes than his experts had deemed possible; Kuznets, who with Raymond Nathan was now at the War Production Board, took charge of military procurement, estimating how and where the American economy could summon up the resources to meet the new targets. They used the national accounts system and accounts of capital formation in devising measures ranging from the transfer of $7 billion of resources from civilian capital formation to war-related purposes, to reduction of consumer demand by increased taxation. Their success in the case of military procurement appeared to demonstrate that a calculable relation could be established between the deployment of national resources and the achievement of national purposes.

Equipped with the intellectual technology of Keynesian macro-economic theory, with the techniques and inscriptions of national income accounting, with the regulatory powers conjured up in the face of total war, accounting had demonstrated its capacity to calculate its way to national objectives. In the post-war American economy, the economists were confident that they could provide for growth in peace as in war, and many new measures of national and international economic activity were devised and tabulated. The measures for operationalizing accounting technologies would certainly entail an increase in the scope of action of the public powers. But, to the extent that they operated by shaping the conditions under which free agents made their choices, this exercise of power for national purposes would not be totalitarian but democratic. And to the extent that they were guided by expertise, it would not be arbitrary but scientific. It appeared as if a democratic society could be governed in the national interest through accounting, expertise and calculation; national income accounting thus took its place within a range of other measures that sought to calibrate the welfare of the nation in order to improve it. The Great Society programmes of the 1960s prompted increasing use of census data for social programmes. 'One man, one vote' entered the national political vocabulary, and it was argued that the bureau had a constitutional duty under the equal protection clause of the Fourteenth Amendment to count everyone. Counting was seen as a central plank of regulatory government.

Ronald Reagan was elected as president as the 1980 census was being completed. His election appears to mark the start of a reversal in the rise and rise of political numbering. Funds for the Census Bureau were

cut; the Office of Federal Statistical Policy and Standards was dis-
banded. The political problematics of Reaganomics and neo-liberalism
are, of course, marked by a profound suspicion of the capacity of
governments to calculate and regulate in the national interest. But, at
the same time, neo-liberalism relies upon and seeks to utilize the calculative capacities of individuals and firms, who, in calculating to serve
their own best interests, will cumulatively serve all our best interests.
The numerical saturation of public discourse in Britain and the USA in
the closing decade of the twentieth century reveals the new potential of
a public habitat of numbers within such modes of government, and the
new importance that is accorded to all those private agencies and consultants who claim that they can transform market conditions into numbers and to make private calculation effective. A new 'privatized'
relationship between numbers and politics has been born.

This privatization was stimulated by the economic consequences of
numbers. Huge amounts of money are committed in the marketplace
on the basis of the figures in national statistical series – hundred of
thousands of dollars change hands in the commodity markets as soon
as data from the Crop Reporting Board of the Department of Agriculture are released. Hence, whilst nineteenth-century arguments stressed
the need for numbers as an aid for governmental legislation and actions,
economists in the late twentieth century argued for a 'public statistical
habitat' to enable private enterprises to calculate actions and decisions.
It is in this context that we should locate the rise of the statistical services
industry in the USA and the UK. Whilst statistics might once have been
a governmental activity, since the middle of the twentieth century it has
become a business. For 'with the technological and economic changes
of the 1970s [emerged] a substantial industry of private firms selling
repackaged public data and privately collected statistics, statistical
models, and analytical skills'.[81] Statistics are now intimately connected
to corporate strategy, through the new discourse which binds economic
success and business expansion to market segmentation and targeted
take-overs and marketing. Statistical information, linking public demographic information on socio-economic and geographical distribution to
all manner of other computerized information, is vital in the programmes to sell different products, in different ways, to different customers.

Neo-liberal rationalities of government may revive the old nineteenth-
century liberal themes of freedom, the market and choice. However,
they become possible bases for a technology of government only in the

[81] Starr and Corson 1987: 415.

presence of a population of personal, social and economic actors who will reason and calculate their freedom. They require a numericized environment in which these free, choosing actors may govern themselves by numbers. And they depend upon the elaboration of an expertise of numbers, embodied in all those professions – economists, accountants, statisticians, demographers – and all those techniques – censuses, surveys, national income tabulations and formulae, accounting practices – which render existence numerical and calculable.

Figuring out democracy

Today the word 'democracy' is uttered reverentially in more and more nations, by more and more diverse political forces, as if embracing democracy were a matter of a philosophical or moral commitment, as if it were a charm that ensured liberty, fairness and justice. Perhaps it is. But democracy, as it has come to operate in the advanced liberal capitalist societies of the West, is more than a set of political ideals, and more than a set of mechanisms for delivering a 'representative' executive and holding them periodically to account. As we are beginning to recognize, democracy, as a way of seeking to exercise and justify power, depends upon a complex set of technologies for linking up the exercise of government with the entities – 'civil society', 'independent power sources', 'private wills' and so forth – upon which it depends. And numbers have been, and remain, indispensable to such technologies of democratic government.

Kenneth Prewitt argues that 'Public statistics in the United States are generated as a part of democratic politics.'[82] For him, this invites inquiry into the ways in which the 'number system' of the United States 'advances or retards democracy, informs or distorts civic discourse, helps or hinders political participation'. In particular, Prewitt argues that democracy entails practices that will call power holders to account, and he cites evidence that voters hold office holders to account less on the grounds of their own personal experience than on the basis of what they know about national economic performance. And, of course, what they know comes to them largely in terms of the 'upward or downward movement of statistical indicators of those important issues for which government has assumed responsibility: unemployment, inflation, balance of trade, interest rates, test scores, poverty levels, crime rates'.[83] Prewitt argues that 'A democratic society is preserved when the public

[82] Prewitt 1987: 262.
[83] Ibid.: 264.

has reliable ways of knowing whether policies are having the announced or promised effect. Is inflation being brought under control? Is a war of attrition being won? Are defence expenditures buying national security? Numbers, a part of this publicly available political intelligence, consequently contribute to the accountability required of a democracy.'[84] Numbers that have integrity, numbers that are safeguarded against political or professional manipulation, are essential elements for informed civic discourse in advanced industrial societies.

Few would disagree. But we need to locate this morality of numbers within its own politico-ethical matrix. Democratic political rationalities that accord significance rational and calculative self-steering of independent citizens in their personal and business activities also must sustain a public environment of numbers within which those citizens may calculate. Democracy, if it be taken seriously as an art of government rather than as philosophy or rhetoric, depends upon the delicate composition of relations of number and numeracy enabling a calculated and calculating government to be exercised over the persons and events to be governed. Democracy in its modern, mass, liberal forms requires a pedagogy of numeracy to keep citizens numerate and calculating, requires experts to inculcate calculative techniques into politicians and entrepreneurs, requires a public habitat of numbers. Democratic mentalities of government prioritize and seek to produce a relationship between numerate citizens, numericized civic discourse and numerical evaluations of government. Democracy can operate as a technology of government to the extent that such a network of numbers can be composed and stabilized. In analyses of democracy, a focus on numbers is instructive, for it helps us turn our eyes from the grand texts of philosophy to the mundane practices of pedagogy, of accounting, of information and polling, and to the mundane knowledges and 'grey sciences' that support them.

[84] Ibid.: 267.

7 Control

What are the costs of our contemporary freedom? And who bears the different portions of those costs? In *Discipline and Punish*, Michel Foucault put forward a compelling vision of the logics of individualization and normalization that were the inescapable other side of liberty.[1] Discipline, as instituted in all those 'moralizing machines' invented in the nineteenth century, was a mode of power that worked through the calculated distribution of bodies, spaces, time, gazes in attempts to fabricate subjects who were simultaneously useful and compliant. Through hierarchical observation and normalizing judgement, institutionalized in prisons, schools, lunatic asylums, reformatories, workhouses and similar assemblages, competences, capacities and controls upon conduct were to be inscribed into the soul of the citizen. The free citizen was one who was able and willing to conduct his or her own conduct according to the norms of civility; the delinquent, the criminal, the insane person, with their specialized institutions of reformation, were the obverse of this individualization and subjectivization of citizenship.

In his 'Postscript on control societies', Gilles Deleuze suggested that Foucault's characterization of 'disciplinary society' was written at the dusk of such societies, which reached their apogee at the beginning of the twentieth century.[2] By the close of the twentieth century, in a process that began slowly but made rapid advances after the Second World War, we had begun to leave disciplinary societies behind: we now lived in 'societies of control'. In such societies, Deleuze suggested, normalization was no longer a matter of the operation of specialist institutionally based disciplinary procedures: the family was splitting apart and could no longer socialize its members, the hospital was breaking down as a

---

[1] Foucault 1977. Of course, others have extrapolated a similar picture, though largely in Foucault's wake, from the work of Weber and Habermas: see, for example, Dandeker 1990.

[2] Deleuze 1995: 177–8. Deleuze's piece was a short article originally published in *L'Autre Journal* in May 1990.

site of confinement of illness and cure, the institutions of education inherited from the nineteenth century were in a more or less terminal crisis. But in their place, a new diagram of control had taken shape.

Rather than being confined, like its subjects, to a succession of institutional sites, the control of conduct was now immanent to all the places in which deviation could occur, inscribed into the dynamics of the practices into which human beings are connected. In disciplinary societies it was a matter of procession from one disciplinary institution to another – school, barracks, factory . . . – each seeking to *mould* conduct by inscribing enduring corporeal and behavioural competences, and persisting practices of self-scrutiny and self-constraint into the soul. Control society is one of constant and never-ending *modulation* where the modulation occurs within the flows and transactions between the forces and capacities of the human subject and the practices in which he or she participates. One is always in continuous training, lifelong learning, perpetual assessment, continual incitement to buy, to improve oneself, constant monitoring of health and never-ending risk management. Control is not centralized but dispersed; it flows through a network of open circuits that are rhizomatic and not hierarchical.

In such a regime of control, Deleuze suggests, we are not dealing with 'individuals' but with 'dividuals': not with subjects with a unique personality that is the expression of some inner fixed quality, but with elements, capacities, potentialities. These are plugged into multiple orbits, identified by unique codes, identification numbers, profiles of preferences, security ratings and so forth: a 'record' containing a whole variety of bits of information on our credentials, activities, qualifications for entry into this or that network. In our societies of control, it is not a question of socializing and disciplining the subject *ab initio*. It is not a question of instituting a regime in which each person is permanently under the alien gaze of the eye of power exercising individualizing surveillance. It is not a matter of apprehending and normalizing the offender *ex post facto*. Conduct is continually monitored and reshaped by logics immanent within all networks of practice. Surveillance is 'designed in' to the flows of everyday existence. The calculated modulation of conduct according to principles of optimization of benign impulses and minimization of malign impulses is dispersed across the time and space of ordinary life.

Of course, these metaphors function more as hypotheses than conclusions. And they are framed in terms that are far too epochal: Foucault's disciplinary societies were not 'disciplined societies', but those where strategies and tactics of discipline were active; likewise, Deleuze's control societies should not be understood sociologically, but in terms of the emergence of new possibilities and the complexification of the old. Understood in this sense, they find some support from researchers working in specific fields. Thus, in relation to psychiatry, Robert Castel has argued that regulatory technologies seek to minimize direct therapeutic intervention, the individualization and normalization of the pathological person, and instead seek the administrative management of populations at risk, anticipating 'possible loci of dangerous irruptions through the identification of sites statistically locatable in relation to norms and means'.[3] The path of prevention is not a eugenic strategy of exclusion and elimination of dangerous elements from the social body: primary prevention, as it is now termed, is a whole programme of political intervention to educate authorities and lay persons so as to act on the conditions which exacerbate the possibilities of mental health problems occurring in the first place. When interventions are necessary, they are administrative rather than therapeutic: they seek 'the technical administration of differences'; they do not target persons, but populations at risk. Thus, for example, Castel cites the GAMIN system for detection of childhood abnormalities, which began to be installed in France in 1976. This made all infants subject to medical examination at regular intervals and collected data on a variety of indications. These ranged from the physical and medical characteristics of the child to information on whether the mother was unmarried, a minor or of foreign nationality. Computers would collate and interpret data from a whole variety of sources to identify risk levels and risk groups across a population, and engage in preventative targeting of particular sites and locales. The presence of a certain number of risk factors, linked to pathology through statistical evidence from earlier research studies, set off an alert which produced a visit to the family from a social worker or other specialist. Intervention was thus pre-emptive and probabilistic, anticipatory and preventive, not based upon the diagnosis of pathology in an individual subject but on actuarial analysis of risk factors. The diagram of post-disciplinary logics of control, in this view, is based upon a dream of the technocratic control of the accidental by continuous monitoring and management of risk.

Similarly, in the context of crime control, Malcolm Feeley and Jonathon Simon have suggested that a 'new penology' is taking shape which is 'markedly less concerned with responsibility, fault, moral sensibility, diagnosis, or intervention and treatment of the individual offender.

---

[3] Castel's argument is set out in detail in *La gestion des risques* (1981): this translation is quoted from Rabinow 1992: 243. His argument is summarized in English in 'From dangerousness to risk' (Castel 1991).

Rather, it is concerned with techniques to identify, classify, and manage groupings sorted by dangerousness. The task is managerial and transformative . . . It seeks to *regulate* levels of deviance, not intervene or respond to individual deviants or social malformations.'[4] This new penology is actuarial in character, seeking to map out distributions of conduct across populations and to arrange strategies to maximize efficiency of the population as a whole. Rather than seeking to normalize individuals by identifying pathological individuals, placing them in reformatory institutions and seeking to move each pathological person towards uniformity, an actuarial regime seeks to 'manage them in place . . . While the disciplinary regime attempts to alter individual behavior and motivation, the actuarial regime alters the physical and social structures within which individuals behave.'[5] This makes power more effective – because changing individuals is difficult and ineffective – and it also makes power less obtrusive – thus diminishing its political and moral fallout. It also makes resistance more difficult, for discipline, in that it produces subjectivities – as prisoners, as patients, as workers, as juvenile delinquents – produces the possibilities for resistance in the name of subjectivity itself. Actuarial practices, in that they do not produce individual or collective identities of this sort, minimize the possibilities for resistance in the name of that identity. The new techniques target offenders as an aggregate; they do not aim to rehabilitate, reintegrate, retrain, provide employment for particular individuals. They seek only to reduce rates of crime and risks posed by groups – such as the urban poor or underclass – by whatever means are appropriate to the risk they prevent. Individual diagnosis and transformations of the soul are irrelevant. Actual conduct is all that is important. Hence imprisonment is a means of enduring incapacitation of those who present a significant risk, whilst, for those who appear to present lower risk, conduct can be managed through measures like probation. Such measures are valued now only to the extent that they can demonstrate themselves as efficient techniques for the more or less permanent management of dangerous sectors of the population.

These arguments are not without their problems, but they do point to the rise of novel possibilities in strategies of control. I suggested in chapter 4 that a new individualization of security could be identified, operating in terms of the responsibilization of individuals, families, organizations for the management of risk, and involving the deployment

---

[4] Feeley and Simon 1992: 452. In fact, Simon began to develop this line of argument in a paper published in 1988 (see n. 5).
[5] Simon 1988: 773.

of a range of novel technologies for acting indirectly and at a distance on the objects to be governed. Risk management strategies are a part of this configuration. They are conceived not in actuarial but in probabilistic terms. And their aim is to act pre-emptively upon potentially problematic zones, to structure them in such a way as to reduce the likelihood of undesirable events or conduct occurring, and to increase the likelihood of those type of events and activities that are desired. They thus attempt to pre-empt or dedramatize conflict by acting upon the physical and social structures within which individuals conduct themselves. They enact a kind of cybernetics of control, in which risk information, risk calculation, risk management and risk reduction are intrinsic to all decisions, whether these be about investment, building design, organizational structure, educational practice or health-related conduct. In these ways of thinking, it is not solely the state that should make such risk calculations: individuals, firms and communities should manage their own riskiness. These technologies of control do not operate by moralization and discipline, nor do they operate through socialization and solidarity. They operate through instrumentalizing a different kind of freedom.

The emergence of such strategies and technologies of control does not, however, amount to a shift to a new type of society. Research suggests a more complex picture. This complexity was captured well by Stan Cohen.[6] Writing in the early 1980s, Cohen sought to characterize the shift in social control strategies that commenced in the late 1960s, often understood in terms of 'decarceration'. The term 'decarceration' was utilized in the sociology of deviance in the 1970s and 1980s to characterize the apparent reduction of the populations incarcerated in reformatories, prisons, asylums and other institutions of sequestration and control, and the development of 'community psychiatry' and community care. Starting from the transformations in prisons and asylums and in programmes and activities of the professionals and specialists of the crime control system, Cohen argued that 'decarceration' did not amount to a reduction in control, not least because the old institutions of incarceration remained, the numbers of professionals involved had increased and the scope of their work had actually both widened and

---

[6] Cohen 1985. Cohen's argument has to be set against those of others who tended to see 'decarceration' as a policy that was economically driven, a response to a 'fiscal crisis of the state', and not as a reconfiguration of control regimes. I develop my own criticisms of this argument in relation to psychiatry in my contribution to *The Power of Psychiatry* which I edited with Peter Miller (Rose 1986).

deepened.[7] It was more accurately understood as a blurring of the boundaries between the 'inside' and the 'outside' of the system of social control, and a widening of the net of control whose mesh simultaneously became finer and whose boundaries became more invisible as it spread to encompass smaller and smaller violations of the normative order. The state had dispersed some of its functions of preventative social control to other institutions: schools, families, neighbourhoods, youth organizations and workplaces. This dispersion did not diminish surveillance; if anything it produced an intensification of the levels of detail in the conduct that was scrutinized and acted upon by reformatory regimes, as the minutiae of the behaviour, demeanour, time-keeping and daily activities of ex-offenders and juveniles were monitored and tracked in 'the community'. Cohen argued that the apparent rejection of the notion of individual 'internal' pathology, which appeared to play a part in many arguments for community corrections, was pretty illusory. The offender was still seen as someone with a deficit to be corrected, albeit now understood as the capacity to manage existence in the external world, social skills, role competence, the ability to obtain and hold down a job and the like. Crime control in the 1980s seemed, in this picture, to be marked by a simultaneous reduction of certain aspects of state-organized penal complex and the extension of others, the emergence of hybrids of commercial and state provision, the rhetorical deployment of the division of public and private combined with its practical and organizational transgression.

The diagnostician of control is thus faced with bewildering complexity rather than a simple shift from discipline to control or from individualization and normalization to actuarial government of groups and popu-

---

[7] Cohen uses the notion of 'social control' in his argument (Cohen 1985). I have some problems with this concept. In chapter 3 we encountered the version that was dominant in American sociology and policy in the first half of the twentieth century. In the radicalized version of the concept that became popular in sociology from the 1960s, social control was the attempt, by the state and its conscious or unconscious agents and institutions, to reduce or eliminate problematic conduct in the name of social pacification and the maintenance of the hegemony of the economic, political, financial and cultural status quo. The concept, in this form, puts too much into the same bag, adopts a state-centred model of power, sees the hand of the state in all control practices, assumes that control works through objectification and the imposition of meaning and that its objective is essentially conservative. Nonetheless, the empirical richness and analytical acuity of Cohen's work ensures that it remains the most penetrating overview of the new control practices that were being invented and deployed in this period.

lations.[8] The discourse of crime control seems to combine incompatible specifications of the problem, and politicians and professionals cycle rapidly through the different options. Proposals stressing the need for individuals and communities to take more responsibility for their own security, whether this be through schemes of 'target hardening' or by setting up neighbourhood watch schemes, coexist with arguments for zero-tolerance policing. Demands for exemplary sanctions against offenders are accompanied by schemes for 'naming, shaming and blaming' focused on the relations between offender and victim. The prisoner is to be incapacitated, or the prisoner is to be taught life skills and entrepreneurship, or the prisoner is to be stigmatized and made to accept his or her moral culpability, or the prisoner is to be helped to reintegrate into his or her community. The spread of community types of correction such as fines, probation orders, community service and so forth goes hand in hand with an inexorable increase in the prison population and the constant expansion of the prison-building programme. Schemes of risk reduction, situational crime control and attempts to identify and modify criminogenic situations portray the criminal as a rational agent who chooses crime in the light of a calculus of potential benefits and costs. Proposals to increase the information, surveillance capacities and investigative skills of police divisions of criminal intelligence portray the criminal as an organized professional lacking normal

[8] This point has been made most emphatically by David Garland, who analyses it in terms of 'the limits of the sovereign State' and the contradictory pressures on governments: on the one hand the urge to escape from the impossible illusion of political omnipotence in crime control; on the other hand, the reluctance to give up the political potency of the myth that law and order can and will be provided by the sovereign state. Different strategies are understood as ways of coping with this dilemma. There are adaptive strategies such as responsibilization (in which individuals, organizations and communities are urged to play their own part in crime control), defining deviance down (by filtering certain types of potentially criminal conduct out of the system), redefining organization success (in terms of secure containment rather than reduction of crime rates, for instance). And there are strategies of denial, of which punitive rhetorics and projects such as boot camps and the like are the most obvious examples. Others have seen it as a sign of post-modern disintegration or as an index of post-liberal politics. In what follows I have drawn particularly on Garland 1996 and on an unpublished paper by Pat O'Malley entitled 'Volatile punishments: contemporary penality and neo-liberal government' (O'Malley 1997). O'Malley suggests that the current inconsistencies and confusion should be accepted as such, and have more to do with political re-adjustments in post-social governance than with either the limits of the sovereign state or a move into post-modernity.

moral controls, who predates in a calculated manner upon the law-abiding. There appears, then, to be no overarching 'post-disciplinary' logic, but rather a multiplication of possibilities and strategies deployed around different problematizations in different sites and with different objectives. And this problem is made more complicated when one accepts that the penal complex represents only one facet of strategies of control: school, family, factory, public architecture and urban planning, leisure facilities, the mass media and much more have been mobilized and instrumentalized governmentally in the name of good citizenship, public order and the control or elimination of criminality, delinquency and anti-social conduct.

This should not surprise us. We should not emulate sociologists by seeking to chart the emergence of a 'post-disciplinary' society. Rather, we should seek to identify the emergence of new control strategies and the reconfiguration of old ones. In what follows, drawing upon the primary research of others, I will attempt little more than an inventory of these. I suggest that we can crudely distinguish two families of control strategies: those of inclusion and those of exclusion. And, as far as strategies of exclusion are concerned, I suggest a further division. On the one hand there are strategies that seek to incorporate the excluded, through a principle of activity, and to re-attach them to the circuits of civility. On the other, there are strategies which accept the inexorability of exclusion for certain individuals and sectors, and seek to manage this population of anti-citizens through measures which seek to neutralize the danger they pose.

Inclusion: circuits of security

It is possible to provide a rough and ready inventory of the control factors that are built into what one might term 'circuits of inclusion'.

The securitization of identity

At the close of the twentieth century, subjects are locked into circuits of control through the multiplication of sites where the exercise of freedom requires proof of legitimate identity.[9] It is impossible to participate in almost any contemporary practice without being prepared to demonstrate identity in ways that inescapably link individuation and control.

---

[9] Among the many studies of the control possibilities inherent in the new information technology are Gandy 1993; D. Gordon 1987; Lyon 1994; Marx 1988; Poster 1990; Webster and Robins 1986.

The modes of identification are multiple: computer-readable passports, driving licences with unique identification codes, social insurance numbers, bank cards, credit cards, debit cards utilized for purchasing goods through EFTPOS (electronic funds transfer at point of sale), cards granting credit at particular stores – the list could be greatly prolonged. Each card identifies the bearer with a virtual identity – a database record storing personal details – whilst at the same time allowing access to various privileges. Each access to such a privilege, for example the purchase of an item using a credit card, entails a further entry upon the database, a further accretion to the virtual identity. Access to other privileges, to mortgages, to credit purchase facilities, to accounts allowing use of telephone, electricity or gas, is dependent upon the provider checking these databases, through specialist intermediaries. Other databases, such as those of criminal records, may be linked into these circuits of information flow. Government agencies use computer-matching facilities to compare data from different sources in order to identify miscreants, for example, those making false claims for social security benefits. Information on driving licences can be linked with police and court records in criminal investigations. Insurance companies check databases held by banks and credit card companies in order to identify bad risks. Proposals are made for national databanks of 'DNA fingerprints' – the ultimate UPI (unique personal identifier).

It is not surprising that many have suggested, on the basis of these and other examples of electronic identification, that we live in a 'surveillance society'. Some see this in terms of the extension of the powers of a controlling state, and point to the increasing use of these techniques by the police and security agencies. I am sceptical about the claims that, by the late twentieth century, citizens of these advanced industrial capitalist societies, despite the veneer of democracy, were entrapped in an 'electronic Panopticon'. Of course, as Gary Marx has suggested, there are undoubtedly totalitarian potentials in the dissemination of networks of surveillance across the territory of everyday life.[10] They overcome the barriers of space and time involved in physical surveillance; they are not labour-intensive; they are of low visibility; they are of high durability; they have high transferability across domains; they are largely involuntary or participated in as an uncalculated side effect of some other action; they are pre-emptive and preventative, denying access to benefits on the basis of what one might do rather than apprehending one after the act; they are amenable to rapid augmentation as new modes of

---

[10] Marx 1988. The characteristics I list are derived from Marx's analysis of the ways in which the new surveillance differs from older forms of control.

identification come on stream. But I tend to agree with those who doubt that we are on our way to a 'maximum security society'.[11]

Such an analysis is based upon a misunderstanding of the forms of control that were inaugurated by nineteenth-century liberalism and a similar misunderstanding of 'advanced liberal' control strategies. It appears to be based on a dystopian and sociologized reading of the diagram of the Panopticon that Foucault utilized in his analysis of discipline. In the first place, it is dystopic in that it understands nineteenth-century disciplinary institutions as installing regimes of perpetual and total surveillance carried out by a central power in the service of dominating individuals and constraining their freedom, and then suggests that across the twentieth century these capacities of vision have been augmented and disseminated across 'the whole of society'.[12] But Panopticism did not model a dominating totalitarian society: it was a diagram of a mode of power that sought to induce a certain relation of human beings to themselves. Discipline, as I have suggested in other places in this book, was not a means of producing terrorized slaves without privacy, but self-managing citizens capable of conducting themselves in freedom, shaping their newly acquired 'private lives' according to norms of civility, and judging their conduct accordingly.

Secondly, the metaphor of the Panopticon did not imply that the nineteenth century saw the construction of totally disciplined society. Discipline modelled a strategy for the regulation of the conduct of citizens that was instantiated to a greater or lesser extent in a variety of institutional forms as part of more or less rationalized attempts to shape the conduct of individuals for certain ends – to reform them, to educate them, to exploit them, to cure them. The analysis here is genealogical not sociological. So, a diagnosis of the new technologies of securitization of identity should not ascribe to them some hidden or covert purpose or function of totalitarian control. On the one hand one needs to identify the specific loci and practices within which conduct has been problematized in ways which have led to the introduction of these new techniques of identification. And, on the other hand, one needs to diagnose, on the basis of such symptoms, the problem space within which they can appear as solutions. What one sees, here, is the emergence, at a whole variety of sites and practices – of consumption, of finance, of police, of health, of insurance – of problems of the individualization of the citizen to which securitization of identity can appear as a solution. The kinds of questions posed are: does this person have sufficient funds to make

---

[11] I tend to agree with Lyon's (1994) assessment of this issue.
[12] E.g. D. Gordon 1987; Poster 1990.

this purchase; is this citizen entitled to enter this national territory; is this person creditworthy; is this individual a potential suspect in this criminal case; is this person a good insurance risk. This is not, I think, an electronic Panopticon. There is no doubt that law enforcement agencies and other similar control agencies will utilize these new sources of information in any ways that they can. They will use them to identify and monitor offenders. They may also utilize them to profile and ident- ify potentially pathological individuals and groups. But the idea of a maximum security society is misleading. Rather than the tentacles of the state spreading across everyday life, the securitization of identity is dispersed and disorganized. And rather than totalizing surveillance, it is better seen as conditional access to circuits of consumption and civility, constant scrutiny of the right of individuals to access certain kinds of flows of consumption goods: recurrent switch points to be passed in order to access the benefits of liberty. On the one hand, this securitiz- ation of identity instils kind of prudent relation to the self as condition for liberty. On the other, in that it refines the criteria for inclusion and specifies them at a finer level, it operates to multiply the possible loci of exclusion.

We can see this in particular in two circuits of everyday life: work and consumption. It is undoubtedly the case that the introduction of information technology systems into the workplace has made possible a level of continuous and molecular surveillance over the activities of individual workers that was logistically impossible in programmes of scientific management and the era of 'time-and-motion' studies. As Shoshanna Zuboff has demonstrated, information systems allow the everyday routines of workers, their pace of work through each moment of the day, their patterns of decision making, their little errors and idio- syncrasies, to be analysed, compared, inscribed, normalized and then managed.[13] New management strategies can be adopted, based upon the invention of a new kind of objectivity about the performance of individual workers. In principle at least, these can be extended from those who carry out routine and repetitive tasks of the variety that were the target of 'Taylorism' to anyone who utilizes a computer for their work. Thus Richard Ericson and Kevin Haggerty have argued that 'in the very process of using communication technologies to accomplish their work, police officers are subject to the surveillance capacities of those technologies, which are able to monitor and risk-profile officer conduct in greater detail than human supervisors can'.[14] Each act of

[13] Zuboff 1988.
[14] Ericson and Haggerty 1997: 394.

data entry can be registered and monitored; each computer keystroke can be counted to see if a clerk is keeping up to production norms. This renders traditional forms of supervision redundant and introduces new ones. Further, as both Zuboff and Ericson and Haggerty argue, the potential of monitoring induces anticipatory compliance with norms and targets, designing in discipline without the potential conflict generated in face-to-face management by disputes over subjective judgements about efficiency.

Is this a super-Panopticon at work? We should avoid a technologically determinist answer to this question. Just because a technology has a potential use, such as that of surveillance, does not imply that this is the use to which it will be put. I have argued in previous chapters that advanced liberal strategies for the government of the productive subject do not understand and regulate the worker as a psycho-physiological machine whose output is to be optimized by surveillance, discipline and sanction. The productive subject is to be governed as a citizen, as an individual striving for meaning in work, seeking identity in work, whose subjective desires for self-actualization are to be harnessed to the firm's aspirations for productivity, efficiency and the like. High levels of surveillance of the labour force actually characterize the least highly developed productive regimes: in these locales – to which repetitive labour-intensive production is exported – exploitation requires rather low technology for its enforcement. Lean production, just-in-time manufacturing, total quality and a regime in which products are directly accountable to customers – these are the strategic priorities of new programmes for the government of production.[15]

Whilst sociologists still imagine the rationalities of work design in the image of Taylorism, the MIT Commission on Industrial Productivity has a very different view:

> Under the new economic citizenship that we envision, workers, managers, and engineers will be continually and broadly trained, masters of their technology, in control of their work environment, and involved in shaping their firm's objectives. No longer will an employee be treated like a cog in a big impersonal machine. From the company's point of view, the work force will be transformed from a cost factor to be minimized into a precious asset to be conserved and cultivated.[16]

In this production regime, new information technology is utilized in a

---

[15] Peter Miller and Ted O'Leary provide a fine account of the new politics of the product and the notions of economic citizenship and corporate governance entailed within it in Miller and O'Leary 1992 and 1994a.

[16] Dertouzos et al. 1989: 135, quoted in Miller and O'Leary 1992: 199.

very different way: to render the inner workings of the activities of production visible to enable them to be managed moment by moment; to eliminate waste; to supply the necessary relays and couplings between the desires of the customer and the characteristics of the product; to require everyone in the enterprise, from the cleaner through the accountant to the manager, to account for themselves from the perspective of the demands of the customer. If one were to draw a diagram of the role of information technology in the government of production here, it would not be that of an electronic Panopticon.

It would be equally misleading to suggest that information technology allows the expansion of the techniques of Taylorism from the workplace to the marketplace.[17] The securitization of identity in consumption regimes operates according to a very different rationale. On the one hand, as I have suggested, securitization polices the points of access to consumption, thus simultaneously securing a space of relative liberty within those borders and generating multiple points of exclusion. On the other, the commoditization of consumer preferences may generate new forms of visibility of the attitudes, aspirations and desires of citizens, but it should, perhaps, be located within a different field: the mobilization of the consumer.[18] It is one strand in a whole array of strategies and tactics that have been developed, over the course of the twentieth century, to 'assemble the subject of consumption': to render the consumer knowable and calculable within an economy of desire, to construct relays and relations between the predilections and passions of the individual and the attributes and image of product. I find myself in agreement with David Lyon here. Through the commercial surveillance aspects of banking, insurance, credit card checking, the datachecking entailed in consumer credit agreements, automatic credit checking at EFTPOS, the strategic use of data on purchasing preferences for targeted marketing on the one hand and retail strategies on the other, consumption regimes simultaneously:

exclude [their] undesirables, the underclass of non-consumers, would-be consumers or flawed consumers. For them is reserved the older, fuller panoptic surveillance, which not only sorts into categories, but closes in automatically on deviants to constrain their options. While consumer surveillance surely does exhibit panoptic traits – unverifiable observation, behavioural classification and so on – the actual mechanism of social integration and criteria for social partici-

[17] This seems to be the argument of Webster and Robins: Webster and Robins 1986, Robins and Webster 1989.

[18] Peter Miller and I have discussed this with reference to strategies of marketing and consumer research in the second half of the twentieth century: see Miller and Rose 1997.

pation are related to 'free choices' made in the marketplace . . . consumers are seduced into conformity by the pleasures of consuming what corporate power has on offer.[19]

In earlier chapters I have argued that, at the close of the twentieth century, citizenship is not primarily realized in a relation with the state nor in a uniform public sphere, but through active engagement in a diversified and dispersed variety of private, corporate and quasi-corporate practices, of which working and shopping are paradigmatic. If we bear in mind such transformations, perhaps we might consider the securitization of identity as a strategy for securing the obligatory access points for active citizenship. This strategy produces, as Deleuze's speculations imply, a ceaseless modulation, the obligation to continuously and repeatedly evidence one's citizenship credentials as one recurrently links oneself into the circuits of civility. In a society of control, a politics of conduct is designed into the fabric of existence itself, into the organization of space, time, visibility, circuits of communication. And these enwrap each individual life decision and action – about labour, purchases, debts, credits, lifestyle, sexual contacts and the like – in a web of incitements, rewards, current sanctions and forebodings of future sanctions which serve to enjoin citizens to maintain particular types of control over their conduct. These assemblages which entail the securitization of identity are not unified, but dispersed, not hierarchical but rhizomatic, not totalized but connected in a web or relays and relations. But in policing the obligatory access points to the practices of inclusion, they inescapably generate novel forms of exclusion.

The securitization of habitat

Sociologists have pointed to the contemporary prominence of the notion of 'risk' as a way of understanding the troubles encountered by individuals and collectivities. Historical sociologies have suggested that the prevalence of the language of risk is a consequence of changes in the contemporary existential condition of humans and their world.[20] In contrast, genealogical studies have analysed risk as part of a *particular style of thinking* born during the nineteenth century. This entailed new ways of understanding and acting upon misfortune *in terms of risk*: risk think-

---

[19] Lyon 1994: 154. Lyon here cites the work of Bauman (1988), Mark Poster (1990) and Clifford Shearing and Phillip Stenning's classic article 'From the Panopticon to Disneyworld' (Shearing and Stenning 1985).
[20] Beck 1992.

ing brought the future into the present and made it calculable. Risk was disciplined, by means of the statistical intelligibility that the collective laws of large numbers seemed to provide.[21] And, as we have seen in previous chapters, the collectivization of risk in the social state is being displaced: individuals, families, firms, organizations, communities are, once again, being urged by politicians and others to *take upon themselves* the responsibility for the security of their property and their persons, and that of their own families. This individualization of risk is intensified by the multiplication of perceptions of risk through media reporting, in which crime risks are posed as an inexcusable intrusion on the right of each individual to a life of untroubled lifestyle maximization.[22] Protection against risk of crime through a investment in measures of security becomes one of the responsibilities of each active individual, each responsible employer, if they are not to feel guilt at failing to protect themselves, their loved ones, their employees against future misfortunes. Nowhere is this more telling than in what we might term 'the securitization of habitat', that is to say, the simultaneous generation of anxiety and insecurity concerning property and personal safety in and around the home, and the marketing of a whole variety of devices and techniques, from insurance policies to burglar alarms, to securitize that habitat.

This strategy for the securitization of habitat is collectivizing as well as individualizing. It is not collectivizing in the earlier social sense, in which a domain of collective security was envisaged to be maintained by the state on behalf of all citizens, through universal measures ranging from social insurance to the enforcement of the criminal law by a unified and socially funded police force. It collectivizes through a different image: that of community. Here, a community is envisaged as a geographical and intersubjective zone, which is to take responsibility for preserving the security of its own members, whether they be the residents of a neighbourhood, the employees of an organization, the consumers and staff of a shopping complex. In this logic, space is reconfigured in the name of security. Risk reduction here takes the form of the construction of different spatio-ethical zones, each of which circumscribes what Clifford Shearing has termed a 'contractual' community.

[21] Hacking 1990; Ewald 1991.

[22] As opposed, for example, to health risks, where the same individualizing logic is at work, inciting a continuous scrutiny of diet and lifestyle in terms of the avoidance of threats to health, but where the intrusion of illness into the life of the health-conscious is seen as unfair, but nonetheless potentially enriching and even ennobling.

And this community assumes – or is forced to assume – responsibility for 'its own' risk management.[23]

One key image here is that of the 'gated community', surrounded by walls, entry and exit controlled by security guards, its internal spaces monitored by security cameras. It is familiar enough to need little amplification. It inaugurates a virtually endless spiral of amplification of risk – as risk is managed in certain secure zones, the perceived riskiness of other unprotected zones is exacerbated. The reconfiguration of notions of risk and security involved here is captured by one tiny example from Britain. As psychiatric care is reorganized along community lines, with patients discharged and managed on the territory of everyday life, public authorities ponder the fate of the vast Victorian asylums which used to house thousands of incarcerated inmates. These typically consist of large building complexes surrounded by open space, ornamental gardens, housing for the attendants and nurses and the other physical accoutrements of moral management. But whatever the moralizing civility of their internal spaces, the perimeter of each asylum was secured: surrounded by walls, gates, guardhouses and the rest in order to ensure the detention of those required to remain within, as well as to re-assure those outside that they were insulated from the contagion and danger represented by the mad. Whilst such asylums were originally built on the outskirts of towns, urban sprawl has turned their sites into valuable suburban land. In Britain at least, the solution has been to sell these sites, together with their buildings (often now subject to environmental protection orders and hence unable to be demolished) to private developers. The buildings themselves are to be turned into luxury apartments, the gardens landscaped, the ominous water towers turned into unique architectural features.[24] But what of the walls and gatehouses? In a reversal that would be laughable if it were not so sad, these are no longer promoted as measures to secure the community outside from the inmate. They are advertised in terms of their capacity to secure the residents of these luxury conversions from the risk posed to them by

[23] Shearing 1995; see also O'Malley 1992.

[24] Think how Enoch Powell, as health minister, described these asylums, in his speech to the Annual Conference of the National Association of Mental Health in 1961 announcing his intention to close them down: 'There they stand, isolated, majestic, imperious, brooded over by the gigantic water-tower and chimney combined, rising unmistakable and daunting out of the countryside – the asylums which our forefathers built with such immense solidity. Do not for a moment underestimate their power of resistance to our assault' (National Association for Mental Health 1961: 6, quoted in Jones 1972: 321–2).

that very community, not least by the mad who once walked those very grounds. High walls, closed circuit video cameras, security guards and the like can now be reframed and represented as measures that will keep threat out rather than keep it in. Within the guarded and gated territory of the community, residents may enact their dreams of lifestyle maximization, their children may roam freely, their dogs may be exercised, their cars parked in safety. Outside the walls, danger lurks, epitomized by the image of the madman.

Such patterns of reconfiguring urban space can be observed in cities as distant as Sydney and Istanbul. On the one hand, they involve a transformation of the work of the security agencies – not merely the private security firms who undertake the labour-intensive work of guarding, patrolling, surveilling and all the rest, but also the public police.[25] They are involved in tracing out the territories for surveillance using high-tech electronic surveillance and data-analysis systems. They use their information technology and database resources to provide information on types of crime and suspects prevalent in particular zones. They alert inhabitants to the dangers of crime through leaflets warning of risks and exhorting alertness and responsibility. They mobilize territories through residential watch programmes. They advise on design and security features of new homes and conversions. They visit schools and colleges. They help make up communities of active citizens committed to the securitization of their habitat.

The collective logics of community are here brought into alliance with the individualized ethos of neo-liberal politics: choice, personal responsibility, control over one's own fate, self-promotion and self-government. They are also brought into line with prevailing anti-political themes in political discourse, in that self-activating communities are promoted as an antidote to the combined depredations of market forces, remote central government, insensitive local authorities and ineffective crime control agencies, which have combined responsibility for the breakdown of law and order at the heart of urban – and rural – existence.[26] New modes of neighbourhood participation, local empowerment and engagement of residents in decisions over their own lives will, it is thought, re-activate self-motivation, self-responsibility and self-reliance in the form of active citizenship within a self-governing community.[27] Government of security here operates through the

---

[25] Once more, I am drawing here upon the work of Richard Ericson and Kevin Haggerty (1997: chs. 7, 8 and 9).

[26] For further discussion of this theme, see chapter 5.

[27] I have examined these themes in more detail in chapter 5.

activation of individual commitments, energies and choices, through personal morality within a community setting. Community is not simply the territory within which crime is to be controlled; it is itself a *means* of government: its ties, bonds, forces and affiliations are to be celebrated, encouraged, nurtured, shaped and instrumentalized in the hope of enhancing the security of each and of all.

The fortress city

The most powerful image of the reconfigurations of urban space at the end of the twentieth century comes from Mike Davis in *City of Quartz*, his 'excavation of the future' through a study of the present and past of Los Angeles.[28] Of course, in 'post-liberal' LA, the richer neighbourhoods isolate themselves behind walls guarded by armed private police and electronic surveillance. But 'Downtown' Los Angeles has also been transformed: redeveloped to segregate a corporate citadel of offices and shopping malls, and their attendant facilities such as car parks and walkways, from the poor neighbourhoods that surround it. Space here is reconfigured in a project of control, to effect a division between zones of inclusion and those of exclusion. Urban design, architecture and the police apparatus have merged into an integrated programme in the name of security. Public space has been destroyed as the American city has been turned not so much 'inside out' as 'outside in'. 'To reduce contact with untouchables, urban redevelopment has converted once vital public streets into traffic sewers and transformed public parks into temporary receptacles for the homeless and wretched . . . street frontage is denuded, pubic activity is sorted into strictly functional compartments, and circulation is internalized in corridors under the gaze of private police.'[29]

As we saw in chapter 2, one of the key spatial strategies of nine-

---

[28] Davis 1990. The term 'post-liberal' is his. The images he paints are familiar not from sociology, but from science fiction, with its depiction of physically gated and secured high-tech zones of civility, safety, tranquillized liberality and sanitized freedom, surrounded by an untamed, wild, hybrid, dangerous and seductive sprawl, where everything can be had for money, seething with sexuality, violence and drugs, home of revolutionaries and predators alike. Whilst the zones of sanitation are policed through electronic surveillance, identity checks, databanks and the like, the sprawl is policed by coercive, violent, military tactics, which owe nothing to liberalism or its predecessors – outside civility lies the war of all against all, and of civility against all that threatens it.

[29] Ibid.: 226.

teenth-century liberalism, maintained in a social form into the twentieth century, involved the casting of a web of civility over public space, to be sustained, at least in part, by the reciprocal gaze of subjects themselves. These public parks, libraries, playgrounds, the streets themselves are increasingly abandoned, desolate and dangerous. They are replaced by an archipelago of secured spaces – shopping malls, arts centres and gourmet restaurant strips. Access to each is guarded, the internal space is under electronic surveillance and private security policing, its architecture and design so organized as to eliminate or expel those who have no legitimate – that is to say, consumerized – reason to be there. In fact, a double exclusion occurs. The Third World proletariat who service these spaces of consumption are herded into ghettos and barrios in the public housing zones that are expelled to the outer rings of the city. And the poor, 'street people', the homeless and workless are expelled to spaces outside the urban enclave, spaces which are increasingly avoided and feared by those who used to walk, shop and visit there.

As with the securitization of habitat, one aspect of Fortress City is the securing of obligatory points of access: offices and malls present the street with their impenetrable exteriors, reflective glass windows, the cold beauty of their cladding and their design. Entry points are minimized, guarded, gated, open only at certain times, scrutinized by video surveillance. Sometimes these require identity proof for entry – swipe cards, ID badges with pictures, security codes. But in shopping and eating areas, where the illusion of openness with security is a commercial requirement, the guarding of access is left to the discretionary judgement of the private security operatives. Parking lots are within the secured precinct, illuminated, patrolled, under closed circuit surveillance. Ideally, respectable citizens can enter their cars within their gated communities, cover the intervening space as rapidly as possible, aware of the ever-present possibility of hijacking, bag-snatching through windows and all the other hazards of the open road, enter a secured zone and de-car once more in securitized civility.

Where enclosure is not possible, in open malls and pedestrian precincts, other measures are used to maintain exclusion. Cameras and security guards identify, apprehend and disperse groups of youths or the huddles of drunks sitting on steps or walls. But where consumption is the objective, coercive security would be a reminder of the fragility and futility of attempts to consume one's way to pleasure. Hence control must be designed-in, embedded in the very structuring of time, space and the environment. These measures need no knowledge of individuals. They are subtle, non-coercive, automatic in their functioning and consensual in their modes of operation.[30] Street furniture is designed to discourage not merely undesirable conduct but undesirable persons. Benches are shaped so that they can be sat on only for short period, not used as beds; grassed areas are landscaped so that they cannot be used as locations for encampment by street persons; artefacts such as flowerbeds, fountains and street sculpture are both aesthetic objects, designed to manifest and induce civility in those who pass, and control objects, designed to direct people to or from certain locations, to secure against the formation of crowds, to turn them instead into disciplined and well-ordered multiplicities. Activities are regulated 'for the safety of all our customers' – where to walk, where to sit, where to eat and drink, which entrance and exit to take. Each employee of these enterprises has the maintenance of security as an objective, the other side, so it seems, of delivering quality service to the customer.

The profession of security is now modified. Architects, store designers, manufacturers of street furniture, management consultants, those running training courses for staff, insurance companies, high-tech designers of video and audio systems now find themselves in the role of experts in security. The task of the actual policing of these civilized spaces is frequently allotted to private security operations, whose industry expanded at a staggering rate over the last two decades of the twentieth century. Davis points to the 'evolving social division of labour between public- and private-sector police services, in which the former act as the necessary supports of the latter … The private sector, exploiting an army of non-union, low-wage employees, has increasingly captured the labour-intensive roles (guard duty, residential patrol, apprehension of retail crime, maintenance of security passages and checkpoints, monitoring of electronic surveillance, and so on) while public law enforcement has retrenched behind supervision of security macro-systems.'[31] Ericson and Haggerty develop this argument and support it empirically.[32] Police become 'knowledge workers' – advisers on risk management in public and private spaces intersecting with a whole range of other professions involved in this task: licensing and certifying security technology, advising on the information technology necessary for securitization, advising on the location of such things as automatic banking machines, underwriting particular alarm systems and much more.

[30] I am drawing here upon the subtle analysis of control in Disneyworld carried out by Shearing and Stenning (1985).
[31] Davis 1990: 250–1.
[32] Ericson and Haggerty 1997.

This securitization of consumption may actually succeed in producing enclaves of contentment and encouraging the pursuit of pleasure. But Davis draws a bleak picture of the exclusory logic that underpins it. 'Downtown hyperstructure . . . is programmed to ensure a seamless continuum of middle-class work, consumption and recreation, without unwonted exposure to Downtown's working-class street environments.' According to an article in *Urban Land* headed 'How to overcome fear of crime in downtowns': 'A downtown can be designed and developed to make visitors feel that it – or a significant portion of it – is attractive and the type of place that "respectable people" like themselves tend to frequent . . . The activities offered in this core area will determine what "type" of people will be strolling its sidewalks; locating offices and housing for middle- and upper-income residents in or near the core area can assure a high percentage of "respectable", law-abiding pedestrians.'[33] Those who are excluded – the new 'dangerous classes' – are forced to consume elsewhere.

Exclusion: circuits of insecurity

The dictionary defines the word 'abjection' as cast-off, rejected, degraded, brought low in position, condition or status, in low repute.[34] It gives another meaning as well: despicable, lacking courage and self-abasing. The last sense is interesting – exactly these characteristics of vile and degraded subjectivity are frequently ascribed to the subjects of practices of security, charity, welfare and reformation. Abjection is an act of force. This force may not be violence, but it entails the recurrent operation of energies that initiate and sustain this casting off or a casting down, this demotion from a mode of existence, this 'becoming abject'. Abjection is a matter of the energies, the practices, the works of division that act upon persons and collectivities such that some ways of being, some forms of existence are cast into a zone of shame, disgrace or debasement, rendered beyond the limits of the liveable, denied the warrant of tolerability, accorded purely a negative value.

Welfare, as we know, was based in part upon a certain notion of citizenship. The subject was a citizen of a race or nation possessing, by virtue of birth, certain common political, social and economic rights or entitlements – not necessarily legal – which would be secured by the state, in return for each citizen fulfilling certain obligations of

---

[33] Milder 1987: 18, quoted in Davis 1990: 231.

[34] I adopt the term 'abjection' from Judith Butler (Butler 1993: 3), but delete the psychoanalytic resonances that are important for her.

responsibility, prudence, self-reliance, and civic duty. Over the closing decades of the twentieth century, as we have seen in previous chapters, this universalizing logic was called into question. We have seen the birth of political mentalities and governmental practices which have served to sharpen and naturalize the divisions between the autonomous and the dependent, the contented and the discontented, the haves and the have-nots. The homeless person in the UK is now designated a 'rough sleeper' – as if the lack of accommodation were a personal lifestyle choice or a symptom of pathology. The unemployed person is now officially designated a 'job seeker', a term which places the problem firmly within the mode of life of the individual. How have these novel practices of abjection been made acceptable and tolerable?

Problematizing exclusion

Since at least the eighteenth century, the political imaginations of most European countries have been haunted by a succession of figures that seem to condense in their person, their name, their image all that is disorder, danger, threat to civility: the vagrant, the pauper, the degener-ate, the unemployable, the residuum, the social problem group. Even over the last decades of the nineteenth century and the first half of the twentieth, when projects to forge universal social citizenship were being formulated and set in place, not all were thought to be includable, notably the mad, the criminal, the persons who refused the bonds of regular labour, but also, in different ways at different times, the child, the African, the woman and the Jew. The political doctrines of universal citizenship do not in themselves eliminate the demand that a boundary be drawn between those who can and those who cannot be citizens. Notions such as 'the residuum', 'the unemployable' and 'the social problem group' were part of the fabric of new liberal thinking in Britain in the early twentieth century: citizenship was not merely a political right but a kind of moral contract granting privileges in return for the fulfil-ment of the obligations to conduct oneself in a certain manner. Those who failed to live up to these obligations through defects of character or will had to be identified and denied their rights of citizenship. 'It is essential', wrote William Beveridge in 1905, 'to maintain the distinction between those who, however irregularly employed, are yet members, though inferior members, of the industrial army and those who are mere parasites, incapable of performing any useful service whatever . . . [The unemployable] must be removed from industry and maintained adequately in public institutions, but with the complete and permanent loss of all citizenship rights – including not only the franchise but civil freedom and fatherhood.'[35]

The aspirations to universality in the rationalities of the welfare state and social security as articulated in the period during and after the 1939-45 war were encapsulated most poignantly in the term 'One Nation'. This was not a prerogative of the centre-left. Here, for example, is Minister for Education R. A. Butler, a Conservative, in 1944, speaking about the Education Act of that year in a film made by the Central Office of Information:

> The effect as I see it will be as much social as educational. I think it will have the effect of welding us all into one nation, when it's got thoroughly worked out, instead of the two nations as Disraeli talked about.[36]

Or here is the Conservative publication *The Right Road for Britain*, in 1949:

> The Social Services are no longer even in theory a form of poor relief. They are a co-operative system of mutual aid and self-help provided by the whole nation and designed to give all the basic minimum of security, of housing, of opportunity, of employment and of living standards below which our duty to one another forbids us to permit anyone to fall.[37]

Of course, welfare citizenship entailed duties and obligations – the obligation to be prepared to enter into employment if offered, or else to risk losing benefit and being required to attend a training centre; the obligation to seek to remain healthy; the obligation upon families not only to have children to reverse the decline of the rate of reproduction of the British race, but also to take their share in their mutual responsibilities to their race by giving each child the best care possible. And, whilst the universalism of such mentalities was an ideal rather than an operational reality, it did regulate the types of response that were appropriate when the 1960s saw 'the rediscovery of poverty', the resurgence of unemployment or the discovery that conditions in the large mental hospitals coupled exclusion with cruelty and degradation of the worst possible kind. The debates over universalism versus selectivity in welfare benefits throughout the 1960s and after – between a minimum standard targeted upon the worst-off, and a universal set of provisions which provided sufficiency for all – still maintained this notion of universal citizenship guaranteed by the state, though they differed in the stress that they

[35] Beveridge 1905: 326–7; see also G. Jones 1982.
[36] Quoted in Timmins 1996: 92.
[37] Quoted ibid.: 249.

placed upon the need to allow and encourage the individual to rise above their fellow citizens by their own industry, genius, thrift or fortune. The supporters of targeting benefits upon the least well-off argued for this on the grounds that more could be done with greater selectivity: only thus could one do away with the slum schools, the slum homes, the slum hospitals, the slum prisons that reproached a modern society.

But at the close of the twentieth century, citizenship is framed in very different terms. Increasingly, the rights and entitlements conferred upon citizens in welfare regimes are criticized because of the dependency which they create in those who are their subjects, the client mentality they encourage, the culture of dependency they produce, in the inhabitants of the empire of 'Giroland'.[38] These arguments first emerged in the United States. 'We tried to provide for the poor and produced more poor instead. We tried to remove the barriers to escape from poverty and inadvertently built a trap.'[39] Thus argued Charles Murray in *Losing Ground*, published in 1984. For Lawrence Mead, the damage seemed to be done not by the benefits themselves, but by the fact that they were 'entitlements' and were thus given regardless of the behaviour of the client.[40] Murray's welfare dependants were rational individuals, calculating that they could earn more or live better by not working, and using the welfare system to their own advantage. But Mead's dependants lacked competence. 'Victims of a culture of dependence spawned by well-meaning but misguided liberal policy, they had lost the capacity to work and to carry out the ordinary duties of citizens.'[41] The War on Poverty and the Great Society programmes in the United States, far from helping the poorest, had created an underclass stripped of self-reliance and self-respect, equipped with a client mentality, degraded and dependent. As *Time Magazine* put it, 'Behind the [ghetto's] crumbling walls lives a large group of people who are more intractable, more socially alien and more hostile than almost anyone had imagined . . . Their bleak environment nurtures values that are often at odds with those of the majority – even the majority of the poor. Thus the underclass produces a highly disproportionate number of the nation's juvenile delinquents, school dropouts, drug addicts and welfare mothers, and much of the adult crime, family disruption, urban decay and demand for social expenditures.'[42] The underclass was a sector formed of long-term wel-

---

[38] Many benefits are paid in the UK in the form of a cheque known as a Giro, which can be drawn on the previously nationalized Post Office Girobank.
[39] Murray 1984: 9.
[40] Mead 1986.
[41] Katz 1993: 15.
[42] *Time*, 29 August 1977, quoted in Katz 1993: 4.

fare recipients, hostile street criminals, hustlers in an alternative under-
ground economy and traumatized alcoholics, vagrants and de-
institutionalized psychiatric patients dominating the wastelands in the
decaying industrial heartland of the cities of North America.

In the UK, a less lurid picture was painted, but it was one in which
the recipients of welfare were still portrayed in terms of a moral problematization: those lured into welfare dependency by the regimes of
social security themselves; those unable to accept their moral responsibilities as citizens for reasons of psychological or other personal inca-
pacity; those who might be enterprising, but wilfully refused to operate
within the values of civility and responsible self-management, such as
New Age Travellers or drug abusers.

Such themes were echoed in the vocabulary of policy pronouncements in the UK in the 1980s. But the new understanding of citizenship
as a matter of active choice was also enunciated, though in a different
way, from a range of other political positions that saw the bureaucracy
of care as failing to address the greatest need, imposing clienthood,
patriarchal authority and social norms upon those who used it, failing
to respect the rights of the consumer or even to provide the most basic
of information. The active consumer of welfare had arrived, and was
increasingly catered for by a plethora of self-help groups, by a variety of
concept houses and voluntary endeavours and by a growing 'for-profit'
market in private care and private insurance.

In the emerging rationalities of welfare reform among the European
parties and institutions of the centre-left, activity is coupled with security in a new way. Duties, obligations and passive rights are counterposed
to opportunities, choices, the engendering of the capacities and competencies for active citizenship in the subject of government, who is
then to be a subject of self-government, individual choice and personal
responsibility. Thus the 1994 report of the Labour Party's Commission
on Social Justice regards the role of a welfare state as to encourage
autonomy and activity on behalf of citizens, and counterposes the Beveridgean welfare state, which became active only when its recipients were
passive, to an 'intelligent' welfare state which secures individuals and
their families against insecurity across a life-cycle and in relation to
specific 'risks' such as illness and unemployment, a welfare state that is
'personalized and flexible, designed to promote individual choice and
personal responsibility'.[43] The language poses a distinction between a
majority who can and do ensure their own well-being and security
through their own active self-promotion and responsibility for

[43] Commission on Social Justice 1994: 223.

themselves and their families, and those who are outside this nexus of activity: the underclass, the marginalized, the truly disadvantaged, the excluded. On the one hand, activity. On the other, exclusion.

Exclusion has become the organizing term for welfare reform in British and European rationalities of social democracy. The old problems of inequality and social justice are analysed in a distinctive and recurring fashion. It is suggested that secular economic changes, exacerbated by policies which have sought to reduce welfare expenditure in the name of competitive tax regimes and the like, have led to the rise of a 'two-thirds, one-third' society, producing a widening gap between the 'included' majority who are seeing their standard of living rising and impoverished minorities who are 'excluded'.[44] In the analyses of social liberals and social market theorists in Europe, in contemporary analyses of deprivation and of poverty, the analytics of abjection have become reframed in this language of exclusion. This has become central to the analytic framework of the European Union, the Organization for Economic Cooperation and Development, UK charitable foundations such as the Joseph Rowntree Foundation and indeed the criticisms and policies of the British Labour Party. In such analyses, exclusion is identified as an inescapable consequence of 'market individualism'. Social problems are recast as 'the problem of the excluded'.[45] The unemployed are understood as those excluded from regular work. Poverty is understood as exclusion from the resources and benefits necessary to participate as a full citizen in the life of the community. And these various forms of exclusion are to be counteracted by strategies of inclusion, for example an 'intelligent welfare state' which gives 'a hand up not a hand out', active labour market policies involving training and job search, even, in the words of the current leader of the Labour Party, enfolding and embracing all in a 'stakeholder economy'.

Despite their great differences in notions of economic causation and personal responsibility, these rationalities for welfare reform being developed by left and right operate with a surprisingly consonant picture of the abjected persons and groups that are their object. On the one hand, they are dispersed. They are no longer seen as part of a single group with common social characteristics, to be managed by a unified 'social service' and 'generic social workers' who can recognize the common roots of all social problems. The excluded have no unity

[44] Levitas 1996.
[45] See, for example, Commission of the European Community 1994; Hutton 1995; Commission for Social Justice 1994; Joseph Rowntree Foundation 1995.

amongst themselves – like Marx's peasants, individualized like potatoes in a sack, incapable of forming themselves into a single class on the basis of a consciousness of their shared expropriation, they cannot represent themselves; they must be represented. The marginalized, the excluded, the underclass are fragmented and divided, comprising all those who are unable or unwilling to manage themselves and capitalize their own existence. Their particular difficulties thus need to be addressed through the activities of a variety of specialists, each of whom is an expert in a particular problem – training schemes for those excluded through unemployment, specialist agencies working with those with disabilities, rehabilitation of addicts undertaken by specialist drug workers, education in social skills by workers with the single homeless, specialized hostels for battered women, for alcoholics etc. Yet on the other hand, these abjected subjects are re-unified ethically and spatially. They are re-unified ethically in that they are accorded a new and active relation to their status in terms of their strategies and capacities for the management of themselves: they have either refused the bonds of civility and self responsibility, or they aspire to them but have not been given the skills, capacities and means. And they are re-unified spatially in that the territory of the social is reconfigured, and the abjected are relocated, in both imagination and strategy, in 'marginalized' spaces: in the decaying council estate, in the chaotic lone parent family, in the shop doorways of inner city streets. It appears as if outside the communities of inclusion exists an array of micro-sectors, micro-cultures of non-citizens, failed citizens, anti-citizens, consisting of those who are unable or unwilling to enterprise their lives or manage their own risk, incapable of exercising responsible self-government, attached either to no moral community or to a community of anti-morality.

Managing risk

A new territory is thus emerging, after the welfare state, for the management of these micro-sectors, traced out by a plethora of quasi-autonomous agencies working within the 'savage spaces', in the 'anti-communities' on the margins, or with those abjected by virtue of their lack of competence or capacity for responsible ethical self-management. There are the 'voluntary' endeavours (often run by users, survivors or philanthropists but funded by various grant regimes) – drug projects, disability organizations, self-help groups, concept houses and so forth (opposition forces transformed into service providers). There are the private and for-profit organizations – old people's homes, hostels and so forth – that make their money from private insurance or from the collection of the state benefits to their individual inmates. There is the huge and murky industry of 'training', where a multitude of private or quasi-private training agencies compete in a market for public contracts and public funds in the quest for profit. Within this new territory of exclusion, the social logics of welfare bureaucracies are replaced by new logics of competition, market segmentation and service management: the management of misery and misfortune can become, once more, a potentially profitable activity.

In this configuration of control, a whole array of control agencies – police, social workers, doctors, psychiatrists, mental health professionals – become, at least in part, connected up with one another in circuits of surveillance and communication designed to minimize the riskiness of the most risky. They form a multiplicity of points for the collection, inscription, accumulation and distribution of information relevant to the management of risk. Whilst social notions of risk were universalizing, these risk agencies focus upon 'the usual suspects' – the poor, the welfare recipients, the petty criminals, discharged psychiatric patients, street people. The logics of risk inescapably locate the careers and identities of such tainted citizens within a regime of surveillance which actually constitutes them all as actually or potentially 'risky' individuals. The incompleteness, fragmentation and failure of risk assessment and risk management is no threat to such logics, merely a perpetual incitement for the incessant improvement of systems, generation of more knowledge, invention of more techniques, all driven by the technological imperative to tame uncertainty and master hazard.

The changing role of mental health professionals exemplifies this well.[46] The territory of operation of contemporary psychiatric professionals, in the UK, USA, Canada and Australia, is virtually defined by the problematic of risk and its control. Britain is not alone in having witnessed a succession of highly publicized 'scandals' of community care in the last ten years that have been debated in terms of risk: the absent or incorrect assessments made by professionals of the risk presented by discharged psychiatric patients living in the community. In these different jurisdictions, a host of regulations, laws and procedures are being enacted and implemented, imposing on psychiatric professionals the requirements for risk assessment of patients on discharge from hospitals, of certain types of prisoners (psychopaths, paedophiles) on discharge from prisons, of psychiatric patients in the community. In thousands of micro-locales, techniques are thus being devised to identify levels of risk,

---

[46] For a more detailed discussion, see Rose 1996f and 1998. I have drawn directly on parts of these two papers in what follows.

signs of risk, indicators of risk and the like and to inscribe these in case notes, care plans and a multitude of other documents. The many professions that are engaged with the subject of psychiatry appear to have, as perhaps their primary contemporary obligation, the administration of individuals in the light of a calculation of their riskiness and in the name of risk reduction and risk management.

Risk management – the identification, assessment, elimination or reduction of the possibility of incurring misfortune or loss – has thus become an integral part of the professional responsibility of each expert of psy. Clinical diagnosis may still take place. But the key judgement that must be made is a different one – what should be done with this person, should her or she be sent to this institution or to that, to this hostel or that sheltered housing scheme, back into the community or back into prison. The logic of prediction comes to replace the logic of diagnosis: the classification of the subjects of psychiatry in terms of likely future conduct, their riskiness to the community and themselves and the identification of the steps necessary to manage that conduct. Mental health professionals are to answer a pair of administrative questions: what is to be done and how can we decide. This does not result in a shift of attention from individuals to the targeting of categories and sub-populations. Indeed, the problem is precisely to deploy actuarial classifications of risk to identify and control risky individuals in order to ascertain who can, and who cannot, be managed within the open circuits of community control. For those who cannot, the psychiatric institutions that remain are defined not in terms of cure nor care, but in terms of the secure containment of risk. Confinement becomes little more than a way of securing the most risky until their riskiness can be fully assessed and controlled. If ever: the spectre of preventive detention re-emerges in relation to a new class of 'monsters' – sexual predators, paedophiles, the incorrigibly anti-social – for whom a whole variety of para-legal forms of confinement are being devised.[47]

Psychiatry has long been as much an administrative as a clinical

---

[47] This is an international phenomenon. In Victoria, Australia, in April 1990, the Community Protection Act was passed in order to legitimate detention of one individual, Garry David, who was considered to be dangerous but did not fall under the ambit of either criminal or mental health law (Greig 1997). In related quasi-psychiatric areas, notably 'paedophilia', issues of preventive detention are being discussed in many national contexts: it appears that the conventions of 'rule of law' must be waived for the protection of the community against a growing number of 'predators', who do not conform to either legalistic or psychiatric models of subjectivity (see Pratt 1999; Simon 1998; Scheingold, Pershing and Olson 1994).

science. One only has to recall its role in relation to concerns about degeneration in the late nineteenth century, in eugenic strategies over the first half of the twentieth century, in the programmes of mental hygiene in the 1930s and in the plans for a comprehensive, preventative health service in the 1950s and 1960s under the sign of community psychiatry. The demand that psychiatry should be concerned with the assessment and administration of risky individuals, rather than with diagnosis, treatment and cure, does not mark a new moment in its political vocation. Nonetheless, its role is revised in the new configuration of control. What is called for is the management of a permanently risky minority on the territory of the community.

In these new circuits of insecurity, mental health workers are but one group of a whole variety of professionals – social workers, probation officers, education welfare officers, health visitors and all the others so often indicted for their failure – who have acquired responsibility for administering the new territory of exclusion. Together they try to manage an ever-extending apparatus for the continuous and unending task of the management of enduringly problematic persons in the name of community security. In this context, the control functions of the public police have also been transformed. Ericson and Haggerty suggest that in the contemporary work of the police 'categories and classifications of risk communication and . . . the technologies for communicating knowledge [about risk] internally and externally' prospectively structure the actions and deliberations of other welfare and medical professionals.[48] Once stabilized in 'communication formats' – more or less systematic rules for the organization and presentation of information and experience – risk classifications tend to become the means by which professionals think, act and justify their actions. In that sense, the very gaze of control professionals and the nature of their encounter with their client, patient or suspect is liable to be formatted by the demands and objectives of risk management. They go so far as to argue that 'Even in medicine the doctor on the ground is a subordinate of expert systems and those who manage them. He or she is one of many contributors to the expert system of risk management that creates the patient's dossier, and therefore lose control over particular outcomes as well as over the progress of cases.'[49] The information so extracted, organized and packaged is then communicated along channels, and with consequences, far removed from those of professional practice.[50]

[48] Ericson and Haggerty 1997: 33.
[49] Ibid.: 37–8.
[50] Cf. Castel 1991: 281.

From this perspective, then, control is no longer merely a matter of repressing or containing those who are individually pathological; it is about the generation of 'knowledge that allows selection of thresholds that define acceptable risks and on forms of inclusion and exclusion based on that knowledge'.[51] Control workers, whether they be police or psychiatrists, thus have a new administrative function – the administration of the marginalia, ensuring community protection through the identification of the riskiness of individuals, actions, forms of life and territories. Hence the increasing emphasis on case conferences, multidisciplinary teams, sharing information, keeping records, making plans, setting targets, establishing networks for the surveillance and documentation of the potentially risky individual on the territory of the community. The respecification of the problem of control as a problem of the management of risk is bound to a revised governmental role for control professionals, to manage dangerous sites and dangerous persons on the territory of the community, under the threat of being held accountable for any harm to 'the general public' – 'normal people' – which might result. This is part of a shift in our conceptions and valuations of normality and civility, in which madness and criminality come to be emblematic of the threat posed to 'the community' by a permanently marginal, excluded, outcast sector. Hence constant work is required to mark out and police new zones of exclusion that are not delineated by the walls of an asylum or the closed doors of the hospital ward. Whilst spatial exclusion can be maintained in sheltered housing, day centres and the like, a new array of dangerous zones of interpenetration come into existence – the shopping mall, the car park, the railway station, the street: spaces requiring a ceaseless labour of administration of differences.

From dependency to activity

As we have seen, contemporary programmes of welfare reform take the ethical reconstruction of the welfare recipient as their central problem. Conservative programmes in the 1980s and early 1990s tended to emphasize the demoralizing consequences of welfare receipt, and to seek to micro-manage the behaviour of welfare recipients in order to remoralize them. Thus they advocated programmes such as 'workfare', to stress the need to reform habits as a condition of receipt of benefits and, ultimately, to seek to get all those physically able to work off benefits entirely. Thus Mayor Rudolph Giuliani of New York argued that

---

[51] Ericson and Haggerty 1997: 41.

welfare recipients should scrub graffiti and clean streets as a condition of benefit; Robert Rector, of the Heritage Foundation, called for 'legislation requir(ing) responsible behavior as a condition of receiving welfare benefits'; Michael Schwartz, of the Free Congress Foundation Center for Family Policy, urged that 'Responsible behavior (marriage) should be rewarded, irresponsible behavior (out-of-wedlock childbearing) should not'; and Governor Tommy Thompson of Wisconsin, architect of the USA's most radical welfare reform experiment, introduced LEARNfare which required that children of welfare recipients attend school as a condition of their parents' receiving benefits.[52] More recently, Conservatives have argued that the task is not merely to 'end welfare as we know it', but to end welfare entirely, and to force individuals who are 'unable support themselves through the job market . . . to fall back upon the resources of family, church, community or private charity'.[53] Governor Thompson's revised scheme Wisconsin Works (or W-2) replaced the principle form of welfare support – Aid to Families with Dependent Children – with a mandatory and time-limited workfare programme for all poor families considered able to work, in which each individual is assessed and directed into a work option which they must accept as a condition for assistance. But liberals too advocated programmes to get individuals off benefit and into work, such as the Jobstart training programme, better child care to allow lone parents to get back into the workforce or Ohio's Learning, Earning and Parenting Program (LEAP) which offered subsidized day care to mothers whilst they returned to education.

These ideas, in uneasy combination, characterize Clinton's federal programme for the reform of welfare in the USA which was developed in the 1990s, as well as those being followed through by the majority of US states. They also characterize the projects of welfare reform undertaken by the Labour administration which came into office in Britain in 1997. In these projects, the new politics of exclusion links up with the emphases on a politics of the 'third sector' and the communitarian and associationalist arguments that I discussed in chapter 5. For, as Tony Blair, then the leader of the Labour Party in opposition, put it in 1996, in an article timed to coincide with the tenth anniversary of the publication of the report of the Archbishop of Canterbury's Special Commission on Urban Priority Areas, 'Britain is today more divided and more insecure than when *Faith in the City* was published . . . The Tories offer a Britain split into two tiers, with affluent communities turned into

[52] All examples quoted from Tanner 1994.
[53] Ibid.: 16.

private fortresses against the world outside. Labour offers the vision of Britain as One Nation – a belief that to help individuals we need to reinvent community for the modern world.'[54]

In this new anti-politics of welfare, communities themselves are urged to take over as much of the responsibility as possible for providing such support through not-for-profit organizations, volunteering, charity and good neighbourliness. In this new schema, thousands of people, from unemployed youth to retired executives, from Christian missionaries to political activists, are to work in multitude of ways to attend to the cultural, welfare and support needs of millions of others, and are to do so through a diversity of institutional forms – private schools, charitable trusts, co-operatives, clubs, associations – which share only one thing in common – they are provided neither by state nor market. This will not only provide many new jobs, mopping up many of those made unemployed by technological advance, but it will make for more receptive and flexible services. And, it appears, such reorganized services will, by virtue of their local and community nature, find their way with less resistance than their predecessors into the very interstices of the problematic sectors. The church hall, the elders of the community, the community centre will achieve the remoralization that eluded the professional welfare worker. These contemporary ethico-political arguments infuse community with vectors of moral authority that tend to reduce, rather than to enhance, the contestability of powers and judgements over conducts and forms of life.

Within such a politics, the aim of welfare interventions should be to encourage and reconstruct self-reliance in both providers and recipients of services. This ambition is shared by neo-liberals, communitarians, third-sector enthusiasts and moralistic market democrats such as Clinton and Blair. Poverty and many other social ills are cast not in economic terms but as fundamentally subjective conditions. This is not a psychological subjectivity with social determinants, as in welfare regimes. It is an ethical subjectivity, and a cultural subjectivity. For community requires all to act by the ethics of virtuous self-responsibility, responsibility for oneself as a member of one's community. Hence the measures for the reform of welfare and criminal justice proposed by the British Labour Party, analogous to those supported by many communitarians in the United States: welfare-to-work, zero tolerance, 'naming, blaming and shaming', parental responsibility for the crimes of their children. This is 'tough love', or in the language of the Labour government in Britain, 'compassion with a hard edge'. The problems of the

---

[54] Blair 1996.

excluded, of the underclass, are to be resolved by a kind of moral re-armament. Indeed, the term 'class' in the notion of the underclass does not carry a logic of social stratification but of moral demarcation. It presupposes that poverty is no longer a question of inequality among 'social' classes: hence 'a politics of conduct is today more salient than a politics of class'.[55] It is through moral reformation, through ethical reconstruction, that the excluded citizen is to be re-attached to a virtuous community.

Central to the strategy of these new forms of control are 'work' and 'family'. One sees, especially in the policies of the current British Labour government, a concerted attempt to reinstate the controls on personal conduct supposedly embodied within the assemblages of paid work and stable family life. The various forms of support provided by the social state, social insurance and social citizenship – entitlements to unemployment benefits, disability benefits, benefits to lone parents to compensate for the absence of a spouse and the like – are now deemed to have undermined self-responsibility by providing alternative, and amoral, modes of support outside the family-work system. Thus a whole variety of little measures, mean and penny-pinching in themselves, are linked by their common strategic orientation: dismantling of the 'social wage', reducing financial support to those falling outside the family form and the wage relationship. Paradoxically, despite the contemporary transformation in the nature of work discussed in chapter 4, the mechanism of employment is prioritized in ethical reconstruction. The shift 'from welfare to workfare' is linked to a cluster of ideas with a nineteenth-century puritan heritage, but given a new ethical gloss: paid work engenders pride and self-respect, or self-esteem, and ties the individual into respectability, identity and community. And despite, or perhaps because of, the evidence that the familialization of sexuality, procreation, habitation and consumption – itself a relatively recent phenomenon – is fragmenting under the pressures of the commercialization of pleasure, the transformation of parenthood into a lifestyle choice, the rise of divorce, remarriage, step-families and other non-familial forms, the family too is to be valorized once more as a mechanism for stabilizing the passions of adults, responsibilizing the parent as a wage earner and instilling the rules of moral order and ethical comportment into children. In these new rationalities of welfare, individuals are to be nodes in little webs of connectedness, connections between the family machine and the employment machine, which will simultaneously provide means of sup-

[55] Mead 1991: 4, quoted in Procacci 1998: 30.

port outside the social state, and means of control of conduct outside the apparatus of social welfare.

Whether intentionally or not, the effect of programmes of welfare-to-work is to produce a sector of the labouring population that is casualized, underprotected against risk, insecure and desocialized.[56] Wage labour itself becomes a generator of insecurity and fragmentation; unionized labour is undercut; the wages paid at the bottom of the labour market drop down to below poverty level. The workfare state is a charitable state: charitable in the sense in which the charity organization societies of the nineteenth century were charitable. Assistance is not a right but is conditional upon demonstration of moral improvement. And, in keeping with the logics of advanced liberalism, in the United States at least, the administration of workfare and welfare-to-work programmes is privatized and undertaken for profit. These regimes entail an intensification of the government of the conduct of the poorest and most underprivileged. Wisconsin is referred to by its promoters as a 'laboratory' for assembling a programme which reshapes social responsibility, no longer 'sheltering people from real-world responsibilities' and 'not requiring people to do anything to receive their cheques' but 'actually helping people become self-sufficient'.[57] As a recent commentator put it, 'At bottom, Wisconsin's welfare-to-work programmes are about ethics rather than money.'[58] Within such programmes for the ethical reconstruction of the excluded, everyone within the ghetto, every member of the underclass, each excluded person should be 'given the opportunity' to achieve full membership in a moral community through work, and to adhere to the core values of honesty, self-reliance and concern for others. Their willingness to do so is to form the object of scrutiny of new moral authorities in the benefits agencies and elsewhere. Those who refuse to become responsible, to govern themselves ethically, have also refused the offer to become members of our moral community. Hence, for them, harsh measures are entirely appropriate. Three strikes and you are out: citizenship becomes conditional upon conduct.

---

[56] This argument was made forcefully by Loic Wacquant at a seminar in London in June 1998 under the auspices of the Finnish Institute and the London School of Economics and Political Science. The seminar was entitled 'Blairism: a beacon for Europe?' I am not convinced that the strategic intention of these programmes was an assault on unionism and wage levels.

[57] T. Thompson 1996.

[58] Kettle 1997: 2.

Technologies of activity

Within this new politics of conduct, the problems of problematic persons are reformulated as moral or ethical problems, that is to say, problems in the ways in which such persons understand and conduct themselves and their existence. This ethical reformulation opens the possibility for a whole range of psychological techniques to be recycled in programmes for governing 'the excluded'. The imperative of activity becomes central once the unemployed person is understood as a 'job seeker' or the homeless person as a 'rough sleeper'. The homeless person may be homeless for a number of reasons, but key among them is the lack of a home or the money to rent or buy one. The rough sleeper, on the other hand, sleeps rough for a range of individual reasons – personal inadequacy, lack of knowledge of alternatives, hand-outs from passers by, wilful refusal of accommodation, drunkenness, drugs, mental illness. Hence the rough sleeper must first be taken off the streets, which may be done by kindness, by bribery or by force, to a hostel or other temporary living space. Here they can be re-educated in the skills of finding accommodation, equipped with the personal skills which seem to lie at the heart of their choice – for choice it must be when there are in fact an excess of hostel places over street sleepers – to sleep rough. The imperative of activity, and the presupposition of an ethic of choice, is central not only to the rationale of policy but also to the reformatory technology to which it is linked.

This is just one example of a whole array of technologies of reformation which seem to operate in terms of the opposition of dependence and passivity with autonomy and activity. Barbara Cruikshank in the United States and Karen Baistow in the UK have drawn attention to the significance of the language of empowerment for professionals operating within such technologies.[59] For empowerment – or the lack of empowerment – codes the subjective substrate of exclusion as lack of self-esteem, self-worth and the skills of self-management necessary to steer oneself as an active individual in the empire of choice. The relations that humans have with themselves are to be the target of professional reconstruction, often backed with the power of law. The beauty of empowerment is that it appears to reject the logics of patronizing dependency that infused earlier welfare modes of expertise. Subjects are to do the work on themselves, not in the name of conformity, but to make them free.

[59] Cruikshank 1994; Baistow 1995.

These new behavioural and cognitive techniques for personal reformation derive, of course, from psychology. It has, perhaps, been insufficiently recognized that, in the 1970s, psychology became a new clinical assemblage, freeing itself from medicine and psychiatry. To its conventional repertoire of tests and diagnostics, it added some highly transferable skills for acting upon the conduct of others. This would not act indirectly on conduct via the gradual reshaping of a psychic economy. It would address specifiable problems, set itself specifiable targets and produce measurable shifts in conduct in short time spans. Behaviourism tried to lose its association with negative and repressive techniques to eliminate undesirable perversions; it tried to become an emancipatory technology for re-establishing the self's control over itself.[60] Cognitive therapy, rational-emotive therapy and a range of similar techniques became the order of the day, with their themes of learned helplessness, self-esteem and self-control – not as inhibition on expression of inner world, but as control over the impressions and actions which steer one through the outer world, an internal locus of control. The binary of dependency and control became a powerful formula for judging the conduct by others, and for judging oneself. Autonomy was now represented in terms of personal power and the capacity to accept responsibility – not to blame others but to recognize your own collusion in that which prevents you from being yourself and, in doing so, to overcome it and achieve responsible autonomy and personal power. High self-esteem was linked to the power to plan one's life as an orderly enterprise and take responsibility for its course and outcome.[61]

These themes are not new; many have a long heritage. But what these developments represent, I think, is the linkage between a way of problematizing the techniques of welfare, in terms of dependence: the production or support of a certain moral – or amoral – form of character in the recipient and the re-activation of this way of problematizing subjectivity, in terms of 'pathologies of the will'. The vocabulary of dependence as a problem of the will provides the common language of description for conditions ranging from lack of work to dependence on alcohol.[62] A problematization at the level of the fiscal and moral management of the population – the costs of dependency culture – is linked to a problematization at the level of individual subjectivity – the threat to individual well-being and to collective security posed by the dependent unemployed youth, welfare recipient, lone mother, disabled person.

---

[60] Baistow 1995.
[61] Cruikshank 1994.
[62] See Sedgwick 1992; N. Fraser and Gordon 1994; Valverde 1998a.

And this is more significant because it connects up with the invention of new control technologies for action on others and self in loci from the marriage guidance session to the prison. For those who can be included, control is now to operate through the rational reconstruction of the will, and of the habits of independence, life planning, self-improvement, autonomous life conduct, so that the individual can be re-inserted into family, work and consumption, and hence into the continuous circuits and flows of control society. But for those who cannot or will not be included, and who are too risky to be managed in open circuits – the repeat offender, the predator, the irredeemably anti-social, the irretrievably monstrous, the paedophile, the psychopath – control will take the form of more or less permanent sequestration.

The penal-welfare complex

The theorists of decarceration in the 1970s suggested that advanced industrial societies were witnessing a sharp decline in the size of the populations who were confined. There has, indeed, been a marked reduction in the numbers of inmates of many publicly run institutions, notably mental hospitals and old people's homes.[63] In the United States, for example, by 1990 the rate of incarceration in state mental hospitals had dropped to less than 50 per 100,000 residents aged fifteen and over, from a peak in 1955 of over 450 per 100,000.[64] The situation is rather more complex, however, not merely because many jurisdictions have introduced compulsory treatment 'in the community', but also because new measures are being implemented for the preventive detention of those thought to present a threat to the public: a new archipelago of confinement without reformation is taking shape. As far as the criminal justice system is concerned, despite the proliferation of non-custodial punishments, there has been no reduction in the prison population in Britain and the United States. By the end of the 1980s, Britain's rate of imprisonment was around 100 persons for every 100,000 population, more than almost any other European state. But the American example is even more striking.[65] In 1996, the incarceration rate for sentenced adult prisoners in the United States had risen to over 400 for every

[63] This 'decarceration' has, in fact, led to a new incarceration, in the grown of a highly lucrative market sector in private residential facilities run for profit.

[64] Mechanic and Rochefort 1996, cited in Caplow and Simon's (1998) article, 'The incarceration mania: a preliminary diagnosis'. I am grateful to Jonathon Simon for allowing me to see this unpublished article, which has informed my argument in this section.

[65] All of the following figures relating to the United States come from Caplow and Simon 1998.

100,000 of the population; where all jail inmates are included, the figure reaches over 600 per 100,000. Almost 1.2 million inmates were serving sentences of a year or more in state and federal prisons, and almost 4 million were on parole or probation: almost 3 per cent of the adult population and 7 per cent of the male adult population were subject to the control practices of the criminal justice system.

There are undoubtedly many reasons for the use of imprisonment in the United States, as elsewhere, and many plausible explanations of the rise in the penalized population can be provided. But I think it is possible to argue that the new regimes of welfare and control that I have described in this chapter entail a new relation between the penal and welfare complexes.[66] The prison and penality more generally have become crucial elements in the government of insecurity. If the United States can be regarded as a test case in this developing diagram of control, the poor, the dispossessed, the unemployed and the recipients of benefits are increasingly 'governed through the crime'.[67] It is not merely that prisoners are overwhelmingly recruited from the ranks of the poor, the uneducated and unaffiliated, as everywhere, and from African-Americans. It is not simply that tough crime control and the virtues of penality have become vital elements in political rhetoric. Nor is it merely that the criminal justice system is used to fight a war that is undoubtedly the longest, costliest and least effective in human history – the 'war on drugs' – although drug convictions have been a powerful contributor to the growth of the penalized population. Rather, it is that the reverse of the responsibilizing moral imperatives of welfare reform is the construction and exclusion of a semi-permanent quasi-criminal population, seen as impervious to the demands of the new morality. Of course, there are innumerable 'interagency' programmes – involving police, welfare agencies, health agencies, school staff, family members and the like – targeting the select few from high-risk youth, habitual offenders and so forth: these redeploy all the moralizing techniques of ethical reconstruction in the attempt to instil the capacity for self-management.[68] But the

---

[66] Prison and regimes of welfare have been intrinsically intertwined since at least the start of the twentieth century but the 'penal-welfare' strategy of the social state was very different, the relation of the penal complex and the social work complex being centred upon individualization, diagnosis, expert treatment, reformation and rehabilitation. Within an explanatory framework that, along one axis at least, attempted to understand the social origins of deviance and inadequacy, care and treatment were to be extended by the state to resocialize the unfortunate individual (Garland 1985).

[67] The phrase is Jonathon Simon's.

[68] Unsurprisingly 'naming, shaming and blaming' – or 'reintegrative shaming' as it is more properly known – has become a great favourite in these

procedures for the selection of these experimental subjects arise out of the detailed profiles maintained by police forces, which identify particularly risky individuals and particularly risky territories on the basis of the compilation of all manner of data on crime, criminal records, offender profiles and the like. In the same movement as the circuits of insecurity exclude the homeless, the workless and all those other non-consumers from the inclusory logics of control, they are consigned to unending management by the agents, agencies and technologies of the new penal complex. Exclusion itself is effectively criminalized, as crime control agencies home in on those very violations that enable survival in the circuits of exclusion: petty theft, drinking alcohol in public, loitering, drugs and so forth. These new circuits cycle individuals from probation to prison because of probation violations, from prison to parole, and back to prison because of parole violations.[69]

Whilst the welfare budgets are cut, the penal budgets expand, and police, magistrates, parole officers and a host of others have become integral to the management of exclusion, playing a key role in the government of insecurity. A penal grid comes to overlay and define zones of exclusion. Once again, Mike Davis captures this strikingly. With the example of the Los Angeles Police Department before him, with its airborne helicopter patrols, equipped with infra-red cameras for night surveillance and 30-million-candlepower spotlights, with jets capable of delivering SWAT teams to trouble spots for instant armed response, and with thousands of residential rooftops painted with identifying street numbers to facilitate identification, he sums up the image, if not the reality, of this control regime: 'good citizens off the streets, enclaved in their high-security private consumption spheres; bad citizens, on the streets (and therefore not engaged in legitimate business), caught in the terrible Jehovan scrutiny of the LAPD's space program'.[70]

Diagrams of control

One should not take Los Angeles as a microcosm of an inherent logic of control. Nor should one confuse the proliferation of control strategies

techniques of ethical reconstruction: whilst John Braithwaite can take much of the credit for the current popularity of the technique, the reasons for its attractiveness lie in this reconfigured strategy of control through ethical reformation (see Braithwaite 1989).

[69] On parole, see Jonathon Simon's study of 'the social control of the underclass' from 1890 to 1990 (Simon 1993).

[70] Davis 1990: 253.

with the formation of a new type of society. But in this rapid inventory, I think we can see the opening up of new ways of thinking and acting, new problematizations, new authorities, new technologies and new conceptions of the subjects of control. These cannot be parcelled out amongst the conventional disciplinary divisions of criminology, social policy, cultural studies and the like. I think that these strategies are linked, in a rather fundamental way, to the new conceptions of freedom that have come to infuse our practices for the government of conduct. They are the other side of the obligations of self-realization through choice and the ethico-politics of community. And it is partly through the analysis of these strategies of control that one can discern the price that is paid, in different ways by different individuals and groups, for what we have come to think of freedom, that is to say, for our current regimes of government through freedom.

Conclusion: beyond government

In the preceding chapters I have explored some of the ways in which the analytics of government can diagnose the multitude of relations of power, knowledge, technique and ethics through which the conduct of human beings is shaped by others and by themselves. But have I not painted a monotonous picture of the successions of ideal types – liberalism, welfare, advanced liberalism . . . ? Do these studies map a history in which it appears that programmes and frameworks dreamed up by authorities are successively imposed on a passive and recipient subject population? Do they not deny the polycentric, multi-vocal, heterogeneous and messy realities of power relations as they are enacted and resisted in a multitude of micro-locales, in favour of the illusory comfort of textual analysis? Do they not ignore the relations of struggle that are so important for political analysis, relations of struggle within rule itself as well as between those who seek to rule and those who are the actual or potential subjects of rule? Do they not exclude by fiat the human agency that must be at the heart of any radical analysis of power in our miserable, corrupt, unequal and unjust present? Have I not ignored the reality that exists 'beyond government'?

No doubt such criticisms point to important issues.[1] Let me try to address some of them by way of a provisional conclusion to a book which is intended to act, above all, as an encouragement to an open and developing programme of research.

The analytics of government are genealogical; they are neither socio-

[1] The most productive criticisms are made in O'Malley, Weir and Shearing 1997, and I have tried to address many of them in this book. Amongst the unproductive criticisms, Curtis (1995) discovers the hand of the 'State' in all he surveys, and B. Frankel (1997) rehearses the claim that behind the superficial phenomena that I have analysed here lies the class struggle and the need to secure the reproduction and viability of particular forms of capital accumulation: he concludes that governmentality studies indirectly endorse the status quo and do not contribute to the development of alternative political movements.

logical nor historicist. They do not narrate a history that takes the form of a succession of underlying unities but seek to unravel the naturalness of problem spaces in the present by tracing the multiple, heterogeneous and contingent conditions which have given rise to them. The rationalities they analyse are not ideal types. As I argued in chapter 1, terms such as 'liberalism' individuate a whole array of different attempts to rationalize the exercise of power. Of course, political discourse does not have the systematic and closed character of disciplined knowledges.[2] It is populated by diverse elements drawn from heterogeneous sources: philosophical doctrines, versions of justice, conceptions of power, notions of social and human reality, beliefs about the efficacy or otherwise of different courses of action and no doubt much else besides. To individuate a rationality is not to construct an ideal type against which a non-ideal reality can be calibrated, but to diagnose the moral, epistemological and linguistic regularities that make it possible to think and say certain things truthfully – and hence to conceive and do certain things politically. Undoubtedly the naming is a creative act, individuating problems, objects, explanations, strategies and justifications in a new way. But the proper name is also an operative element in political thought itself, which troubles itself 'reflexively' over what it is, for example, to govern in a 'liberal' way.

The programmes, strategies and technologies which have been described in previous chapters arise out of a complex field of contestation. Their problems, languages, judgements and strategies are rarely invented *ab initio*, but accumulated from practical rationalities already developed in particular sites. Their techniques and devices are thus frequently assembled from what happens to be available, turning it to account for new purposes, although they stimulate, in their turn, a great deal of invention and innovation. Ian Hunter has made this point most forcefully, arguing that historically contingent institutions such as mass schooling are improvised from available moral, intellectual and practical techniques in attempts to assemble pragmatic solutions to deal with specific exigencies and limited problems.[3] Much evidence bears this out. Hunter's example is the 'popular' school, which emerged in a number of European nations out of the intersection of eighteenth-century political objectives for the mass moral training of the population in order to advance the strength and prosperity of the state, and the institutions and practices of Christian pastoral guidance which had a quite different history and set of ambitions. The central operative principle of state

[2] See Rose and Miller 1992: 178–81.
[3] Hunter 1996: 148.

schooling emerged out of this contingent lash-up: self-realization became a disciplinary objective through the redeployment of the Christian techniques of pastoral guidance for secular purposes.[4]

Other examples support this emphasis upon contingency and specificity. In Britain, for example, the nineteenth-century problem of working-class pedagogy arose out of a multitude of attempts by churchmen, philanthropists and organizations of working people themselves, seeking to educate their children and to campaign for the extension of their own experiments in pedagogy on a wider scale: only later were these diverse and often radical lines of development to be captured, reorganized and rationalized within a programme of universal education which combined these aspirations with others to do with order, civility and domestication. Similarly, the contemporary problem of the government of madness and mental health in terms of risk emerges out of the contingent interconnections amongst diverse elements each of which has its own history: the problematization of 'random' violence on the inner city streets, tragedies aired in the forum of the law courts, struggles between and within the different professional groups involved (doctors, nurses, social workers, administrators), disputes between national government and local authorities over finance, arguments over the increasing cost of upkeep of hospital buildings, deliberations by the law courts over cases of murder or suicide committed by discharged psychiatric patients, the invention of new drugs, exposures of institutionalization by sociologists and social workers, public enquiries into untoward incidents, financial problems of advanced industrial societies, the success of unions of psychiatric nurses in increasing their pay levels and quasi-professionalization, campaigns by the US civil rights movement couched in terms of rights, the rise of campaigning groups seeking increased incarceration of the mentally ill in the name of their own care and protection. The list could be extended.

Programmes and technologies of government, then, are assemblages which may have a rationality, but this is not one of a coherence of origin or singular essence. Foucault suggested that the French legal system was like one of the machines constructed by Tinguely – full of parts that come from elsewhere, strange couplings, chance relations, cogs and levers that aren't connected, that don't work, and yet somehow produce judgements, prisoners, sanctions and much more.[5] To analyse, then, is not to seek for a hidden unity behind this complex diversity. Quite the reverse. It is to reveal the historicity and the contingency of the truths

---

[4] Hunter 1996: 149.
[5] This remark is cited in C. Gordon 1980: 257.

that have come to define the limits of our contemporary ways of under-standing ourselves, individually and collectively, and the programmes and procedures assembled to govern ourselves. By doing so, it is to disturb and destabilize these regimes, to identify some of the weak points and lines of fracture in our present where thought might insert itself in order to make a difference. Such work, as Graham Burchell has put it, 'produces – or invites – a modification of the historian's and others' relationship to truth through the problematization of what is given to us as necessary to think and do. It is at this level that it produces both its critical effect (making it more difficult for us to think and act in accustomed ways) and its positive effect (clearing a space for the possibility of thinking otherwise, for a consideration of the conditions for a real transformation of what we are).'[6] Its aim, therefore, is to reshape and expand the terms of political debate, enabling different questions to be asked, enlarging the space of legitimate contestation, modifying the relation of the different participants to the truths in the name of which they govern or are governed.

Thus empirical studies of government – of the regulation of madness, health, welfare, production, sexuality, childhood, pedagogy and so forth – do not simplify: they generate complexity. One aspect of this complexity has proved particularly troubling to those schooled in Marx-ism or critical theory. This is because it requires us to abandon, once and for all, those binary divisions that have structured our political thinking and our theorizing about the political for so long: domination and emancipation; power and resistance; strategy and tactics; Same and Other; civility and desire. Empirical studies of regulatory problematiza-tions, ambitions, programmes, strategies and techniques require us to jettison the division between a logic that structures and territorializes 'from above' according to protocols that are not our own, and a more or less spontaneous anti-logic 'from below' that expresses our own needs, desires, aspirations. Each such binary suggests a principle of division between those political, technical and ethical strategies that have made up our present and those that have opposed them. This way of dividing the matter is illusory. There is not a single discourse or strategy of power confronted by forces of resistance, but a set of conflicting points and issues of opposition, alliance and division of labour. And our present has arisen as much from the logics of contestation as from any imperatives of control.

Nineteenth-century liberal doctrines and techniques posed them-selves as a critical rejoinder to overweening state power. The early

[6] G. Burchell 1996: 32–3.

twentieth-century politics of solidarism in France and the related social democratic and social liberal politics of England posed themselves in opposition to both the fragmentary and anomic consequences of an industrial system that was beyond control, and the centralizing and anti-liberal aspirations of socialist collectivism. Feminist critiques of the patriarchal powers of fathers and husbands helped shape the domesticated nuclear family and the powers that are accorded to women in the site of domesticity. Radical critiques of welfare since the 1960s, articulated from both left and right, contested the power, status and professional advancement that had been accrued by a professional caste, doing well from doing (not much) good. Our present arises as much out of these moments of critique as out of some relentless logic of regulation.

Consider, for example, the government of madness. Those who have problematized madness and intervened upon it in its various incarnations since the late eighteenth century have included politicians, theologians, psychiatrists, nurses, lawyers, therapists, psychologists, social workers and many other 'experts'. These authorities are diverse and disputatious. Many contesting views have been elaborated from within each of these groupings, and strange alliances formed between them. But those who problematize and seek to intervene are not simply 'authorities'. A multitude of other groupings and collectivities have also had their say in the government of madness – press campaigns, pressure groups, groups established by individuals whose family members have been damaged psychiatric patients or damaged by psychiatric patients, local residents protesting about hostels for discharged psychiatric patients in their areas, pressure groups campaigning around other issues for whom psychiatric patients are a problem – for the homeless or for prisoners, for radicals contesting the powers of doctors and so forth. Some of these may be 'heroes of their own lives', as Linda Gordon has put it in another context.[7] Some may be villains in the lives of others. Individuals and organizations who have criticized and contested the government of madness, and the truths upon which it has rested, have played key roles in configuring the ways in which madness is governed today, and this includes, of course, the subjects of government themselves.

It is only in relation to a dream of unification – of epochs, societies, systems – that the existence of dispersed conflicts – over ideals, goals, values, types of person we are or wish to be – seems surprising. These

---

[7] Linda Gordon (1989) uses this term to refer to the role of victims and assailants in the family violence cases that she traces from 1880 to 1960.

contestations are not between power and its others, but between diverse programmes, logics, dreams and ideals, codified, organized and rationalized to a greater or lesser extent. We need no 'theory of resistance' to account for contestation, any more than we need an epistemology to account for the production of truth effects – except if we wish to use our theory to ratify some acts of contestation and to devalue others.

But perhaps, in a present when old forms of political mobilization – the party, the programme, the electoral mandate – are losing their attraction, and when a host of new forms of politics are taking shape, it may be untimely to address ourselves to politics of contestation itself, to seek to diagnose the historically shaped limits of both our democratic and our revolutionary political imagination. Without resurrecting yet another binary, an analysis of the forms of contestation might help us understand the ways in which something new is created, a difference is introduced into history in the form of a politics. In particular, it might help us amplify some of those mobile lines of force which have, historically, taken shape on the margins of politics. This is not to say that creativity is never found in traditional political forms. But it is to suggest that something might be learnt from those insurgent, minority or subaltern forces that have often refused to codify themselves, that have resisted the temptations of party and programme, that have taken shape in the shadows, interstices and oversights of conventional politics and that have so often acted as laboratories for alternative futures.

The notion of resistance, at least as it has conventionally functioned within the analyses of self-proclaimed radicals, is too simple and flattening for such an analysis. It is merely the obverse of a one-dimensional notion of power as domination. And it seems to imply a subject who resists out of an act of bravery or heroism. But however noble the sentiment, in the politics of innovation and creation, courage is redundant. It is not a question of the assertion of the agency inscribed within an individual or collective subject. If one were trying to characterize the creativity of what one might term, after Deleuze and Guattari, a 'minor' or 'minority' politics, one would not seek to identify particular agents of a radical politics – be they classes, races or genders – or to distinguish once and for all the forces of reaction from those of progression in terms of fixed identities.[8] Rather, one would examine the ways in which creativity arises out of the situation of human beings engaged in particular relations of force and meaning, and what is made out of the possibilities of that location. These minor engagements do not have the arrogance

---

[8] I am grateful to Nick Thoburn for many discussions about these issues of 'minor politics' that have shaped my way of thinking about them.

of programmatic politics – perhaps even refuse their designation as politics at all. They are cautious, modest, pragmatic, experimental, stuttering, tentative. They are concerned with the here and now, not with some fantasized future, with small concerns, petty details, the everyday and not the transcendental. They frequently arise in 'cramped spaces' – within a set of relations that are intolerable, where movement is impossible, where change is blocked and voice is strangulated. And, in relation to these little territories of the everyday, they seek to engender a small reworking of their own spaces of action. But the feminist politics that was conducted under the slogan of 'the personal is political' is the most obvious example from our recent past of the ways in which such a molecular and minor engagement with cramped space can connect up with a whole series of other circuits and cause them to fluctuate, waver and reconfigure in wholly unexpected ways.

But it is not a question of a radical distinction of a politics of the minor and a traditional or majoritarian kind of politics. On the one hand, the creativity of a minor trajectory is all too brief: as both feminism and the green movement have shown, lines of flight rapidly get recuperated, organized, systematized, programmatized. On the other hand, there are moments of minoring, of breaking away, creating something new within the most traditional political forms, as when new practices of mobilization and protest are invented within the most organized of strikes, where new and mobile subjectivities form, swarm and dissipate in mass mobilizations, marches and demonstrations, where, in the heart of the routine theatricals of parliamentary elections, a prime minister seeking re-election comes face to face with an ordinary citizen who refuses deference and dares to speak the truth. The mobilizations of forces represented by traditional politics – the politics of parties, of manifestos, of electoral assemblies, laws, policies and the like – are certainly timely, in the relations to truth, to ourselves, to others and to our future that they presuppose. Undoubtedly, many will aspire to engage with these forces in the hope that they can help invent ways to govern better. But perhaps the real powers of invention lie in those untimely mobilizations which can introduce new possibilities into our thought: marginal, eccentric, minority movements, millenarians, syndicalists, situationists, autonomists, rough and ready assemblages of forces such as those in the UK contesting road building or animal abuse, international environmental movements such as Greenpeace, radical medical endeavours such as Médecins sans Frontières.

It would probably be unwise to try to distil some essence of creative politics from the history of minor and major engagements. But it would undoubtedly be instructive to anatomize the diverse forms that the political imagination has taken in our recent past, in order to learn something for our present and our future. Such an analysis would have to ask questions that are rather different from those addressed in this book. What *forms of collectivization or massification* are involved: groups, movements, collectivities, solidarities and so forth? To what extent are these collectivizations disciplined – through training, parties, hierarchies and the like – or mobile, fluid, more or less situational, as in the forms of collectivization that take shape at demonstrations, or in peace camps or occupations of sites scheduled for road building or housing development? What *relation to truth* do such movements establish – do they depend upon a basis in veridical knowledge for their authority, as for example in Marxism; upon charismatic types of authority, as in millenarian sects; upon legal and juridical forms of reasoning as in demands for rights; upon alternative forms of expertise as in many environmental contests; in 'self-evidence' as when defenders of nature or animals establish their arguments by 'bearing witness' through showing devastation or cruelty; or upon claims to a different kind of expertise based in experience, as in the 'users' and 'consumers' movements in psychiatry? How are the *objects of contestation* formed? Sometimes the objects under contest are *creations* of regulation, such as the domesticated nuclear family or the asylum. Sometimes the objects form as a kind of inverse of regulation, as in contests over the health care systems that arose in the twentieth century on the grounds that they were, in fact, systems organized around a norm of illness rather than a norm of health. What are the *rhetorics of contestation*, and what mechanisms do they use for generating truths? Such mechanisms are very different from those involved in veridical discourses, which today are regulated meticulously by procedures of training, credentialization and control of the apparatus of publications. What is the *telos* of these struggles and how are these end points justified: efficiency, equality, dignity, health, autonomy? Here one should not underestimate the role of utopias and dystopias in political mobilization. What is the *techne of struggle*: one could imagine a whole study of the diverse forms of political mobilization popular on the left – the party form, the conference, the demonstration, the speech from the platform, the barricades . . . What is the relation between the telos and the *form of the struggle* – to what extent are these consistent, or to what extent must the struggle itself take a different form from its objective, subordinating all present autonomy within the party, for example, in the name of a 'real' autonomy to come. Of particular significance today might be the rise and fall of the disciplined collective form of political mobilization, the party, the trades union, in favour of a series of more direct experiments in living which have an immediate aesthetic quality: road protests, campaigns to reclaim the streets, to halt exports of live veal calves, to save an area of woodland from development as a housing estate. Finally, what kind of *art of activity* does it produce in those who engage in it – an art which is sometimes the product of long discipline, which sometimes involves a whole ascetics as in left-wing politics of the 1960s, but which is sometimes a spontaneous moment of revolt, of saying no to power, as in the manifestations of 'people's power' which brought down the dictatorship in the Philippines, or the uprisings of previously and subsequently stolid citizens which finally swept away the Berlin Wall?

Of course there is a whole literature which devotes itself to just such sociologies of social movements. But the kinds of studies which go under the sign of histories of the present have a genealogical, rather than a sociological ambition. Through destabilizing and denaturalizing the present, they aim to help maximize the capacity of individuals and collectivities to shape the knowledges, contest the authorities and configure the practices that govern them in the name of their nature, their freedom and their identity. They seek a transvaluation of values, or at least to provide some of the conceptual tools and arguments which might enable a revaluation of those values by which we are ruled or governed, showing the humble and mundane origins of the supposedly pure and transcendent, revealing the lies, falsehoods, deceptions and self-deceptions which are inherent within these attempts to govern us for our own good, the costs as well as the benefits entailed, for example, in the nineteenth-century valorization of self-discipline as the counterpart to political liberty, or the late twentieth-century valorization of an image of personal freedom marked out in terms such as autonomy, choice and self-realization as a counterpart to entrepreneurship, innovation and national competitiveness. So what would be the ethos of studies of alternative political imaginations?

Perhaps Foucault's own fragmentary ideas about aesthetic politics might provoke us here. Thomas Osborne has pointed out that, for Foucault, an aesthetic politics was not a celebration of a politics of individual dandyism.[9] The suggestion that we might each try to make our own life 'a work of art' was an invitation to creativity and experimentation, not a retreat to consumerized narcissism. This life politics was defined, in part, by what it was *not* – it was *not conducted under the sign of a morality* (in the name of a heteronomous moral code), *not conducted under the sign of an epistemology* (in the name of a hidden truth or desire

---

[9] Thomas Osborne makes this argument in a number of recent papers (1996a, 1996b) and at greater length in his (1998) book *Aspects of Enlightenment*.

revealed by knowledge which it was one's aspiration to realize), *not con-ducted under the sign of a regime of authority* (subordination to the organ-izational demands of a party) and *not conducted in relation to an absolute end point* at some future time (to which the present must be subordinated). Rather than subordinate oneself in the name of an exter-nal code, truth, authority or goal, such a politics would operate under a different slogan: each person's life should be its own telos. It would thus have its own minimal normativity: we should oppose all that which stands in the way of life being its own telos. This would not be an anthropology or an essentialism of the human: there is no essence here serving as the basis for critique, and waiting to be realized. But perhaps it would embody a certain 'vitalism'. It would, that is to say, be in favour of life, of 'the obstinate, stubborn and indomitable will to live', of the conditions that make possible the challenge to existing modes of life and the creation of new modes of existence.[10] For perhaps we could say that every style of government also implies a way of living, a form of life, a mode of existence. An ethic of how one is governed is also an ethic of how one governs others, of how one governs oneself. And diagnostic reason must try, in some way, to provide some conditions for evaluating this form of life, not judging it against a criterion of good and bad, but discerning the possibilities and the limits for ways of existing that it embodies. Such a political vitalism would certainly take sides: it would take the side of an active art of living. It would ask for a politics which is itself an active art of living. And it would accord itself the right, per-haps the duty, to oppose all that which blocks or subverts the capacity of others asserting for themselves their own vitalism, their own will to live through the active shaping of their lives.

Of course, one needs no ground for politics, still less for a recognition that political imprisonment, torture, corruption, virulent nationalism and the like are worth opposing. But such an ethic of vitalism would be an antidote to the apparent depoliticizing consequences of anti-essentialist political thought and to any implication that such analyses can sanction only a *realpolitik*. For we can be 'against' identity, 'against' ideas of a human essence, 'against' the humanist conception of the indi-vidual subject, but in favour of life. Some ways of governing are intoler-able precisely because they exclude the possibility – at least for some

---

[10] I think that this is what Deleuze is arguing in his essay 'To have done with judgement' from which this quote is drawn (Deleuze 1997: 133), and my thoughts here are a clumsy paraphrase of his. Daniel Smith discusses this aspect of Deleuze's thought in his introduction to that volume (D. W. Smith 1997).

who are subject to them – that their life should become its own telos, that they should be able to practise an active art of living. We may not share an essence, a soul, an identity or any other fixed attributes with others. But there is one status that we do share, and that is our status as subjects of government. That is to say, like so many others, we are inhabitants of regimes that act upon our own conduct in the proclaimed interest of our individual and collective well-being. To the extent that we are governed in our own name, we have a right to contest the evils that are done to us in the name of government, a right that we acquire from our birth and life at the point of convergence of practices of government themselves.[11]

In showing us that what we take to be solid and inevitable is less so than we believe, genealogies of power and freedom also show us that we do not know what human beings are capable of, and that it has been, and is, possible for even the most unlikely subjects, in the most unpropitious circumstances, to act upon their limits in the name of no principle but that of their own life. Above all, such analyses seek to open, but not to close, the space within which human beings, being the kinds of creatures they have become, can exercise their political responsibilities.

[11] Thomas Osborne (1996a, 1998) suggests this is the position that Foucault develops in many of his shorter interviews posthumously collected in *Dits et écrits* (Foucault 1994).

Bibliography

Abrams, P. 1968, *The Origins of British Sociology 1834–1914*, Chicago: University of Chicago Press.

Adler, M. and Asquith, S. (eds.) 1981, *Discretion and Welfare*, London: Heinemann.

Agamben, G. 1993, *The Coming Community*, Minneapolis: University of Minnesota Press.

Alonso, W. and Starr, P. (eds.) 1987, *The Politics of Numbers*, New York: Russell Sage Foundation.

Andrew, D. 1989, *Philanthropy and Police: London Charity in the Eighteenth Century*, Princeton: Princeton University Press.

Armstrong, D. 1983, *Political Anatomy of the Body*, Cambridge: Cambridge University Press.

Arnold, D. 1994, 'The colonial prison: power, knowledge and penology in nineteenth-century India', *Subaltern Studies* 8: 148–87.

Atkinson, A. 1997, *The Europeans in Australia: A History*, vol. I, Melbourne: Oxford University Press.

Atkinson, D. 1994, *The Common Sense of Community*, London: Demos.

Bachelard, G. 1951, *L'activité rationaliste de la physique contemporaine*, Paris: PUF.

Bacon, R. and Eltis, W. 1976, *Britain's Economic Problems: Too Few Producers?*, London: Macmillan.

Badie, B. and Birnbaum, P. 1983, *The Sociology of the State*, Chicago: University of Chicago Press.

Baistow, K. 1995, 'Liberation or regulation?: some paradoxes of empowerment', *Critical Social Policy* 42: 34–46.

Baker, K. M. 1975, *Condorcet: From Natural Philosophy to Social Mathematics*, Chicago: University of Chicago Press.

Barron, A. 1996, 'The governance of schooling: genealogies of control and empowerment in the reform of public education', *Studies in Law, Politics and Society* 15: 167–204.

Barry, A., Osborne, T. and Rose, N. (eds.) 1996, *Foucault and Political Reason*, London: UCL Press.

Baudrillard, J. 1983, *In the Shadow of the Silent Majorities or 'the Death of the Social'*, New York: Semiotexte.

Bauman, Z. 1988, *Freedom*, Milton Keynes: Open University Press.

1989, *Modernity and the Holocaust*, Cambridge: Polity.

Beck, U. 1992, *Risk Society: Towards a New Modernity*, London: Sage.

Becker, G. S. 1976, *The Economic Approach to Human Behavior*, Chicago: University of Chicago Press.

Bell, V. 1993, 'Governing childhood', *Economy and Society* 22, 3: 390–405.

Bellah, R. et al. 1985, *Habits of the Heart: Middle America Observed*, Berkeley: University of California Press.

Bennett, T. 1988, 'The exhibitionary complex', *New Formations* 4: 73–103.

1995, *The Birth of the Museum: History, Theory, Politics*, London: Routledge.

Bentham, J. 1830, *Emancipate Your Colonies: Addressed to the National Convention of France 1793 Shewing the Uselessness and Mischevousness of Distant Dependencies to An European State*, London: Robert Heward.

1843, *Works*, vol. IV, edited by John Bowring, London: Tait.

Berlin, I. [1958] 1969, 'Two concepts of liberty', in Berlin, *Four Essays on Liberty*, pp. 118–72, Oxford: Oxford University Press.

Beveridge, W. 1905, 'The problems of the unemployed', *Sociological Papers* 3: 324–31.

1942, *Social Insurance and Allied Services*, Cmd. 6404, London: HMSO.

Bijker, W. and Law, J. (eds.) 1992, *Shaping Technology, Building Society: Studies in Sociotechnical Change*, Cambridge, MA: MIT Press.

Blair, T. 1996, 'Battle for Britain', *Guardian* 29 January 1996.

Bodin, J. [1606] 1962, *Six Bookes of a Commonweale*, facsimile reprint of the English translation of 1606, edited by K. D. McRae, Cambridge, MA: Harvard University Press.

Booth, W. 1892–7, *Life and Labour of the People in London*, 10 vols., London: Macmillan.

Bosanquet, B. (ed.) 1895, *Aspects of the Social Problem*, London: Macmillan.

Braithwaite, J. 1989, *Crime, Shame and Reintegration*, Cambridge: Cambridge University Press.

British Inspector of Inebriates 1911, *Report of the Inspector . . . for 1909*, British Parliamentary Papers, 29, Part I: 18–19.

Brown, J. 1757, *An Estimate of the Manners and Principles of the Times*, London: n.p.

Brown, P. 1989, *The Body and Society: Men, Women and Sexual Renunciation in Early Christianity*, London: Faber.

Brown, W. 1995, *States of Injury: Power and Freedom in Late Modernity*, Princeton: Princeton University Press.

Buck, P. 1982, 'People who counted: political arithmetic in the eighteenth century', *Isis* 73: 28–45.

Bulmer, M., Bales, K. and Sklar, K. K. (eds.) 1991, *The Social Survey in Historical Perspective, 1880–1940*, Cambridge: Cambridge University Press.

Bulpitt, J. 1986, 'The discipline of the New Democracy: Mrs Thatcher's domestic statecraft', *Political Studies* 34: 19–34.

Burchell, D. 1995, 'Genealogies of the citizen: virtue, manners and the modern activity of citizenship', *Economy and Society* 24, 4: 540–58.

1998, ' "The mutable minds of particular men": the emergence of "economic science" and contemporary economic policy', in Dean and Hindess 1998, pp. 194–209.

Burchell, G. 1981, 'Putting the child in its place', *I&C* 8: 73–96.

1991, ' "Peculiar interests": governing the system of natural liberty', in G. Burchell, Gordon and Miller 1991, pp. 119–50.

1996, 'Liberal government and techniques of the self', in Barry, Osborne and Rose 1996, pp. 19–36.

Burchell, G., Gordon, C. and Miller, P. (eds.) 1991, *The Foucault Effect: Studies in Governmentality*, Hemel Hempstead: Harvester Wheatsheaf.

Burke, P. 1991, *Social Orders and Social Classes in Europe Since 1500: Studies in Social Stratification*, London: Longmans.

Burn, W. L. 1949, 'Free trade in land: an aspect of the Irish Question', *Transactions of the Royal Historical Society* 4th series, 31: 61–74.

Butler, J. 1993, *Bodies That Matter*, New York: Routledge.

Callon, M. 1986, 'Some elements of a sociology of translation', in J. Law (ed.), *Power, Action and Belief: A New Sociology of Knowledge?*, pp. 196–233, London: Routledge and Kegan Paul.

Callon, M. and Latour, B. 1981, 'Unscrewing the Big Leviathan: how actors macro-structure reality and how sociologists help them to do so', in K. Knorr-Cetina and A. Cicourel (eds.), *Advances in Social Theory and Methodology: Toward an Integration of Micro- and Macro-Sociologies*, pp. 277–303, Boston: Routledge & Kegan Paul.

Callon, M., Latour, B. and Rip, A. 1986, *Mapping the Dynamics of Science and Technology*, London: Macmillan.

Canguilhem, G. 1978, *On the Normal and the Pathological*, translated by C. R. Fawcett, Dordrecht: Reidel.

1994, *A Vital Rationalist*, edited by F. Delaporte, New York: Zone.

Caplow, T. and Simon, J. 1998, 'The incarceration mania: a preliminary diagnosis', unpublished manuscript, May 1998.

Carpenter, M. 1872, *Reformatory Prison Discipline as Developed by the Rt. Hon. Sir Walter Croften in the Irish Convict Prisons*, London: Longmans, Green, Reader and Dwyer.

Carpenter, W. B. 1842, *Principles of Human Physiology*, London: John Churchill.

Castel, F., Castel, R. and Lovell, A. 1986, *The Psychiatric Society*, New York: Columbia University Press.

Castel, R. 1981, *La gestion des risques: de l'anti-psychiatrie a l'après-psychanalyse*, Paris: Edition de Minuit.

1988, *The Regulation of Madness*, Cambridge: Polity.

1991, 'From dangerousness to risk', in G. Burchell, Gordon and Miller 1991, pp. 281–98.

1995, *Les métamorphoses de la question sociale*, Paris: Fayard.

Chambers, W. 1861–2, *Manuals for the Working Classes: [Robert] Chambers Social Science Tracts Embracing Subjects Connected with Social, Political and Sanitary Economy*, vol. II, *Of Political and Social Economy*, London: Chambers.

Chancellor of the Exchequer 1961, *Control of Public Expenditure*, Cmnd. 1432, London: HMSO.

Chartier, R. (ed.) 1989, *A History of Private Life*, vol. III, *Passions of the Renaissance*, translated by A. Goldhammer, Cambridge, MA: Belknap Press of Harvard University Press.

Churchill, W. S. 1909, *Liberalism and the Social Problem (Speeches 1906–1909)*, 2nd edn, London: Hodder and Stoughton.

Clarke, P. 1978, *Liberals and Social Democrats*, Cambridge: Cambridge University Press.

Cline-Cohen, P. 1982, *A Calculating People: The Spread of Numeracy in Early America*, Chicago: University of Chicago Press.

Clouston, T. 1906, *The Hygiene of Mind*, London: Methuen.

Cohen, S. 1985, *Visions of Social Control*, Cambridge: Polity.

Cohn, B. 1990, *An Anthropologist Among the Historians and Other Essays*, Delhi: Oxford University Press.

Coleman, J. 1990, *Foundations of Social Theory*, Cambridge, MA: Harvard University Press.

Colley, L. 1996, *Britons: Forging the Nation 1707–1837*, London: Vintage.

Collini, S. 1979, *Liberalism and Sociology*, Cambridge: Cambridge University Press.

1991, *Public Moralists: Political Thought and Intellectual Life in Britain, 1850–1930*, Oxford: Oxford University Press.

Commission of the European Community 1993, *European Social Policy: Options for the Union*, Brussels and Luxembourg: Commission of the European Community.

1994, *European Social Policy: A Way Forward For The Union*, White Paper, COM(94) 333 final, Brussels and Luxembourg: Commission of the European Community.

Commission on Social Justice 1994, *Social Justice: Strategies for National Renewal*, London: Vintage.

Committee on the Civil Service 1968, *Report*, Cmnd. 3638, London: HMSO.

Communitarian Network 1996, *The Responsive Communitarian Platform: Rights and Responsibilities*, at http://www.gwu.edu/~ccps/RCPlatform.html.

Condorcet (Marie-Jean-Antoine-Nicolas Caritat, Marquis de Condorcet) [1794] 1795, *Esquisse d'un Tableau Historique de Progrès de l'Esprit Humain (ouvrage posthume)*, Paris: n.p.

Conk, M. 1987, 'The 1980 census in historical perspective', in Alonso and Starr 1987, pp. 155–86.

Connolly, W. 1983, *The Terms of Political Discourse*, Princeton: Princeton University Press.

1995, *The Ethos of Pluralization*, Minneapolis: University of Minnesota Press.

Coward, R. and Ellis, J. 1976, *Language and Materialism*, London: Routledge and Kegan Paul.

Crary, J. and Kwinter, S. (eds.) 1992, *Incorporations*, New York: Zone.

Cromer, Earl of 1908, *Modern Egypt*, 2 vols., New York: Macmillan.

Cruikshank, B. 1994, 'The will to empower: technologies of citizenship and the War on Poverty', *Socialist Review* 23, 4: 29–55.

1998, 'Moral disentitlement: personal autonomy and political reproduction', in Hänninen 1998, pp. 145–71.

Cullen, M. 1975, *The Statistical Movement in Early Victorian Britain*, Hassocks, Sussex: Harvester.

Curtis, B. 1995, 'Taking the state back out: Rose and Miller on political power', *British Journal of Sociology* 46, 4: 575–89.

Dandeker, C. 1990, *Surveillance, Power and Modernity*, Cambridge: Polity.

Danziger, K. 1990, *Constructing the Subject*, Cambridge: Cambridge University Press.

Daston, L. 1994, 'Historical epistemology', in J. Chandler, A. I. Davidson and H. Harootunian (eds.), *Questions of Evidence: Proof, Practice and Persuasion Across the Disciplines*, pp. 282–9, Chicago: University of Chicago Press.

Davis, M. 1990, *City of Quartz: Excavating the Future in Los Angeles*, London: Verso.

de Swaan, A. 1990, *The Management of Normality*, London: Routledge.

Dean, M. 1991, *The Constitution of Poverty*, London: Routledge.

1994, *Critical and Effective Histories*, London: Routledge.

1995, 'Governing the unemployed self in an active society', *Economy and Society* 24, 4: 559–83.

1996, 'Putting the technological into government', *History of the Human Sciences* 9, 3: 47–68.

1999, *Governmentality*, London: Sage.

Dean, M. and Hindess, B. 1998, *Governing Australia: Studies in Contemporary Rationalities of Government*, Cambridge: Cambridge University Press.

Defert, D. 1991, ' "Popular life" and insurance technology', in G. Burchell, Gordon and Miller 1991, pp. 211–34.

Deleuze, G. 1979, 'Foreword', in Donzelot 1979, pp. ix–xvii.

1988, *Foucault*, Minneapolis: University of Minnesota Press.

1994a, *Difference and Repetition*, translated by P. Patton, London: Athlone Press.

1994b, *What Is Philosophy?*, translated by G. Burchell and H. Tomlinson, London: Verso.

1995, 'Postscript on control societies', in Deleuze, *Negotiations*, translated by M. Joughin, pp. 177–82, New York: Columbia University Press.

1997, *Essays Critical and Clinical*, translated by D. W. Smith and M. A. Greco, Minneapolis: University of Minnesota Press.

Deleuze, G. and Guattari, F. 1987, *A Thousand Plateaus*, translated by B. Massumi, Minneapolis: University of Minnesota Press.

Deleuze, G. and Parnet, C. 1987, *Dialogues*, London: Athlone.

Dertouzos, M. L., Lester, R. K. and Solow, R. M. 1989, *Made in America: Regaining the Cutting Edge*, Cambridge, MA: MIT Press.

Donald, J. 1992, *Sentimental Education: Schooling, Popular Culture and the Regulation of Liberty*, London: Verso.

Donzelot, J. 1979, *The Policing of Families: Welfare Versus the State*, London: Hutchinson.

1981, 'Pleasure in work', *I&C* 9: 3–28.

1984, *L'invention du social*, Paris: Vrin.

1991, 'The mobilisation of society', in G. Burchell, Gordon and Miller 1991, pp. 169–80.

Donzelot, J. and Estebe, P. (eds.) 1994, *L'état animateur: essai sur la politique de la ville*, Paris: Esprit.

Dreyfuss, H. and Rabinow, P. 1983, *Michel Foucault: Between Structuralism and Hermeneutics*, Brighton: Harvester Press.

Drucker, P. 1995, 'Really reinventing government', *Atlantic Monthly* 275, 2: 49–61.

du Gay, P. 1996, 'Organizing identity: entrepreneurial governance and public management', in Hall and du Gay 1996, pp. 151–69.

Duby, G. (ed.) 1988, *A History of Private Life*, vol. II, *Revelations of the Medieval World*, translated by A. Goldhammer, Cambridge, MA: Belknap Press of Harvard University Press.

Dumm, T. 1996, *Michel Foucault and the Politics of Freedom*, Thousand Oaks, CA: Sage.

Duncan, O. D. 1984, *Notes on Social Measurement: Historical and Critical*, New York: Russell Sage Foundation.

Durkheim, E. [1895] 1964, *The Rules of Sociological Method*, New York: Free Press.

Eden, R. (ed.) 1989, *The New Deal and Its Legacy*, New York: Greenwood.

Elias, N. 1969, *The Court Society*, Oxford: Basil Blackwell.

1982, *The Civilizing Process: State Formation and Civilization*, Oxford: Basil Blackwell.

Engels, F. [1844] 1976, *The Conditions of the Working Class in England in 1844*, in K. Marx and Engels, *Collected Works*, vol. IV, pp. 295–583, London: Lawrence and Wishart.

Eräsaari, R. 1993, *Essays on Non-Conventional Community*, Jyväskylä: University of Jyväskylä.

Ericson, R. and Haggerty, K. 1997, *Policing the Risk Society*, Toronto: University of Toronto Press.

Etzioni, A. 1993, *The Spirit of Community*, New York: Crown.

1997, *The New Golden Rule: Community and Morality in a Democratic Society*, London: Profile.

Evans, P., Rueschmeyer, D. and Skocpol, T. 1985, *Bringing the State Back In*, Cambridge: Cambridge University Press.

Ewald, F. 1986, *L'état providence*, Paris: Grasset.

1991, 'Insurance and risk', in G. Burchell, Gordon and Miller 1991, pp. 197–210.

Ewen, S. 1976, *Captains of Consciousness*, New York: Basic Books.

1988, *All Consuming Images*, New York: Basic Books.

Fabian Society 1946, *Population and the People: A National Policy*, London: Fabian Society.

Farr, W. 1895, *Vital Statistics*, edited by N. A. Humphries, London: Office of the Sanitary Institute.

Feeley, M. and Simon, J. 1992, 'The new penology: notes on the emerging strategy of corrections and its implications', *Criminology* 30, 4: 449–74.

1994, 'Actuarial justice: power/knowledge in contemporary criminal justice', in D. Nelken (ed.), *The Futures of Criminology*, pp. 173–201, London: Sage.

Finegold, K. and Skocpol, T. 1995, *State and Party in America's New Deal*, Madison: University of Wisconsin Press.

Finer, S. 1972, 'The transmission of Benthamite ideas', in G. Sutherland (ed.), *Studies in the Growth of Nineteenth-Century Government*, pp. 11–32, Totowa, NJ: Rowman and Littlefield.

Foucault, M. 1970, *The Order of Things: An Archaeology of the Human Sciences*, translated by A. Sheridan, London: Tavistock.

1972a, *Histoire de la folie a l'âge classique*, Paris: Gallimard.

1972b, 'Orders of discourse', translated by R. Swyer, *Social Science Information* 10: 7–30.

1973, *The Birth of the Clinic: An Archaeology of Medical Perception*, translated by A. Sheridan, London: Tavistock.

1977, *Discipline and Punish: The Birth of the Prison*, translated by A. Sheridan, London: Allen Lane.

1979a, *The History of Sexuality*, vol. I, *An Introduction*, translated by R. Hurley, London: Allen Lane.

1979b, 'On governmentality', *I&C* 6: 5–22.

1980a, *Michel Foucault: Power/Knowledge*, edited by C. Gordon, Brighton: Harvester.

1980b, 'The politics of health in the eighteenth century', in Foucault 1980a, pp. 166–82.

1981, 'Omnes et singulatim: towards a criticism of political reason', in S. McMurrin (ed.), *The Tanner Lectures on Human Values*, vol. II, pp. 225–54, Salt Lake City: University of Utah Press.

1986, 'Nietzsche, genealogy, history', in Foucault, *The Foucault Reader*, edited by P. Rabinow, pp. 76–100, London: Penguin.

1988, 'Technologies of the self', in L. H. Martin, H. Gutman and P. H. Hutton (eds.), *Technologies of the Self*, pp. 16–49, London: Tavistock.

1991, 'Governmentality', in G. Burchell, Gordon and Miller 1991, pp. 87–104.

1994, *Dits et écrits*, 4 vols., Paris: Gallimard.

1997, 'The ethics of the concern for self as a practice of freedom', in Foucault, *Ethics: Subjectivity and Truth*, edited by P. Rabinow, pp. 281–301, New York: New Press.

Frankel, B. 1997, 'Confronting neoliberal regimes: the post-Marxist embrace of populism and realpolitik', *New Left Review* 226: 57–92.

Frankel, L. K. and Dawson, M. M. 1910, *Workingmen's Insurance in Europe*, New York: Charities Publication Committee.

Fraser, N. 1995, 'From redistribution to recognition?: dilemmas of justice in a "post-socialist" age', *New Left Review* 212: 68–93.

Fraser, N. and Gordon, L. 1994, 'A genealogy of *dependency*: tracing a keyword of the US welfare state', *Signs* 19, 2: 311–36.

Fraser, S. and Gerstle, G. 1989, *The Rise and Fall of the New Deal Order, 1930–1980*, Princeton: Princeton University Press.

Freeden, M. 1978, *The New Liberalism*, Oxford: Oxford University Press.

Friedman, M. and Friedman, R. 1980, *Free to Choose*, New York : Harcourt Brace Jovanovich.

Fukuyama, F. 1996, *Trust: The Social Virtues and the Creation of Prosperity*, London: Penguin.

Furner, M. O. 1993, 'The Republican tradition and the new liberalism: social investigation, state building and social learning in the Gilded Age', in M. J. Lacey and M. O. Furner (eds.), *The State and Social Investigation in Britain and the United States*, pp. 171–241, Cambridge: Woodrow Wilson Center Press and Cambridge University Press.

Gallup, G. and Rae, S. F. 1940, *The Pulse of Democracy: The Public Opinion Poll and How It Works*, New York: Simon and Schuster.

Gandall, K. and Kotkin, S. 1985, 'Governing work and social life in the USA and the USSR', unpublished typescript, University of California, Berkeley, September 1985.

Gandy, O. 1993, *The Panoptic Sort: Towards a Political Economy of Information*, Boulder, CO: Westview.

Garland, D. 1985, *Punishment and Welfare*, Aldershot: Gower.

1996, 'The limits of the sovereign state: strategies of crime control in contemporary society', *British Journal of Criminology* 36, 1: 445–71.

Gaukroger, S. 1976, 'Bachelard and the problem of epistemological analysis', *Studies in History and Philosophy of Science* 7: 189–244.

Geertz, C. 1973, *The Interpretation of Cultures*, New York: Basic Books.

Giddens, A. 1991, *Modernity and Self-Identity*, Cambridge: Polity.

1998, *The Third Way*, Cambridge: Polity.

Gilman, S. 1985, *Difference and Pathology: Stereotypes of Sexuality, Race and Madness*, Ithaca, NY: Cornell University Press.

Glass, D. V. 1973, *Numbering the People: The Great Demography Controversy*, London: Gordon and Cremonesi.

Godwin, W. [1793] 1976, *Enquiry Concerning Political Justice*, Harmondsworth: Penguin.

Goodman, N. 1978, *Ways of Worldmaking*, Indianapolis: Hackett.

Gordon, C. 1980, 'Afterword', in Foucault 1980a, pp. 229–59.

1987, 'The soul of the citizen: Max Weber and Michel Foucault', in S. Whimster and S. Lash (eds.), *Max Weber, Rationality and Modernity*, pp. 293–316, London: Allen and Unwin.

1991, 'Governmental rationality: an introduction', in G. Burchell, Gordon and Miller 1991, pp. 1–52.

Gordon, D. 1987, 'The electronic Panopticon: a case-study of the development of the National Criminal Records System', *Politics and Society* 15: 483–511.

Gordon, L. 1989, *Heroes of Their Own Lives: The Politics and History of Family Violence*, London: Virago.

Graunt, J. 1662, *Natural and political observations mentioned in a following index, and made upon the Bills of Mortality, by John Graunt, citizen of London. With reference to the government, religion, trade, growth, ayre, diseases, and the several changes of the said City*, London: printed by Tho. Roycroft, for John Martin, James Allestry and Tho. Dicas.

Gray, J. 1995, *Enlightenment's Wake: Politics and Culture at the Close of the Modern Age*, London: Routledge.

1996, *After Social Democracy*, London: Demos.

1997, *Endgames: Questions in Late Modern Political Thought*, Cambridge: Polity.

Greco, M. 1993, 'Psychosomatic subjects and "the duty to be well"', *Economy and Society* 22, 3: 357–72.

Greenblatt, S. 1980, *Renaissance Self-Fashioning: From More to Shakespeare*, Chicago: University of Chicago Press.

Greig, D. 1997, 'The politics of dangerousness', in S. A. Gerull and W. Lucas (eds.), *Serious Violent Offenders: Sentencing, Psychiatry and Law Reform*, pp. 47–66, Canberra: Australian Institute of Criminology.

Gullick, L. 1936, 'Introduction', in L. Harrison and E. Lane, *After Repeal: A Study of Liquor Control Legislation*, pp. i–xxxv, New York: Harper.

Hacking, I. 1975, *The Emergence of Probability*, Cambridge: Cambridge University Press.

1981, 'How should we do the history of statistics?', *I&C* 8: 15–26.

1983, *Representing and Intervening*, Cambridge: Cambridge University Press.

1986, 'Making up people', in T. C. Heller, M. Sosna and D. E. Wellbery (eds.), *Reconstructing Individualism: Autonomy, Individuality and the Self in Western Thought*, pp. 222–36, Stanford: Stanford University Press.

1988, 'The participant irrealist at large in the laboratory', *British Journal for the Philosophy of Science* 39: 277–94.

⊀1990, *The Taming of Chance*, Cambridge: Cambridge University Press.

1991, 'How should we do the history of statistics?', in G. Burchell, Gordon and Miller 1991, pp. 181–96.

1992, 'World-making by kind-making: child abuse for example', in M. Douglas and D. Hull (eds.), *How Classification Works: Nelson Goodman Among the Social Sciences*, pp. 180–238, Edinburgh: Edinburgh University Press.

. Hall, P. 1986, *Governing the Economy*, Cambridge: Polity.

Hall, S. and du Gay, P. (eds.) 1996, *Questions of Cultural Identity*, London: Sage.

Haller, M. H. 1963, *Eugenics*, New Brunswick, NJ: Rutgers University Press.

Hamilton, G. and Sutton, J. 1989, 'The problem of control in the weak state: domination in the United States, 1880–1920', *Theory and Society* 18: 1–46.

Hänninen, S. (ed.) 1998, *Displacement of Social Policies*, Jyväskylä: SoPhi, University of Jyväskylä.

Hardt, M. 1995, 'The withering of civil society', *Social Text* 14: 27–44.

Harris, J. 1972, *Unemployment and Politics: A Study in English Social Policy 1886–1914*, Oxford: Oxford University Press.

1977, *William Beveridge: A Biography*, Oxford: Clarendon Press.

Hayek, F. A. 1944, *The Road to Serfdom*, London: Routledge & Kegan Paul.

1979, *Law, Legislation and Liberty*, vol. III, *The Political Order of a Free People*, London: Routledge and Kegan Paul.

Heelas, P., Lash, S. and Morris, P. (eds.) 1996, *Detraditionalization*, Oxford: Blackwell.

Heelas, P. and Morris, P. (eds.) 1992, *The Values of the Enterprise Culture: The Moral Debate*, London: Routledge.

Himmelfarb, G. 1994, *The Demoralization of Society: From Victorian Virtues to Modern Values*, New York: Vintage.

1995a, 'Beyond social policy: remoralizing America', *Wall Street Journal* 7 February 1995.

⚫1995b, *The Demoralization of Society: From Victorian Virtues to Modern Values*, revised edn, London: Institute of Economic Affairs.

Hindess, B. 1994, 'Governing what economy?', paper delivered to Governing Australia conference, Sydney, November 1994 (revised version published as Hindess 1998b).

1996a, *Discourses of Power: From Hobbes to Foucault*, Oxford: Blackwell.

1996b, 'Liberalism, socialism and democracy: variations on a governmental theme', in Barry, Osborne and Rose 1996, pp. 65–80.

1996c, 'Multiculturalism and citizenship', unpublished manuscript.

1997, 'Fears of intrusion: anti-political motifs in Western political discourse', in A. Schedler (ed.), *The End of Politics: Explorations into Modern Anti-Politics*, pp. 21–39, Basingstoke: Macmillan.

1998a, 'Divide and govern', in R. Ericson (ed.), *Governing Modern Societies*, forthcoming.

1998b, 'Neo-liberalism and the national economy', in Dean and Hindess 1998, pp. 210–26.

Hirschman, A. O. 1991, *The Rhetoric of Reaction*, Cambridge, MA: Belknap Harvard.

Hirst, P. 1994, *Associative Democracy: New Forms of Economic and Social Governance*, Cambridge: Polity.

Hirst, P. and Thompson, G. 1992, *Globalization in Question*, Cambridge: Polity.

Hirst, P. and Zeitlin, J. (eds.) 1988, *Reversing Industrial Decline: Industrial Structure and Policy in Britain and Her Competitors*, Oxford: Berg.

Hobson, J. 1901, *The Social Problem: Life and Work*, London: Nisbet.

1914, *Work and Wealth: A Human Valuation*, New York: Macmillan.

Hofstadter, R. 1955, *Social Darwinism in American Thought*, Boston: Beacon Press.

Hood, C. 1991, 'A public management for all seasons', *Public Administration* 69, 1: 3–19.

Hooghe, L. (ed.) 1996, *Cohesion Policy and European Integration: Building Multi-Level Governance*, Oxford: Oxford University Press.

Hopwood, A. G. 1986, 'Management accounting and organizational action: an introduction', in M. Bromwich and A. G. Hopwood (eds.), *Research and Current Issues in Management Accounting*, pp. 9–30, London: Pitman.

1988, 'Accounting and the domain of the public: some observations on current developments. The Price Waterhouse Public Lecture on Accounting, University of Leeds, 1985', in A. G. Hopwood, *Accounting from the Outside: The Collected Papers of Anthony G. Hopwood*, edited with an introduction by A. G. Hopwood, pp. 259–77, New York: Garland.

Hopwood, A. G. and Miller, P. (eds.) 1994, *Accounting as Social and Institutional Practice*, Cambridge: Cambridge University Press.

Hubback, E. M. 1947, *The Population of Britain*, London: n.p.

Hughes, T. P. 1983, *Networks of Power*, Baltimore: Johns Hopkins University Press.

Hunter, I. 1988, *Culture and Government: The Emergence of Literary Education*, London: Macmillan.

1993, 'The pastoral bureaucracy: towards a less principled understanding of state schooling', in D. Meredyth and D. Tyler (eds.), *Child and Citizen: Genealogies of Schooling and Subjectivity*, pp. 237–88, Brisbane: Institute for Cultural Policy, Griffith University.

1994, *Rethinking the School*, St Leonards, Australia: Allen and Unwin.

1996, 'Assembling the school', in Barry, Osborne and Rose 1996, pp. 143–66.

1998, 'Uncivil society: liberal government and the deconfessionalisation of politics', in Dean and Hindess 1998, pp. 242–64.

Hutton, W. 1995, *The State We're In*, London: Cape.

Ignatieff, M. 1979, *A Just Measure of Pain*, London: Macmillan.

Isin, E. 1992, *Cities Without Citizens*, Montreal: Black Rose Press.

Ivison, D. 1993, 'Liberal conduct', *History of the Human Sciences* 6, 3: 25–59.

1995, 'The art of political liberalism', *Canadian Journal of Political Science* 28, 2: 203–26.

1997a, 'The secret history of public reason: Hobbes to Rawls', *History of Political Thought* 18, 1: 125–47.

1997b, *The Self at Liberty: Political Argument and the Arts of Government*, Ithaca, NY: Cornell University Press.

Jacob, F. 1974, *The Logic of Living Systems*, translated by B. Spillman, London: Allen Lane.

Jefferson, T. [1790] 1961, 'Second State of the Report of Weights and Measures', April-May 1790, in Julian P. Boyd (ed.), *The Papers of Thomas Jefferson*, vol. XVI, pp. 628–48, Princeton: Princeton University Press.

Jones, G. 1982, 'Eugenics and social policy between the wars', *Historical Journal* 25, 3: 726–7.

Jones, K. 1972, *A History of the Mental Health Services*, London: Routledge and Kegan Paul.

Jones, K. and Williamson, K. 1979, 'The birth of the schoolroom', *I&C* 6: 59–110.

Joseph Rowntree Foundation 1995, *Enquiry into Income and Wealth*, 2 vols., York: Joseph Rowntree Foundation.

Joyce, P. 1994, 'The end of social history', *Social History* 20, 1: 73–91.

(ed.) 1995a, *Class: A Reader*, Oxford: Oxford University Press.

1995b, *Democratic Subjects: The Self and the Social in the Nineteenth Century*, Cambridge: Cambridge University Press.

Katz, M. 1993, ' "Underclass" as metaphor', in Katz (ed.), *The 'Underclass' Debate*, pp. 3–26, Princeton: Princeton University Press.

Kay, L. 1993, *The Molecular Vision of Life: CalTech, the Rockefeller Foundation and the Rise of the New Biology*, New York: Oxford University Press.

Keane, J. 1984, *Public Life and Late Capitalism: Towards a Socialist Theory of Democracy*, Cambridge: Cambridge University Press.

1988, *Democracy and Civil Society*, London: Verso.

Keat, R. and Abercrombie, N. (eds.) 1991, *Enterprise Culture*, London: Routledge.

Kelman, S. 1987, 'The political foundation of American statistical policy', in Alonso and Starr 1987, pp. 275–302.

Kendall, G. 1997, 'Governing at a distance: Anglo-Australian relations, 1840–1870', *Australian Journal of Political Science* 32, 2: 223–35.

Kettle, M. 1997, 'Where a chill wind blows in from the real world', *Guardian* 29 December 1997: 2.

Kevles, D. 1985, *In the Name of Eugenics: Genetics and the Uses of Human Heredity*, Berkeley: University of California Press.

Keynes, J. M. 1926, *The End of Laissez-Faire*, London: Hogarth Press.

Klein, R. 1983, *The Politics of the National Health Service*, London: Longman.

Knemeyer, F.-L. 1980, 'Polizei', *Economy and Society* 9, 2: 172–96.

Kooiman, J. (ed.) 1993, *Modern Governance: New Government-Society Interactions*, London: Sage.

Kühl, S. 1994, *The Nazi Connection: Eugenics, American Racism and German National Socialism*, New York: Oxford University Press.

Kula, W. 1986, *Measures and Men*, translated by R. Szreter, Princeton: Princeton University Press.

Kuznets, S. 1933, 'National income', *Encyclopedia of the Social Sciences*, vol. XI, pp. 205–24, New York: Macmillan.

Lash, S. and Urry, J. 1994, *Economies of Signs and Spaces*, London: Routledge.

Latour, B. 1986, 'Visualization and cognition: thinking with eyes and hands', *Knowledge and Society* 6: 1–40.

1987, *Science in Action*, Milton Keynes: Open University Press.

1988, *Irréductions* (published with *The Pasteurisation of France*), Cambridge, MA: Harvard University Press.

Latour, B. and Woolgar, S. 1979, *Laboratory Life: The Social Construction of Scientific Facts*, London: Sage.

Law, J. (ed.) 1991, *A Sociology of Monsters: Essays on Power, Technology and Domination*, London: Routledge.

Le Bon, G. 1895, *The Crowd: A Study of the Popular Mind*, London: Fisher Unwin.

Lefebvre, H. 1991, *The Production of Space*, Oxford: Basil Blackwell.

Leftwich, A. 1994, 'Governance, the state and the politics of development', *Development and Change* 25, 2: 363–86.

Leiss, W., Kline, S. and Jhally, S. 1986, *Social Communication in Advertising*, London: Methuen.

Levitas, R. 1996, 'The concept of social exclusion and the new Durkheimian hegemony', *Critical Social Policy* 16, 1: 5–20.

Lukes, S. 1973, *Emile Durkheim: His Life and Work*, Harmondsworth: Penguin.

Lumley, F. 1925, *Means of Social Control*, New York: Century.

Lyon, D. 1994, *The Electronic Eye: The Rise of Surveillance Society*, Cambridge: Polity.

McCulloch, J. 1995, *Colonial Psychiatry and 'the African Mind'*, Cambridge: Cambridge University Press.

MacDonagh, O. 1958, 'The nineteenth-century revolution in government', *Historical Journal* 1: 52–67.

1977a, *Early Victorian Government, 1830–1870*, London: Weidenfeld and Nicholson.

1977b, *Ireland: The Union and Its Aftermath*, London: Allen and Unwin.

MacIntyre, A. 1981, *After Virtue: A Study in Moral Theory*, London: Duckworth.

Mackenzie, D. 1981, *Statistics in Britain 1865–1930: The Social Construction of Scientific Knowledge*, Edinburgh: Edinburgh University Press.

MacLeod, R. (ed.) 1988, *Government and Expertise: Specialists, Administrators and Professionals, 1860–1919*, Cambridge: Cambridge University Press.

Malthus, T. [1798] 1970, *An Essay on the Principle of Population*, Harmondsworth: Penguin.

Markus, T. 1993, *Buildings and Power: Freedom and Control in the Origin of Modern Building Types*, London: Routledge.

Marshall, T. H. [1949] 1992, 'Citizenship and social class', in Marshall and T. Bottomore, *Citizenship and Social Class*, pp. 3–51, London: Pluto Press.

1975, *Social Policy*, 2nd edn, London: Hutchinson.

Marx, G. 1988, *Undercover: Police Surveillance in America*, Berkeley: University of California Press.

Mayhew, Henry [1851] 1969, *The Unknown Mayhew: Selections from the 'Morning Chronicle'*, edited by E. P. Thompson and E. Yeo, London: Merlin.

Mayo, E. 1933, *The Human Problems of an Industrial Civilization*, New York: Macmillan.

Mead, L. 1986, *Beyond Entitlement: The Social Obligations of Citizenship*, New York: Free Press.

1991, 'The new politics of the new poverty', *Public Interest* 105: 3–20.

Mechanic, D. and Rochefort, D. 1996, 'Comparative mental health systems', *Annual Review of Sociology* 22: 239–70.

Melton, J. van Horn, 1991, *Language, Class and History*, Oxford: Blackwell.

1995, ' "Society" and "the public sphere" in eighteenth- and nineteenth-century Germany', in Joyce 1995a, pp. 192–201.

Meuret, D. 1981, 'Political economy and the legitimation of the state', *I&C* 9: 29–38.

1988, 'A political genealogy of political economy', *Economy and Society* 17, 2: 225–50.

Middlemas, K. 1979, *Politics in Industrial Society: The Experience of the British System Since 1911*, London: Deutsch.

Milder, N. D. 1987, 'Crime and downtown revitalization', *Urban Land* September 1987.

Mill, J. S. [1859] 1975, *On Liberty*, in *Three Essays*, Oxford: Oxford University Press.

Miller, P. 1986, 'The psychotherapy of employment and unemployment', in Miller and Rose 1986, pp. 143–76.

1987, *Domination and Power*, London: Routledge.

1990, 'On the interrelations between accounting and the state', *Accounting, Organizations and Society* 15, 4: 315–38.

1992, 'Accounting and objectivity: the invention of calculating selves and calculable spaces', *Annals of Scholarship* 9, 1–2: 61–86.

1994, 'Accounting and objectivity: the invention of calculating selves and calculable spaces', in A. Megill (ed.), *Rethinking Objectivity*, pp. 239–64, Durham, NC: Duke University Press.

Miller, P. and O'Leary, T. 1987, 'Accounting and the construction of the governable person', *Accounting, Organizations and Society* 12: 235–65.

1989, 'Hierarchies and American ideals, 1900–1940', *Academy of Management Review* 14: 235–65.

1992, 'Accounting expertise and the politics of the product: economic citizenship and modes of corporate governance', *Accounting, Organizations and Society* 17: 187–206.

1994a, 'Accounting, "economic citizenship", and the spatial reordering of manufacture', *Accounting, Organizations and Society* 19: 15–43.

1994b, 'The factory as laboratory', *Science in Context* 7, 3: 469–96.

1994c, 'Governing the calculable person', in Hopwood and Miller 1994, pp. 98–115.

Miller, P. and Rose, N. (eds.) 1986, *The Power of Psychiatry*, Cambridge: Polity.

1990, 'Governing economic life', *Economy and Society* 19, 1: 1–31.

1995a, 'Political thought and the limits of orthodoxy: a response to Curtis', *British Journal of Sociology* 46, 4: 590–7.

1995b, 'Production, identity and democracy', *Theory and Society* 24: 427–67.

1997, 'Mobilizing the consumer: assembling the subject of consumption', *Theory, Culture and Society* 14, 1: 1–36.

Minson, J. and Meredyth, D. forthcoming, *Constituents of Culture: Citizens and Cultural Governance*, London: Sage.

Mitchell, T. 1988, *Colonising Egypt*, Cambridge: Cambridge University Press.

Montesquieu (Charles de Secondat, Baron de Montesquieu) [1721] 1971, *The Persian Letters*, translated by C. Betts, Harmondsworth: Penguin.

[1748] 1900, *The Spirit of Laws*, translated by T. Nugent, New York: Colonial Press.

Morgenstern, O. 1963, *On the Accuracy of Economic Observations*, 2nd edn, Princeton: Princeton University Press.

Moscovici, S. 1988, *The Age of the Crowd: An Historical Treatise on Mass Psychology*, Cambridge: Cambridge University Press.

Mosse, G. 1978, *Toward the Final Solution*, London: Dent.

Mouffe, C. 1992, 'Democratic citizenship and the political community', in Mouffe (ed.), *Dimensions of Radical Democracy*, pp. 225–39, London: Verso.

Mulhall, S. and Swift, A. 1997, *Liberals and Communitarians*, 2nd edn, Oxford: Blackwell.

Murray, C. 1984, *Losing Ground: American Social Policy 1950–1980*, New York: Basic Books.

Nancy, J.-L. 1991, *The Inoperative Community*, Minneapolis: University of Minnesota Press.

National Association for Mental Health 1961, *Report of the Annual Conference of 1961*, London: National Association for Mental Health.

National Committee for Mental Hygiene 1929, *Twenty Years of Mental Hygiene, 1909–1929*, New York: American Foundation for Mental Hygiene.

Nietzsche, F. 1983, *Untimely Meditations*, translated by R. J. Hollingdale, Cambridge: Cambridge University Press.

O'Connor, J. 1972, *The Fiscal Crisis of the State*, New York: St Martin's Press.

O'Malley, P. 1992, 'Risk, power and crime prevention', *Economy and Society* 21, 3: 252–75.

1995, 'The prudential man cometh: life insurance, liberalism and the government of thrift', paper presented to the Annual Meeting of the Law and Society Association, Toronto, June 1995.

1996a, 'Indigenous governance', *Economy and Society* 26: 301–26.

1996b, 'Risk and responsibility', in Barry, Osborne and Rose 1996, pp. 189–208.

1997, 'Volatile punishments: contemporary penality and the neo-liberal government', unpublished manuscript.

O'Malley, P., Weir, L. and Shearing, C. 1997, 'Governmentality, criticism, politics', *Economy and Society* 26, 4: 501–7.

OECD 1990, *Labour Market Policies for the 1990s*, Paris: OECD.

Oestreich, G. 1982, *Neostoicism and the Early Modern State*, Cambridge: Cambridge University Press.

Osborne, D. and Gaebler, T. 1992, *Reinventing Government: How the Entrepreneurial Spirit Is Transforming the Public Sector*, Reading, MA: Addison-Wesley.

Osborne, T. 1993, 'Liberalism, neo-liberalism and the liberal profession of medicine', *Economy and Society* 22, 3: 345–56.

1994, 'Bureaucracy as a vocation: governmentality and administration in nineteenth-century Britain', *Journal of Historical Sociology* 7, 3: 289–313.

1996a, 'Foucault and the idea of an aesthetic politics', public lecture, Stockholm, September 1996.

1996b, 'Governmentality versus sociology', unpublished paper delivered to seminar on governmentality, Stockholm, September 1996.

1998, *Aspects of Enlightenment: Social Theory and the Ethics of Truth*, London: UCL Press.

Osborne, T. and Rose, N. 1997, 'In the name of society, or three theses on the history of social thought', *History of the Human Sciences* 10, 3: 87–104.

1998, *Society and the Life Sciences*, special issue of *Economy and Society in Honour of Georges Canguilhem*, *Economy and Society* 27, 2 and 3.

forthcoming, 'Do the social sciences create phenomena?: the example of public opinion research'. *British Journal of Sociology*.

Parton, N. 1995, 'Neglect as child protection: the political context and the practical outcomes', *Children and Society* 9, 1: 67–89.

1996, 'Social work, risk and "the blaming system"', in Parton (ed.), *Social Theory, Social Change and Social Work*, pp. 98–114, London: Routledge.

Pasquino, P. 1991, 'Theatrum politicum: the genealogy of capital – police and the state of prosperity', in G. Burchell, Gordon and Miller 1991, pp. 105–18.

Patten, C. 1995, 'Refiguring social space', in L. Nicholson and S. Seidman (eds.), *Social Postmodernism: Beyond Identity Politics*, pp. 216–49, Cambridge: Cambridge University Press.

Patterson, O. 1991, *Freedom*, vol. I, *Freedom in the Making of Western Culture*, London: I. B. Tauris.

Pelling, H. 1965, *Origins of the Labour Party*, 2nd edn, Oxford: Oxford University Press.

Perelman, C. and Obrechts-Tyteca, L. 1971, *The New Rhetoric: A Treatise on Argumentation*, Notre Dame, IN: University of Notre Dame Press.

Perlman, M. 1987, 'Political purpose and the national accounts', in Alonso and Starr 1987, pp. 133–52.

Perrot, M. (ed.) 1990, *A History of Private Life*, vol. IV, *From the Fires of Revolution to the Great War*, Cambridge, MA: Belknap Press of Harvard University Press.

Petersen, W. 1987, 'Politics and the measurement of ethnicity', in Alonso and Starr 1987, pp. 187–234.

Petty, W. 1648, *The Advice of WP [Sir William Petty] to Mr Samuel Hartlib, for the Advancement of Some Particular Parts of Learning*, reprinted in *The Harleian Miscellany, 1810*, vol. VI, pp. 1–14, London: Robert Dutton.

Peukert, D. 1987, *Inside Nazi Germany: Conformity, Opposition and Racism in Everyday Life*, translated by R. Deveson, New Haven: Yale University Press.

Pick, D. 1989, *Faces of Degeneration: A European Disorder c. 1848–c. 1918*, Cambridge: Cambridge University Press.

Piore, M. and Sabel, C. 1984, *The Second Industrial Divide*, New York: Basic Books.

Platt, A. 1969, *The Child Savers: The Invention of Delinquency*, Chicago: University of Chicago Press.

Pocock, J. G. A. 1985, *Commerce, Virtue and History*, Cambridge: Cambridge University Press.

Polanyi, K. 1957, *The Great Transformation: The Political and Economic Origins of Our Time*, Boston: Beacon Press.

Poovey, M. 1995, *Making a Social Body*, Chicago: University of Chicago Press.

Porter, P. 1983, 'Sydney Cove 1788', in *Peter Porter's Collected Poems*, pp. 50–1, Oxford: Oxford University Press.

Porter, T. 1986, *The Rise of Statistical Thinking, 1820–1900*, Princeton: Princeton University Press.

1990, 'Quantification as a social technology', paper delivered to the *History of the Present* Research Network, London, 1990.

1992, 'Quantification and the accounting ideal in science', *Social Studies of Science* 22: 633–52.

1996, *Trust in Numbers: The Invention of Objectivity*, Princeton: Princeton University Press.

Poster, M. 1990, *Mode of Information*, Cambridge: Polity.

Power, M. 1993, 'The audit society', paper delivered to *History of the Present* Research Network, London, 1993.

1994a, *The Audit Explosion*, London: Demos.

1994b, 'The audit society', in Hopwood and Miller 1994, pp. 299–316.

1997, *The Audit Society: Rituals of Verification*, Oxford: Oxford University Press.

Pratt, J. 1999, 'Sex crime and the new punitiveness', *International Journal of Law and Psychiatry*.

Prewitt, K. 1987, 'Public statistics and democratic politics', in Alonso and Starr 1987, pp. 261–74.

Procacci, G. 1989, 'Sociology and its poor', *Politics and Society* 17: 163–87.

1991, 'Social economy and the government of poverty', in G. Burchell, Gordon and Miller 1991, pp. 151–68.

1993, *Gouverner la misère: la question sociale en France 1789–1848*, Paris: Editions du Seuil.

1998, 'Poor citizens: social citizenship and the crisis of welfare states', in Hänninen 1998, pp. 7–30.

Proctor, R. 1988, *Racial Hygiene: Medicine Under the Nazis*, Cambridge, MA: Harvard University Press.

Prost, A. and Gerard, V. (eds.) 1991, *A History of Private Life*, vol. V, *Riddles of Identity in Modern Times*, translated by A. Goldhammer, Cambridge, MA: Belknap Press of Harvard University Press.

Proudhon, P.-J. [1851] 1923, *General Idea of the Revolution in the Nineteenth Century*, translated by John Beverley Robinson, London: Freedom Press.

Putnam, R. 1995a, 'Bowling alone: America's declining social capital', *Journal of Democracy* 6, 1: 65–78.

1995b, 'Tuning in, tuning out: the strange disappearance of social capital in America', *PS: Political Science and Politics* December 1995: 664–83.

Quetelet, A. [1835] 1842, *A Treatise on Man and the Development of His Faculties*, translated by R. Knox, Edinburgh: n.p.

Rabinow, P. 1989, *French Modern: Norms and Forms of the Social Environment*, Cambridge, MA: MIT Press.

1992, 'Artificiality and enlightenment: from sociobiology to biosociality', in Crary and Winter 1992, pp. 234–51.

Raeff, M. 1983, *The Well-Ordered Police State: Social and Institutional Change Through Law in the Germanies and Russia, 1699–1800*, New Haven and London: Yale University Press.

Rajchman, J. 1991, *Truth and Eros: Foucault, Lacan and the Question of Ethics*, New York: Routledge.

Rawson, R. W. 1839, 'An enquiry into the statistics of crime in England and Wales', *Journal of the Statistical Society of London* 2: 316–44.

Reich, C. 1964, 'Individual rights and social welfare', *Yale Law Journal* 74: 1245–57.

Reich, R. 1992, *The Work of Nations: Preparing Ourselves for 21st-Century Capitalism*, New York: Vintage.

Rhein, C. 1982, 'La gèographie: discipline scolaire et/ou science sociale? 1860–1920', *Revue française de sociology* 23: 223–51.

Rhodes, R. A. W. 1994, 'The hollowing out of the state', *Political Quarterly* 65: 138–51.

1995, *The New Governance: Governing Without Government*, State of Britain Seminar Series, London: ESRC.

Richter, M. 1977, *The Political Theory of Montesquieu*, Cambridge: Cambridge University Press.

Rickman, J. 1800, 'Thoughts on the utility and facility of ascertaining the population of England', *Commercial and Agricultural Magazine* 2: 391–9.

Rieff, P. 1966, *The Triumph of the Therapeutic*, London: Chatto and Windus.

Rifkin, J. 1995, *The End of Work: The Decline of the Global Labor Force and the Dawn of the Post-Market Era*, New York: Tarcher/Putnam.

Riley, D. 1983, *War in the Nursery*, London: Virago.

1988, *Am I That Name: Feminism and the Category of 'Women' in History*, London: Macmillan.

Robins, K. and Webster, F. 1989, 'Plan and control: towards a cultural history of the information society', *Theory and Society* 18: 323–51.

Rose, N. 1985, *The Psychological Complex: Psychology, Politics and Society in England 1869–1939*, London: Routledge and Kegan Paul.

1986, 'Psychiatry: the discipline of mental health', in Miller and Rose 1986, pp. 43–84.

1987, 'Beyond the public/private division: law, power and the family', *Journal of Law and Society* 14, 1: 61–76.

1988, 'Calculable minds and manageable individuals', *History of the Human Sciences* 1, 2: 179–200.

1990, *Governing the Soul: The Shaping of the Private Self*, London: Routledge.

1991, 'Governing by numbers: figuring out democracy', *Accounting, Organizations and Society* 16, 7: 673–92.

1992a, 'Governing the enterprising self', in Heelas and Morris 1992, pp. 141–64.

1992b, 'Towards a critical sociology of freedom', inaugural lecture, Goldsmiths College, 5 May 1992, London: Goldsmiths College, excerpted in Joyce 1995a, pp. 213–24.

1993, 'Government, authority and expertise in advanced liberalism', *Economy and Society* 22, 3: 283–99.

1994a, 'Expertise and the government of conduct', *Studies in Law, Politics and Society* 14: 359–67.

1994b, 'Medicine, history and the present', in R. Porter and C. Jones (eds.), *Reassessing Foucault*, pp. 48–72, London: Routledge.

1996a, 'Authority and the genealogy of subjectivity', in Heelas, Morris and Lash 1996, pp. 294–327.

1996b, 'The death of the social?: refiguring the territory of government', *Economy and Society* 25, 3: 327–56.

1996c, 'Governing "advanced" liberal democracies', in Barry, Osborne and Rose 1996, pp. 37–64.

1996d, 'Identity, genealogy, history', in Hall and du Gay 1996, pp. 128–50.

1996e, *Inventing Our Selves: Psychology, Power and Personhood*, New York: Cambridge University Press.

1996f, 'Psychiatry as a political science: advanced liberalism and the administration of risk', *History of the Human Sciences* 9, 2: 1–23.

1997a, 'Between authority and liberty: civil society, communitarianism, third sector', presented to the Annual Conference of the Finnish Social Policy Association, November 1997; published as 'Vallan ja vapauden välissä: hyveen hallinta vapaasa yhteiskunassa', *Janus* (Journal of the Finnish Society for Social Policy) 1998, 6, 1: 1–33.

1997b, 'The crisis of "the social": beyond the social question', in Hänninen 1998, pp. 54–99.

1998, 'Governing risky individuals: the role of psychiatry in new regimes of control', *Psychiatry, Psychology and Law* 5, 2: 1–19.

Rose, N. and Miller, P. 1992, 'Political power beyond the state: problematics of government', *British Journal of Sociology* 43, 2: 172–205.

Rosenau, J. 1997, *Along the Domestic-Foreign Frontier: Exploring Governance in a Turbulent World*, Cambridge: Cambridge University Press.

Ross, E. A. 1901, *Social Control: A Survey of the Foundations of Order*, New York: Macmillan.

Rubinow, I. M. 1913, *Social Insurance With Special Reference to American Conditions*, New York: Henry Holt & Co.

Rüstow, A. [1950, 1952, 1957] 1980, *Freedom and Domination: A Historical Critique of Civilization*, translated by S. Attanasio, Princeton: Princeton University Press.

Sandel, M. 1982, *Liberalism and the Limits of Justice*, Cambridge: Cambridge University Press.

Scheingold, S., Pershing, J. and Olson, T. 1994, 'Sexual violence, victim advocacy and republican criminology', *Law and Society Review* 28, 4: 729–63.

Schofield, P. (ed.) 1995, *Colonies, Commerce and Constitutional Law: Rid Yourself of Ultramaria and Other Writings on Spain and Spanish America*, Oxford: Oxford University Press.

Schott, K. 1982, 'The rise of Keynesian economics: Britain 1940–1964', *Economy and Society* 11, 3: 292–316.

Schwartz, H. 1997, 'On the origin of the phrase "social problems" ', *Social Problems* 44, 2: 276–96.

Scott, D. 1995, 'Colonial governmentality', *Social Text* 5, 3: 191–220.

Searle, G. 1971, *The Quest for National Efficiency*, Oxford: Blackwell.

Sedgwick, E. 1992, 'Epidemics of the will', in Crary and Kwinter 1992, pp. 582–95.

Serres, M. 1982, *Hermes: Literature, Science, Philosophy*, edited by J. V. Harari and D. F. Bell, Baltimore: Johns Hopkins University Press.

Shapiro, M. (ed.) 1984, *Language and Politics*, London: Blackwell.

  1997, 'Bowling blind: post-liberal civil society and the worlds of neo-Toquevillean social theory', *Theory and Event* 1, 1 at http://128.220.50.88/journals/theory-&-event/v001/1.1shapiro.html.

Shearing, C. 1995, 'Reinventing policing: police as governance', in O. Marenin (ed.), *Policing Change: Changing Police*, pp. 285–307, New York: Garland Press.

Shearing, C. and Stenning, P. 1985, 'From the Panopticon to Disneyworld: the development of discipline', in E. Doob and E. L. Greenspan (eds.), *Perspectives in Criminal Law*, pp. 335–49, Aurora: Canada Law Books.

Simon, J. 1988, 'The ideological effects of actuarial practices', *Law and Society Review* 22, 4: 771–800.

  1993, *Poor Discipline: Parole and the Social Control of the Underclass, 1890–1990*, Chicago: University of Chicago Press.

  1996, 'Megan's Law: governing through crime in a democratic society', unpublished manuscript, June 1996.

  1998, 'Managing the monstrous: sex offenders and the new penology', *Psychology, Public Policy and Law* 4: 1–16.

Skocpol, T. 1992, *Protecting Soldiers and Mothers: The Political Origins of Social Policy in the United States*, Cambridge, MA: Belknap Harvard.

Skowronek, S. 1982, *Building a New American State: The Expansion of National Administrative Capacities, 1877–1920*, Cambridge: Cambridge University Press.

Smith, Adam [1759] 1982, *The Theory of Moral Sentiments*, edited by D. D. Raphael and A. L. Macfie, Indianapolis: Liberty Press.

Smith, Alison 1997, 'Military formations: the government of military conduct', unpublished Ph.D thesis, Australian National University, Canberra, Australia.

Smith, D. W. 1997, 'Introduction', in Deleuze 1997, pp. xi–lvi.

Smith, R. 1992, *Inhibition*, Berkeley: University of California Press.

Spencer, H. 1884, *The Man vs the State*, London and Edinburgh: Williams and Norgate.

Starr, P. 1987, 'The sociology of official statistics', in Alonso and Starr 1987, pp. 7–58.

Starr, P. and Corson, R. 1987, 'Who will have the numbers?: the rise of the statistical services industry and the politics of public data', in Alonso and Starr 1987, pp. 415–48.

Statistical Society of London 1838, 'Queries of the Statistical Society of London relating to strikes', *Journal of the Statistical Society of London* 1: 11–13.

Stedman Jones, G. 1983, 'Working-class culture and working-class politics in London 1870–1900', in Stedman Jones, *Languages of Class: Studies in English Working-Class History 1832–1982*, pp. 179–238, Cambridge: Cambridge University Press.

Stenson, K. 1993, 'Community policing as a governmental technology', *Economy and Society* 22, 3: 373–89.

Stokes, E. 1959, *The English Utilitarians and India*, Oxford: Clarendon.

Stoler, A. L. 1995, *Race and the Education of Desire*, Durham, NC: Duke University Press.

Stow, D. 1834, *Moral Training, Infant and Juvenile, as Applicable to the Condition of the Population of Large Towns*, 2nd edn, enlarged, Glasgow: n.p.

Strathern, M. 1992, *After Nature: English Kinship in the Late Twentieth Century*, Cambridge: Cambridge University Press.

Swenarton, M. 1981, *Homes Fit for Heroes*, London: Heinemann.

Tanner, M. 1994, 'Ending welfare as we know it', *Policy Analysis* 212, 7 July 1994, at http://www.cato.org/pubs/pas/pa-212.htm.

Taylor, C. 1955, *Philosophy and the Human Sciences*, Cambridge: Cambridge University Press.

1989a, 'Cross-purposes: the liberal-communitarian debate', in N. Rosenblum (ed.), *Liberalism and the Moral Life*, pp. 159–82, Cambridge, MA: Harvard University Press.

1989b, *Sources of the Self: The Making of the Modern Identity*, Cambridge: Cambridge University Press.

Taylor, F. W. 1913, *The Principles of Scientific Management*, New York: Harper and Brothers.

Thatcher, M. 1980, 'The Airey Neave Memorial Lecture', *Commentary* 1, 2: 7–14.

Thevenot, L. 1984, 'Rules and implements: investment in forms', *Social Science Information* 23, 1: 1–45.

Thompson, E. P. 1967, 'Time, work discipline and industrial capitalism', *Past and Present* 38: 56–97.

Thompson, G. 1997, 'Where goes economics and the economies?', *Economy and Society* 26, 4: 599–610.

1998, 'Encountering economics and accounting: some skirmishes and engagements', *Accounting, Organizations and Society* 23, 3: 283–323.

Thompson, T. 1996, *Power to the People*, New York: Harper Collins.

Timmins, N. 1996, *The Five Giants: A Biography of the Welfare State*, London: Fontana.

Tocqueville, A. de. [1835, 1840] 1969, *Democracy in America*, edited by J. P. Maier, translated by G. Lawrence, Garden City, NY: Anchor.

Tomlinson, J. 1981a, *Problems of British Economic Policy 1870–1945*, London: Methuen.

1981b, 'Why was there never a "Keynesian Revolution" in economic policy?', *Economy and Society* 10, 1: 72–87.

Tonkiss, F. 1998. 'Corporations and economic governance: the use of "publicly sponsored capital" in British economic management', unpublished manuscript.

Tribe, K. 1978, *Land, Labour and Economic Discourse*, London: Routledge.

Tudor-Walters 1918, *Report of the Committee . . . to Consider Questions of Building Construction in Connection with the Provision of Dwellings for the Working Classes in England and Wales . . .* (The Tudor Walters Report), London: HMSO.

Tully, J. 1988, *Meaning and Context: Quentin Skinner and His Critics*, Princeton: Princeton University Press.

  1989, 'Governing conduct', in E. Leites (ed.), *Conscience and Casuistry in Early Modern Europe*, pp. 12–71, Cambridge: Cambridge University Press.

  1993, *An Approach to Political Philosophy: Locke in Contexts*, Cambridge: Cambridge University Press.

  1995, *Strange Multiplicity: Constitutionalism in an Age of Diversity*, Cambridge: Cambridge University Press.

UK Department of Trade and Industry 1995, *Forging Ahead*, London: HMSO.

Valverde, M. 1991, *The Age of Light, Soap and Water*, Toronto: McClelland and Stewart.

  1996a, 'Despotism and ethical liberal government', *Economy and Society* 25, 3: 357–72.

  1996b, 'The dialectic of the familiar and the unfamiliar: the "jungle" in early slum travel writing', *Sociology* 30, 3: 493–509.

  1997, '"Slavery from within": the invention of alcoholism and the question of free will', *Social History* 22, 3: 251–68.

  1998a, *Diseases of the Will: Alcohol and the Dilemmas of Freedom*, Cambridge: Cambridge University Press.

  1998b, 'Governing out of habit: from "habitual inebriates" to "addictive personalities"', *Studies in Law, Politics and Society* 18: 217–42.

  1998c, 'Liquor licensing and the governance of consumption', paper presented to meeting of Law and Society, Aspen, CO, June 1998.

Van Ginneken, J. 1994, *Crowds, Psychology and Politics 1871–1899*, Cambridge: Cambridge University Press.

Van Til, J. 1988, *Mapping the Third Sector: Volunteerism in a Changing Social Economy*, New York: The Foundation Center.

Veyne, P. (ed.) 1987, *A History of Private Life*, vol. I, *From Pagan Rome to Byzantium*, translated by A. Goldhammer, Cambridge, MA: Belknap Press of Harvard University Press.

  1990, *Bread and Circuses: Historical Sociology and Political Pluralism*, abridged with an introduction by O. Murray, translated by B. Pearce, London: Allen Lane, Penguin Press.

  1997, 'Foucault revolutionises history', in A. Davidson (ed.), *Foucault and His Interlocutors*, pp. 146–82, Chicago: University of Chicago Press.

Walker, F. A. 1899, *Discussions in Economics and Statistics*, edited by D. R. Dewey, New York: H. Holt and Co.

Walters, W. 1994a, 'The discovery of "unemployment"', *Economy and Society* 23, 3: 265–90.

1994b, 'Social technologies after the welfare state', paper delivered to *History of the Present* conference, London, Goldsmiths College, April 1994.

1996, 'The demise of unemployment', *Politics and Society* 24, 3: 197–220.

1997, 'The active society: new designs for social policy', *Policy and Politics* 25, 3: 221–34.

Walzer, M. 1983, *Spheres of Justice*, New York: Basic Books.

Weber, M. 1978, *Economy and Society*, Berkeley: University of California Press.

Webster, F. and Robins, K. 1986, *Information Technology: A Luddite Analysis*, Norwood, NJ: Ablex.

Weir, M. and Skocpol, T. 1985, ' "Keynesian" responses to the Great Depression in Sweden, Britain, and the United States', in Evans, Rueschmeyer and Skocpol 1985, pp. 107–63.

Wilensky, H. 1967, *Organizational Intelligence*, New York: Basic Books.

Winch, D. 1969, *Economics and Policy: A Historical Study*, London: Hodder & Stoughton.

Winnicott, D. W. [1944] 1964, 'Support for normal parents', in Winnicott, *The Child, the Family and the Outside World*, pp. 173–6, Harmondsworth: Penguin.

Worcester, J. E. 1838, *The American Almanac and Repository of Useful Knowledge*, Boston: Charles Bowen.

Wuthnow, R. 1994, *Sharing the Journey: Support Groups and America's New Quest for Community*, New York: Free Press.

Yeatman, A. 1995, 'Interpreting contemporary contractualism', in J. Boston (ed.), *The State Under Contract*, pp. 124–39, Wellington, NZ: Bridget Williams.

Younghusband, E. 1978, *Social Work in Britain, 1950–1975*, London: Allen and Unwin.

Zifcak, S. 1994, *New Managerialism: Administrative Reform in Whitehall and Canberra*, Buckingham: Open University Press.

Zuboff, S. 1988, *In the Age of the Smart Machine*, New York: Basic Books.

Zukin, S. 1991, *Landscapes of Power*, Berkeley: University of California Press.

Zwart, H. 1996, 'Cultivation or intervention: Foucault's moral assessment of the human sciences', unpublished paper given at Symposium on Ethics and the History of the Human Sciences, Groningen, November 1996.

Index

abjection, 253
Abrams, Philip, 113n
access points, for active citizenship, 241, 245–6, 251
accountability, 150–5, 232
accounting,
    and accountability, 151–3; relations of, 211–12
accuracy, politics of, 199
activity,
    art of, 282; from dependency to, 263–7; technologies of, 268–70
actor network theory, 52n
actuarial regime, versus disciplinary regime, 235–6
administration,
    expert, 111; of others and of ourselves, 5
administrative agencies, of the state, 120
advanced liberal, use of term, 139–40
advanced liberalism, 12, 84, 137–66
    control techniques of, 12, 147, 235–43; diagram of, 141–2
aesthetic politics, 282–4
Agamben, Giorgio, 196
agency,
    multiple forms of, 59, 72, 274; recognition of capacity for, 1, 4
alienation, 46, 78, 120
alignments, see translation
allegiance,
    and identities, 190–1; networks of, 177
Alonso, William, 198, 199n
Althusser, Louis, 146
American exceptionalism, 118–19
American Journal of Insanity, 220
Americas, 107–8, 110
anarchy and autonomy, 180–1
Andrew, D., 24–5n
anomie, 46, 120, 172
anti–political themes, 2, 173–4
architecture, 73, 103

Aristotle, on good life, 169–70
arithmetic, political, 202–3, 225
Arnold, D., 109
asceticism, 96–7
Aschenwall, Gottfried, *Statistik*, 201
assessment, perpetual, 234
associationalism, 170, 180–2
asylums, 72, 103
    transformation of Victorian, 248–9
Atkinson, Alan, 110
attitude surveys, 85, 166, 189
audits, 146, 147, 153–5, 165
Australia, 107, 110
authorities,
    calculating, 215–21; heterogeneity of, 21, 66; political authorization of independent, 49–51; and political rule, 6–7
authority,
    contestability of regimes of, 60, 282; dethroning of traditional, 173; expert, 132–3; and bureaucratic, 147–56; legitimate, 1, 26–7; materializing relations of, 103; relation of liberty to, 184–7; and truth, 8–9, 281
autonomization, and responsibilization, 154–5, 174, 214–15
autonomy, 269–70
    alignments with political aims, 49–51; freedom as, 83–5; norm of, 93; potential, 281–2; security and, 184–7; of the will, 10; see also professional autonomy

Bachelard, Gaston, 55
Badie, B., 119n
Baistow, Karen, 268
Baker, Keith Michael, 201n
Baudrillard, Jean, 100
Bauman, Zygmunt, 41n, 66
Beck, Ulrich, 41n
Becker, Gary, 141n